PRINCIPLES OF SOCIOLOGY (1, PT. 2);

PRINCIPLES OF SOCIOLOGY (1, PT. 2);

Herbert Spencer

www.General-Books.net

Publication Data:

Title: Principles of Sociology
Volume: 1, pt. 2
Author: Herbert Spencer
General Books publication date: 2009
Original publication date: 1896
Original Publisher: D. Appleton and Co.
Subjects: Sociology
Philosophy / History Surveys / Modern
Social Science / General
Social Science / Customs Traditions
Social Science / Methodology
Social Science / Research
Social Science / Sociology / General

CONTENTS

1

SECTION 1

CHAPTER L

WHAT IS A SOCIETY ?

§ 212. This question has to be asked and answered at the outset. Until we have decided whether or not to regard a society as an entity ; and until we have decided whether, if regarded as an entity, a society is to be classed as absolutely unlike all other entities or as like some others ; our conception of the subject-matter before us remains vague.

It may be said that a society is but a collective name for a number of individuals. Carrying the controversy between nominalism and realism into another sphere, a nominalist might affirm that just as there exist only the members of a species, while the species considered apart from them has no existence; so the units of a society alone exist, while the existence of the society is but verbal. Instancing a lecturer's audience as an aggregate which by disappearing at the close of the lecture, proves itself to be not a thing but only a certain arrangement of persons, he might argue that the like holds of the citizens forming a nation.

But without disputing the other steps of his argument, the last step may be denied. The arrangement, temporary in the one case, is permanent in the other ; and it is the permanence of the relations among component parts which constitutes the individuality of a whole as distinguished from the individualities of its parts. A mass broken into fragments ceases to be a thing; while, conversely, the stones, bricks, and wood, previously separate, become the thmg called a house if connected in fixed ways.

Thus we consistently regard a society as an entity, because, though formed of discrete units, a certain concreteness in the aggregate of them is implied by the general persistence of the arrangements among them throughout the area occupied. And it is this trait which yields our idea of a society. For, withholding the name from an ever-changing cluster such as primitive men form, we apply it only where some constancy in the distribution of parts has resulted from settled life.

§ 213. But now, regarding a society as a thing, what kind of thing must we call it ? It seems totally unlike every object with which our senses acquaint us. Any likeness it may possibly have to other objects, cannot be manifest to perception, but can be discerned only by reason. If the constant relations among its parts make it an entity; the question arises whether these constant relations among its parts are akin to the constant relations among the parts of other entities. Between a society and anything else, the only conceivable resemblance must be one due to *parallelism of -principle in the arrangement of components.*

There are two great classes of aggregates with which the social aggregate may be compared – the inorganic and the organic. Are the attributes of a society in any way like those of a not-living body ? or are they in any way like those of a living body ? or are they entirely unlike those of both ?

The fipst of these questions needs only to be asked to be answered in the negative. A whole of which the parts are alive, cannot, in its general characters, be like lifeless wholes. The second question, not to be thus promptly answered, is to be answered in the affirmative. The reasons for asserting that the permanent relations among the parts of a society, are analogous to the permanent relations among the parts of a living body, we have now to consider.

CHAPTER II.

A SOCIETY IS AN ORGANISM.

§ 214. When we say that growth is common to social aggregates and organic aggregates, we do not thus entirely exclude community with inorganic aggregates. Some of these, as crystals, grow in a visible manner ; and all of them, on the hypothesis of evolution, have arisen by integration at some time or other. Nevertheless, compared with things we call inanimate, living bodies and societies so conspicuously exhibit augmentation of mass, that we may fairly regard this as characterizing them both. Many organisms grow throughout their lives; and the rest grow throughout considerable parts of their lives. Social growth usually continues either up to times when the societies divide, or up to times when they are overwhelmed.

Here, then, is the first trait by which societies ally themselves with the organic world and substantially distinguish htemselves from the inorganic world.

§ 215. It is also a character of social bodies, as of living bodies, that while they increase in size they increase in structure. Like a low animal, the embryo of a high one has few distinguishable parts; but while it is acquiring greater mass, its parts multiply and differentiate. It is thus with a society. At first the unlikenesses among its groups of units are inconspicuous in number and degree; but as populationaugments, divisions and sub-divisions become more numerous and more decided. Further, in the social organism as in the individual organism, differentiations cease only with that completion of the type which marks maturity and precedes decay.

Though in inorganic aggregates also, as in the entire Solar System and in each of its members, structural differentiations accompany the integrations; yet these are so relatively slow, and so relatively simple, that they may be disregarded. The multiplication of contrasted parts in bodies politic and in living bodies, ia so great that it substantially constitutes another common character which marks them off from inorganic bodies.

o"

§ 216. This community will be more fully appreciated on observing that progressive differentiation of structures *is* accompanied by progressive differentiation of functions.

The divisions, primary, secondary, and tertiary, which arise in a developing animal, do not assume their major and minor unlikenesses to no purpose. Along with diversities in their shapes and compositions go diversities in the actions they perform: they grow into unlike organs having unlike duties. Assuming the entire function of absorbing nutriment at the same time that it takes on its structural characters, the alimentary system becomes gradually marked off into contrasted portions; each of which has a special function forming part of the general function. A limb, instrumental to locomotion or prehension, acquires divisions and sub-divisions which perform their leading and their subsidiary shares in this office. So is it with the parts into which a society divides. A dominant class arising does not simply become unlike the rest, but assumes control over the rest; and when this class separates iuto the more and the less dominant, these, again, begin to discharge distinct parts of the entire control. With the classes whose actions are controlled it is the same. The various groups into which they fall havevarious occupations: each of such groups also, within itself, acquiring minor contrasts of parts along with minor contrasts of duties.

And here we see more clearly how the two classes ot things v/e are comparing, distinguish themselves from things of other classes; for such differences of structure as slowly arise in inorganic aggregates, are not accompanied by what we can fairly call differences of function.

§ 217. Why in a body politic and in a living body, these unlike actions of unlike parts are properly regarded by us as functions, while we cannot so regard the unlike actions of unlike parts in an inorganic body, we shall perceive on turning to the next and most distinctive common trait.

Evolution establishes in them both, not differences simply, but definitely-connected differences – differences such that each makes the others possible. The parts of an inorganic aggregate are so related that one may change greatly without appreciably affecting the rest. It is otherwise with the parts of an organic aggregate or of a social aggregate. In either of these, the changes in the parts are mutually determined, ami the changed actions of the parts are mutually dependent. In both, too, this mutuality increases as the evolution advances. The lowest type of animal is all stomach, all respiratory surface, all limb. Development of a type having appendages by which to move about or lay hold of food, can take place only if these appendages, losing power to absorb nutriment directly from surrounding bodies, are supplied with nutriment by parts which retain the power of absorption. A respiratory surface to which the circulating fluids are brought to be aerated, can be formed only on condition that the concomitant loss of ability to supply itself with materials for repair and growth, is made good by the development of a structure bringing these materials. Similarly in a society. What we call with perfect propriety its organization, necessarily implies traits of the same kind. While rudimentary, a society is all warrior, all hunter, all hut-builder, all tool-maker: every part fulfils for itself all needs. Progress to a stage characterized by a permanent army, can go on only as there arise arrangements for supplying that army with food, clothes, and munitions of war by the rest. If here the population occupies itself solely with agriculture and there with mining – if these manufacture goods while those distribute them, it must be on condition that in exchange for a special kind of service rendered by each part to other parts, these other parts severally give due proportions of their services.

This division of labour, first dwelt on by political economists as a social phenomenon, and thereupon recognized by biologists as a phenomenon of living bodies, which they called the "physiological division of labour," is that which in the society, as in the animal, makes it a living whole. Scarcely can I emphasize enough the truth that in respect of this fundamental trait, a social organism and an individual organism are entirely alike. When we see that in a mammal, arresting the lungs quickly brings the heart to a stand; that if the stomach fails absolutely in its office all other parts by-and-by cease to act; that paralysis of its limbs entails on the body at large death from want of food, or inability to escape ; that loss of even such small organs as the eyes, deprives the rest of a service essential to their preservation; we cannot but admit that mutual dependence of parts is an essential characteristic. And when, in a society, we see that the workers in iron stop if the miners do not supply materials; that makers of clothes cannot carry on their business in the absence of those who spin and weave textile fabries ; that the manufacturing community will cease to act unless the food-producing and food-distributing agencies are acting; that the controlling powers, governments, bureaux, judicial officers, police, must fail to keep order when the necessaries of life are not supplied to them by Lhe parts kept in order; we are obliged to say that thismutual dependence of parts is similarly rigorous. Unlike as the two kinds of aggregates otherwise are, they are alike in respect of this fundamental character, and the characters implied by it,

§ 218. How the combined actions of mutually-dependent parts constitute life of the whole, and how there hence results a parallelism between social life and animal life, we see still more clearly on learning that the life of every visible organism is constituted by the lives of units too minute to be seen by the unaided eye.

An undeniable illustration is furnished by the strange order *Myxomycdes*. The spores or germs produced by one of these forms, become ciliated monads, which, after a time of active locomotion, change into shapes like those of amcebai, move about, take in nutriment, grow, multiply by fission. Then these amreba-form individuals swarm together, begin to coalesce into groups, and these groups to coalesce with one another: making a mass sometimes barely visible, sometimes as big as the hand. This *plasmodium,* irregular, mostly reticulated, and in substance gelatinous, itself exhibits movements of its parts like those of a gigantic rhizopod' creeping slowly over surfaces of decaying matters, and -even up the stems of plants. Here, then, union of many minute living individuals to form a relatively vast aggregate in which their individualities are apparently lost, but the life of which results from combination of their lives, is demonstrable.

In other cases, instead of units which, originally discrete, lose their individualities by aggregation, we have units which, arising by multiplication from the same germ, do not part company, but nevertheless display their separate lives very clearly. A growing sponge has its horny fibres clothed with a gelatinous substance; and the microscope shows this to consist of moving monads. We cannot deny life to the sponge as a whole, for it shows us some corporate

actions. The outer amoeba-form units partially lose their individualities by fusion into a protective layer or skin; the supporting framework of fibres is produced by the joint agency of the monads; and from their joint agency also result those currents of water which are drawn in through the smaller orifices and expelled through the larger. But while there is thus shown a feeble aggregate life, the lives of the myriads of component units are very little subordinated: these units form, as it were, a nation having scarcely any sub-division of functions. Or, in the words of Professor Huxley, "the sponge represents a kind of subaqueous city, where the people are arranged about the streets and roads, in such a manner, that each can easily appropriate his food from the water as it passes along." Again, in the hydroid polype *Myriothda*, " pseudopodial processes are being constantly projected from the walls of the alimentary canal into its cavity;" and these Dr. Allman regards as processes from the cells forming the walls, which lay hold of alimentary matter just as those of an amoeba do. The like may be seen in certain planarian worms.

Even in the highest animals there remains traceable this relation between the aggregate life and the lives of components. Blood is a liquid in which, along with nutritive matters, circulate innumerable living units – the blood corpuscles. These have severally their life-histories. During its first stage each of them, then known as a white corpuscle, makes independent movements like those of an amoeba; it "may be fed with coloured food, which, will then be seen to have accumulated in the interior;" " and in some cases the colourless blood-corpuscles have actually been seen to devour their more diminutive companions, the red ones." Nor is this individual life of the units provable only where flotation in a liquid allows its signs to be readily seen. Sundry mucous surfaces, as those of the air passages, are covered with what is called ciliated epithelium – a layer of minute elongated cells packed side by side, andeach bearing on its exposed end several cilia continually in motion. The wavings of these cilia are essentially like those of the monads which live in the passages running through a sponge; and just as the joint action of these ciliated sponge-monads propels the current of water, so does the joint action of the ciliated epithelinm-cells move forward the mucous secretion covering them. If there needs further proof that these epithelinm-cells have independent lives, we have it in the fact that when detached and placed in a fit menstruum, they "move about with considerable rapidity for some time, by the continued vibrations of the cilia with which they are furnished."

On thus seeing that an ordinary living organism may be regarded as a nation of units which live individually, and have many of them considerable degrees of independence, we shall have the less difficulty in regarding a nation of human beings as an organism.

§ 219. The relation between the lives of the units and the life of the aggregate, has a further character common to the two cases. By a catastrophe the life of the aggregate may be destroyed without immediately destroying the lives of all its units; while, on the other hand, if no catastrophe abridges it, the life of the aggregate is far longer than the lives of its units.

In a cold-blooded animal, ciliated cells perform their motions with perfect regularity long after the creature they are part of has become motionless. Muscular fibres retain their power of contracting under stimulation. The cells of secreting organs go on pouring out their product if blood is artificially supplied to them. And the components of an entire organ, as the heart, continue tfoeir co-operation for many hours after its detachment. Similarly, arrest

of those commercial activities, governmental co-ordinations, etc., which constitute the corporate life of a nation, may be

caused, say by an inroad of barbarians, without immediately stopping the actions of all the units. Certain classes of these, especially the widely-diffused ones engaged in food- production, may long survive and carry on their individual occupations.

On the other hand, the minute living elements composing a developed animal, severally evolve, play their parts, decay, and are replaced, while the animal as a whole continues. In the deep layer of the skin, cells are formed by fission which, as they enlarge, are thrust outwards, and, becoming flattened to form the epidermis, eventually exfoliate, while the younger ones beneath take their places. Liver-cells, growing by imbibition of matters from which they separate the bile, presently die, and their vacant seats are occupied by another generation. Even bone, though so dense and seemingly inert, is permeated by blood-vessels carrying materials to replace old components by new ones. And the replacement, rapid in some tissues and in others slow, goes on at such rate that during the continued existence of the entire body, each portion of it has been many times over produced and destroyed. Thus it is

also with a society and its units. Integrity of the whole as of each large division is perennially maintained, notwithstanding the deaths of component citizens. The fabric of living persons which, in a manufacturing town, produces some commodity for national use, remains after a century as large a fabric, though all the masters and workers who a century ago composed it have long since disappeared. Even with minor parts of this industrial structure the like holds. A firm that dates from past generations, still carrying on business in the name of its founder, has had all its members and *employes* changed one by one, perhaps several times over; while the firm has continued to occupy the same place and to maintain like relations with buyers and sellers. Throughout we find this. Governing bodies, general and local, ecclesiastical corporations, armies, institutions of all orders down to guilds, clubs, philanthropic associations, etc.,

show us a continuity of life exceeding that of the persons constituting them. Nay, more. As part of the same law, we see that the existence of the society at large exceeds in duration that of some of these compound parts. Private unions, local public bodies, secondary national institutions, towns carrying on special industries, may decay, while the nation, maintaining its integrity, evolves in mass and structure.

In both cases, too, the mutually-dependent functions of the various divisions, being severally made up of the actions of many units, it results that these units dying one by one, are replaced without the function in which they share being sensibly affected. In a muscle, each sarcous element wearing out in its turn, is removed and a substitution made while the rest carry on their combined contractions as usual; and the retirement of a public official or death of a shopman, perturbs inappreciably the business of the department, or activity of the industry, in which he had a share.

Hence arises in the social organism, as in the individual organism, a life of the whole quite unlike the lives of the units; though it is a life produced by them.

§ 220.   From these likenesses between the social organism and the individual organism, we must now turn to an extreme unlikeness. The parts of an animal form a concrete whole; but the parts of a society form a whole which is discrete. While the living units composing the one are bound together in close contact, the living units composing the other are free, are not in contact, and are more or less widely dispersed. How, then, can there be any parallelism ?

Though this difference is fundamental and apparently puts comparison out of the question, yet examination proves it to be less than it seems. Presently I shall have to point out that complete admission of it consists with maintenance of the alleged analogy; but we will first observe how one who thought it needful, might argue that even in this respect there is a smaller contrast than a cursory glance shows.

He might urge that the physically-coherent body of an animal is not composed all through of living units ; but that it consists in large measure of differentiated parts which the vitally active parts have formed, a. nd which thereafter become serai-vital and in some cases un-vitul. Taking as an example the protoplasmic layer underlying the skin, he might say that while this consists of truly living units, the cells produced in it, changing into epithelium scales, become inert protective structures; and pointing to the insensitive nails, hair, horns, etc., arising from this layer, he might show that such parts, though components of the organism, are hardly living components. Carrying out the argument, he would contend that elsewhere in the body there exist such protoplasmic layers, from which grow the tissues composing the various organs – layers which alone remain fully alive, while the structures evolved from them lose their vitality in proportion as they are specialized: instancing cartilage, tendon, and connective tissue, as showing this in conspicuous ways. From all which he would draw the inference that though the body forms a coherent whole, its essential units, taken by themselves, form a whole which is coherent only throughout the protoplasmic layers.

And then would follow the facts showing that the social organism, rightly conceived, is much less discontinuous than it seems. He would contend that as, in the individual organism, we include with the fully living parts, the less living and not living parts which co-operate in the total activities; so, in the social organism, we must include not only those most highly vitalized units, the human beings, who chiefly determine its phenomena, but also the various kinds of domestic animals, lower in the scale of life, which, under the control of man, co-operate with him, and even those far inferior structures, the plants, which, propagated by human agency, supply materials for animal and human activities. In defence of this view he would point out how largely these lower classes of organisms, co-existing

with men in societies, affect the structures and activities of the societies – how the traits of the pastoral type depend on the natures of the creatures reared; and how in settled societies the plants producing food, materials for textile fabrics, etc., determine certain kinds of social arrangements and actions. After which he might insist that since the physical characters, mental natures, and daily doings, of the human units, are, in part, moulded by relations to these animals and vegetals, which, living by their aid and aiding them to live, enter so much into social life as even to be cared for by legislation, these lower forms cannot rightly be excluded from the conception of the social organism. Hence would come his conclusion that when, with human beings, are incorporated the less vitalized beings, animal and vegetal, covering the surface occupied by the society, there results an aggregate having a continuity of parts more nearly approaching to that of an individual organism; and which is also like it in being composed of local aggregations of highly vitalized units, imbedded in a vast aggregation of units of various lower degrees of vitality, which are, in a sense, produced by, modified by, and arranged by, the higher units.

But without accepting this view, and admitting that the discreteness of the social organism stands in marked contrast with the concreteness of the individual organism, the objection may still be adequately met.

§ 221. Though coherence among its parts is a prerequisite to that co-operation by which the life of an individual organism is carried on; and though the members of a social organism, not forming a concrete whole, cannot maintain co-operation by means of physical influences directly propagated from part to part; yet they can and do maintain co-operation by another agency. Not in contact, they nevertheless affect one another through intervening spaces, both by emotional language and by the language, oraland written, of the intellect. For carrying on mutually- dependent actions, it is requisite that impulses, adjusted in their kinds, amounts, and times, shall be conveyed from part to part. This requisite is fulfilled in living bodies by molecular waves, that are indefinitely diffused in low types, nud in high types are earned along definite channels (the function of which has been significantly called *intetr- nuncial).* It is fulfilled in societies by the signs of feelings and thoughts, conveyed from person to person; at first in vague ways and only through short distances, but afterwards more definitely and through greater distances. That is to say, the inter-nuncial function, not achievable by stimuli physically transferred, is nevertheless achieved by language – emotional and intellectual.

That mutual dependence of parts which constitutes organization is thus effectually established. Though discrete instead of concrete, the social aggregate is rendered a living whole.

§ 222. But now, on pursuing the course of thought opened by this objection and the answer to it, we arrive at an implied contrast of great significance – a contrast fundamentally affecting our idea of the ends to be achieved by social life.

Though the discreteness of a social organism does not prevent sub-division of functions and mutual dependence of parts, yet it does prevent that differentiation by which one part becomes an organ of feeling and thought, while other parts become insensitive. High animals of whatever class are distinguished from low ones by complex and well-integrated nervous systems. While in inferior types the minute scattered ganglia may be said to exist for the benefit of other structures, the concentrated ganglia in superior types are the structures for the benefit of which the rest may be said to exist. Though a developed nervous system so directs the actions of . the whole body as to preserve its integrity; yetthe welfare of the nervous system is the ultimate object of all these actions: damage to any other organ being serious in proportion as it immediately or remotely entails that pain or loss of pleasure which the nervous system suffers. But the discreteness of a society negatives differentiations carried to this extreme. In an individual organism the minute living units, most of them permanently localized, growing up, working, reproducing, and dying away in their respective places, are in successive generations moulded to their respective functions; so that some become specially sentient and others entirely insentient. But it is otherwise in a social organism, -The units of this, out of contact and much less rigidly held in their relative positions, cannot be so much differentiated as to become feelingless units and units which mouopolize feeling. There are,

indeed, traces of such a differentiation. Human beings are unlike in the amounts of sensation and enution producible in them by like causes: here callousness, here susceptibility, is a characteristic. The mechanically-working and hard- living units are less sensitive than the mentally-working and more protected units. But while the regulative structures of the social organism tend, like those of the individual organism, to become specialized as seats of feeling, the tendency is checked by want of that physical cohesion which brings fixity of function; and it is also checked by the continued need for feeling in the mechanically-working units for the due discharge of their functions.

Hence, then, a cardinal difference in the two kinds of organisms. In the one, consciousness is concentrated in a small part of the aggregate. In the other, it is diffused throughout the aggregate: all the units possess the capacities for happiness and misery, if not in equal degrees, still in degrees that approximate. As, then, there is no social sensorinm, the welfare of the aggregate, considered apart from that of the units, is not an end to be sought . The society exists for the benefit of its members; not its members for the benefit of the society. It has ever to be remembered that great as may be the efforts made for the prosperity of the body politic, yet the claims of the body politic are nothing in themselves, and become something only in so far as they embody the claims of its component individuals.

§ 223. From this last consideration, which is a digression rather than a part of the argument, let us now return and sum up the reasons for regarding a society as an organism.

It undergoes continuous-growth. As it grows, its parts become unlike: it exhibits increase of structure. The unlike parts simultancously assume activities of unlike kinds. These activities are not simply different, but their differences are so related as to make one another possible. The reciprocal aid thus given causes mutual dependence of the parts. And the mutually-dependent parts, living by and for one another, form an aggregate constituted on the same general principle as is an individual organism.

The analogy of a society to an organism becomes still clearer on learning that every organism of appreciable size is a society; and on further learning that in both, the lives of the units continue for some time if the life of the aggregate is suddenly arrested, while if the aggregate is not destroyed by violence, its life greatly exceeds in duration the lives of its units. Though the two are contrasted as respectively discrete and concrete, and though there results a difference in the ends subserved by the organization, there does not result a difference in the laws of the organization: the required mutual influences of the parts, not transmissible in a direct way, being, in a society, transmitted in an indirect way.

Having thus considered in their most general forms the reasons for regarding a society as an organism, we are prepared for following out the comparison in detail.

CHAPTER IIL

SOCIAL GROWTH.

§ 224. Societies, like living bodies, begin as germs – originate from masses which are extremely minute in comparison with the masses some of them eventually reach. That out of small wandering hordes have arisen the largest societies, is a conclusion not to be contested. The implements of pre-historic peoples, ruder even than existing savages use, imply absence of those arts by which alone great aggregations of men are made possible. Religious ceremonies that survived among ancient historic races, pointed back to a time when the progenitors of those races had flint knives, and got fire by nibbing together pieces of wood; and must have lived in such small clusters as are alone possible before the rise of agriculture.

The implication is that by integrations, direct and indirect, there have in course of time been produced social aggregates a. million times in size the aggregates which alone existed in the remote past. Here, then, is a growth reminding us, by its degree, of growth in living bodies.

§ 225. Between this trait of organic evolution and the answering trait of super-organic evolution, there is a further parallelism: the growths in aggregates of different classes are extremely various in their amounts.

Glancing over the entire assemblage of animal *types,* we sec that the members of one large class, the *Protozoa,* rarely increase beyond that microscopic size with which every higher animal begins. Among the multitudinous kinds of *Ccelenterata,* the masses range from that of the small Hydra to that of the large Medusa. The ammlose and molluscous types, respectively show us immense contrasts between their superior and inferior members. And the vertebrate animals, much larger on the average than the rest, display among themselves enormous differences.

Kindred unlikenesses of size strike us when we contemplate the entire assemblage of human societies. Scattered over many regions there are minute hordes – still extant samples of the primordial type of society. We have Vood- Veddahs living sometimes in pairs, and only now and then assembling; we have Bushmen wandering about in families, and forming larger groups but occasionally; we have Fuegians clustered by the dozen or the score. Tribes of Australians, of Tasmanians, of Andamanese, are variable within the limits of perhaps twenty to fifty. And similarly, if the region is inhospitable, as with the Esquimaux, or if the arts of life are undeveloped, as with the Digger-Indians, or if adjacent higher races are obstacles to growth, as with Indian

Hill-tribes like the Juangs, this limitation to primitive size continues. "Where a fruitful soil affords much food, and where a more settled life, leading to agriculture, again increases the supply of food, we meet with larger social aggregates: instance those in the Polynesian Islands and in many parts of Africa, Here a hundred or two, here several thousands, here many thousands, are held together more or less completely as one mass. And then in the highest societies, instead of partially-aggregated thousands, we have completely-aggregated millions.

§ 226. The growths of individual and social organisms are allied in another respect. In each case size augments by two processes, which go on sometimes separately, sometimes together. There is increase by simple multiplication of units, causing enlargement of the group; there is increase by union of groups, and again by union of groups of groups. The first parallelism is too simple to need illustration; but the facts which show us the second must be set forth.

Organic integration, treated of at length in the *Principles of Biology,* §§ 180 – 211, must be here summarized to make the comparison intelligible. The compounding and re-compounding, as shown us throughout the vegetal kingdom, may be taken first, as most easily followed. Plants of

the lowest orders are minute cells, some kinds of which in their myriads colour stagnant waters, and others compose the green films on damp surfaces. By clusterings of such cells are formed small threads, dises, globes, etc.; as well as amorphous masses and laminated masses. One of these last (called a thallus when scarcely at all differentiated, as in a sea-weed, and called a frond in cryptogams that have some structure), is an extensive but simple group of the protophytes first named. Temporarily united in certain low cryptogams, fronds become permanently united in higher cryptogams: then forming a series of foliar surfaces joined by a creepirg stem. Out of this comes the phsenogamic axis – a shoot with its foliar organs or leaves. That is to say, there is now a permanent cluster of clusters. And then, as these axes develop lateral axes, and as these again branch, the compounding advances to higher stages. In the animal- kingdom the like happens; though in a less regular and more disguised manner. The smallest animal, like the smallest plant, is essentially a minute group of living molecules. There are many forms and stages showing us the clustering of such smallest animals. Sometimes, as in the compound *Vorticdlce* and in the Sponges, their individualities are scarcely at all masked; but as evolution of the composite aggregate advances, the individualities of the component aggregates become less distinct. In some *Cwleutcrata,* though

they retain considerable independence, which they show by moving about like *Amcebce* when separated, they have their individualities mainly merged in that of the aggregate formed of them: instance the common Hydra. Tertiary aggregates similarly result from the massing of secondary ones. Sundry modes and phases of the process are observable among coelenterate types. There is the branched hydroid, in which the individual polypes preserve their identities, and the polypidom merely holds them together; and there are forms, such as *Vddla,* in which the polypes have been so modified and fused, that their individualities were long unrecognized. Again, among the *Molluseoida* we have feebly-united tertiary aggregates in the *Salpidae;* while we have, in the *Botryllidce,* masses in which the tertiary aggregate, greatly consolidated, obscures the individualities of the secondary aggregates. So, too, is it with certain nnnuloid types; and, as I have sought to show, with the *Aunulosa* generally. *(Prin. of Biol.,* § 205.)

Social growth proceeds by an analogous compounding and re-compounding. The primitive social group, like the primitive group of living molecules with which organic evolution begins, never attains any considerable size by simple increase. Where, as among Fuegians, the supplies of wild food yielded by an inclement habitat will not enable more than a score or so to live in the same place – where, as among Andamanese, limited to a strip of shore backed by impenetrable bush, forty is about the number of individuals who can find prey without going too far from their temporary abode – where, as among Bushmen, wandering over barren tracts, small hordes are alone possible, and even families " are sometimes obliged to separate, since the same spot will not afford sufficient sustenance for all;" we have extreme instances of the limitation of simple groups, and the formation of migrating groups when the limit is passed. Even in tolerably productive habitats, fission of the groups is eventually necessitated in a kindred manner. Spreading as its numbei

increases, a primitive tribe presently reaches a diffusion at which its parts become incoherent; and it then gradually separates into tribes that become distinct as fast as their continually-diverging dialects pass into different languages. Often nothing further happens than repetition of this. Conflicts of tribes, dwindlings or extinctions of some, growths and spontaneous divisions of others, continue. The

formation of a larger society results only by the joining of such smaller societies ; which occurs without obliterating the divisions previously caused by separations. This process may be seen now going on among uncivilized races, as it once went on among the ancestors of the civilized races. Instead of absolute independence of small hordes, such as the lowest savages show us, more advanced savages show us slight cohesions among larger hordes. In North America each of the three great tribes of Comanches consists of various bands, having such feeble combination only, as results from the personal character of the great chief. So of the Dakotahs there are, according to Burton, seven principal bands, each including minor bands, numbering altogether, according to Catlin, forty-two. And in like manner the five Iroquois nations had severally cight tribes. Closer unions of these slightly-coherent original groups arise under favourable conditions ; but they only now and then become permanent. A common form of the process is that described by Mason as occurring among the Karens. " Each village, with its scant domain, is an independent state, and every chief a prince; but now and then a little Napoleon arises, who subdues a kingdom to himself, and builds up an empire. The dynasties, however, last only with the controlling mind." The like happens in Africa. Livingstone says – "Formerly all the Maganja were united under the government of their great Chief, Uudi; ... but after Undi's death it fell to pieces. . . . This has been the inevitable fate of every African Empire from time immemorial." Only occasionally does there result a compound social aggregate that endures

for a considerable period, as Dahomey or as Ashanteet which *is* " an assemblage of states owing a kind of feudal obedience to the sovereign." The histories of Madagascar and of sundry Polynesian islands also display these transitory compound groups, out of which at length come in some cases permanent ones. During the earliest times of the extinct civilized races, like stages were passed through. In the words of Maspero, Egypt was "divided at first into a great number of tribes, which at several points simultancously began to establish small independent states, every one of which had its laws and its worship." The compound groups of Greeks first formed, were those minor ones resulting from the subjugation of weaker towns by stronger neighbouring towns. And in Northern Europe during pagan days, the numerous German tribes, each with its cantonal divisions, illustrated this second stage of aggregation. After

such compound societies are consolidated, repetition of the process on a larger scale produces doubly-compound societies; which, usually cohering but feebly, become in some cases quite coherent. Maspero infers that the Egyptian nomes described above as resulting from integrations of tribes, coalesced into the two great principalities, Upper Egypt and Lower Egypt, which were eventually united: the small states becoming provinces. The boasting records of Meso- potamian kings similarly show us this union of unions going on. So, too, in Greece the integration at first occurring locally, began afterwards to combine the minor societies into two confederacies. During Eoman days there arose for defensive purposes federations of tribes, which eventually consolidated; and subsequently these were compounded into still larger aggregates. Before and after the Christian era, the like happened throughout Northern Europe. Then after a period of vague and varying combinations, there came, in later times, as is well illustrated by French history, a massing of small feudal territories into provinces, and a subsequent massing of these into kingdoms.

So that in both organic and super-organic growths, we see a process of compounding and re-compounding earned to various stages. In both cases, after some consolidation of the smallest aggregates there comes the process of forming larger aggregates by union of them; and in both cases repetition of this process makes secondary aggregates into tertiary ones.

§ 227. Organic growth and super-organic growth have yet another analogy. As above said, increase by multiplication of individuals in a group, and increase by union of groups, may go on simultaneously; and it does this in both cases.

The original clusters, animal and social, are not only small, but they lack density. Creatures of low types occupy large spaces considering the small quantities of animal substance they contain; and low-type societies spread over areas that are wide relatively to the numbers of their component individuals. But as integration in animals is shown by concentration as well as by increase of bulk; so that social integration which results from the clustering of clusters, is joined with augmentation of the number contained by each cluster. If we contrast the sprinklings in regions inhabited by wild tribes with the crowds filling equal regions in Europe; or if we contrast the density of population in England under the Heptarchy with its present density; we see that besides the growth produced by union of groups there has gone on interstitial growth. Just as the higher animal has become not only larger than the lower but r. iore *solid ;* so, too, has the higher society.

Social growth, then, equally with the growth of a living body, shows us the fundamental trait of evolution under a twofold aspect. Integration is displayed both in the formation of a larger mass, and in the progress of such mass towards that coherence due to closeness of parts.

It is proper to add, however, that there is a mode of socialgrowth to which organic growth affords no parallel – that caused by the migration of units from one society to another. Among many primitive groups and a few developed ones, this is a considerable factor; but, generally, its effect bears so small a ratio to the effects of growth by increase of population and coalescence of groups, that it does not much qualify the analogy.

CHAPTER IV.

SOCIAL STRUCTURES.

§ 228. In societies, as in living bodies, increase of mass is habitually accompanied by increase of structure. Along with that integration which is the primary trait of evolution, both exhibit in high degrees the secondary trait, differentiation.

The association of these two characters in animals was described in the *Principles of Biology,* § 44. Excluding certain low kinds of them whose activities are little above those of plants, we recognized the general law that large aggregates have high organizations. The qualifications of this law which go along with differences of medium, of habitat, of type, are numerous; but when made they leave intact the truth that for carrying on the combined life of an extensive mass, involved arrangements are required. So, too, is it with societies. As we

progress from small groups to larger; from simple groups to compound groups ; from compound groups to doubly compound ones; the unlikeuesses of parts increase. The social aggregate, homogeneous when minute, habitually gains in heterogeneity along with each increment of growth; and to reach great size must acquire great complexity. Let us glance at the leading stages.

Naturally in a state like that of the Cayaguas or Wood- Indians of South America, so little social that " one family lives at a distance from another," social organization is impossible; and even whcre there is some slight association of families, organization does not arise while they are few and wandering. Groups of Esquimaux, of Australians, of Bushmen, of Fuegians, are without even that primary contrast of parts implied by settled chieftainship. Their members are subject to no control bub such as is temporarily acquired by the stronger, or more cunning, or more experienced: not even a permanent nucleus is present. Habitually where larger simple groups exist, we find some kind of head. Though not a uniform rule (for, as we shall hereafter see, the genesis of a controlling agency depends on the nature of the social activities), this is a general rule. The headless clusters, wholly ungoverned, are incoherent, and separate before they acquire considerable sizes; but along with maintenance of an aggregate approaching to, or exceeding, a hundred, we ordinarily find a simple or compound ruling agency – one or more men claiming and exercising authority that is natural, or supernatural, or both. This is the first social differentiation. Soon after it there

frequently comes another, tending to form a division between regulative and operative parts. In the lowest tribes this is rudely represented only by the contrast in *status* between the sexes: the men, having unchecked control, carry on such external activities as the tribe shows us, chiefly in war; while the women are made drudges who perform the less skilled parts of the process of sustentation. But that tribal growth, and establishment of chieftainship, which gives military superiority, presently causes enlargement of the operative part by adding captives to it. This begins unobtrusively. While in battle the men are killed, and often afterwards eaten, the non-combatants are enslaved. Patagonians, for example, make slaves of women and children taken in war. Later, and especially when cannibalism ceases, comes the enslavement of male captives; whence results, in some cases, an operative part clearly marked offfrom the regulative part. Among the Chinooks, " slaves do all the laborious work." "We read that the Beluchi, avoiding the hard labour of cultivation, impose it on the Jutts, the ancient inhabitants whom they have subjugated. Beecham says it is usual on the Gold Coast to make the slaves clear the ground for cultivation. And among the Felatahs " slaves are numerous: the males are employed in weaving, collecting wood or grass, or on any other kind of work; some of the women are engaged in spinning ... in preparing the yaru for the loom, others in pounding and grinding corn, etc."

Along with. that increase of mass caused by union of primary social aggregates into a secondary one, a further unlikeness of parts arises. The holding together of the compound cluster implies a head of the whole as well as heads of the parts; and a differentiation analogous to that which originally produced a chief, now produces a chief of chiefs. Sometimes the combination is made for defence against a common foe, and sometimes it results from conquest by one tribe of the rest. In this last case the predominant tribe, in maintaining its supremacy, develops more highly its military character: thus becoming unlike the others.

After such clusters of clusters have been so consolidated that their united powers can he wielded by one governing agency, there come alliances with, or subjugations of, other clusters of clusters, ending from time to time in coalescence. When this happens there results still greater complexity in the governing agency, with its king, local rulers, and petty chiefs; and at the same time, there arise more marked divisions of classes – military, priestly, slave, etc. Clearly, then, complication of structure accompanies increase of mass.

§ 229. This increase of heterogeneity, which in both classes of aggregates goes along with growth, presents another trait in common. Beyond unlikenesses of parts due to development of the co-ordinating agencies, there presently follow unlikenesses among the agencies coordinated – the organs of alimentation, etc., in the one case, and the industrial structures in the other.

When animal-ajTcrrpejates of the lowest order unite to form one of a higher order, and when, again, these secondary aggregates are compounded into tertiary aggregates, each component is at first similar to the other components; but in the course of evolution dissimilarities arise and become more and more decided. Among the *Ccelentcrata* the stages are clearly indicated. From the sides of a common hydra, bud out young ones which, "when fully developed, separate from their parent. In the compound hydroids the young polypes produced in like manner, remain permanently attached, and, themselves repeating the process, presently form a branched aggregate. When the members of the compound group lead similar and almost independent lives, as in various rooted genera, they remain similar: save those of them which become reproductive organs. But in the floating and swimming clusters, formed by a kindred process, the differently-conditioned members become different, while assuming different functions. It is thus with the

minor social groups combined into a major social group. Each tribe originally had within itself such feebly-marked industrial divisions as sufficed for its low kind of life; and these were like those of each other tribe. But union facilitates exchange of commodities; and if, as mostly happens, the component tribes severally occupy localities favourable to unlike kinds of production, unlike occupations are initiated, and there result unlikenesses of industrial structures. Even between tribes not united, as those of Australia, barter of products furnished by their respective habitats goes on so long as war does not hinder. And evidently when there is reached such a stage of integration as in Madagascar, or as in the chief Negro states of Africa, the internal peace that follows subordination to one government makes commercial intercourse easy. The like parts being permanently held together, mutual dependence becomespossible; and along with growing mutual dependence the parts grow unlike.

§ 230. The advance of organization which thus follows the advance of aggregation, alike in individual organisms and in social organisms, conforms in both cases to the same general law: differentiations proceed from the more general to the more speciaL. First broad and simple contrasts of parts; then within each of the parts primarily contrasted, changes which make unlike divisions of them; then within each of these unlike divisions, minor unlikenesses; and so on continually.

The successive stages in the development of a vertebrate column, illustrate this law in animals. At the outset an elongated depression of the blastoderm, called the " primitive groove," represents the entire cerebro-spinal axis: as yet there are no marks of vertebra, nor even a contrast between the part which is to become head and the part which is to become back-bone. Presently the ridges bounding this groove, growing up and folding over more rapidly at the anterior end, which at the same time widens, begin to make the skull distinguishable from the spine; and the commencement of segmentation in the spinal part, while the cephalic part remains unsegmented, strengthens the contrast. Within each of these main divisions minor divisions soon arise. The rudimentary craninm, Lending forward, simultaneously acquires three dilatations indicating the contained nervous centres; while the segmentation of the spinal column, spreading to its ends, produces an almost-uniform series of " proto-vertebrse." At first these proto-vertebrae not only differ very little from one another, but each is relatively simple – a quadrate mass. Gradually this almost-uniform series falls into unlike divisions – the cervical group, the dorsal group, the lumbar group; and while the series of vertebrae is thus becoming specialized in its different regions, each vertebra is changing from that general form which it atfirst had in common with the rest, to the more special form eventually distinguishing it from the rest. Throughout the embryo there are, at the same time, going on kindred processes ; which, first making each large part unlike all other large parts, then make the parts of that part unlike one another. During social evolution analogous meta

morphoses may everywhere be traced. The rise of the structure exercising religious control will serve as an example. In simple tribes, and in clusters of tribes during their early stages of aggregation, we find men who are at once sorcerers, priests, diviners, exorcists, doctors, – men who deal with supposed supernatural beings in all the various possible ways: propitiating them, seeking knowledge and aid from them, commanding them, subduing them. Along with advance in social integration, there come both differences of function and differences of rank. In Tanua " there are rain-makers . . . and a host of other ' sacred men;'" in Fiji there are not only priests, but seers; among the Sandwich Islanders there are diviners as well as priests 5 among the New Zealanders, Thomson distinguishes between priests and sorcerers; and among the Kaffirs, besides diviners and rain-makers, there are two classes of doctors who respectively rely on supernatural and on natural agents in curing their patients. More advanced societies, as those of ancient America, show us still greater multiformity of this once-uniform group. In Mexico, for example, the medical class, descending from a class of sorcerers who dealt antagonistically with the supernatural agents supposed to cause disease, were distinct from the priests, whose dealings with supernatural agents were propitiatory. Further, the sacerdotal class included several kinds, dividing the religious offices among them – sacrificers, diviners, singers, composers of hymns, instructors of youth ; and then there were also gradations of rank in each. This progress from general to special in priesthoods, has, in the higher nations, led to such marked distinctions that the original kinships areforgotten. The priest-astrologers of ancient races were initiators of the scientific class, now variously specialized ; from the priest-doctors of old have come the medical class with its chief division and minor divisions; while within the clerical class proper, have arisen not only various ranks from Pope down to acolyte, but various kinds of functionaries – dean, priest, deacon, chorister, as well as others classed as curates and chaplains. Similarly if we trace the genesis of any industrial structure; as that which from primitive blacksmiths who smelt their own iron as well as make implements from it, brings us to our iron-manufacturing districts, where preparation of the metal *is* separated into smelting, refining, puddling, rolling, and where turning this metal into implements is divided into various businesses.

The transformation here illustrated, is, indeed, an aspect of that transformation of the homogeneous into the heterogeneous which everywhere characterizes evolution; but the truth to be noted is that it characterizes the evolution of individual organisms and of social organisms in especially high degrees.

§ 231. Closer study of the facts shows us another striking parallelism. Organs in animals and organs in societies have internal arrangements framed on the same principle.

Differing from one another as the viscera of a living creature do in many respects, they have several traits in common. Each viscus contains appliances for conveying nutriment to its parts, for bringing it materials on which to operate, for carrying away the product, for draining off waste matters; as also for regulating its activity. Though liver and kidneys are unlike in their general appearances and minute structures, as well as in the offices they fulfil, the one as much as the other has a system of arteries, a system of veins, a system of lymphaties – has branched channels through which its excretions escape, and nervesfor exciting and checking it. In large measure the like is true of those higher organs which, instead of elaborating and purifying and distributing the blood, aid the general life by carrying on external actions – the nervous and muscular organs. These, too, have their ducts for bringing prepared materials, ducts for drafting off vitiated materials, ducts for carrying away effete matters; as also their controlling nerve-cells and fibres. So that, along with the many marked differences of structure, there are these marked communities of structure.

It is the same in a society. The clustered citizens forming an organ which produces some commodity for national use, or which otherwise satisfies national wants, has within it subservient structures substantially like those of each other organ carrying on each other function. Be it a cotton- weaving district or a district where cutlery is made, it has a set of agencies which bring the raw material, and a set of agencies which collect and send away the manufactured articles; it has an apparatus of major and minor channels through which the necessaries of life are drafted out of the general stocks circulating through the kingdom, and brought home to the local workers and those who direct them; it has appliances, postal and other, for bringing those impulses by which the industry of the place is excited or checked; it- has local controlling powers, political and ecclesiastical, by which order is maintained and healthful action furthered. So, too, when, from a district which secretes certain goods, we turn to a sea-port which absorbs and sends out goods, we find the distributing and restraining agencies are mostly the same. Even where the social organ, instead of carrying on a material activity, has, like a university, the office of preparing certain classes of units for social functions of particular kinds, this general type of structure is repeated: the appliances for local sustentation and regulation, differing in some respects, are similar in essentials – there are like classes of distributors, like classesfor civil control, and a specially-developed class for ecclesiastical control.

On observing that this community of structure among social organs, like the community of structure among organs in a living body, necessarily accompanies mutual dependence, we shall see even more clearly than hitherto, how great is the likeness of nature between individual organization and social organization.

§ 232. One more structural analogy must he named. The formation of organs in a living body proceeds in ways which we may distinguish as primary, secondary, and tertiary; and, paralleling them, there are primary, secondary, and tertiary ways in which social organs are formed. We will look at each of the three parallelisms by itself.

In animals of low types, bile is secreted, not by a liver, but by separate cells imbedded in the wall of the intestine at one pait. These cells individually perform their function of separating certain matters from the blood, and individually pour out what they separate. No organ, strictly so-called, exists; but only a number of units not yet aggregated into an organ. This is analogous to the incipient form of an industrial structure in a society. At first each worker carries on his occupation alone, and himself disposes of the product to consumers. The arrangement still extant in our villages, where the cobbler at his own fireside makes and sells boots, and where the blacksmith single-handed does what iron-work is needed by his neighbours, exemplifies the primitive type of every producing structure. Among savages slight differentiations arise from individual aptitudes. Even of the degraded Fuegians, Fitz- roy tells us that " one becomes an adept with the spear; another with the sling; another with a bow and arrows." As like differences of skill among members of primitive tribes, cause some to become makers of special things, ib results that necessarily the industrial organ begins as asocial unit. Where, as among the Shasta Indians of California, arrow-making is a distinct profession, it is clear that manipulative superiority being the cause of the differentiation, the worker is at first single. And during subsequent periods of growth, even in small settled communities, this type continues. The statement that among the Coast Negroes, " the most ingenious man in the village is usually the blacksmith, joiner, architect, and weaver," while it shows ns artizan-functions in an undifferentiated stage, also shows us how completely individual is the artizan-structure: the implication being that as the society grows, it is by the addition of more such individuals, severally carrying on their occupations independently, that the additional demand is met.

By two simultaneous changes, an incipient secreting organ in an animal reaches that higher structure with which our next comparison may be made. The cells pass from a scattered cluster into a compact cluster; and they severally become compound. In place of a single cell elaborating and emitting its special product, we now have a small elongated sac containing a family of cells; and this, through an opening at one end, gives exit to their products. At the same time there is formed an integrated group of such follicles, each containing secreting units and having its separate orifice of discharge. To this type of in

dividual organ, we find, in semi-civilized societies, a type of social organ closely corresponding. In one of these settled and growing communities, the demands upon individual workers, now more specialized in their occupations, have become unceasing; and each worker, occasionally piessed by work, makes helpers of his children. This practice, beginning incidentally, establishes itself; and eventually it grows into an imperative custom that each man shall bring up his boys to his own trade. Illustrations of this stage are numerous. Skilled occupations, "like every other calling and oilice in Peru, always descended from father to son. The division of castes, in this particular, was as precise as that which existed in Egypt or Hindostan." In Mexico, too, " the sons in general learned the trades of their fathers, and embraced their professions." The like was true of the industrial structures of European nations in early times. J5y the Theodosian code, a Itoman youth "was compelled to follow the employment of his father . . . and the suitor who sought the hand of the daughter could only obtain his bride by becoming wedded to the calling of her family." In mediaeval France handicrafts were inherited; and the old English periods were characterized by a like usage. Branching of the family through generations into a number of kindred families carrying on the same occupation, produced the germ of the guild; and the related families who monopolized each industry formed a cluster habitually occupying the same quarter. Hence the still extant names of many streets in English towns – " Fellmonger, Horse- monger, and Fleshmonger, Shoewright and Shieldwright, Turner and Salter Streets:" a segregation like thut which still persists in Oriental bazaars. And now, on observing how one of these industrial quarters was composed of many allied families, each containing sous working under direction of a father, who while sharing in the work sold the produce, and who, if the family and business were large, became mainly a channel taking in raw material and giving out the manufactured article, we see that there existed an analogy to the kind of glandular organ described above, which consists of a number of adjacent cell-containing follicles having separate mouths.

A third stage of the analogy may be traced. Along with that incrsase of a glandular organ necessitated by the more active functions of a more developed animal, there goes a change of structure consequent on augmentation of bulk. If the follicles multiply while their ducts have all to be brought to one spot, it results that their orifices, increasingly numerous, occupy a larger area of the wall of thecavity which receives the discharge; and if lateral extension of this area is negatived by the functional requirements, it results that the needful area is gained hy formation of a ciEcum. Further need of the same kind leads to secondary caeca diverging from this main ccecum; which hence becomes, in part, a duct. Thus is at length evolved a large viscus, such as a liver, having a single main duct with ramifying branches running throughout its mass. Now we

rise from the above-described kind of industrial organ by parallel stages to a higher kind. There is no sudden leap from the household-type to the factory-type, but a gradual transition. The first step is shown us in those rules of trade- guilds under which, to the members of the family, might be added an apprentice (possibly at first a relation), who, as Brentano says, "became a member of the family of his master, who instructed him in his trade, and who, like a father, had to watch over his morals, as well as his work:" practically, an adopted son. This modification having been established, there followed the employing of apprentices who had changed into journeymen. With development of this modified household-group, the master grew into a seller of goods made, not by his own family only, but by others; and, as his business enlarged, necessarily ceased to be a worker, and became wholly a distributor – a channel through which went out the products, not of a few sons, but of many unrelated artizans. This led the way to establishments in which the employed far outnumbered the members of the family; until at length, with the use of mechanical power, came the factory: a series of rooms, each containing a crowd of producing units, and sending its tributary stream of product to join other streams before reaching the single place of exit. Finally, in greatly-developed industrial organs, we see many factories clustered in the same town, and others in adjacent towns; to and from which, along branching roads, come the raw materials and go the bales of cloth, calico, etc.

There are instances in which a new industry passes throughthese stages in the course of a few generations; as happened with the stocking-manufacture. In the Midland counties, fifty years ago, the rattle and burr of a solitary stocking- frame came from a road-side cottage every here and there t the single worker made and sold his product. Presently arose work-shops in which several such looms might be heard going: there was the father and his sons, with perhaps a journeyman. At length grew up the large building containing many looms driven by a steam-engine; and finally many such large buildings in the same town.

§ 233. These structural analogies reach a final phase that is still more striking. In both cases there is a contrast between the original mode of development and a substituted later mode.

In the general course. of organic evolution from low types to high, there have been passed through by insensible modifications all the stages above described; but now, in the individual evolution of an organism of high type, these stages are greatly abridged, and an organ is produced by a comparatively direct process. Thus the liver of a mammalian embryo is formed by the accumulation of numerous cells, which presently grow into a mass projecting from the wall of the intestine; while

simultaneously there dips down into it a caecum from the intestine. Transformation of this csecum into the hepatic duct takes place at the same time that within the mass of cells there arise minor ducts, connected with this main duct; and there meanwhile go on other changes which, during evolution of the organ through successively higher types, came one after another. In the formation of industrial
organs the like happens. Now that the factory system is well-established – now that it has become ingrained in the social constitution, we see direct assumptions of it in all industries for which its fitness has been shown. If at one place the discovery of ore prompts the setting up of ironworks, or at another a special kind of water facilitatesbrewing, there is no passing through the early stages of single worker, family, clustered families, and so on; but there is a sudden drafting of materials and men to the spot, followed by formation of a producing structure on the advanced type. Nay, not one large establishment only is thus evolved after the direct manner, but a cluster of large establishments. At Barrow-in-Furness we see a town with its iron-works, its importing and exporting businesses, its extensive docks and means of communication, all in the space of a few years framed after that type which it has taken centuries to develop through successive modifications.

An allied but even more marked change in the evolutionary process, is also common to both cases. Just as in the embryo of a high animal, various organs have their important parts laid down out of their original order, in anticipation, as it were; so, with the body at large, it happens that entire organs which, during the serial genesis of the type, came comparatively late, come in the evolving individual comparatively soon. This, which Prof. Haeckel has called heterochrony, is shown us in the early marking out of the brain in a mammalian embryo, though in the lowest vertebrate animal, no brain ever exists; or, again, in the segmentation of the spinal column before any alimentary system is formed, though, in a proto-vertebrate, even when its alimentary system is completed, there are but feeble signs of segmentation. The analogous change
of order in social evolution, is shown us by new societies which inherit the confirmed habits of old ones. Instance the United States, where a town in the far west, laid down in its streets and plots, has its hotel, church, post-olficej built while there are but few houses; and where a railway is run through the wilderness in anticipation of settlements. Or instance Australia, where a few years after the huts of gold-diggers begin to cluster round new mines, there is established a printing-office and journal; though, in the mother-country, centuries passed before a town of like size developed a like agency.

CHAPTER V.
SOCIAL FUNCTIONS.

§ 234. Changes of structures cannot Occitt without changes of functions. Much that was said in the last chapter might, therefore, be said here with substituted terms. Indeed, as in societies many changes of structure are more indicated by changes of function than directly seen, it may be said that these last have been already described by implication.

There are, however, certain functional traits not manifestly implied by traits of structure. To these a few pages must be devoted.

§ 235. If organization consists in such a construction of the whole that its parts can carry on mutually-dependent actions, then in proportion as organization is high there must go a dependence of each part upon the rest so great that separation is fatal; and conversely. This truth is equally well shown in the individual organism and in the social organism.

The lowest animal-aggregates are so constituted that each portion, similar to every other in appearance, carries on similar actions ; and here spontaneous or artificial separation interferes scarcely at all with the life of either separated portion. When the faintly-differentiated speck of protoplasm forming a llhizopod is accidentally divided, each divisiongoes on as before. So, too, is it with those aggregates of the second order in which the components remain substantially alike. The ciliated monads clothing the horny fibres of a living sponge, need one another's aid so little that, when the sponge is cut in two, each half carries on its processes without interruption. Even where some unlikeuess has arisen among the units, as in the familiar polype, the perturbation caused by division is but temporary: the two or more portions resulting, need only a little time for the units to rearrange themselves into fit forms before resuming their ordinary simple actions. The like happens for the

like reason with the lowest social aggregates. A headless wandering group of primitive men divides without any inconvenience. Each man, at once warrior, hunter, and maker of his own weapons, hut, etc., with a squaw who has iu. every case the like drudgeries to carry on, needs concert with his fellows only in war and to some extent in the chase; and, except for fighting, concert with half the tribe is as good as concert with the whole. Even where tho slight differentiation implied by chieftainship exists, little inconvenience results from voluntary or enforced separation. Either before or after a part of the tribe migrates, some man becomes head, and such low social life as is possible recommences.

With highly-organized aggregates of either kind it is very different . We cannot cut a mammal in two without causing immediate death. Twisting off the head of a fowl is fatal. Not even a reptile, though it may survive the loss of its tail, can live when its body is divided. And among annulose creatures it similarly happens that though in some inferior genera, bisection does not kill either half, it kills both in an insect, an arachnid, or a crustacean. If

in high societies the eflect of mutilation is less than in high animals, still it is great. Middlesex separated from its surroundings would in a few days have all its social processes stopped by lack of supplies. Cut off the cotton-district fromLiverpool and other ports, and there would come arrest of itsi industry followed by mortality of its people. Let a division be made between the coal-mining populations and adjacent populations which smelt metals or make broadcloth by machinery, and both, forthwith dying socially by arrest of their actions, would begin to die individually. Though when a civilized society is so divided that part of it is left without a central controlling agency, it may presently evolve one; yet there is meanwhile much risk of dissolution, and before re-organization is efficient, a long period of disorder and weakness must be passed through.

So that the *consensus* of functions becomes closer as evolution advances. In low aggregates, both individual and social, the actions of the parts are but little dependent on one another; whereas in developed aggregates of both kinds, that combination of actions which constitutes the life of the whole, makes possible the component actions which constitute the lives of the parts.

§ 236. Another corollary, manifest *a priori* and proved *a posteriori*, must be named. Where parts are little differentiated, they can readily perform one another's functions; but where much differentiated they can perform one another's functions very imperfectly, or not at all.

Again the common polype furnishes a clear illustration. One of these sack-shaped creatures admits of being turned inside out, so that the skin becomes stomach and the stomach becomes skin : each thereupon beginning to do the work of the other. The higher we rise in the scale of organization the less practicable do we find such exchanges. Still, to some extent, substitutions of functions remain possible in highly developed creatures. Even in man the skin shows a trace of its original absorptive power, now monopolized by the alimentary canal: it takes into the system certain small amounts of matter rubbed on to it. Such vicarious actions are, however, most manifest between parts having functions that are still allied. If, for instance, thu bile-excreting function of the liver is impeded, other excretory organ?, the kidneys and the skin, become channels through which bile is got rid of. If a cancer in the ceso- pha/rus prevents swallowing, the arrested food, dilating the oesophagus, forms a pouch, in which imperfect digestion is set up. But these small abilities of the differentiated parts to discharge one another's duties, are not displayed where they have diverged more widely. Though mucous membrane, continuous with skin at various orifices, will, if everted, assume to a considerable extent the characters and powers of skin, yet serous membrane will not; nor can bone or muscle undertake, for any of the viscera, portions of their functions if they fail.

In social organisms, low and high, we find these relatively great and relatively small powers of substitution. Of course, where each member of the tribe repeats every other in his mode of life, there are no unlike functions to be exchanged ; and where there has arisen only that small differentiation implied by the barter of weapons for other articles, between one member of the tribe skilled in weapon-making and others less skilled, the destruction of this specially-skilled member entails no great evil; since the rest can severally do for themselves that which he did for them, though net quite so well. Even in settled societies of considerable sizes, we find the like holds to a great degree. Of the ancient Mexicans, Zurita says – "Every Indian knows all handicrafts which do not require great skill or delicate instruments;" and in Peru each man " was expected to be acquainted with the various handicrafts essential to domestic comfort:" the parts of the societies were so slightly differentiated in their occupations, that assumption of one another's occupations remained practicable. But in societies like our own, specialized industrially and otherwise in high degrees, the actions of one part which fails in its function cannot be assumed by other parts. Even the relatively-unskilled farmlabourers, were they to strike, would have their duties very inadequately performed by the urban population; and our iron manufactures would be stopped if their trained artizans, refusing to work, had to be replaced by peasants or hands from cotton-factories. Still less could the higher function?, legislative, judicial, etc., be effectually performed by coal- miners and navvies.

Evidently the same reason for this contrast holds in the two cases. In proportion as the imits forming any part of an individual organism are limited to one kind of action, as that of absorbing, or secreting, or contracting, or conveying an impulse, and become adapted to that action, they lose adaptation to other actions; and in the social organism the discipline required for effectually discharging a special duty, causes uufitness for discharging special duties widely unlike it.

§ 207. Beyond these two chief functional analogies between individual organisms and social organisms, that when they are little evolved, division or mutilation causes small inconvenience, but when they are much evolved it causes great perturbation or death, and that in low types of either kind the parts can assume one another's functions, but cannot in high types; sundry consequent functional analogies might be enlarged on did space permit.

There is the truth that in both kinds of organisms the vitality increases as fast as the functions become specialized. In either case, before there exist structures severally adapted for the unlike actions, these are ill-performed; and in tho absence of developed appliances for furthering it, the utilization of one another's services is but slight. But along with advance of organization, every part, more limited in its office, performs its office better; the means of exchanging benefits become greater; each aids all, and all aid each with increasing efficiency; and the total activity we call life, individual or national, augments.

Much, too, remains to be said about the parallelism between the changes by which the functions become specialized; but this, along with other parallelisms, will best be seen on following out, as we will now do, the evolution of the several great systems of organs, individual and social: considering their respective structural and functional traits together.

2

SECTION 2

CHAPTER VL
SYSTEMS OF ORGANS.

§ 237a. The hypothesis of evolution implies a truth which was established independently of it – the truth that all animals, however unlike they finally become, begin their developments in like ways. The first structural changes, once passed through in common by divergent types, arc repeated in the early changes undergone by every new individual of each type. Admitting some exceptions, chiefly among parasites, this is recognized as a general law.

This common method of development among individual organisms, we may expect to find paralleled by some common method among social organisms; and our expectation will be verified.

§ 238. In *First Principles* (§§ 149 – 152) and in the *Principles of Biology* (§§ 287 – 9) were described the primary organic differentiations which arise in correspondence with the primary contrasts of conditions among the parts, as outer and inner. Neglecting earlier stages, let us pass to those which show us the resulting systems of organs in their simple forms.

The aggregated units composing the lowest ccelenterate animal, have become so arranged that there is an outer layer of them directly exposed to the surrounding medinm with
its inhabitants, and an inner layer lining the digestive cavity
directly exposed only to the food. From units of the outer layer are formed those tentacles by which small creatures are caught, and those thread-cells, as they are called, whence are ejected minute weapons against invading larger creatures; while by units of the inner layer is poured out the solvent which prepares the food for that absorption afterwards effected by them, both for their own sustentation and for the sustentation of the rest. Here we have in its first stage the fundamental distinction which pervades the animal kingdom, between the external parts which deal with environing existences – earth, air, prey, enemies, – and the internal parts which utilize for the benefit of the entire body the nutritious substances which the external parts have secured. Among the higher *Codenterata* a complication occurs. In place of each single layer of units there is a double layer, and between the two double layers a space. This space, partially separate from the stomach in creatures of this type, becomes completely shut off in types above it . In these last the outer double layer forms the wall of the body; the inner double layer bounds the alimentary cavity; and the space between them, containing absorbed nutriment, is the so-called peri-visceral sac. Though the above-described two simple layers with their intervening protoplasm, are but *analogous to* the outer and inner systems of higher animals, these two double layers, with the intervening cavity, are *homologous with* the outer and inner systems of higher animals. For in the course of evolution the outer double layer gives rise to the skeleton, the nervo-muscular system, the organs of sense, the protecting structures, etc.; while the inner double layer becomes the alimentary canal, with its' numerous appended organs which almost monopolize the cavity of the body.

Early stages which are in principle analogous, occur in the evolution of social organisms. "When from low tribes entirely undifi'erentiated, we pass to tribes next above them, we fiud classes of masters and slaves – masters who, as warriorscarry on the offensive and defensive activities and thus especially stand in relations to environing agencies; and slaves who carry on inner activities for the general sustentation, primarily of their masters and secondarily of themselves. Of course this contrast is at first vague. Where the tribe subsists mainly on wild animals, its dominant men, being hunters as well as warriors, take a large share in procuring food; and such few captives as are made by war, become men who discharge the less skilled and more laborious parts of the process of sustentation. But along with establishment of the agricultural state, the differentiation grows more appreciable. Though members of the dominant class, superintending the labour of their slaves in the fields, sometimes join in it; yet the subject-class is habitually the one immediately in contact with the food- supply, and the dominant class, more remote from the food- supply, is becoming directive only, with respect to internal actions, while it is both executive and directive with respect to external actions, offensive and defensive. A
society thus composed of two strata in contact, complicates by the rise of grades within each stratum. For small tribes the structure just described suffices ; but where there are formed aggregates of tribes, necessarily having more- developed

governmental and militant agencies, with accompanying more-developed industrial agencies supporting them, the higher and lower strata severally begin to differentiate internally. The superior class, besides minor distinctions which arise locally, originates everywhere a supplementary class of personal adherents who are mostly also warriors; while the inferior class begins to separate into bond and free. Various of the Malayo-Polynesian societies bhow us this stage. Among the East Africans, the Congo people, the Coast Negroes, the Inland Negroes, we find the same general sub-division – the king with his relatives, the class of chiefs, the common people, the slaves ; of which the first two with their immediate dependents carry on the corporate actions of the society, and the second two those actions of a relatively-separate order which yield it all the necessaries of life.

§ 239. In both individual and social organisms, after the outer and inner systems have been marked off from one another, there begins to arise a third system, lying between the two and facilitating their co-operation. Mutual dependence of the primarily-contrasted parts, implies intermediation; and in proportion as they develop, the apparatus for exchanging products and influences must develop too. Thia we find it does.

In the low ccelenterate animal first described, consisting of inner and outer layers with intervening protoplasm, the nutritive matter which members of the inner layer have absorbed from prey caught by members of the outer layer, is transmitted almost directly to these members of the outer layer. Not so, however, in the superior type. Between the double-layered body-wall and the double-layered alimentary cavity, there is now a partially-separate peri-visceral sac; and this serves as a reservoir for the digested matters from which the surrounding tissues take up their shares of prepared food. Here we have the rudiment of a distributing system. Higher in the animal series, as in *Mollusea,* this peri-visceral sac, quite shut off, has ramifications running throughout the body, carrying nutriment to its chief organs ; and in the central part of the sac is a contractile tube which, by its occasional pulses, causes irregular movements in the nutritive fluid. Further advances are shown by the lengthening and branching of this tube, until, dividing and sub-dividing, it becomes a set of blood-vessels, while its central part becomes a heart . As this change progresses, the nutriment taken up by the alimentary structures, is better distributed by these vascular structures to the outer and inner organs in proportion to their needs. Evidently this distributing system must arise between the two pre-existing

systems; and it necessarily ramifies in proportion as the parts to which it carries materials become more remote, more numerous, and severally more complex.

The like happens in societies. The lowest types have no distributing systems – no roads or traders exist. The two original classes are in contact. Any slaves possessed by a member of the dominant class, stand in such direct relation to him that the transfer of products takes place without intervening persons; and each family being self-sufficing, there need no agents through whom to effect exchanges of products between families. Even after these two primary divisions become partially subdivided, we find that so long as the social aggregate is a congeries of tribes severally carrying on within themselves the needful productive activities, a distributing system is scarcely traceable: occasional assemblings for barter alone occur. But as fast as consolidation of such tribes makes possible the localization of industries, there begins to show itself an appliance for transferring commodities; consisting now of single hawkers, now of travelling companies of traders, and growing with the formation of roads into an organized system of wholesale and retail distribution which spreads everywhere.

§ 240. There are, then, parallelisms between these three great systems in the two kinds of organisms. Moreover, they arise in the social organism in the same order as in the individual organism; and for the same reasons.

A society lives by appropriating matters from the earth – the mineral matters used for buildings, fuel, etc., the vegetal matters raised on its surface for food and clothing, the animal matters elaborated from these with or without human regulation ; and the lowest social stratum is the one through which such matters are taken up and delivered to agents who pass them into the general current of commodities: the higher part of this lowest stratum being that which, in workshops and factories, elaborates some of these materialsbefore they go to consumers. Clearly, then, the classes engaged in manual occupations play the same part in the function of social sustentation, as is played by the components of the alimentary organs in the sustentation of a living body. No less certain is it that the entire

class of men engaged in buying and selling commodities of all kinds, on large and small scales, and in sending them along gradually-formed channels to all districts, towns, and individuals, so enabling them to make good the waste caused by action, is, along with those channels, fulfilling an office essentially like that fulfilled in a living body by the vascular system; which, to every structure and every unit of it, brings a current of nutritive matters proportionate to its activity. And it is equally manifest that while in the living body, the brain, the organs of sense, and the limbs guided by them, distant in position from the alimentary surfaces, are fed through the tortuous channels of the vascular system; so the controlling parts of a society, most remote from the operative parts, have brought to them through courses of distribution often extremely indirect, the needful supplies of consumable articles.

That the order of evolution is necessarily the same in the two cases, is just as clear. In a creature which is both very small and very inactive, like a hydra, direct passage of nutriment from the inner layer to the outer layer by absorption suffices. But in proportion as the outer structures, becoming more active, expend more, simple absorption from adjacent tissues no longer meets the resulting waste; and in proportion as the mass becomes larger, and the parts which prepare nutriment consequently more remote from the parts which consume it, there arises the need for a means of transfer. Until the two original systems have been marked off from one another, this tertiary system has no function ; and when the two original systems arise, they cannot develop far without corresponding development of thiatertiary system. In the evolution of the social

organism we see the like. Where there exist only a class of masters and a class of slaves, in direct contact, an appliance for transferring products has no place; but a larger society having classes exercising various regulative functions, and localities devoted to different industries, not only affords a place for a transferring system, but can grow and complicate only on condition that this transferring system makes proportionate advances.

And now, having observed the relations among these three great systems, we may trace out the evolution of each by itself.

3

SECTION 3

CHAPTER VIL
THE SUSTAINING SYSTEM.

§ 241. The parts carrying on alimentation in a living body and the parts carrying on productive industries in the body politic, constitute, in either case, a sustaining system : sustentation is the office they have in common. These parts are differentiated in conformity with certain laws which arc common to individual organisms and social organisms; and of these laws the most general is that which concerns localization of their divisions.

As a typical example of this localization in vegetal organisms, may be named the ordinary contrast between the underground parts and the above-ground parts – the first absorbing water and mineral constituents, and the last, by the aid of light, depriving the atmospheric carbonic acid of its carbon. That this distinction of functions is originally caused by the relations of the two parts to environing agents, is proved by the facts that if not covered with an opaque bark, the root-part, when above the surface, becomes green nnd decomposes carbonic acid, while, conversely, branches bent down and imbedded in the ground develop rootlets. That- is to say, unlikeness of their conditions determines this difference between the nutritive actions which these two great divisions of the plant carry on for the good of the whole. Among animals (with the exception

of certain *eutozoa* which, being immersed in nutritive matters, feed themselves through their outer surfaces) the outer surfaces take no share in alimentation. As already shown, the primary differentiation, establishing in the external layers a monopoly of those activities which their position makes possible, establishes in the internal layers a monopoly of those activities by which the swallowed prey is utilized. Here we have to note how the general process of utilization is divided among the parts of the alimentary canal, in conformity with their respective relations to nutritive matters. The course of evolution will be roughly conceived on recalling the antithesis between the uniform digestive tube with undivided function which an inferior creature possesses, and the multiform digestive apparatus, with great and small divisions of function, which a bird or mammal possesses. Secured in a solid form, the food has first to be triturated; and hence triturating appliances when formed, come at, or near, the beginning of the series of structures – teeth where they exist, or a gizzard where they do not. Crushed to pieces, the ingested substances must be further reduced before absorption can begin; and their presence in an incompletely broken down state, therefore throws on a succeeding portion of the alimentary canal the duty of completing the disintegration in a contractile sac, furnished with glands secreting solvent liquids. The pulp produced in this sac entails on the next part of the canal a different office. There can no longer be trituration, or dissolution of large fragments into minute shreds; and any further preparation must consist in the addition of secretions which fit the matters for absorption. Preparation being now completed, there remains nothing to do but take up what is prepared – the arrival at a certain part of the alimentary canal in an absorbable state, determines in that part the absorbing function. And similarly, though indirectly, with the localization of the great appended glands *(Prin. of Biol.,* § 298 – 9).' In the social organism localization of the various indus-

tries which jointly sustain the whole, is determined in an analogous manner. Primarily, the relations to different parts of the organic and inorganic environments, usually not alike over the whole area the society covers, initiate differences in the occupations carried on. And, secondarily, the nearness to districts which have had their industries thus fixed, fixes the positions of other industries which especially require their products. The first of these localizations is traceable even among the semi-civilized. Jackson describes some of the Fiji Islands as famous for wooden implements, others for mats and baskets, others for pots and pigments – unlikenesses between the natural products of the islands being the causes; as also in Samoa, where Turner says net-making is " confined principally to the inland villages," and ascribes this to " proximity to the raw material." The slightly-advanced societies of Africa show us kindred differentiations, having kindred origins. In Loango," the sea-coasts are frequented by regular professed fishermen," and there are also men who live near the sea and make salt by " evaporating sea-water over a fire." Here local facilities manifestly fix these occupations; as they doubtless do in that Ashantee town which is devoted to pottery. The extinct societies of America had more numerous such instances. Lorenzana says – "An extensive commerce is carried on in this salt [saltpetre] by the Mexicans of Yxtapaluca and Yxtapalapa, which mean the places where salt, or *Yxtatl,* is gathered ;" and when we read in Clavigero of the potters of Cholula, the stone-cutters of Tenajocan, the fishers of Cuitlahuac, and the florists of Xochimilco, we cannot doubt that these several businesses grew up in places which respectively furnished natural advantages for canyiug them on. So of the Ancient Peruvians we are told that "the shoes were made in the provinces where aloes were most abundant, for they were made of the leaves of a tree called *mayucy.* The arms also were supplied by the provinces where the materials for

making them were most abundant." By showing ns the generality of the law, these instances give point to the evidence around us. Familiarity must not make us overlook the meaning of the facts that the population fringing our shores is, by virtue of its position, led into occupations directly or indirectly maritime – fishing, sailing, shipbuilding – while certain coast-towns are, by physical circumstances, differentiated into places of import and export; and that the inland population, mostly raising this or that kind of food as soil and climate determine, has its energies otherwise turned by proximity to the raw material, here to quarrying stone or slate, here to brick-making, and in other places to raising minerals. Then,

as above implied, there result the secondary localizations favoured by these. Where not drawn by natural advantages in the way of water-power, manufactures in general cluster in or around regions where abundance of coal makes steam- power cheap. And if two materials are needed, the localization is determined by them jointly; as with the nail-making industry at Stourbridge, where both iron and coal are close at hand ; as in Birmingham, with its multifarious hardwares, which is similarly adjacent to the sources of these two chief raw materials; as in Manchester, which lies near the chief cotton port and on a coal region; as in Sheffield, which, besides the five streams yielding its water-power, and its adjacency to supplies of iron, coal, and charcoal, has at hand " the best grit in the world for grindstones."

§ 242. Tin's localization of organs devoted to the preparation of those matters which the organism, individual or social, needs for sustentation, exhibits a further common trait. Alimentary structures differentiate and develop in a manner quite unlike that followed by regulating structures.

Tho common trait referred to is most visible where the two kinds of aggregates respectively consisted at first of similar segments, which gradually became consolidated.

Among animals the annulose type best shows us this transformation with all its concomitants. The segments, or somites, as they are called, forming a low type of aquatic worm, such as a *Syllis,* repeat one another's structures. Each has its enlargement of the alimentary canal; each its contractile dilatation of the great blood-vessel; each its portion of the double nervous cord, with ganglia when these exist; each its branches from the nervous and vascular trunks answering to those of its neighbours; each its similarly answering set of muscles; each its pair of openings through the body-wall; and so on throughout, even to the organs of reproduction. Externally, too, they have like locomotive appendages, like branchiae, and sometimes even like pairs of eyes *(Prin. of Biol.,* § 205). But when we come to the higher *Aunulosa,* such as Crustaceans and Insects, the somites of which, much more integrated, are some of them so completely fused that their divisions are no longer traceable, we find that the alimentary organs have entirely lost their original relations to the somites. In a moth or a cockroach, the abdomen of which is still externally segmented, these internal parts which carry on sustentation do not, as in the annelid, repeat one another in each segment; but the crop, stomach, glands, intestines, severally extend themselves through two, three, four, or more segments. Meanwhile it is observable that the nervous centres carrying on co-ordination, though now partially unlike in the successive segments, have not lost their original relations to the segments. Though in a moth the anterior ganglia, controlling the external activities, have become a good deal displaced and integrated; yet the ganglia of the abdominal segments, now relatively small, remain in their localities.

With the industrial structures which arise in a large society formed by permanent consolidation of small societies, the like happens: they extend themselves without reference to political divisions, great or little. We have around us a Builiciency of illustrations. Just noting the partial differentiations of the agricultural system, here characterized by predominance of cereal produce, here by the raising of cattle, and in mountainous parts by sheep-farming – differences which have no reference to county-boundaries – we may note more especially how the areas devoted to this or that manufacture, are wholly unrelated to the original limits of political groups, and to whatever limits were politically established afterwards. We have an iron-secreting district occupying part of Worcestershire, part of Staffordshire, part of Warwickshire. The cotton manufacture is not restricted to Lancashire, but takes in a northern district of Derbyshire. And in the coal and iron region round Newcastle and Durham it is the same. So, too, of the smaller political divisions and the smaller parts of our industrial structures. A manufacturing town grows without regard to parish- boundaries ; which are, indeed, often traversed by the premises of single establishments. On a larger scale the like is shown us by our great city. London overruns many parishes; and its increase is not checked by the division between Middlesex and Surrey. Occasionally it is observable that even national boundaries fail to prevent this consequence of industrial localization: instance the fact named by llallam, that "the woollen manufacture spread from Flanders along the banks of the Ehine, and into the northern provinces of France." Meanwhile the controlling structures, however much they change their proportions, do not thus lose their relations to the original segments. The regulating agencies of our counties continue to represent what were once independent governments. In the old English period the county was an area ruled by a *comes* or earl. According to Bp. Stubbs," the constitutional machinery of the shire thus represents either the national organi/ation of the several divisions created by West Saxon conquest; or that of the early settlements which united in the Mercian kingdom as it advanced westwards; or the re-arrangement by the West Saxon dynasty of the whole of England on the principles

already at work in its own shires." Similarly respecting the eighty small Gaulish states which originally occupied the area of France, M. Fustel de Coulanges says – " Ni les Eomaius n i les Germains, ni la fe'odalite' ni la monarchic n'ont de"truit ces unites vivaces;" which up to the time of the Revolution remained substantially, as *"provinces "* and *"pays,"* the minor local governments,

§ 243. This community of traits between the developments of sustaining structures in an individual organism and in a social organism, requires to be expressed apart from detail before its full meaning can be seen.

What is the course of evolution in the digestive system of an animal as most generally stated ? That the entire alimentary canal becomes adapted in structure and function to the matters, animal or vegetal, brought in contact with its interior; and, further, that its several parts acquire fitnesses for dealing with these matters at successive stages of their preparation. That is, the foreign substances serving for sustentation, on which its interior operates, determine the geceral and special characters of that interior. And what, stated in terms similarly general, is the course of evolution in the industrial system of a society ? That as a whole it takes on activities and correlative structures, determined by the minerals, animals, and vegetals, with which its workers are in contact; and that industrial specializations in parts of its population, are determined by differences, organic or inorganic, in the local products those parts have to deal with.

The truth that while the material environment, yielding in various degrees and with various advantages consumable things, thus determines the industrial differentiations, I have, in passing, joined with a brief indication of the truth that differentiations of the regulative or governmental structures are not thus determined. The significance of this antithesis remains to be pointed out when the evolution of those governmental structures is traced.

4

SECTION 4

CHAPTER VIII.
THE DISTRIBUTING SYSTEM.

§ 244. In the last chapter but one, where the relatioufi between the three great systems of organs were described, it was pointed out that neither in an animal nor in a society can development of the sustaining system or of the regulating system go on without concomitant development of the distributing system. Transition from a partially-coherent group of tribes which are severally self-sufficing, to a completely-coherent group in which industrial differences havo arisen, cannot take place without the rise of an agency for transferring commodities; any more than a cluster of similar polypites can be changed into such a combination as we see in *Diphyes,* without some modification facilitating conveyance of nutriment from its feeding members to its swimming members. A mediaeval society formed of slightly-subordinated feudal states, each having besides its local lord its several kinds of workers and traders within itself, just as an annelid is formed of segments, each having besides its ganglia its own appendages, branchiae, and simple alimentary Iract; can no more pass into an integrated society having localized industries, without the development of roads and commercial classes, than the annelid can evolve into a crustacean or insect, characterized by many unlikenessea of parts and actions, without the growth of a vascular system.

Here, then, we have to observe the implied parallelisms

between the distributing systems, individual and social, in their successive stages.

§ 245. Protozoa of the rhizopod type are without channels of communication from part to part. The close proximity of the parts, the likeness of function among the parts, and their great variability of relative position, make a distributing system alike useless and impracticable. Even such animal aggregates as *Myxomycetes,* which are of considerable extent but are homogeneous, have no permeable lines for the distribution of nutriment. So is it with low societies. Tribes that are small, migratory, and without division of labour, by each of these characters negative the formation of channels for intercourse. A group of a dozen or two, have among themselves such small and indefinite communications as scarcely to make tracks between huts; when migratory, as they mostly are, the beaten paths they begin forming at each temporary abode are soon overgrown; and even where they are settled, if they are scattered and have no unlikc- nesses of occupations, the movements of individuals from place to place are so trifling as to leave but faint traces.

Animal aggregates of which the parts, differently related to conditions, assume different functions, must have channels for transfer which develop as the aggregates grow. Through the mere double-walled sac constituting a hydra, nutritive matter absorbed by the inner layer, may reach the outer layer without visible openings: passing, as we may assume, along lines of least resistance which, once opened, are continually followed and made more permeable. With advance to larger aggregates having parts further from the stomach, there comes first a branching stomach – a gastric cavity that sends ramifications throughout the body. Distribution of crude nutritive matters through such gastric sinuses occurs in the *Medusae* and again in the *Planarue.* But in those higher types characterized by a peii-visceral sac containing the filtered nutriment, this, which is therudiment of ?, vascular system, becomes the cavity out of which there diverge channels ramifying through the tissues – *la.:n. nce* probably formed by the draughts of liquid caused by local demands, and established by the repetitions of such draughts. With societies, as with living

bodies, channels of communication are produced by the movements which they afterwards facilitate: each transit making subsequent transits easier. Sometimes lines opened by animals are followed; as by the Nagas, who use the tracks made through the jungle by wild beasts. Similarly caused, the early paths of men are scarcely better than these.' The roads of the Bechuanas are " with difficulty to be distinguished from those made by the quaghas and antelopes." Throughout Eastern Africa " the most frequented routes are foot-tracks like goat-walks." And in Abyssinia, a high road "is only a track worn by use, and a little larger than the sheep-paths, from the fact of more feet passing over it." Even with such social growth as produces towns carrying on much intercourse, there is at first nothing more than an undesigned production of a less resistant channel by force of much passing. Describing the road between the old and new capitals of the Bechuanas, Burchell says – " This consists of a number of footpaths wide enough only for a single person, and running either parallel to each other, or crossing very obliquely. I counted from twelve to about eighteen or twenty of these paths, within the breadth of a few yards."

In animal organisms, ascending from the stage in which there is a mere oozing of nutritive liquids through the most permeable places in the tissues, to the stage in which occasional currents move feebly through indefinite sinuses, we come at length to the stage in which there are regular motions of blood along vessels having definite walls. As before pointed out, the formation of a true vascular system begins in the central regions and spreads to the periphery. At first there arises in the peri-visceral sac a short open- mouthed tube, by the rhythmical contractions of whichagitation is kept up in the surrounding liquid, now entering one end of this pulsating tube and now the other; and gradually this primitive heart, elongating and giving off smaller contractile vessels which ramify into the *lacuna,* originates a vascular system. The like happens with channels of communication through the social organism: indefinite *lacunce,* as we see that they are all at the outset, fitst acquire definite boundaries in the parts where there is most traffic. Of East African roads, which are commonly like goat-walks, Burton says that " where fields and villages abound they are closed with rough hedges, horizontal tree- trunks, and even rude stockades, to prevent trespassing and pilferage." So, too, in Dahomey, though the roads are mostly footpaths, yet " the roads to the coast, except in a few places, are good enough for wheeled vehicles," while "the road, six or seven miles long, separating the two capitals, may compare with the broadest in England." And from the capital of Ashantee, described as having broad, clean streets, there radiate towards distant parts of the territory eight pathways, cut by successive kings through the forest – doubtless replacing the primitive paths made by traffic. Ignoring Roman roads, which were not produced by local evolution, we may trace in our own history this centrifugal development of channels of communication. The paving of the central parts of London did not begin till after the eleventh century; and, having got as far outwards as Holborn at the beginning of the fifteenth century, it spread into some of the suburbs during the sixteenth century. In Henry VHIth's reign a way, when too deep and miry to be traversed, was " merely abandoned and a new track selected." Up to about 1750 the great north road from London was a turnpike for the first 100 miles, and " north of that point there was only a narrow causeway fit for pack-horses, flanked with clay sloughs on either side." At the same time, in North-England and Mid-England, the roads were " still for the most part entirely unenclosed." Then macadamization, an improvement belonging to our own century, beginning with main lines of communication, gradually extended itself first to all turnpike roads, then to parish roads, and finally to private roads.

Further analogies may be indicated. "With increased pressure of traffic has come, in addition to the road, the railway; which, in place of a single channel for movement in both directions, habitually has a double channel – up-line and down-line – analogous to the double set of tubes through which, in a superior animal, blood proceeds from the centre and towards the centre. As in the finished vascular system the great blood-vessels are the most direct, the divergent secondary ones less direct, the branches from these more crooked still, and the capillaries the most tortuous of all; so we see that these chief lines of transit through a society are the straiglitest, high roads less straight, parish roads more devious, and so on down to cart-tracks through fields. One more strange

parallel exists. In considerably-developed animals, as many *Mollusea,* though the vascular system is so far complete in its central parts that the arteries have muscular coats, and are lined with " pavement epithelinm," it remains incomplete at its peripheral parts: the small blood-vessels terminate in *lacuncB* of the primitive kind. Similarly in the developed distributing system of a society, while the main channels are definitely bounded and have surfaces fitted for bearing the wear and tear of great traffic, the divergent channels carrying less traffic are less highly structured; and the re-divergent ones, becoming less finished as they ramify, everywhere end in *laciauz* – unfenced, unmetalled tracks for cart, horse, or pedestrian, through field or wood, over moor and mountain.

Notice must also be taken of the significant fact that in proportion as organisms, individual and social, develop largely the appliances for conflict with other organisms, these channels of distribution arise not for internal sustentationonly, bnt partly, and often mainly, for transferring materials from the sustaining parts to the expending parts. As in an animal with a large nervo-museular system, arteries are formed more for carrying blood from the viscera to the brain and limbs than for carrying blood from one viscus to another ; so in a kingdom with activities predominantly militant, the chief roads are those made for purposes of offence and defence. The consumption of men and supplies in war, makes more necessary than all others the roads which take them; and they are the first to assume defmiteness. We see this in the above-named royal roads in Ashantee ; again in the ancient Peruvian royal roads for conveying troops; and we are reminded of the relation in the empire of the Romans, between finished roads and military activity at remote points. The principle, however, remains the same: be it in the commercial railways of England or the military railways of Russia, the channels arise between places of supply and places of demand, though the consumption may be here in peace and there in war.

§ 246. When from the channels which carry, in the one case blood-corpuscles and serum, and in the other case men and commodities, we turn to the movements along them, we meet with further analogies.

Devoid of canals for distribution, animals of low types show us nothing but an extremely slow, as well as irregular, diffusion through the tissues; and so in primitive societies, where nothing beyond a small amount of barter goes on, the exchanged products are dispersed very gradually and in indefinite ways: the movements are feeble, and do not constitute anything like circulation. On ascending to such a type as an ascidian, having a peri-visceral sac with pulsating vessel in it, we see a distribution of nutriment which cannot be called circulation, but which approaches to it. The pulsations, setting up in the surrounding fluid such waves as send feeble currents through the sinuses and*lacuncf,* jresently undergo a reversal, causing movement in the opposite direction. This alternation of waves, now setting towards a certain part which thereupon becomes congested, and presently setting away from it towards parts which have been drained, is analogous to the first movements of distribution in developing societies. We do not begin with constant currents in the same directions; but we begin with periodical currents, now directed to certain spots and then away from them. That which, when established, we know as a fair, is the commercial wave in its first form. We find it in slightly-advanced societies. The Sandwich Islanders met on the Wairuku river at stated times to exchange their products ; and the Fijians of different islands, assembled occasionally at a fixed place for barter. Of course, with the increase of population the streams of people and commodities which set at intervals to and from certain places, become more frequent. The semi-civilized African kingdoms show us stages. On the Lower Niger, " every town has a market generally once in four days," and at different parts of the river a large fair about once a fortnight. In other cases, as at Sansanding, besides some daily sale there was a great market once a week, to which crowds from the surrounding country came. And then in the largest places, such as Timbuctoo, constant distribution has replaced periodic distribution. So, too, in the Batta territory, Sumatra, there are assemblings for traffic every fourth day; and in Madagascar, besides the daily market in the capital, there are markets at longer intervals in the provincial towns. Ancient American societies displayed this stage passing into a higher. Among the Chibchas, along with constant traffic, the greatest traffic was at eight- day intervals; and Mexico, besides daily markets, had larger markets every five days, which, in adjacent cities, were at different dates: there being meanwhile merchants who, Sahagun says, " go through the whole country . . . buying in one district and selling in others " – so fore-shadowinga more developed system. Clearly these occasional assemblings and dispersings, shortening their intervals until they reach a daily bringing of products by some and buying by others, thus grow into a regular series of frequent waves, transferring things from places of supply to places of demand. Our own history shows how such slow periodic repletions arid depletions, now in this locality and now in that, pass gradually into a rapid circulation. In early English times the great fairs, annual and other, formed the chief means of distribution, and remained important down to the seventeenth century, when not only villages but even small towns, devoid of shops, were irregularly supplied by hawkers who had obtained their stocks at these gatherings. Along with increased population, larger industrial centres, and improved channels of communication, local supply became easier; and so, frequent markets more and more fulfilled the purpose of infrequent fairs. Afterwards in chief places and for chief commodities, markets themselves multiplied; becoming in some cases daily. Finally came a constant distribution such that of some foods there is to each town an influx every morning; and of milk even more than one in the day. The transitions from times when the movements of people and goods between places were private, slow, and infrequent, to times when there began to run at intervals of several days public vehicles moving at four miles an hour, and then to times when these shortened their intervals and increased their speed while their lines of movement multiplied, ending in our own times when along each line of rails there go at high speed a dozen waves daily that ara relatively vast; sufficiently show us how the social circulation progresses from feeble, slow, irregular movements to a rapid, regular, and powerful pulse.

§ 247. If from the channels of communication and the movements along them, we turn to the circulating currentsthemselves, and consider their natures and their relations to the parts, we still meet with analogies.

Relatively simple in a low animal, the nutritive fluid becomes in a high animal relatively complex – a heterogeneous combination of general and special materials required by, and produced by, the several parts. Similarly, the currents of commodities, if they can be so called, which move from place to place in a low society, are little varied in composition; but as we advance to high societies, the variety of components in the currents continually increases. Moreover, the parallelism of composition holds in another way; for in both cases relative simplicity is joined with crudity, whereas relative complexity in both cases results from elaboration. In low animal types the product of a rude digestion is carried in an unprepared state through extensions of the gastric cavity to the neighbourhoods of the parts which need it; but in developed types the products are refined before they are distributed – protein substances of several kinds, fats, sugar, etc. And while the blood is thus made heterogeneous by containing many matters fitted for use, and while its heterogeneity is increased by the swarms of white and red corpuscles which take part in the processes of purification, etc., it is made more heterogeneous still by the inorganic constituents which aid molecular change, as well as by the effete products of molecular change on their ways to places of exit. If, in like manner, with the currents in a low society, we contrast the currents in an advanced society, we see that here, too, the greate:- heterogeneity is mainly caused by the many kinds of manufactured articles fitted for consumption; and though certain waste products of social life do not return into the circulating currents, but are carried off by under-ground channels, yet other waste products are carried off along those ordinary channels of circulation which bring materials for consumption. Next we have to note the specialactions which the local structures exert on the general current of commodities. While in a living body the organs severally take from the blood everywhere carried through them, the materials needed for their sustentation, those which are occupied in excretion and secretion also severally take from the blood particular ingredients, which they either cast out or compound. A salivary gland forms from the matters it appropriates, a liquid which changes starch into sugar and by doing this aids the subsequent preparation of food; the gastric follicles elaborate and pour out acids, etc., which help to dissolve the contents of the stomach; the liver, separating certain waste products from the blood, throws them into the intestine as bile, along with that glycogen it forms from other components which is to be re-absorbed; and the units of these several organs live, grow, and multiply, by carrying on their several businesses. So is it with social organs. While all of them, under restrictions to be hereafter specified, absorb from the distributed supply of commodities shares needful for their sustentation, such of them as carry on manufactures, large or small, also select from the heterogeneous streams of things that run everywhere, the mateiials which they transform ; and afterwards return into these streams the elaborated products. Ignoring for the moment the familiar aspect of sale and purchase, under which these transactions present themselves to us, and contemplating simply the physical process, we see that each industrial structure, allowing various materials to pass through its streets untouched, takes out of the mixed current those it is fitted to act upon; and throws into the circulating stock of things, the articles it has prepared for general consumption.

The fact that competition is common to the two cases must also bo observed. Though commonly thought of as a phenomenon exclusively social, competition exists in a living body – not so obviously between parts that carry on the same function, as between parts that carry on differentfunctions. The general stock of nutriment circulating through an organism has to support the whole. Each organ appropriates a portion of this general stock for repair and growth. Whatever each takes diminishes by so much the amount available for the rest. All other organs therefore, jointly and individually, compete for blood with each organ. So that though the welfare of each is indirectly bound up with that of the rest; yet, directly, each is antagonistic to the rest . Hence it happens that extreme cerebral action so drafts away the blood as to stop digestion; that, conversely, the visceral demand for blood after a heavy meal often so drains the brain as to cause sleep; and that extremely violent exertion, carrying an excessive amount of blood to the motor organs, may arrest digestion, or diminish thought and feeling, or both. While these facts prove that there is competition, they also prove that the exalted function of a part caused by demands made on it, determines the flow of blood to it. Though, as we shall hereafter see, there is in the higher organisms a kind of regulation which secures a more prompt balancing of supplies and demands under this competitive arrangement, yet, primarily, the balancing results from the setting of blood towards parts in proportion to their activities. Morbid growths, which not only draw to themselves much blood but develop in themselves vascular structures to distribute it, show us how local tissue- formation (which under normal conditions measures the waste of tissue in discharging function) is itself a cause of increased supply of materials. Now we have daily

proof that in a society, not only individuals but classes, local and general, severally appropriate from the total stock of commodities as much as they can; and that their several abilities to appropriate, normally depend on their several states of activity. If less iron is wanted for export or home consumption, furnaces are blown out, men are discharged, and there flows towards the district a diminished stream of the things required for nutrition: causing arrestof growth and, if continued, even decay. When a cotton famine entails greater need for woollens, the increased activity of the factories producing them, while it leads to the drawing in of more raw material and sending out of more manufactured goods, determines towards the cloth districts augmented supplies of all kinds – men, money, consumable commodities; and there results enlargement of old factories and building of new ones. Evidently this process in each social organ, as in each individual organ, results from the tendency of the units to absorb all they can from the common stock of materials for sustentation; and evidently the resulting competition, not between units simply but between organs, causes in a society, as in a living body, high nutrition and growth of parts called into greatest activity by the requirements of the rest.

§ 248. Of course, along with these likenesses there go differences, due to the contrast named at the outset between the concreteness of an individual organism and the discreteness of a social organism. I may name, first, a difference which accompanies the likeness last dwelt upon.

If the persons forming a body-politic were mostly fixed in their positions, as are the units forming an individual body, the feeding of them would have to be similarly effected. Their respective shares of nutriment, not simply brought to their neighbourhood, would have to be taken home to them. A process such as that by which certain kinds of food are daily carried round to houses by a class of locomotive units, would be the universal process. But as members of the body politic, though having stationary habitations and working places, are themselves locomotive, it results that the process of distribution is effected partly in this way and partly by their own agency. Further, there results

from the same general cause, a difference between the ways in which motion is given to the circulating currents in the two cases. Physical cohesion of the parts in an individual livingbody, makes possible the propulsion of the nutritive liquid by a contractile organ; but lacking this physical cohesion, and lacking too the required metamorphosis of units, the body-politic cannot have its currents of commodities thus moved: though remotely produced by other forces, their motion has to be proximately produced by forces within the currents themselves.

After recognizing these unlikenesses, however, we see that they do but qualify the essential likenesses. In both cases so long as there is little or no differentiation of parts there is little or no need for channels of communication among the parts; and even a differentiation, when such only that the unlike parts remain in close contact, does not demand appliances for transfer. But when the division of labour, physiological or sociological, has so far progressed that parts at some distance from one another co-operate, the growth of channels of distribution, with agents effecting distribution, becomes necessary; and the development of the distributing system has to keep pace with the other developments. A like necessity implies a like parallelism between the progressing circulations in the two cases. Feeble activities, small amounts of exchange, obstacles to transfer, unite in preventing at first anything more than very slow and irregular repletions and depletions, now at one place now at another; but with multiplication of parts increasingly specialized in their functions, increasingly efficient therefore, and combining to produce an increased amount of general life, there goes an increased need for large distributions in constant directions. Irregular, weak, and Blow movements at long intervals, are changed into a regular rapid rhythm by strong and unceasing local demands. Yet more. With the advance of the aggregate, individual or social, to a greater heterogeneity, there goes advancing heterogeneity in the circulating currents ; which at first containing few crude matters, contain at last many prepared matters. In botli cases, too, structureswhich elaborate the requisites for sustentation, stand to these currents in like relations – take from them the raw materials on which they have to operate, and directly or indirectly deliver into them again the products; and in both cases these structures, competing with one another for their shares of the circulating stock of consumable matters, are enabled to appropriate, to repair themselves, and to grow, in proportion to their performances of functions.

Stated most generally, the truth we have to carry with us is that the distributing system in the social organism, as in the individual organism, has its development determined by the necessities of transfer among inter-dependent parts. Lying between the two original systems, which carry on respectively the outer dealings with surrounding existences, and the inner dealings with materials required for sustentation, its structure becomes adapted to the requirements of this carrying function between the two great systems as wholes, and between the sub-divisions of each.

5

SECTION 5

CHAPTER IX.

THE REGULATING SYSTEM.

§ 249. When observing how the great systems of organs, individual and social, are originally marked off from one another, we recognized the truth that the inner and outer parts become respectively adapted to those functions which their respective positions necessitate – the one having to deal with environing actions and agents, the other having to use internally-placed materials. We have seen how the evolution of interior structures is determined by the natures and distributions of these matters they are in contact with. We have now to see how the evolution of the structures carrying on outer actions is determined by the characters of things existing around.

Stated in a more concrete form, the general fact to be here set forth is, that while the alimentary systems of animals and the industrial systems of societies, are developed into fitness for dealing with the substances, organic and inorganic, used for sustentation, the regulating and expending systems (nervo-motor in the one, and governmental-military in the other) are developed into fitness for dealing with surrounding organisms, individual or social – other animals to be caught or escaped from, hostile societies to be conquered or resisted. In both cases that organization which fits the aggregate for acting as a whole in conflict with other aggregates, indirectly results from the carrying on of conflicts with other aggregates.

§ 2oO. To be slow of speed is to be caught by an enemy; to be wanting in swiftness is to fail in catching prey: death being in either "case the result Sharp sight saves the herbivorous animal from a distant carnivore; and is an essential aid to the eagle's successful swoop on a creature far below. Obviously it is the same with quickness of hearing and delicacy of scent; the same with all improvements of limbs that increase the power, the agility, the accuracy of movements ; the same with all appliances for attack and defence – claws, teeth, horns, etc. And equally true must it be that each advance in that nervous system winch, using the information coming through the senses, excites and guides these external organs, becomes established by giving an advantage to its possessor in presence of prey, enemies, and competitors. On glancing up from low types of animals having but rudimentary eyes and small powers of motion, to high types of animals having wide vision, considerable intelligence, and great activity, it becomes undeniable that where loss of life is entailed on the first by these defects, life is preserved in the last by these superiorities. The implication, then, is that successive improvements of the organs of sense and motion, and of the internal co-ordinating apparatus which uses them, have indirectly resulted from the antagonisms and competitions of organisms with one another.

A parallel truth is disclosed on watching how there evolves the regulating system of a political aggregate, and how there are developed those appliances for offence and defence put in action by it. Everywhere the wars between societies originate governmental structures, and are causes of all such improvements in those structures as increase the efficiency of corporate action against environing societies. Observe, first, the conditions under which there is an absenceof this agency furthering combination; and then observe the conditions under which this agency begins to show itself.

Where food is scarce, diffusion great, and co-operation consequently hindered, there is no established chieftainship. The Fuegians, the Cayaguas or Wood-Indians of South America, the Jungle-Veddahs of Ceylon, the Bushmen of South Africa, are instances. They do not form unions for defence, and have no recognized authorities: personal predominance of a temporary kind, such as tends to arise in every group, being the only approach to it. So of the Esquimaux, necessarily much scattered, Hearne says – "they live in a state of perfect freedom; no one apparently claiming tho superiority over, or acknowledging the least subordination to, another:" joined with which fact stands the fact that they do not know what war means. In like manner where barrenness of territory negatives anything more than occasional assemblings, as with the Chippewayans, there is nothing like chieftainship beyond the effect due to character; and this is very small. Elsewhere adequate con

centration is negatived by the natures of the people. They are too little social or too little subordinate. It is thus with the Ahors, a Hill-tribe of India, who, "as they themselves say, are like tigers, two cannot dwell in one den," and who have their houses " scattered singly or in groups of two and three." It is thus, too, as before pointed out (§ 35), with the Mantras of the Malay peninsula, who separate if they dispute. Here both the diffusion and the disposition causing the diffusion, check the evolution of a political head. But it is not only in cases like these that governmental co-ordination is absent. It is absent also among tribes which are settled and considerably more advanced, provided they are not given to war. Among such Papuans as the Arafuras and the Dal- rymple Islanders, there are but nominal chiefs: the people living " in such peace and brotherly love with one another " that they need no control but the decisions of their eldersThe Todas, too, wholly without military organization, and described as peaceable, mild, friendly, have no political headships. So again is it with the placable Bodo and Dhimals; described as being honest, truthful, entirely free from revenge, cruelty, and violence, and as having headmen whose authorities are scarcely more than nominal . To which, as similarly significant, I may add that the Lepchas, referred to by Sir J. Hooker as " amiable and obliging," are said by Campbell to be " wonderfully honest," " singularly forgiving of injuries," " making mutual amends and concessions;" while at the same time "they are averse to soldiering, and cannot be induced to enlist in our army," and are so little subordinate that they fly to the jungle and live on roots rather than submit to injustice.

Now observe how the headless state is changed and political co-ordination initiated. Edwards says the Caribs in time of peace admitted no supremacy; but, he adds, " in war, experience had taught them that subordination was as requisite as courage." So, too, describing the confederations of tribes among the Caribs, Humboldt compares them with " those warlike hordes who see no advantage in the ties of society but for common defence." Of the Creeks, whose subordination to authority is but slight, Schoolcraft says " it would be difficult, if not impossible, to impress on the community at large the necessity of any social compact, that should be binding upon it longer than common danger threatened them." Again, Bonwick says – " Chieftains undoubtedly did exist among the Tasmanians, though they were neither hereditary nor elective. They were, nevertheless, recognized, especially in time of war, as leaders of the tribes. . . . After the cessation of hostilities they retired ... to the quietude of every-day forest life." In other cases we find a permanent change produced. Kotze- bue says the Kamschadales "acknowledged no chief;" while another statement is that the principal authority was that of " the old men, or those who were remarkable for theirbravery." And then it is remarked that these statements refer to the time before the Russian conquest – before there had been combined opposition to an enemy. This

development of simple headship in a tribe by conflict with other tribes, we find advancing into compound headship along with larger antagonisms of race with race. Of the Pata- goninns Falkner tells us that though the tribes " are at continual variance among themselves, yet they often join together against the Spaniards." It was the same with the North American Indians. The confederacy of the six nations, which cohered under a settled system of co-operation, resulted from a war with the English. Stages in the genesis of a compound controlling agency by conflict with other societies are shown us by the Polynesians. In Samoa eight or ten village-communities, which are in other respects independent,

"unite by common conseat, and form a district, or state, for mutual protection. . . . When war *is* threatened *by* another district, no single village ean act alone ; . . . Some of these districts or states have thcir king; others eaunot agree on the choice of one; . . . there is no such thing as a king, or even a district, whose power extends all over the group." Yet in cnse of war, they sometimes combine in twos or threes.

Early histories of the civilized similarly show us how union of smaller social aggre-gates for offensive or defensive purposes, necessitating co-ordination of their actions, tends to initiate a central co-ordinating agency. Instance the Hebrew monarchy: the previously-separate tribes of Israelites became a nation subordinate to Saul and David, during wars with the Moabites, Ammonites, Edomites and Philistines. Instance the case of the Greeks: the growth of the Athenian hegemony into mastership, and the organization, political and naval, which accompanied it, was a concomitant of the continued activity of the confederacy against external enemies. Instance in later times the development of governments among Teutonic peoples. At the beginning of the Christian era there were only chieftainships of separate tribes; and, during wars, tem-porary greater chieftainships of allied forces. Between the first and the fifth centuries the federations made to resist or invade the Roman empire did not evolve permanent heads; but in the fifth century the prolonged military activities of these federations ended in transforming these military leaders into kings over consolidated states.

As this differentiation by -which there arises first a temporary and then a permanent military head, who passes insensibly into a political head, is initiated by conflict with adjacent societies, it naturally happens that his political power increases as military activity continues. Everywhere, providing extreme diffusion does not prevent, we find this connexion between predatory activity and submission to despotic rule. Asia shows it in the Kirghiz tribes, who are slave-hunters and robbers, and of whose mauaps, once elective but now hereditary, the Michells say – " The word Manap literally means a tyrant, in the ancient Greek sense. It was at first the proper name of an elder distinguished for his cruelty and unrelenting spirit; from him the appellation became general to all Kirghiz rulers." Africa shows it in the cannibal Niam-niams, whose king is unlimited lord of persons and things; or again in the sanguinary Dahomans with their Amazon army, and in the warlike Ashantees, all trained to arms: both of them under governments so absolute that the highest officials are slaves to the king. Polynesia shows it in the ferocious Fijiaus, whose tribes are ever fighting with one another, and among whom loyalty to absolute rulers is the extremest imaginable – even so extreme that people of a slave district " said it was their duty to become food and sacrifices for the chiefs." This

relation between the degree of power in the political head and the degree of mil-itancy, has, indeed, been made familiar to us in the histories of ancient and modern civilized races. The connexion is implied in the Assyrian inscriptions as well as in the frescoes and papyri of Egypt. The case of Pausanias and other such cases, were regarded by the Spartans themselves as showing the tendency of generals to become despots – as showing, that is, the tendency of active operations against adjacent so-cieties to generate centralized political power. How the imperativeness fostered by continuous command of armies thus passes into political imperativeness, has been agaia and again shown us in later histories.

Here, then, the induction we have to carry with us is that as in the individual organism that nervo-muscular apparatus which carries on conflict with environing organisms, begins with, and is developed by, that conflict; so the governmental-military organization of a society, is initiated by, and evolves along with, the warfare between societies. Or, to speak more strictly, there is thus evolved that part of its governmental organization which conduces to efficient cooperation against other societies.

§ 251. The development of the regulating system may now be dealt with. Let us first trace the governmental agency through its stages of complication.

In small and little-differentiated aggregates, individual and social, the structure which co-ordinates does not become complex : neither the need for it nor the materials for forming and supporting it, exist. Eut complexity begins in compound aggregates. In either case its commencement is seen in the rise of *a* superior co-ordinating centre exercising control over inferior centres. Among animals the

Annulosa illustrate this most clearly. la an annelid the like nervous structures of the like successive segments, are but little subordinated to any chief ganglion or group of ganglia. But along with that evolution which, integrating and differentiating the segments, produces a higher annulose animal, there arise at the end which moves foremost, more developed senses and appendages for action, as well as a cluster of ganglia connected with them; and along with formation of this goes an increasing control exercised by itover the ganglia of the posterior segments. Not very strongly marked in sucb little-integrated types as centipedes, a nervous centralization of this kind becomes great in such integrated types as the higher crustaceans and the arachnida. So is it in the progress from compound

social aggregates that are loosely coherent to those that are consolidated. Manifestly during those early stages in which the chief of a conquering tribe succeeds only in making the chiefs of adjacent tribes tributary while he lives, the political centralization is but slight; and hence, as in cases before referred to in Africa and elsewhere, the powers of the local centres re-assert themselves when they can throw off their temporary subordination. Many races which have got beyond the stage of separate simple tribes, show us, along with various degrees of cohesion, various stages in the subjection of local governing centres to a general governing centre. When first visited, the Sandwich Islanders had a king with turbulent chiefs, lormerly independent; and in Tahiti there was similarly a monarch with secondary rulers but little subordinate. So was it with the New Zealanders; and so was it with the Malagasy until a century since. The nature of the political organization during such stages, is shown us by the relative degrees of power which the general and special centres exercise over the people of each division. Thus of the Tahitians we read that the power of the chief was supreme in his own district, and greater than that of the king over the whole. Lichteu- stein tella us of the Koossas that "they are all vassals of the king, chiefs, as well as those under them; but the subjects are generally so blindly attached to their chiefs, that they will follow them against the king." " Scarcely would the slave of an Ashantee chief," says Craickshank, "obey the mandate of his king, without the special concurrence of his immediate master." And concerning the three grades of chiefs among the Araucanians, Thompson says of those who rule the smallest divisions that " their authority is lessprecarious" than that of the higher officers. These few instances, which might readily be multiplied, remind us of the relations between major and minor political centres in feudal times; when there were long periods during which the subjection of barons to kings was being established – during which failures of cohesion and re-assertions of local authority occurred – during which there was loyalty to the district ruler greater than that to the general ruler.

And now let us note deliberately, what was before implied, that this subordination of local governing centres to a general governing centre, accompanies co-operation of the components of the compound aggregate in its conflicts with other like aggregates. Between such superior *Anuulosa* as the winged insects and clawed crustaceans above described as having centralized nervous systems, and the inferior *Anuulosa* composed of many similar segments with feeble limbs, the contrast is not only in the absence from these last of centralized nervous systems, but also in the absence of offensive and defensive appliances of efficient kinds. In the high types, nervous subordination of the posterior segments to the anterior, has accompanied the growth of those anterior appendages which preserve the aggregate of segments in its dealings with prey and enemies; and this centralization of the nervous structure has resulted from the co-operation of these external organs. It is thus also with the political centraliza tions which become permanent. So long as the subordination is established by internal conflict of the divisions with one another, and hence involves antagonism among them, it remains unstable; but it tends towards stability in proportion as the regulating agents, major and minor, are habituated to combined action against external enemies. The recent changes in Germany have re-illustrated under our eyes this political centralization by combination in war, which was so abundantly illustrated in the Middle Ages by the rise of monarchical governments over numerous fiefs.

How tins compound regulating agency for internal control, results from combined external actions of the compound aggregate in war, we may understand on remembering that at first the army and the nation are substantially the same. As in each primitive tribe the men are all warriors, so, during early stages of civilization the military body is co-extensive with the adult male population excluding only the slaves – co-extensive with all that part of the society which has political life. In fact the army is the nation mobilized, and the nation the quiescent army. Hence men who are local rulers while at home, and leaders of their respective bauds of dependents when fighting a common foe under direction of a general leader, become minor heads disciplined in subordination to the major head; and as they carry more or less of this subordination home with them, the military organization developed during war survives as the political organization during peace.

Chiefly, however, we have here to note that in the compound regulating system evolved during the formation of a compound social aggregate, what were originally independent local centres of regulation become dependent local centres, serving as deputies under command of the general centre; just as the local ganglia above described become agents acting under direction of the cephalic ganglia.

§ 252. This formation of a compound regulating system characterized by a dominant centre and subordinate centres, is accompanied, in both individual organisms and social organisms, by increasing size and complexity of the dominant centre.

In an animal, along with development of senses to yield information and limbs to be guided in conformity with it, so that by their co-operation prey may be caught and enemies escaped, there must arise one place to which the various kinds of information are brought, and from which are issued the adjusted motor impulses; and, in proportion as evolution of the senses and limbs progresses, this centre which utilizes increasingly-varied information and directs better- combined movements, necessarily comes to have more numerous unlike parts and a greater total mass. Ascending through the annulose sub-kingdom, we find a growing aggregation of optic, auditory, and other ganglia receiving stimuli, together with the ganglia controlling the chief legs, claws, etc. And so in the vertebrate series, beginning in its lowest member with an almost uniform cord formed of local centres undirected by a brain, we rise finally to a cord appended to an integrated cluster of minor centres through which are issued the commands of certain supreme centres growing out of them. In a society it similarly happens that the political agency which gains predominance, is gradually augmented and complicated by additional parts for additional functions. The chief of chiefs begins to require helpers in carrying on control. He gathers round him some who get information, some with whom he consults, some who execute his commands. No longer a governing unit, he becomes the nucleus in a cluster of governing units. Various stages in this compounding, proceeding generally from the temporary to the permanent, may be observed. la the Sandwich Islands the king and governor have each a number of chiefs who attend on them and execute their orders. The Tahitian king had a prime minister, as well as a few chiefs to give advice; and in Samoa, too, each village chief has a sort of prime minister. Africa shows us stages in this progress from simple personal government to government through agents. Among the Beetjuans (a Bechuana people) the king executes "his own sentence, even when the criminal is condemned to death;" and Lichteustein tells us of another group of Bechuanas (the Maatjaping) that, his people being disorderly, the monarch " swung his tremendous *sjambok* of rhinoceros leather, striking on all sides, till he tairly drove the whole multitude before him:" being thereupon imitated by his courtiers. And then of the

Bachapin government, belonging to this same race, we learn that the duty of the chief's brother " was to convey the chiefs orders wherever the case demanded, and to see them put in execution." Among the Koossas, governed by a king and vassal chiefs, every chief has councillors, and " the great council of the king is composed of the chiefs of particular kraals." Again, the Zulu sovereign shares his power with two soldiers of his choice, and these form the supreme judges of the country. The appendages which add to the size and complexity of the governing centre in the larger African kingdoms are many and fully established. In Dahomey, besides two premiers and various functionaries surrounding the king, there are two judges, of whom one or other is " almost constantly with the king, informing him of every circumstance that passes;" and, according to Jjurton, every official is provided with a second in command, who is in reality a spy. Though the king joins in judging causes, and though when his executioners bungle he himself shows them how to cut off heads, yet he has agents around him into whose hands these functions are gradually lapsing; as, in the compound nervous structures above described, there are appended centres through which information is communicated, and appended centres through which the decisions pass into execution. How in civilized nations analogous developments have taken place – how among ourselves William the Conqueror made his"justiciar" supreme administrator of law and finance, having under him a body of Secretaries of whom the chief was called Chancellor ; how the justiciar became Prime Minister and his staff a supremo court, employed alike on financial and judicial affairs and in revision of laws; how this in course of time became specialized and complicated by appendages; needs not to be shown in detail. Always the central governing agency while being enlarged, is made increasingly heterogeneous by the multiplication of parts having specialized functions. And theu, as in nervous evolution after a certain complication of

the directive and executive centres is reached, there begin to grow deliberative centres, which, at first unobtrusive, eventually predominate; so in political evolution, those assemblies which contemplate the remoter results of political actions, beginning as small additions to the central governing agency, outgrow the rest. It is manifest that these latest and highest governing centres perform in the two cases analogous functions. As in a man the cerebrum, while absorbed in the guidance of conduct at large, mainly in reference to the future, leaves the lower, simpler, older centres to direct the ordinary movements and even the mechanical occupations; so the deliberative assembly of a nation, not attending to those routine actions in the body politic controlled by the various administrative agencies, is occupied with general requirements and the balancing of many interests which do not concern only the passing moment . It is to be observed, also, that these high centres in the two cases, are neither the immediate recipients of information nor the immediate issuers of commands; but receive from inferior agencies the facts which guide their decisions, and through other inferior agencies get those decisions carried into execution. The cerebrum is not a centre of sensation or of motion; but has the function of using the information brought through the sensory centres, for determining the actions to be excited by the motor centres. And in like manner a developed legislative body, though not incapable of getting impressions directly from the facts, is habitually guided by impressions indirectly gained through petitions, through the press, through reports of committees and commissions, through the heads of ministerial departments; and the judgments it arrives at are executed not under its immediate direction but under the immediate direction of subordinate centres, ministerial, judicial, etc.

One further concomitant may be added. During evolution of the supreme regulating centres, individual and social, the older parts become relatively automatic. A simpleganglion with its afferent and efferent fibres, receives stimuli and issues impulses unhelped and unchecked; hut when there gather round it ganglia through which different kinds of impressions come to it, and others through which go from it impulses causing different motions, it he- comes dependent on these, and in part an agent for transforming the sensory excitements of the first into the motor discharges of the last. As the supplementary parts multiply, and the impressions sent by them to the original centre, increasing in number and variety, involve multiplied impulses sent through the appended motor centres, this original centre becomes more and more a channel through which, in an increasingly-mechanical way, special stimuli lead to appropriate actions. Take, for example, three stages in the vertebrate animal. We have first an almost uniform spinal cord, to the successive portions of which are joined the sensory and motor nerves supplying the successive portions of the body: the spinal cord is here the supreme regulator. Then in the nervous system of vertebrates somewhat more advanced, the medulla oblongata and the sensory ganglia at the anterior part of this spinal cord, taking a relatively large share in receiving those guiding impressions which lead to motor discharges from its posterior part, tend to make this subordinate and its actions mechanical: the sensory ganglia have now become the chief rulers. And when in the course of evolution the cerebrum and cerebellum grow, the sensory ganglia with the co-ordinating motor centre to which they were joined, Japse into mere receivers of stimuli and conveyers of impulses: the last-formed centres acquire supremacy, and those preceding them are their servants. Thus is it with kings,

ministries, and legislative bodies. As the original political head, acquiring larger functions, gathers agents around him. who bring data for decisions and undertake execution of them, he falls more and more into the hands of these agents – has his judgments in great degree made for himby informers and advisers, and his deputed acts modified by executive officers: the ministry begins to rule through the original ruler. At a later stage the evolution of legislative bodies is followed by the subordination of ministries; who, holding their places by the support of majorities, are substantially the agents executing the wills of those majorities. And while the ministry is thus becoming less deliberative and more executive, as the monarch did pie- viously, the monarch is becoming more automatic: royal functions are performed by commission; royal speeches are but nominally such; royal assents are practically matters of form. This general truth, which our own constitutional history so well illustrates, was illustrated in another way during the development of Athenian institutions, political, judicial, and administrative: the older classes of functionaries survived, but fell into subordinate positions, performing duties of a comparatively routine kind.

§ 253. From the general structures of regulating systems, and from the structures of their great centres of control, we must now turn to the appliances through whioh control is exercised. For co-ordinating the actions of an aggregate, individual or social, there must be not only a governing centre, but there must also be media of communication through which this centre may affect the parts.

Ascending stages of animal organization carry ns from types in which this require- ment is scarcely at all fulfilled, to types in which it is fulfilled effectually. Aggregates of very humble orders, as Sponges, *Thalla-s&icollce,* etc., without co-ordinating cen- tres of any kind, are also without means of transferring impulses from part to part; and there is no co-operation of parts to meet an outer action. In *Ilydrozoa* and *Acti- nozoa,* not possessing visible centres of co-ordination' slow adjustments result from the diffusion of molecular changes from part to part through the body: contraction of the whole creature presently follows rough handling of thetentacles, while contact of the tentacles with nutritive matter causes a gradual elosing of them around it. Here by the propagation of some influence among them, the parts are made to co-operate toi the general good, feebly and sluggishly. In *Polyzoa,* along with the rise of dis- tinct nerve- centres, there is a rise of distinct nerve-fibres, conveying impulses rapidly along definite lines, instead of slowly through the substance in general. Hence comes a relatively prompt co-operation ot parts to deal with sudden external actions. And as these internuncial lines multiply, becoming at the same time well adjusted in their connexions, they make possible those varied co-ordinations which developed nervous centres direct. Analogous stages in social evolution are sufficiently manifest. Over a territory covered by groups devoid of political organization, news of an inroad spreads from person to person, taking long to diffuse over the whole area; and the inability of the scattered mass to co-operate, is involved as much by the absence of internuncial agencies as by the absence of regulating centres. But along with such slight political co-ordination as union for defence produces, there arise appliances for influencing the actions ot distant allies. Even the Fuegians light fires to communicate intelligence. The Tasmanians, too, made use ot signal fires, as do also the Trmnese; and this method of producing a vague co-ordination among the parts in certain emergencies, is found among other uncivilized races. As we advance, and as more definite combinations of more varied kinds have to be effected for offence and defence, messengers are employed. Among the Fijians, for instance, men are sent with news and commands, and use certain mnemonic aids. The New Zealanders " occasionally conveyed information to distant tribes during war by marks on gourds." In such comparatively advanced states aa those of Ancient America, this method of sending news was greatly developed. The Mexicans had couriers who at full speed ran six-mile stages, and so carried intelligence, it is said, even 300 miles in a day; and the Peruvians, besides their fire and smoke signals in time of rebellion, had runners of the same kind. So, too, was it with the Persians. Herodotus writes: –

" Nothing mortal travels so fnst as these Persian messengers. The eatire plau is a Persian invention ; and this is the method of it. Along the whole line of road there are men (they say) stationed with horses," and the message " is borne from hand to hand along the whole line, like the light in the torch-race, which the Greeks celebrate to Vulean."

Thus what is in its early stage a slow propagation of impulses from unit to unit throughout a society, becomes, as we advance, a more rapid propagation along settled lines: so making quick and definitely-adjusted combinations possible. Moreover, we must note that this part of the regulating system, like its other parts, is initiated by the necessities of co-operation against alien societies. As in later times among Highland clans, the fast runner, bearing the fiery cross, carried a command to arm; so, in early English times, the messages were primarily those between rulers and their agents, and habitually concerned military affairs. Save in these cases (and even state-messengers could not move swiftly along the bad roads of early days) the propagation of intelligence through the body-politic was very slow. The slowness continued down to comparatively late periods Queen Elizabeth's death was not known in some parts of Devon until after the Court had gone out of mourning; and the news of the appointment of Cromwell as Protector took nineteen days to reach Bridgwater. Nor have we to remark only the tardy spread of the influences required for co-operation of parts. The smallness and uniformity of these influences have also to be noted in contrast with their subsequent greatness and multiformity. Instead of the courier bearing a single despatch, military or political, from one ruling agent to another, at irregular intervals in few places; there come eventually, through despatches of

multitudinous letters daily and several times a-day, in all directions through every class, swift transits of impulses, no less voluminous than varied, all instrumental to co-operation. Two other internuncial agencies of more developed kinds are afterwards added Out of the letter, when it had become comparatively frequent among the educated classes, there came the news-letter: at first a partially-printed sheet issued on the occurrence of an important event, and having an unprinted space left for a written letter. From this, dropping its blank part, and passing from the occasional into the periodic, came the newspaper. And the newspaper has grown in size, in multitudinousness, in variety, in frequency, until the feeble and slow waves of intelligence at long and irregular intervals, have become the powerful, regular, rapid waves by which, twice and thrice daily, millions of people receive throughout the kingdom stimulations and checks of all kinds, furthering quick and balanced adjustments of conduct. Finally there arises a far swifter propagation of stimuli serving to coordinate social actions, political, military, commercial, etc. Beginning with the semaphore-telegraph, which, reminding us in principle of the signal-fires ot savages, differed by its ability to convey not single vague ideas only, but numerous, complex, and distinct ideas, we end with the electric-telegraph, immeasurably more rapid, through which go quite definite messages, infinite in variety and of every degree of complexity. And in place of u few such semaphore-telegraphs, transmitting, chiefly for governmental purposes, impulses in a few directions, there has come a multiplicity of lines of instant communication in all directions, subserving all purposes. Moreover, by the agency of these latest internuncial structures, the social organism, though discrete, has acquired a promptness of co-ordination equal to, and indeed exceeding, the promptness of co-ordination in concrete organisms. It was before pointed out (§ 221) that social units, though forming a discontinuous aggregate, achieve by language a transmission of impulses which, in individual aggregates, isachieved by nerves. But now, utilizing the molecular continuity of wires, the impulses are conveyed throughout the body-politic much faster than they would be were it a solid living whole. Including times occupied by taking messages to and from the offices in each place, any citizen in Edinburgh may give motion to any citizen in London, in less Uian one-fourth of the time a nervous discharge would take to pass from one to the other, were they joined by living tissue. Nor should we omit the fact that parallelism

in the requirements, has caused something like parallelism in the arrangements, of the internuncial lines. Out of great social centres emerge many large clusters of wires, from which, as they get further away, diverge at intervals minor clusters, and these presently give off re-diverging clusters; just as main bundles of nerves on their way towards the periphery, from time to time emit lateral bundles, and these again others. Moreover, the distribution presents the analogy that near chief centres these great clusters of internuncial lines go side by side with the main channels of communication – railways and roads – but frequently part from these as they ramify; in the same way that in the central parts of a vertebrate animal, nerve-trunks habitually accompany arteries, while towards the periphery the proximity of nerves and arteries is not maintained: the only constant association being also similar in the two cases; for the one telegi-aph- wiro which accompanies the railway system throughout eveiy ramification, is the wire which checks and excites its traffic, as the one nerve which everywhere accompanies an artery, is the vaso-motor nerve regulating the circulation in it. Once more, it is a noteworthy fact that in

both cases insulation characterizes the interuuncial lines. Utterly unlike as are the molecular waves conveyed, it is needful in both cases that they should be limited to the channels provided. Though in the aerial telegraph-wires insulation is otherwise effected, in under-ground wires it is ffected in a way analogous to that seen in nerve-fibres. Many wires united in a bundle are separated from one another by sheaths of non-conducting substance; as the nerve- fibres that run side by side in the same trunk, are separated from one another by their respective medullary sheaths.

The general result, then, is that in societies, as in living bodies, the increasing mutual dependence of parts, implying an increasingly-efficient regulating system, therefore implies not only developed regulating centres, but also means by which the influences of such centres may be propagated. And we see that as, under one of its aspects, organic evolution shows us more and more efficient internuncial appliances subserving regulation, so, too, does social evolution.

§ 254. There is one other remarkable and important parallelism. In both kinds of organisms the regulating system, during evolution, divides into two systems, to which is finally added a third partially-independent system; and the differentiations of these systems have common causes in the two cases.

The general law of organization, abundantly illustrated in foregoing chapters, is that distinct duties entail distinct structures; that from the strongest functional contrasts come the greatest structural differences; and that within each of the leading systems of organs first divided from one another in conformity with this principle, secondary divisions arise in conformity with the same principle. The implication is, then, that if in an organism, individual or social, the function of regulation falls into two divisions which are widely unlike, the regulating apparatus will differentiate into correspondingly-unlike parts, carrying on theii unlike functions in great measure independently. This we shall find it does.

The fundamental division in a developed animal, we have seen to be that between the outer set of organs which deal with the environment and the inner set of organs which carry on susteutation. Tor efficient mutual aid itfa requisite, not only that the actions of these inner and outer sets, considered as wholes, shall be co-ordinated; but also that each set shall have the actions of its several parts co-ordinated with one another. Prey can be caught or enemies escaped, only if the bones and muscles of each limb work together properly – only if all the limbs effectually co-operate – only if they jointly adjust their motions to the tactual, visual, and auditory impressions; and to combine these many actions of the various uensory and motor agents, there must be a nervous system that is large and complex in proportion as the actions combined are powerful, multiplied, and involved. Like in principle, though much less elaborate, is the combination required among the actions of the sustaining structures. It the masticated food is not swallowed when thrust to the entrance of the gullet, digestion cannot begin ; if when food is in the stomach contractions, but no secretions, take place, or if the pouring out of gastric juices is not accompanied by due rhythmical movements, digestion is arrested; if the great appended glands send into the intestines not enough of their respective products, or send them at wrong times, or in wrong proportions, digestion is left imperfect; and so with the many minor simultaneous and successive processes which go to make up the general function. Hence there must be some nervous structure which, by its inter- ouncial excitations and inhibitions, shall maintain the co- 3rdination. Now observe how widely unlike are the two kinds of co-ordination to be effected. The external domgs must be quick in their changes. Swift motions, sudden variations of direction, instant stoppages, are needful. Muscular contractions must be exactly adjusted to preserve the balance, achieve the leap, evade the swoop. Moreover, involved combinations are implied; for the forces to be simultaneously dealt with are many and various. Again, the involved combinations, changing from moment to moment, rarely recur; because the circumstances arerarely twice alike. And once more, not the needs of the moment only, have to be met, but also the needs of a future more or less distant. Nothing of the kind holds with the internal co-ordinations. The same series of processes has to be gone through after eveiy meal – varying somewhat with the quantity of food, with its quality, and with the degree to which it has been masticated. No quick, special, and exact adaptations are required; but only a general proportion and tolerable order among actions which are not precise in their beginnings, amounts, or endings. Hence for the sustaining organs there arises a regulating apparatus of a strongly contrasted character, which eventually becomes substantially separate. The sympathetic system of nerves, or " nervous system of organic life," whether or not originally derived from the cerebro-spinal system, is, in developed vertebrates, practically independent. Though perpetually influenced by the higher system which, working the muscular structures, causes the chief expenditure, and though in its turn influencing this higher system, the two carry on their functions apart: they affect one another chiefly by general demands and general checks. Only over the heart and lungs, which are indispensable co- operators with both the sustaining organs and the expending organs, do we find that the superior and inferior nervoua systems exercise a divided control. The heart, excited by the cerebro-spinal system in proportion to the supply of blood required for external action, is also excited by the sympathetic when a meal has made a supply of blood needful for digestion; and the lungs which (because their expansion has to be effected partly by thoracic muscles belonging to the outer system of organs) largely depend for their movements on cerebro-spinal nerves, are nevertheless also excited by the sympathetic when the alimentary organs are at work. And here, as showing the tendency there is for all these comparatively-constant vital processes to fall under a nervous control unlike that which directs the ever-varying outer processes, it may be remarked that such influences as

trie cerebro-spinal system exerts on the heart and lungs differ greatly from its higher directive actions – are mainly reflex and unconscious. Volition fails to modify the heart's pulsations; and though an act of will may temporarily increase or decrease respiration, yet the average respiratory movements are not thus changeable, but during waking and sleeping are automatically determined. To which

facts let me add that the broad contrast here illustrated in the highest or vertebrate type, is illustrated also in the higher members of the annulose type. Insects, too, have visceral nervous systems substantially distinguished from the nervous systems which co-ordinate outer actions. And thus we are shown that separation of the two functionally-contrasted regulating systems in animals, is a concomitant of greater evolution.

A parallel contrast of duties produces a parallel differentiation of structures during the evolution of social organisms. Single in low societies as in low animals, the regulating system in high societies as in high animals becomes divided into two systems; which, though they perpetually affect one another, carry on their respective controls with substantial independence. Observe the like causes for these like effects. Success in conflicts with other socie

ties implies quickness, combination, and special adjustments to ever-varying circumstances. Information of an enemy's movements must be swiftly conveyed ; forces must be rapidly drafted to particular spots; supplies fit in kinds and quantities must be provided; military manauivres must be harmonized; and to these ends there must be a centralized agency that is instantly obeyed. Quite otherwise is it with the structures carrying on sustentation. Though the actions of these have to be somewhat varied upon occasion, especially to meet war-demands, yet their general actions are comparatively uniform. The several kinds of food raised have to meet a consumption which changes within moderate limits only ; for clothing the demands are tolerablyconstant, and alter in their proportions not suddenly but slowly; and so with commodities of less necessary kinds: rapidity, speciality, and exactness, do not characterize the required co-ordinations. Hence a place for another kind of regulating system. Such a system evolves as fast as the sustaining system itself evolves. Let us note its progress. In early stages the occupations are

often such as to prevent division between the control of defensive actions and the control of sustaining actions, because the two are closely allied. Among the Mandans the families joined in hunting, and divided the spoil equally: showing us that the war with beasts carried on for joint benefit, was so nearly allied to the war with men carried on for joint benefit, that both remained public affairs. Similarly with the Comanches, the guarding of a tribe's cattle is carried on in the same manner as military guarding; and since the community of individual interests in this protection of cattle from enemies, is like the community of interests in personal protection, unity in the two kinds of government continues. Moreover in simple tribes which are under rulers of any kinds, what authority exists is unlimited in range, and includes industrial actions as well as others. If there are merely wives for slaves, or if there is a slave-class, the dominant individuals who carry on outer attack and defence, also direct in person such labour as is performed; and where a chief having considerable power has arisen, he not only leads in war but orders the daily activities during peace. The Gonds, the Bhils, the Nagas, the Mishmis. the Kalmucks, and many other simple tribes, show us this identity of the political and industrial governments. A partial advance, leading to some distinction, does not separate the two in a definite way. Thus among the Kookies the rajah claims and regulates work, superintends village removals, and apportions the land each family has to clear on a new site; among the Santals the head man partially controls the people's labour; and among the Khonds he acts as

chief merchant. Polynesia presents like facts. The New Zealand chiefs superintend agricultural and building operations ; the Sandwich Islanders have a market, in which " the price is regulated by the chiefs;" trade in Tonga also " is evidently under [the chief's] supervision;" and the Ka- dayan chiefs " settle the price of rice." So again in Celebes, the days for working in the plantations are decided by the political agency, and the people go at beat of gong; so again in East Africa, the times of sosving and harvest depend on the chiefs will, and among the Inland Negroes the " market is arranged according to the directions of the chiefs;" so again in some parts of Ancient. America, as San Salvador, where the cazique directed the plantings; and so again in some parts of America at the present time. Those who trade with the Mundurucus " have first to distribute their wares . . . amongst the minor chiefs," and then wait some months " for repayment in produce;" and the Patagonians could not sell any of their arms to Wilkes's party without asking the chiefs permission. In other societies, and especially in those which are considerably developed, we find this union of political and industrial rule becoming modified: the agency, otherwise the same, is doubled. Thus among the Sakarran Dyaks there is a "trading chief" in addition to two principal chiefs; among the Dahomans there is a commercial chief ill Whydah; and there are industrial chiefs in Fiji, where, in other respects, social organization is considerably advanced. At a later stage the commercial chief passes into the government officer exercising stringent supervision. In Ancient Guatemala a State-functionary fixed the prices in the markets; and in Mexico, agents of the State saw that lands did not remain uncultivated. Facts of this kind introduce us to the stages passed through by European societies. Up to the 10th century each domain in France had its bond, or only partially-free, workmen and artizans, directed by the seigneur and paid in meals and goods; between the

lltlx and 14th centuries the feudal superiors, ecclesiastical or lay, regulated production and distribution to such extent that industrial and commercial licences had to be purchased from them; in the subsequent monarchical stage, it was a legal maxim that " the right to labour is a royal right, which the prince may sell and subjects can buy;" and onwards to the time of the Revolution, the country swarmed with officials who authorized occupations, dictated processes, examined products: since which times State- control has greatly diminished, and the adjustments of industry to the nation's needs have been otherwise effected. Still better does our own history show us this progressive differentiation. In the Old English period the heads of guilds were identical with the local political heads – ealdormeu, wick-, port-, or burgh-reeves; and the guild was itself in part a political body. Purchases and bargains had to be made in presence of officials. Agricultural and manufacturing processes were prescribed by law. Dictations of kindred kinds, though decreasing, continued to late times. Down to the 16th century there were metropolitan and local councils, politically authorized, which determined prices, fixed wages, etc. But during subsequent generations, restrictions and bounties disappeared; usury laws were abolished ; liberty of commercial combination increased.

And now if, with those early stages in which the rudimentary industrial organization is ruled by the chief, and with those intermediate stages in which, as it develops, it pets a partially-separate political control, we contrast a late stage like our own, characterized by an industrial organization which has become predominant, we find that this has evolved for itself a substantially-independent control. There is now no h'xing of prices by the State; nor is there prescribing of methods. Subject to but slight hindrances from a few licences, citizens adopt what occupations they please; buy and sell where they please. The amounts grown and manufactured, imported and exported, are unregulated by lawsjimprovements are not enforced nor bad processes legislatively interdicted; but meu, carrying on their businesses as they think best, are simply required by law to fulfil their contracts and commanded not to aggress upon their neighbours. Under what system, then, are their industrial activities adjusted to the requirements? Under an iuternuncial system through which the various industrial structures receive from one another stimuli or checks caused by rises or falls in the consumptions of their respective products; and through which they jointly receive a stimulus when there is suddenly an extra consumption for war - purposes. Markets in the chief towns, where bargaining settles the prices of grain and cattle, of cottons and woollens, of metals and coal, show dealers the varying relations of supply and demand; and the reports of their transactions, diffused by the press, prompt each locality to increase or decrease of its special function. Moreover, while the several districts have their activities thus partially regulated by their local centres of business, the metropolis, where all these districts are represented by houses and agencies, has its central markets and its exchange, in which is effected such an averaging of the demands of all kinds, present and future, as keeps a due balance among the activities of the several industries. That is to say, there has arisen, in addition to the political regulating system, an industrial regulating system which carries on its co-ordinating function independently – a separate plexus of connected ganglia.

As above hinted, a third regulating system, partially distinguishable from the others, arises in both cases. For the prompt adjustment of functions to needs, supplies of the required consumable matters must be rapidly drafted to the places where activities are set up. If an organ in the individual body or in the body-politic, suddenly called into great action, could get materials for its nutrition or its secretion, or both, only through the ordinary quiet flow ofthe distributing currents, its enhanced action would Boon flag. That it may continue responding to the increased demand, there must be an extra influx of the materials used in its actions – it must have *credit* in advance of function discharged. In the individual organism this end

is achieved by the vaso-motor nervous system. The fibres of this ramify everywhere along with the arteries, which they enlarge or contract in conformity with stimuli sent along them. The general law, as discovered by Ludwig and Loven, is that when by the nerves of sensation there is sent inwards that impression which accompanies the activity of a part, there is reflected back to the part, along its vaso- motor nerves, an influence by which its minute arteries are suddenly dilated; and at the same time, through the vaso- motor nerves going to all inactive parts, there is sent an influence which slightly constricts the arteries supplying them: thus diminishing the flow of blood where it is not wanted, that the flow may be increased where it is wanted. In the social organism, or rather in such

a developed social organism as our own in modern times, this kind of regulation is effected by the system of banks and associated financial bodies which lend out capital. When a local industry, called into unusual activity by increased consumption of its products, makes demands first of all on local banks, these, in response to the impressions caused by the rising activity conspicuous around them, open more freely those channels for capital which they command; and presently, with further rise of prosperity, the impression propagated to the financial centres in London produces an extension of the local credit, so that there takes place a dilatation of the in-flowing streams of men and commodities. While, at the same time, to meet this local need for capital, various industries elsewhere, not thus excited, and therefore not able to offer such good interest, get diminished supplies: some constriction of the circulation through them takes place. This third regulating system, observe, vaso-

motor in the one case and monetary in the other, is substantially independent. Evidence exists that there are local vaso-motor centres possessing local control, as there are local monetary centres; and though there seems to be in each case a chief centre, difficult to distinguish amid tho other regulating structures with which it is entangled, yec it is functionally separate. Though it may be bound up with the chief regulating system by which outer actions are controlled, it is not subject to that system. Volition in the one case cannot alter these local supplies of blood; and legislation in the other, ceasing to perturb as it once did the movements of capital, now leaves it almost entirely alone: even the State, with the structures under its direct control, standing to the financial corporations in the position of a customer, just as the brain and limbs do to the vaso-motor centres. Nor does this ruler of the circulation form part of that second regulating system which controls the organs carrying on sustcntation, individual or social. The viscera get blood only by permission of these nerve-centres commanding their arteries, and if the outer organs are greatly exerted, the supply is shut off from the inner organs; and similarly the industrial system, with that centralized apparatus which balances its actions, cannot of itself draft capital here or there, but does this indirectly only through the impressions yielded by it to Lombard-street.

§ 255.   Thus the increasing mutual dependence of parts, which both kinds of organisms display as they evolve, necessitates a further series of remarkable paral-lelisms. Co-operation being in either case impossible without appliances by which the co-operating parts shall have their actions adjusted, it inevitably happens that in the body-politic, as in the living body, there arises a regulating system; and within itself this differentiates as the sets of organs evolve.

The co-operation most urgent from the outset, is that required for dealing with environing enemies and prey. Hence the first regulating centre, individual and social, is initiated as a means to this co-operation; and its development progresses with the activity of this co-operation. As compound aggregates are formed by integration of simplo ones, there arise in either case supreme regulating centres and subordinate ones; and the supreme centres begin to enlarge and complicate. While doubly-compound and trebly- compound aggregates show us further developments in complication and subordination, they show us, also, better inter- nuncial appliances, ending in those which, convey instant information and instant command.

To this chief regulating system, controlling the organs which carry on outer actions, there is, in either case, added during the progress of evolution, a regulating system for the inner organs carrying on sustentation; and this gradually establishes itself as independent. Naturally it comes later than the other. Complete utilization of materials for sustentation being less urgent, and implying co-ordination relatively simple, has its controlling appliances less rapidly developed than those which aie concerned with the catching of prey and the defence against enemies.

And then the third or distributing system, which, though necessarily arising after the others, is indispensable to the considerable development of them, eventually gets a regulating apparatus peculiar to itself.

CHAPTER X.

SOCIAL TYPES AND CONSTITUTIONS.

§ 256. A Glance at the respective antecedents of individual organisms and social organisms, shows why the last admit of no such definite classification as the first. Through a thousand generations a species of plant or animal leads suhstantially the same kind of life; and its successive members inherit the acquired adaptations. When changed conditions cause divergences of forms once alike, the accumulating differences arising in descendants only superficially disguise the original identity – do not prevent the grouping of the several species into a genus; nor do wider divergences that began earlier, prevent the grouping of genera into orders and orders into classes. It is otherwise with societies. Hordes of primitive men, dividing and subdividing, do, indeed, show us successions of small social aggregates leading like lives, inheriting such low structures as had resulted, and repeating those structures. But higher social aggregates propagate their respective types in much less decided ways. Though colonies tend to grow like their parent-societies, yet the parent-societies are so comparatively plastic, and the influences of new habitats on the derived societies are so great, that divergences of structure are inevitable. In the absence of definite organizations established during the similar lives of many societies descendingone from another, there cannot be the precise distinctions implied by complete classification.

Two cardinal kinds of differences there are, however, of which we may avail ourselves for grouping societies in a natural manner. Primarily we may arrange them according to their degrees of composition, as simple, compound, doubly-compound, trebly-compound; and secondarily, though in a less specific way, we may divide them into the predominantly militant and the predominantly industrial – those in which the organization for offence and defence is most largely developed, and those in which the sustaining organization is most largely developed.

§ 257. We have seen that social evolution begins with small simple aggregates ; that it progresses by the clustering of these into larger aggregates ; and that after being consolidated, such clusters are united with others like themselves into still larger aggregates. Our classification, then, must begin with societies of the first or simplest order.

We cannot in all cases say with precision what constitutes a simple society; for, in common with products of evolution generally, societies present transitional stages which negative sharp divisions. As the multiplying members of a group spread and diverge gradually, it is not always easy to decide when the groups into which they fall become distinct. Here, inhabiting a barren region, the descendants of common ancestors have to divide while yet the constituent families are near akin; and there, in a more fertile region, the group may hold together until clusters of families remotely akin are formed: clusters which, diffusing slowly, are held by a common bond that slowly weakens. By and by comes the complication arising from the presence of slaves not of the same ancestry, or of an ancestry but distantly allied; and these, though they may not be political units, must be recognized as units sociologically considered. Then there is the kindred complication arising where an invading tribe becomes a dominant class. Our only course is to regard as a simple society, one which forms a single working whole unsubjected to any other, and of which the parts co-operate with or without a regulating centre, for certain public ends. Here is a table, presenting with as much definiteness as may be, the chief divisions and sub-divisions of such simple societies.

(´. Headless.

'Nomadic: – (huating) Fuegians, some Australians, Wood-Veddahs, Bushmen, Ghepangs and Kusundaa of Nepal.

Semi-settled: – most Esquimaux.

Settled: – Arafuraa, Laud Djaks of Upper Sarawak
River.

ro W

fNomadic: – (huating) some Australians, Tasmaniaua.   HEADSHII'1   1 *Semi-settled:* – some Caribs.

j5ettled: – some Uaupes of the upper Bio Negro.

Nomadic: – (huating) Andamanese, Abipones, Snckca,
Chippewayans, (pastoral) some Bedouins.

Semi-settled: – some Esquimaux, Chinooks, Cbippewaa
(at preseat), some Kamschadales, Village Veddaha,
Bodo and Uhimals.

Settled; – Guiana tribes, Handans, Coroados, New
Guinea people, Tanuese, Vateans, ItyaLs, Toilna,
Nagas, Karens, Saatuls.

f Nomadic: –

Stable I *Semi-settled:* – some Caribs, Patagonians, New Calo Headship.] donians, Kaffirs.

(Settled: – Guarunis, Pueblos.

On contemplating these uncivilized societies which,

though alike as being uncompounded, differ in their sizes and structures, certain generally-associated traits may be noted. Of the groups without political organization, or with but vague traces of it, the lowest are those small wandering ones which live on the wild food sparsely distributed in forests, over barren tracts, or along sea-shores. Where small simple societies remain without chiefs though settled, it is where circumstances allow them to be habitually peaceful. Glancing down the table we find reason for inferring that the changes from the hunting life to the pastoral, and from the pastoral to the agricultural, favour increase of population, the development of political organization, of industrial organization, and of the arts ; though these causes do not of themselves produce these results.

Nomadio: – (pastoral) some Bedouins.

Settled: –

'Nomadic: – (huating) Dacotahs, (huating and pastoral) Comanclies, (pastoral) Kalmuiks.

Semi-settled: – Ostyaks, Belueliis, Kookies, Bhils, Congo- people (passing iato doubly compound), Teutons before 5th century.

Settled: – Chippewas (in past times), Creeks, Man-
dracus, Tupis, Khonds, some New Guinea people,
Sumatrans, Malagasy (till recently), Coast Negroes,

Inland Negroes, some Abyssinians, Homeric Greeks,
Kingdoms of the Heptarchy, Teutons in 5th ceatury,
Fiefs of 10th century.
'Nomadic: – (pastoral) Kirghiz.
Semi-settled: – Bechuanas, Zulus.
Settled: – TJaup&, Fijians (when first visited), Hew
Zealanders, . Sandwich Islanders (in Cook's time)
Javans, Hotteutots, Dahomans, Ashaatees, some
Abjssinians, Ancieat Yucatanese, New Granada
people, Honduras people, Chibclms, some town
Arubs.

The second table, given on the preceding page, contains societies which have passed to a slight extent, or considerably, or wholly, into a state in which the simple groups have their respective chiefs under a supreme chief. The stability or instability alleged of the headship in these cases, refers to the headship of the composite group, and not to the headships of the component groups. As might be expected, stability of this compound headship becomes more marked as the original unsettled state passes into the completely settled state: the nomadic life obviously making it difficult to keep the heads of groups subordinate to a general head. Though not in all cases accompanied by considerable organization, this coalescence evidently conduces to organization. The completely- settled compound societies are mostly characterized by division into ranks, four, five, or six, clearly marked off; by established ecclesiastical arrangements; by industrial structures that show advancing division of labour, general and local; by buildings of some permanence clustered into places of some size; and by improved appliances of life generally.

In the succeeding table are placed societies formed by the re-compounding of these compound groups, or in which many governments of the types tabulated above have become subject to a still higher government. The first notable fact is that these doubly-compound societies are all completely settled. Along with their greater integration we see in many cases, though not uniformly, a more elaborate and stringent political organization. Where complete stability of political headship over these doubly-compound societies has been established, there ia mostly, too, a developed ecclesiastical hierarchy. While becoming more complex by division of labour, the industrial organization has in many cases assumed a caste structure. To a greater or less extent, custom has passed into positive law; and religious observances have grown definite, rigid, and complex. Towns and roads have become general; and considerable progress in knowledge and the arts has taken place.

ti-settled?
: – Samoaus.
'Semi-settled: –
Settled: – Tahitiaus, Tongaus, Javnus (oceanouAlN), Fijiaus (since fire-arms), Malagasy (in rccuut times), Athenian Confederacy, Spartan Confederacy, Teutonic Kingdoms from 6th to 9th centuries, Greater Fiefs in France of the 13th century.
Semi-settled: –

Settled: – Iroquois, Araueaniaus, Sandwich Islanders (since Cook's time), Ancient Vera Paz and Bogota pcoples, Guatemalaus, Ancient Peruvians, Wah- habees (Arab), Oman (Arab), Aneient Egyptian Kingdom, England after the 10th century.

There remain to be added the great civilized nations which need no tabular form, since they mostly fall under one head – trebly compound. Ancient Mexico, the Assyrian Empire, the Egyptian Empire, the Roman Empire, Great Britain, France, Germany, Italy, Russia, may severally be regarded as having reached this stage of composition, or perhaps, in some cases, a still higher stage. Only in respect of the stabilities of their governments may they possibly require classing apart – not their political stabilities in the ordinary sense, but their stabilities in the sense of continuing to be the supreme centres of these great aggregates. So defining this trait, the ancient trebly-compound societies have mostly to be classed as unstable; and of the modern, the Kingdom of Italy and the German Empire have to be tested by time.

As already indicated, this classification must not be taken as more than an approximation to the truth. In some cases the data furnished by travellers and others are inadequate; in some cases their accounts are conflicting; in some cases the composition is so far transitional that it is dimcult to say tmder which of two heads it should come. Here the gens or tho phratry may he distinguished as a local community; and here these groups of near or remote kinsmen are so mingled with other such groups as practically to form parts of one community. Evidently the like combination of several such communities, passing through stages of increasing cohesion, leaves it sometimes doubtful whether they are to be regarded as many or as one. And when, as with the larger social aggregates, there have been successive conquests, resulting unions, subsequent dissolutions, and reunions otherwise composed, the original lines of structure become so confused or lost that it is difficult to class the ultimate product.

But there emerge certain generalizations which we may safely accept . The stages of compounding and re-compounding have to be passed through in succession. *No* tribe becomes a nation by simple growth; and no great society is formed by the direct union of the smallest societies. Above the simple group the first stage is a compound group inconsiderable in size. The mutual dependence of parts which constitutes it a working whole, cannot exist without some development of lines of intercourse and appliances for combined action; and this must be achieved over a narrow area before it can be achieved over a wide one. When a compound society has been consolidated by the co-operation of its component groups in war under a single head – when it has simultaneously differentiated somewhat its social ranks and industries, and proportionately developed its arts, which all of them conduce in some way to better co-operation, the compound society becomes practically a single one. Other societies of the same order, each having similarly reached a stage of organization alike required and made possible by this co-ordination of actions throughout a larger mass, now form bodies from which, by conquest or by federation in war, may be formed societies of the doubly-compound type. The consolidation of these hasagain an accompanying advance of organization distinctive of it – an organization for which it affords the scope and which makes it practicable – an organization having a higher complexity in its regulative, distributive, and industrial systems. And nt later stages, by kindred steps, arise still larger aggregates having still more complex structures, In this order has social evolution gone on, and only in this order does it appear to be possible. Whatever imperfections and incongruities the above classification has, do not hide these general facts – that there are societies of these different grades of composition; that those of the same grade have general resemblances in their structures; and that they arise in t-ie order shown.

§ 258. We pass now to the classification based on unlike- nesses between the kinds of social activity which predominate, and on the resulting nnlikenesses of organization. The two social types thus essentially contrasted are the militant and the industrial.

It is doubtless true that no definite separation of these can be made. Excluding a few simple groups such as the Esquimaux, inhabiting places where they are safe from invasion, all societies, simple and compound, are occasionally or habitually in antagonism with other societies; and, as we have seen, tend to evolve structures for carrying on offensive and defensive actions. At the same time sus- tentation is necessary; and there is always an organization, slight or decided, for achieving it. But while the two systems in social organisms, as in individual organisms, co-exist in all but the rudimentary forms, they vary immensely in the ratios they bear to one another. In some cases the structures carrying on external actions are largely developed; the sustaining system exists solely for their benefit; and the activities are militant. In other cases there is predominance of the structures carrying on sus- tentation; offensive and defensive structures are maintained only to protect them; and the activities are indus-trial. At the one extreme we have those warlike tribes which, subsisting mainly by the chase, make the appliances for dealing with enemies serve also for procuring food, and have sustaining systems represented only by their women, who are their slave-classes; while, at the other extreme we have the type, as yet only partially evolved, in which the agricultural, manufacturing, and commercial organizations form the chief part of the society, and, in the absence of external enemies, the appliances for offence and defence are either rudimentary or absent. Transitional as are nearly all the societies we have to study, we may yet clearly distinguish the constitutional traits of these opposite types, characterized by predominance of the outer and inner systems respectively.

Having glanced at the two thus placed in contrast, it will be most convenient to contemplate each by itself.

§ 2o9. As before pointed out, the militant type is one in which the army is the nation mobilized while the nation is the quiescent army, and which, therefore, acquires a structure common to army and nation. "We shall most clearly understand its nature by observing in detail this parallelism between the military organization and the social organization at large.

Already we have had ample proof that centralized control is the primary trait acquired by every body of fighting men, be it horde of savages, band of brigands, or mass of soldiers. And this centralized control, necessitated during war, characterizes the government during peace. Among the uncivilized there is a marked tendency for the military chief to become also the political head (the medicine man being his only competitor); and in a conquering race of savages his political headship becomes fixed. In semi- civilized societies the conquering commander and the despotic king are the same; and they remain the same in civilized societies down to late times.

The connexion ia well shownwhere in the same race, along with a contrast between the habitual activities we fmd contrasted forms of government . Thus the powers of the patriarchal chiefs of Kaffir tribes are not great; but the Zulus, who have become a conquering division of the Kaffirs, are under an absolute monarch. Of advanced savages the Fijians may be named as well showing this relation between habitual war and despotic rule: the persons and property of subjects are entirely at the king's or chief's disposal . We have seen that it is the same in the warlike African states, Dahomey and Ashantee. The ancient Mexicans, again, whose highest profession was that of aims, and whose eligible prince became king only by feats in war, had an autocratic government, which, according to Clavigero, became more stringent as the territory was enlarged by conquest. Similarly, the unmitigated despotism under which the Peruvians lived, had been established during the spread of the Ynca conquests. And that race is not the cause, we are shown by this recurrence in ancient America of a relation so familiar in ancient states of the Old "World. The absoluteness of a commander-in-chief goes along with absolute control exercised by his generals over their subordinates, and by their subordinates over the men under them: all are slaves to those above and despots to those below. This structure repeats itself in the accompanying social arrangements. There are precise gradations of rank in the community and complete submission of each rank to the ranks above it. We see this in the society already instanced as showing among advanced savages the development of the militant type. In Fiji six classes are enumerated, from king down to slaves, as sharply marked off. Similarly in Madagascar, where despotism has been in late times established by war, there are several grades and castes. Among the Dahomans, given in so great a degree to bloodshed of all kinds, "the army, or, what is nearly synonymous, the nation," says Burton, " is divided, both male and female, into twowings;" and then, of the various ranks enumerated, all are characterized as legally slaves of the king. In Ashantee, too, where his officers are required to die when the king dies, we have a kindred condition. Of old, among the aggressive Persians, grades were strongly marked. So was it in warlike ancient Mexico: besides three classes of nobility, and besides the mercantile classes, there were three agricultural classes down to the serfs – all in precise subordination. In Peru, also, below the Ynca there were grades of nobility – lords over lords. Moreover, in each town the inhabitants were registered in decades under a decurion, five of these under a superior, two such under a higher one, five of these centurions under a head, two of these heads under one who thus ruled a thousand men, and for every ten thousand there was a governor of Ynca race: the political rule being thus completely regimental. Till lately, another illustration was furnished by Japan. That there were kindred, if less elaborate, structures in ancient militant states of the Old World, scarcely needs saying; and that like structures were repeated in mediaeval times, when a large nation like France had under the monarch several grades of feudal lords, vassals to those above and suzerains to those below, with serfs under the lowest, again shows us that everywhere the militant type has sharply-marked social gradations as it has sharply-marked military gradations. Along with this natural government

there goes a like form of supernatural government. I do not mean merely that in the ideal other-worlds of militant societies, the ranks and powers are conceived as like those of the real world around, though this also is to be noted; but I refer to the militant character of the religion. Ever in antagonism with other societies, the life is a life of enmity and the religion a religion of enmity. The duty of blood-revenge, most sacred of all with the savage, continues to be the dominant duty as the militant type of society evolves. The chief, baulked of his vengeance, dies enjoininghis successors to avenge him; his ghost is propitiated by fulfilling his commands ; the slaying of his enemies becomes the highest action; trophies are brought to his grave in token of fulfilment; and, as tradition grows, he becomes the god worshipped with bloody sacrifices. Everywhere we find evidence. The Fijians offer the bodies of their victims killed in war to the war-god before cooking them. In Dahomey, where the militant type is so far developed that women are warriors, men are almost daily sacrificed by the monarch to please his dead father; and the ghosts of old kings are invoked for aid in war by blood sprinkled on their tombs. The war-god of the Mexicans (originally a conqueror), the most revered of their gods, had his idol fed with human flesh: wars being undertaken to supply him with victims. And similarly in Peru, where there were habitual human sacrifices, men taken captive were immolated to the father of the Yncas, the Sun. How militant societies of old in the East similarly evolved deities who were similarly propitiated by bloody rites, needs merely indicating. Habitually their mythologies represent gods as conquerors; habitually their gods are named "the strong one," "the destroyer," "the avenger," "god of battles," "lord of hosts," "man of war," and so forth. As we read in Assyrian inscriptions, wars were commenced by their alleged will; and, as we read elsewhere, peoples were massacred wholesale in professed obedience to them. How its theological government, like its political government, is essentially military, we see even in late and qualified forms of the militant type; for down to the present time absolute subordination, like that of soldier to commander, is the supreme virtue, and disobedience the crime for which eternal torture is threatened. Similarly with the accompanying ecclesiastical organization. Generally where the militant type is highly developed, the political head and the ecclesiastical head are identical – the king, chief descendant of his ancestor who has become a god, is also chief propitiator of him. It wasso in ancient Peru; and in Acolhuacan (Mexico) tho high-priest was the king's second son. The Egyptian wall-paintings show us kings performing sacrifices; as do also the Assyrian. Babylonian records harmonize with Hebrew traditions in telling us of priest-kings. In Lydia it was the same: Crœsus was king and priest. In Sparta, too, the kings, while military chiefs, were also high priests; and a trace of the like original relation existed in Rome. A system of subordination essentially akin to the military, has habitually characterized the accompanying priesthoods. The Fijians have an hereditary priesthood forming a hierarchy. In Tahiti, where the high-priest was often royal, there were grades of hereditary priests belonging to each social rank. In ancient Mexico the priesthoods of different gods had different ranks, and there were three ranks within each priesthood; and in ancient Peru, besides the royal chief priest, there were priests of the conquering race set over various classes of inferior priests. A like type of structure, with subjection of rank to rank, has characterized priesthoods in the ancient and modern belligerent societies of the Old World. A kind of government essentially the same is traceable throughout the sustaining organization also, so long as the social type remains predominantly militant. Beginning with simple societies in which the slave-class furnishes the warrior-class with the necessaries of life, we have already seen that during subsequent stages of evolution the industrial part of the society continues to be essentially a permanent commissariat, existing solely to supply the needs of the governmental-military structures, and having left over for itself only enough for bare maintenance. Hence the development of political regulation over its activities, has been in fact the extension throughout it of that military rule which, as a permanent commissariat, it naturally had. An extreme instance is furnished us by the ancient Peruvians, whose political and industrial governments were identical – whose kinds and quantities of labourfor every *class* in every locality, were prescribed by lawg enforced by State-officers – who had work legally dictated even for their young children, their blind, and their lame, and who were publicly chastised for idleness: regimental discipline being applied to industry just as our modern advocate of strong government would have it now. The lato Japanese system, completely military in origin and nature, similarly permeated industry: great and small things – houses, ships, down even to mats – were prescribed in theii structures. In the warlike monarchy of Madagascar the artizan classes are in the employ of government, and no man can change his occupation or locality under pain of death. Without multiplication of cases, these typical ones, reminding the reader of the extent to which even in modern fighting States industrial activities are officially regulated, will sufficiently show the principle. Not industry only,

but life at large, is, in militant societies, subject to kindred discipline. Before its recent collapse the government of Japan enforced sumptuary laws on each class, mercantile and other, up to the provincial governors, who must rise, dine, go out, give audience, and retire to rest at prescribed hours; and the native literature specifies regulations of a scarcely credible minuteness. In ancient Peru, officers " minutely inspected the houses, to see that the man, as well as his wife, kept the household in proper order, and preserved a due state of discipline among their children;" and householders were rewarded or chastised accordingly. Among the Egyptians of old each person had, at fixed intervals, to report to the local authority his name, abode, and mode of living. Sparta, too, yields an example of a society specially organized for offence and defence, in which the private conduct of citizens in all its details was under public control, enforced by spies and censors. Though regulations so stringent have not characterized the militant type in more recent ages, yet we need but recall the laws regulating food and dress, the restraints on locomotion, the prohibitions ofsome games and dictation of others, *to* indicate the parallelism of principle. Even now where the military organization has been kept in vigour by military activities, as in France, we are shown by the peremptory control of journals and suppression of meetings, by the regimental uniformity of education, by the official administration of the fine arts, the way in which its characteristic regulating system ramifies everywhere. And then, lastly, is to be noted the

theory concerning the relation between the State and the individual, with its accompanying sentiment. This structure, which adapts a society for combined action against other societies, is associated with the belief that its members exist for the benefit of the whole and not the whole for the benefit of its members. As in an army the liberty of the soldier is denied and only his duty as a member of the mass insisted on; as in a permanently encamped army like the Spartan nation, the laws recognize no personal interests, but patriotic ones only ; so in the militant type throughout, the claims of the unit are nothing and the claims of the aggregate everything. Absolute subjection to authority is the supreme virtue and resistance to it a crime. Other offences may be condoned, but disloyalty is an unpardonable offence. If we take the sentiments of the sanguinary Fijians, among whom loyalty is so intense that a man stands unbound to be knocked on the head, himself saying that what the king wills must be done; or those of the Dahomans, among whom the highest officials are the king's slaves, and on his decease his women sacrifice one another that they may all follow him; or those of the ancient Peruvians, among whom with a dead Ynca, or great Curaca, were buried alive his favourite attendants and wives that they might go to serve him in the other world; or those of the ancient Persians, among whom a father, seeing his innocent son shot by the king in pure wantonness, " felicitated " the king " on the excellence of his archery," and among whom bastinadoed subjects "declared themselves delighted because his majesty had condescendedto recollect them;" we are sufficiently shown that in this social type, the sentiment which prompts assertion of personal rights in opposition to a ruling power, scarcely exists.

Thus the trait characterizing the militant structure throughout, is that its units are coerced into thoir various combined actions. As the soldier's will is so suspended that he becomes in everything the agent of his officer's will; so *ia* the will of the citizen in all transactions, private and public, overruled by that of the government. The co-operation by which the life of the militant society is maintained, is a *compulsory* co-operation. The social structure adapted for dealing with surrounding hostile societies is under a centralized regulating system, to which all the parts are completely subject; just as in the individual organism the outer organs are completely subject to the chief nervous centre.

§ 260. The traits of the industrial type have to be generalized from inadequate and entangled data. Antagonism more or less constant with other societies, having been almost everywhere and always the condition of each society, a social structure fitted for offence and defence exists in nearly all cases, and disguises the structure which social sustentation alone otherwise originates. Such conception as may be formed of it has to be formed from what we find in the few simple societies which have been habitually peaceful, and in the advanced compound societies which, though once habitually militant, have become gradually less so.

Already I have referred to the chiefless Arafuras, living in " peace and brotherly love with one another," of whom we are told that "they recognize the right of property in the fullest sense of the word, without there being any authority among them than the decisions of their elders, according to the customs of thoir forefathers." That is, there has grown up a recognition of mutual claims and personal rights, with voluntary submission to a tacitly-elected representative go emment formed of the most experienced. Among theTodas " who lead a peaceful, tranquil life," disputes are " settled either by arbitration" or by " a council of five." The amiable Bodo and Dhimals, said to be wholly umnilitary, display an essentially-free social form. They have nothing but powerless head men, and are without slaves or servants; but they give mutual assistance in clearing ground and housebuilding : there is voluntary exchange of services – giving of equivalents of labour. The Mishmis again, described as quiet, inoffensive, not warlike, and only occasionally uniting in self- defence, have scarcely any political organization. Their village communities under merely nominal chiefs acknowledge no common chief of the tribe, and the rule is democratic: crimes are judged by an assembly. Naturally few, if any,

cases occur in which societies of this type have evolved into larger societies without passing into the militant type; for, as we have seen, the consolidation of simple aggregates into a compound aggregate habitually results from war, defensive or offensive, which, if continued, evolves a centralized authority with its coercive institutions. The Pueblos, however, industrious and peaceful agriculturists, who, building their unique villages, or compound houses containing 2,000 people, in such ways as to " wall out black barbarism," fight only when invaded, show us a democratic form of government: " the governor and Ids council are elected annually by the people." The case of Samoa, too, may be named as showing to some extent how, in one of these compound communities where the warlike activity is now not considerable, decline in the rigidity of political control has gone along with some evolution of the industrial type. Chiefs and minor heads, partly hereditary, partly elective, are held responsible for the conduct of affairs: there are village-parliaments and district-parliaments. Along with, this we find a considerably-developed sustaining organization separate from the political – masters who have apprentices, employ journeymen, and pay wages; and when payment for work is inadequate, there are even strikes upheld by a tacit trades-unionism. Passing

to more evolved societies it must be observed, first, that the distinctive traits of the industrial type do not become marked, even where the industrial activity is considerable, so long as the industrial government remains identified with the political. In Phoenicia, for example, the foreign wholesale trade seems to have belonged mostly to the State, the kings, and the nobles. Ezekiel describes the king of Tyrus as a prudent commercial prince, who finds out the precious metals in their hidden seats, enriches himself by getting them, and increases these riches by traffic. Clearly, where the political and military heads have thus themselves become the heads of the industrial organization, the traits distinctive of it are prevented from showing themselves. Of ancient societies to be named in connexion with the relation between industrial activities and free institutions, Athens will be at once thought of; and, by contrast with other Greek States, it showed this relation as clearly as can be expected. Up to the time of Solon all these communities were under either oligarchies or despots. Those of them in which war continued to be the honoured occupation while industry was despised, retained this political type; but in Athens, where industry was regarded with comparative respect, where it was encouraged by Solon, and where immigrant artizans found a home, there grew up an industrial organization which distinguished the Athenian society from adjacent societies, while it was also distinguished from them by those democratic institutions that simultancously developed. Turning to later times, the relation between a social *n'yime* predominantly industrial and a less coercive form of rule, is shown us by the Hanse Towns, by the towns of the Low Countries out of which the Dutch Eepublic arose, and in high degrees by ourselves, by the United States, and by our colonies. Along with wars less frequent and these carried on at a distance; and along with an accompanying growth of agriculture, manufactures, and commerce, beyond that of continental states more militaryin habit; there has gone in England a development of free institutions. As further implying that the two are related as cause and consequence, there may be noted the fact that the regions whence changes towards greater political liberty have come, are the leading industrial regions; and that rural districts, less characterized by constant trading transactions, have retained longer the earlier type with its appropriate sentiments and ideas. In the form of ecclesiastical

government we see parallel changes. Where the industrial activities and structures evolve, this branch of the regulating system, no longer as in the militant type a rigid hierarchy little by little loses strength, while there grows up one of a different kind: sentiments and institutions both relaxing. Eight of private judgment in religious matters gradually establishes itself along with establishment of political rights. In place of a uniform belief imperatively enforced, there come multiform beliefs voluntarily accepted; and the ever- multiplying bodies espousing these beliefs, instead of being governed despotically, govern themselves after a manner more or less representative. Military conformity coercively maintained gives place to a varied non-conformity maintained by willing union. The industrial organization itself, which thus as it becomes predominant affects all the rest, of course shows us in an especial degree this change of structure. From the primitive condition under which the master maintains slaves to work for him, there is a transition through stages of increasing freedom to a condition like our own, in which all who work and employ, buy and sell, are entirely independent; and in which there is an unchecked power of forming unions that rule themselves on democratic principles. Combinations of workmen and counter-combinations of employers, no less than political societies and leagues for carrying on this or that agitation, show us tho representative mode of government; which characterizes also every joint-stock company, for mining, banking, railway- making, or other commercial enterprise. Further.

we see that as in the militant type the mode of regulation ramifies into all minor departments of social activity, so here does the industrial mode of regulation. Multitudinous objects are achieved by spontaneously-evolved combinations, of citizens governed representatively. The tendency to this kind of organization is so ingrained that for every proposed end the proposed means is a society ruled by an elected committee headed by an elected chairman – philanthropic associations of multitudinous kinds, literary institutions, libraries, clubs, bodies for fostering the various sciences and arts, etc., etc. Along with all which traits there go senti

ments and ideas concerning the relation between the citizen and the State, opposite to those accompanying the militant type. In place of the doctrine that the duty of obedience to the governing agent is unqualified, there arises the doctrine that the will of the citizens is supreme and the governing agent exists merely to carry out their will. Thus subordinated in position, the regulating power is also restricted in range. Instead of having an authority extending over actions of all kinds, it is shut out from large classes of actions. Its control over ways of living in respect to food, clothing, amusements, is repudiated; it is not allowed to dictate modes of production nor to regulate trade. Nor is

this alL It becomes a duty to resist irresponsible government, and also to resist the excesses of responsible government. There arises a tendency in minorities to disobey even the legislature deputed by the majority, when it interferes in certain ways ; and their oppositions to laws they condemn as inequitable, from time to time cause abolitions of them. With which changes of political theory and accompanying sentiment, is joined a belief, implied or avowed, that the combined actions of the social aggregate have for their end to maintain the conditions under which individual lives may be satisfactorily carried on; in place of the old belief that individual lives have for their end the maintenance of tlua aggregate's combined actions.

These pervading traits in which the industrial type differs so widely from the militant type, originate in those relations of individuals implied by industrial activities, which are wholly unlike those implied hy militant activities. All trading transactions, whether between masters and workmen, buyers and sellers of commodities, or professional men and those they aid, are effected by free exchange. For some benefit which A's business enables him to give, B willingly yields up an equivalent benefit: if not in the form of something he has produced, then in the form of money gained by his occupation. This relation, in which the mutual rendering of services is unforced and jieither individual subordinated, becomes the predominant relation throughout society in proportion as the industrial activities predominate. Daily determining the thoughts and sentiments, daily disciplining all in asserting their own claims while forcing them to recognize the correlative claims of others, it produces social units whose mental structures and habits mould social arrangements into corresponding forms. There results a type characterized throughout by that same individual freedom which every commercial transaction implies. The co-operation by which the multiform activities of the society are carried on, becomes a *voluntary* co-operation. And while the developed sustaining system which gives to a social organism the industrial type, acquires for itself, like the developed sustaining system of an animal, a regulating apparatus of a diffused or uncentralized kind; it tends also to decentralize the primary regulating apparatus, by making it derive from more numerous classes its deputed powers.

§ 261. The essential traits of these two social types are in most cases obscured, both by the antecedents arid by the coexisting circumstances. Every society has been, at each past period, and is at present, conditioned in a way more or less unlike the ways in which others have been and are conditioned. Hence the production of structures characterizingone or other of these opposed types, is, in every instance, furthered, or hindered, or modified, in a special manner. Observe the several kinds of causes.

There is, first, the deeply-organized character of the particular race, coming down from those pre-historic times during which the diffusion of mankind and differentiation of the varieties of man, took place. Very difficult to change, this must in every case qualify differently the tendency towards assumption of either type.

There is, next, the effect due to the immediately-preceding mode of life and social type. Nearly always the society we have to study contains decayed institutions and habits belonging to an ancestral society otherwise circumstanced; and these pervert more or less the effects of circumstances subsequently existing.

Again, there are the peculiarities of the habitat in respect of contour, soil, climate, flora, fauna, severally affecting in one mode or other the activities, whether militant or industrial ; and severally hindering or aiding, in some special way, the development of either type.

Yet further, there are the complications caused by the particular organizations and practices of surrounding societies. For, supposing the amount of offensive or defensive action to be the same, the nature of it depends in each case on the nature of the antagonist action; and hence its reactive effects on structure vary with the character of the antagonist. Add to this that direct imitation of adjacent societies is a factor of some moment.

There remains to be named an element of complication more potent perhaps than any of these – one which of itself often goes far to determine the type as militant, and which iu every case profoundly modifies the social arrangements. I refer to the mixture of races caused by conquest or otherwise. We may properly treat of it separately under the head of social constitution – not, of course, constitution politically understood, but constitution understood as referring to therelative homogeneity or heterogeneity of the units constituting the social aggregate.

§ 262. As the nature of the aggregate, partially determined by environing conditions, is in other respects determined by the natures of its units, where its units are of diverse natures the degrees of contrast between the two or more kinds of them, and the degrees of union among them, must greatly affect the results. Are they of unallied races or of races near akin; and do they remain separate or do they mix ?

Clearly where it has happened that a conquering race, continuing to govern a subject race, has developed the militant regulating system throughout the whole social structure, and for ages habituated its units to compulsory co-operation – where it has also happened that the correlative ecclesiastical system with its appropriate cult, has given to absolute subordination the religious sanction – and especially where, as in China, each individual is educated by the governing power and stamped with the appropriate ideas of duty which it is heresy to question; it becomes impossible for any considerable change to be wrought in the social structure by other influences. It is the law of all organization that as it becomes complete it becomes rigid. Only where incompleteness implies a remaining plasticity, is it possible for the type to develop from the original militant form to the form which industrial activity generates. Especially where the

two races, contrasted in their natures, do not mix, social cooperation implies a compulsory regulating system: the militant form of structure which the dominant impose ramifies throughout. Ancient Peru furnished an extreme case; and the Ottoman empire may be instanced. Social constitutions of this kind, in which races having aptitudes for forming unlike structures co-exist, are in states of unstable equilibrinm. Any considerable shock dissolves the organization ; and in the absence of unity of tendency, re-establishment of it is difficult if not impossible. In caseswhere the conquering and conquered, though widely unlike, intermarry extensively, a kindred effect is produced in another way. The conflicting tendencies towards different social types, instead of existing in separate individuals, now exist in the same individual . The half-caste, inheriting from one line of ancestry proclivities adapted to one set of institutions, and from the other line of ancestry proclivities adapted to another set of institutions, is not fitted for either. He is a unit whose nature has not been moulded by any social type, and therefore cannot, with others like himself, evolve any social type. Modern Mexico and the South American Republics, with their perpetual revolutions, show us the result. It is observable, too, that where races of

strongly-contrasted natures have mixed more or less, or, remaining but little mixed, occupy adjacent areas subject to the same government, the equilibrium maintained so long as that government keeps up the coercive form, shows itself to be unstable when the coercion relaxes. Spain with its diverse peoples, Basque, Celtic, Gothic, Moorish, Jewish, partially mingled and partially localized, shows us this result.

Small differences, however, seem advantageous. Sundry instances point to the conclusion that a society formed from nearly-allied peoples of which the conquering eventually mingles with the conquered, is relatively well fitted for progress. From their fusion results a community which, determined in its leading traits by the character common to the two, is prevented by their differences of character from being determined in its minor traits – is left capable of taking on new arrangements wrought by new influences: medium plasticity allows those changes of struct are constituting advance in heterogeneity. One example is furnished us by the Hebrews; who, notwithstanding their boasted purity of blood, resulted from a mixing of many Semitic varieties in the country east of the Nile, and who, both in their wanderings and after the conquest of Palestine, went on amalgamating kindred tribes. Another is supplied by theAthenians, whose progress had for antecedent the mingling of numerous immigrants from other Greek states with the Greeks of the locality. The fusion by conquest of the Romans with other Aryan tribes, Sabini, Sabelli, and Samnites, preceded the first ascending stage of the Roman civilization. And our own country, peopled by different divisions of the Aryan race, and mainly by varieties of Scandinavians, again illustrates this effect produced by the mixture of units sufficiently alike to co-operate in the same social system, but sufficiently unlike to prevent that social system from becoming forthwith definite in structure.

Admitting that the evidence where so many causes are in operation cannot be satisfactorily disentangled, and claiming only probability for these inductions respecting social constitutions, it remains to point out their analogy to certain inductions respecting the constitutions of individual living things. Between organisms widely unlike in kind, no progeny can arise: the physiological units contributed by them respectively to form a fertilized germ, cannot work together so as to produce a new organism. Evidently as, while multiplying, each class of units tends to build itself into its peculiar type of structure, their conflict prevents the formation of any structure. If the two organisms are less unlike in kind – belonging, say, to the same genus though to different species – the two structures which their two groups of physiological units tend to build up, being tolerably similar, these can, and do, co-operate in making an organism that is intermediate. But this, though it will work, is imperfect in its latest-evolved parts: there results a mule incapable of propagating. If, instead of different species, remote varieties are united, the intermediate organism is not infertile; but many facts suggest the conclusion that infertility results in subsequent generations: the incongruous working of the united structures, though longer in showing itself, comes out ultimately. And then, finally, if instead of remote varieties, varieties nearly allied aipounited, a permanently-fertile breed results; and while the slight differences of the two kinds of physiological units are not such as to prevent harmonious co-operation, they are such as conduce to plasticity and unusually vigorous growth. Here, then, seems a parallel to the conclusion indicated above, that hybrid societies are imperfectly organizable – cannot grow into forms completely stable; while societies which have been evolved from mixtures of nearly-allied varieties of man, can assume stable structures, and have an advantagcous modifiability.

§ 263. "We class societies, then, in two ways; both having to be kept in mind when interpreting social phenomena.

First, they have to be arranged in the order of their integration, as simple, compound, doubly-compound, trebly- compound.   And along with the increasing degrees of evolution implied by these ascending stages of composition, we have to recognize the increasing degrees of evolution implied by growing heterogeneity, general and local.

Much less definite is the division to be made among societies according as one or other of their great systems of organs is supreme. Omitting those lowest types which show no differentiations at all, we have but few exceptions to the rule that each society has structures for carrying on conflict with other societies and structures for carrying on sustentation; and as the ratios between these admit of all gradations, it results that Do specific classification can be based on their relative developments. Nevertheless, as the militant type, characterized by predominance of the one, is framed on the principle of compulsory co-operation, while the industrial type, characterized by predominance of the other, is framed on the principle of voluntary co-operation, the two types, when severally evolved to their extreme forms, are diametrically opposed ; and the contrasts between their traits are among the most important with which Sociology has to deal.

Were this the fit place, some pages might be added respecting a possible future social type, differing as much from the industrial as this does from the militant – a type which, having a sustaining system more fully developed than any we know at present, will use the products of industry neither for maintaining a militant organization nor exclusively for material aggrandizement; but will devote them to the carrying on of higher activities. As the contrast between the militant and the industrial types, is indicated by inversion of the belief that individuals exist for the benefit of the State into the belief that the State exists for the benefit of individuals; so the contrast between the industrial type and the type likely to be evolved from it, is indicated by inversion of the belief that life is for work into the belief that work is for life. But we are here concerned with inductions derived from societies that have been and are, and cannot enter upon speculations respecting societies that may be. Merely naming as a sign, the multiplication of institutions and appliances for intellectual and aesthetic culture, and for kindred activities not of a directly life-sustaining kind but of a kind having gratification for their immediate purpose, I can here say no more.

Returning from this parenthetical suggestion, there remains the remark that to the complications caused by crossings of the two classifications set forth, have to be added the complications caused by unions of races widely unlike or little unlike;

which here mix not at all, there partially, and in other cases wholly. Respecting these kinds of constitutions, we have considerable warrant for concluding that the hybrid kind, essentially unstable, admits of being organized only on the principle of compulsory co-operation; since units much opposed in their natures cannot work together spontaneously. While, conversely, the kind characterized by likeness in its units is relatively stable; and under fit conditions may evolve into the industrial type: especially if the likeness is qualified by slight differences.

6

SECTION 6

CHAPTER XI.
SOCIAL METAMORPHOSE. S.

§ 264. Verification of the general view set fort), in tho last chapter, is gained by observing the alterations ot' social structures which follow alterations of social activities; and here again we find analogies between social organisms and individual organisms. In both there is metamorphosis consequent on change from a wandering life to a settled life; in both there is metamorphosis consequent on change from a life exercising mainly the inner or sustaining system, to a life exercising the outer or expending system; and in both there is a reverse metamorphosis.

The young of many invertebrate creatures, annulose and molluscous, pass through early stages during which they move about actively. Presently comes a settling down in tome fit habitat, a dwindling away of the locomotive organs and the guiding appliances which they had, a growth of those other organs now needed for appropriating such food as the environment supplies, and a rapid enlargement of the sustaining system. A transformation opposite in nature, is made familiar to us by the passage from larva to imago in insects. Surrounded by food, the future moth or fly develops almost exclusively its sustaining system; has but rudimentary limbs or none at all; and has proportionately imperfect senses. After growing immensely and accumulating much plastic material, it begins to uufold its external organs with their appropriate regulating apparatus, while its organs of nutrition decrease; and it thus fits itself for active dealings with environing existences.

The one truth, common to these opposite kinds of metamorphoses, which here concerns us, is that the two great systems of structures for carrying on outer activities and inner activities respectively, severally dwindle or develop according to the life the aggregate leads. Though in the absence of social types fixed by repeated inheritance, we cannot have social metamorphoses thus definitely related to changes of life arising in definite order, analogy implies that which we have already seen reason to infer; namely, that the outer and inner structures with their regulating systems, severally increase or diminish according as the activities become more militant or more industrial.

§ 265. Before observing how metamorphoses are caused, let us observe how they are hindered. I have implied above that where it has not derived a specific structure from a line of ancestral societies leading similar lives, a society cannot undergo metamorphoses in a precise manner and order: the effects of surrounding influences predominate over the effects of inherited tendencies. Here may fitly be pointed out the converse truth, that where societies descending one from another in a series, have pursued like careers, there results a type so far settled in its cycle of development, maturity, and decay, that it resists metamorphosis.

Uncivilized tribes in general may be cited in illustration. They show little tendency to alter their social activities and structures under changed circumstances, but die out rather than adapt themselves. Even with superior varieties of men this happens; as, for example, with the wandering hordes of Arabs. Modern Bedouins show us a form of society which, so far as the evidence enables us to judge, has remained substantially the same these 3000 years or more, spite of contact with adjacent civilizations; and there is evidencethat in some Semites the nomadic type had, even in ancient times, become so ingrained as to express itself in the religion. Tims we have the Rechabite injunction – "Neither shall ye build house, nor sow corn, nor plant vineyard, nor have any, but all your days ye shall dwell in tents;" and Mr. E. W. Robertson points out that –

"One of the laws of the ancient Nabatean confederacy made it a capital crime to sow corn, to build a house, or plant a tree. ... It was a fixed and settled principle in the nomad to reduce the country he invaded to the condition of a waste and open pasturage. . . . He looked upon such a course as a religious duty."

Change from the migratory to the settled state, hindered by persistence of the primitive social type, is also otherwise hindered. Describing the Hill Tribes on the Kuladyne River, Arraean, Lieut. Latter says : –

" A piece of ground rarely yields more than one crop; in each successive year other spots are in like mauner chosen, till all those around the village are exhausted ; a move is then made to another locality, fresh habitations are erected, and the same process gone through. These migrations occur about every third year, and they are the means by which long periods of time are calculated ; thus a Toungtha will tell you that such and such an event occurred so many migrations since."

Evidently a practice of this kind, prompted partly by the restlessness inherited from ancestral nomads, is partly due to undeveloped agriculture – to the absence of those means by which, in a thickly-peopled country, the soil is made permanently fertile. This intermediate state between the wandering and the stationary is common through-out Africa. It is remarked that " society in Africa is a plant of herbaceous character, without any solid or enduring stem; rank in growth, rapid in decay, and admitting of being burned down annually without any diminution of its general productiveness." Reade tells us that " the natives of Equatorial Africa are perpetually changing the sites of their villages." Of the Bechuanas, Thompson says – " Their towns are often so considerable as to contain many thousand people; and yet they are removable at the caprice of thechief, like an Arab camp." And a like state of things existed in primitive Europe : families and small communities iu each tribe, migrated from one part of the tribal territory to another. Thus from the temporary villages of hunters like the North American Indians, and from the tempornry encampments of pastoral hordes, the transition to settled agricultural communities is very gradual: the earlier mode of life, frequently resumed, is but slowly outgrown.

"When studying the social metamorphoses that follow altered social activities, we have therefore to bear in mind those resistances to change which the inherited social type offers, and also those resistances to change caused by partial continuance of old conditions. Further, we may anticipate reversion if the old conditions begin again to predominate.

§ 266. Of chief interest to ns here are the transformations of the militant into the industrial and the industrial into the militant. And especially we have to note how the industrial type, partially developed in a few cases, retrogrades towards the militant type if international conflicts recur.

When comparing these two types we saw how the compulsory co-operation which military activity necessitates, is contrasted with the voluntary co-operation which a de-veloped industrial activity necessitates; and we saw that where the coercive regulating system proper to the one has not become too rigid, the non-coercive regulating system proper to the other begins to show itself as industry nourishes unchecked by var. The great liberalization of political arrangements which occurred among ourselves during the long peace that commenced in 1815, furnishes an illustration. An example of this metamorphosis is supplied by Norway, too, in which country absence of war and growth of free institutions have gone together. But our attention is demanded chiefly by the proofs that revived belligerent habits re-develop the militant type of structure.

Not dwelling on the instances to be fou11d in ancienthistory, nor on the twine-repeated lapse of the rising Dutch Republic into a monarchy under the reactive in-fluences of war, nor on the reversion from parliamentary government to despotic government which resulted from the wars of the Protectorate among ourselves, nor on the effect which n career of conquest had in changing the first French Eepublic into a military despotism; it will suffice if we contemplate the evidence yielded in recent years. How, since the establishment of a stronger centralized power in Germany by war, a more coercive *regime* has shown itself, we see in the dealings of Bismarck with the ecclesiastical powers; in the laying down by Moltke of the doctrine that both for safety from foreign attack and guardianship of order at home, it is needful that the supplies for the army should not be dependent on a parliamentary vote; and again in the measures lately taken for centralizing the State-control of German railways. In France we have as usual the chief soldier becoming the chief ruler; the maintenance, in many parts, of that state of siege which originated with the war; and the continuance by a nominally-free form of government of many restrictions upon freedom. But the kindred changes of late undergone by our own society, furnish the clearest illustrations; because the industrial type having developed here further than on the Continent, there is more scope for retrogression.

Actual wars and preparations for possible wars, have conspired to produce these changes. In the first place, since the accession of Louis Napoleon, which initiated the change, we have had the Crimean war, the war entailed by the Indian Mutiny, the China war, and the more recent wars in Abyssinia and Ashantee. In the second place, and chiefly, there has been the re-development of military organization and feeling here, caused by re-development of them abroad. That in nations as in individuals a threatening attitude begets an attitude of defence, is a truth that needs no proof, And since this was written the Afghan, Zulu, and Egyptian wars.

Hence among ourselves the recent growth of expenditure for army and navy, the making of fortifications, the formation of the volunteer force, the establishment of permanent camps, the repetition of autumn manceuvres, the building of military stations throughout the kingdom.

Of the traits accompanying this reversion towards the militant type, we have first to note the revival of predatory activities. Always a structure assumed for defensive action, available also for offensive action, tends to initiate it.   As in Athens the military and naval organization which was developed in coping witli a foreign enemy, thereafter began to exercise itself aggressively ; as in France the trinmphant army of the Republic, formed to resist invasion, forthwith became an invader; so is it habitually – so is it now with ourselves. In China, India, Polynesia, Africa, the East Indian Archipelago, reasons – never wanting to the aggressor – are given for widening our empire : without force if it may be, and with force if needful. After annexing the Fiji Islands, voluntarily ceded only because there was no practicable alternative, there comes now the proposal to take possession of Samoa. Accepting in exchange for another, a territory subject to a treaty, we ignore the treaty and make the assertion of it a ground for war with the Ashantees. In Sherbro our agreements with native chiefs having brought about universal disorder, we send a body of soldiers to suppress it, and presently will allege the necessity of extending our rule over a larger area. So again in Perak. A resident sent to advise becomes a resident who dictates; appoints as sultan the most plastic candidate in place of one preferred by the chiefs; arouses resistance which becomes a plea for using force; finds usurpation of the government needful; has his proclamation torn down by a native, who is thereupon stabbed by the resident's servant; the resident is himself killed as a consequence; then (nothing being eaid of the murder of the native), the murder of the resident leads to outcries for vengeance, and a militaryexpedition establishes British rule. Be it in the slaying of Karen tribes who resist surveyors of their territory, or be it in the demand made on the Chinese in pursuance of the doctrine that a British traveller, sacred wherever he may choose to intrude, shall have his death avenged on some one, we everywhere find pretexts for quarrels which lead to acquisitions. In the House of Commons and in the Press, the same spirit is shown. During the debate on the Suez-Canal purchase, our Prime Minister, referring to the possible annexation of Egypt, said that the English people, wishing the Empire to be maintained, " will not be alarmed even if it be increased;" and was cheered for so saying. And recently, urging that it is time to blot out Dahomey, the weekly organ of filibustering Christianity exclaims – " Let us take Whydah, and leave the savage to recover it."

And now, having observed this re-development of armed forces and revival of the predatory spirit, we may note that which chiefly concerns us – the return towards the militant type in our institutions generally – the extension of centralized administration and of compulsory regulation. In the first place we see it within the governmental organization itself: the functions of courts-martial on naval disasters are usurped by the head of the naval department; the powers of the Indian Government are peremptorily restricted by a minister at home; and county governing bodies, seeking to put part of their county burdens on the nation at large, are simultaneously yielding up part of their powers. Military officialism everywhere tends to usurp the place of civil officialism. We have military heads of the metropolitan and provincial police; military men hold offices under the Board of Works and in the Art department; the inspectors of railways are military men; and some municipal bodies in the provinces are appointing majors and captains to minor civil offices in their gift: an inevitable result being a style of administration which asserta authority more and regards individual claims

less. The spirit of sucli a system we see in the design and execution of the Contagious Diseases Acts – Acts which emanated from the military and naval departments, which over-ride those guarantees of individual freedom provided by constitutional forms, and which are administered by a central police not responsible to local authorities. Akin in spirit is the general sanitary dictation which, extending for these many years, has now ended in the formation of several hundred districts officered by medical men, partly paid by the central government and under its supervision. Within the organization of the medical profession itself we see a congruous change: independent bodies who give diplomas are no longer to be tolerated, but there must be unification – a single standard of examination. Poor-Law administration, again, has been growing more centralized: boards of guardians having had their freedom of action gradually restricted by orders from the Local Government Board. Moreover, while the regulating centres in London have been absorbing the functions of provincial regulating centres, these have in their turn been usurping those of local trading companies. In sundry towns municipal bodies have become distributors of gas and water; and now it is urged (significantly enough by a military enthusiats) that the same should be done in London. Nay, these public agents have become builders too. The supplying of small houses having, by law-enforced cost of construction, been made unremunerative to private persons, is now in provincial towns to be undertaken by the municipalities ; and in London the Metropolitan Board having proposed that the rate-payers should spend so much to build houses for the poor in the Holborn district, the Secretary of State says they must spend more! Of like meaning is the fact that our system of telegraphs, developed as a part of the industrial organization, has become a part of the governmental organization. And then similarly showing the tendency towards increase of govern-

mental structures at the expense of industrial structures, there has been an active advocacy of State-purchase of railways – an advocacy which has been for the present suspended only because of the national loss entailed by purchase of the telegraphs. How pervading is the influence we see in the schemes of a coercive philanthropy, which, invoking State-power to improve people's conduct, disregards the proofs that the restrictions on conduct enacted of old, and in later times abolished as tyrannical, habitually had kindred motives. Men are to be made temperate by impediments to drinking – shall be less free than hitherto to buy and sell certain articles. Instead of extending the principle proper to the industrial type, of providing quick and costless remedies for injuries, minor as well as major, which citizens inflict on one another, legislators extend the principle of preventing them by inspection. The arrangements in mines, factories, ships, lodging-houses, bakehouses, down even to water-closets in private dwellings, are prescribed by laws carried out by officials. Not by quick and certain penalty for breach of contract is adulteration to be remedied, but by public analyzers. Benefits are not to be bought by men with the money their efficient work brings them, which is the law of voluntary co-operation, but benefits are given irrespective of effort expended: without regard to their deserts, men shall be provided at the public cost with free libraries, free local museums, etc.; and from the savings of the more worthy shall be taken by the tax- gatherer means of supplying the less worthy who have not saved. Along with the tacit assumption that State-authority over citizens has no assignable limits, which is an assumption proper to the militant type, there goes an unhesitating faith in State-judgment, also proper to the militant type. Bodily welfare and mental welfare are consigned to it without the least doubt of its capacity. Having by struggles through centuries deposed a power which, for their alleged eternal good, forced on men its teachings, we invoke another power

to force its teachings on men for their alleged temporal good. The compulsion once supposed to be justified in religious instruction by the infallible judgment of a Pope, is now supposed to be justified in secular instruction by the infallible judgment of a Parliament; and thus, under penalty of imprisonment for resistance, there is established an education bad in matter, bad in manner, bad in order.

Inevitably along with this partial reversion to the compulsory social system which accompanies partial reversion to the militant type of structure, there goes an appropriate change of sentiments. In essence Toryism stands for the control of the State *verms* the freedom of the individual; and in essence Liberalism stands for the freedom of the individual *versus* the control of the State. But whereas, during the previous peaceful period, individual liberty was extended by abolishing religious disabilities, establishing free-trade, removing impediments from the press, etc. ; since the reversion began, the party which effected these changes has vied with the opposite party in multiplying State-administrations which diminish individual liberty. How far the principles of free government have been disregarded, and how directly this change is sequent upon the feeling which militant action fosters, is conclusively shown by the Suez-Canal business. A step which, to say nothing of the pecuniary cost, committed the nation to entanglements of a serious kind, was taken by its ministry in such manner that its representative body had a nominal, but no real, power of reversing it; and instead of protest against this disregard of constitutional principles, there came general applause. The excuse accepted by all was the military exigency. The prompt action of the co-ordinating centre by. which offensive and defensive operations are directed, was said to necessitate this ignoring of Parliament and this suspension of self-government . And the general sentiment, responding to the alleged need for keeping our hold on a conquered territory, not onlyforgave but rejoiced over this return towards military rule.

§ 267. Of course social metamorphoses are in every case complicated and obscured by special causes never twice a like. Where rapid growth is going on, the changes of structure accompanying increase of mass are involved with the changes of structure resulting from modification of type. Further, disentanglement of the facts is made difficult when the two great systems of organs for sustentation and external action are evolving simultaneously. This is our own case. That re-development of structures for external action which we have been tracing, and that partial return to a congruous social system, have not arrested the development of the sustaining structures aud that social system they foster. Hence sundry changes opposite to those enumerated above. While the revival of ecclesiasticism having for cardinal principle subordination to authority, has harmonized with this reversion towards the militant type, the increase of divisions in the Church, the assertions of individual judgment, and the relaxations of dogma, have harmonized with the contrary movement. While new educational organizations tending towards regimental uniformity, are by each fresh Act of Parliament made more rigid, the old educational organizations in public schools and universities, are being made more plastic and less uniform. While there have been increasing interferences with the employment of labour, wholly at variance with the principles of voluntary co-operation, they have not yet gone far enough to reverse the free-trade policy which industrial evolution has been extending. The interpretation appears to be that while the old compulsory system of regulation has been abolished where its pressure had become intolerable, this re-development of it is going on where its pressure has not yet been felt.

Moreover, the vast transformation suddenly caused by railways and telegraphs, adds to the difficulty of tracingmetamorphoses of the kinds we are considering. Within a generation the social organism has passed from a stage like that of a cold-blooded creature with feeble circulation and rudimentary nerves, to a stage like that of a warm-blooded creature with efficient vascular system and a developed nervous apparatus. To this more than to any other cause, are due the great changes in habits, beliefs, and sentiments, characterizing our generation. Manifestly, this rapid evolution of the distributing and internuncial structures, has aided the growth of both the industrial organization and the militant organization. While productive activities have been facilitated, there has been a furtherance of that centralization characterizing the social type required for offensive and defensive actions.

But notwithstanding these disguising complexities, if we contrast the period from 1815 to 1850 with the period from 1850 to the present time, we cannot fail to see that along with increased armaments, more frequent conflicts, and revived military sentiment, there has been a spread of compulsory regulations. While nominally extended by the giving of votes, the freedom of the individual has been in many ways actually diminished; both by restrictions which ever-multiplying officials are appointed to insist on, and by the forcible taking of money to secure for him, or others at his expense, benefits previously left to be secured by each for himself. And undeniably this is a return towards that coercive discipline which pervades the whole social life where the militant type is predominant.

In metamorphoses, then, so far as they are traceable, we discern general truths harmonizing with those disclosed by comparisons of types. With social organisms, as with individual organisms, the structure becomes adapted to the activity. In the one case as in the other, if circumstances entail a fundamental change in the mode of activity, there by-and-by results a fundamental change in the form of structure. And in both cases there is a reversion towards the old type if there is a resumption of the old activity.

7

SECTION 7

CHAPTER XII.

QUALIFICATIONS AND SUMMARY.

5 268. One who made the analogies between individual organization and social organization his special subject, might carry them further in several directions.

He might illustrate the general truth that as fast as structure approaches completeness, uiodifiability diminishes and growth ends. The finished animal, moulded in all details, resists change by the sum of those forces which have evolved its parts into their respective shapes; and the finished society does the like. In either case results, at length, rigidity. Every organ of the one and institution of the other becomes, as maturity is neared, more coherent and definite, and offers a greater obstacle to alterations required either by increase of size or variation of conditions.

Then he might enlarge on the fact that, as in individual organisms so in social organisms, after the structures proper to the type have fully evolved there presently begins a slow decay. He could not, indeed, furnish satisfactory proof of this; since among ancient societies, essentially militant in their activities, dissolution by conquest habitually prevented the cycles of changes from being completed; and since modern societies are passing through their cycles. But the minor parts of modern societies, especially during those earlier times when local development was little implicated with general development, would yield him evidence. Hemight instance the fact that ancient corporate towns, with their guilds and regulations of industry, gradually made more numerous and stringent, slowly dwindled, and gave way before towns in which the absence of privileged classes permitted freedom of industry: the rigid old structure having its function usurped by a plastic new one. In each institution, private or public, he might point to the ever-multiplying usages and hye-laws, severally introduced to fit the actions to the passing time, but eventually making adaptation to a coming time impracticable. And he might infer that a like fate awaits each entire society, which, as its adjustments to present circumstances are finished, loses power to re-adjust itself to the circumstances of the future: eventually disappearing, if not by violence, then by a decline conseqnent on inability to compete with younger and more modifiable societies.

Were his speculative audacity sufficient, he might end by alleging parallelisms between the processes of reproduction in the two cases. Among primitive societies which habitually multiply by fission, but are by conquest occasionally fused, group with group, after which there is presently a recurrence of fission, he might trace an analogy to what happens in the lowest types of organisms, which, multiplying fissiparously, from time to time reverse the process by that fusion which naturalists call conjugation. Then he might point out that in either case the larger and stationary types propagate by the dispersion of germs. Adult organisms which are fixed, send off groups of such units as they are themselves composed of, to settle down elsewhere and grow into organisms like themselves, as settled societies send off their groups of colonists. And he might even say that as union of the germinal group detached from one organism with a group detached from a similar organism, is either essential to, or conducive to, the vigorous evolution of a new organism; so the mixture of colonists derived from one society with others derived from a kindred society, is, if not essential to, stillconducive to, the evolution of a new society more plastic than the old ones from which the mingled units were derived. But without committing ourselves to any such further adventurous suggestions, we may leave the comparison as it stands in preceding chapters.

§ 269. This comparison has justified to a degree that could scarcely have been anticipated, the idea propounded by certain philosophers and implied even in popular language. Naturally it happened that this idea took at first crude forms. Let us glance at some of them.

In the *Republic* of Plato, asserting the fact, not even yet adequately recognized, that " the States are as the men are; they grow out of human characters," Socrates is represented as arguing – " then if the constitutions of States are five, the dispositions of individual minds will also be five:" an absurd corollary from a rational proposition. Division of labour is described as a social need; but it is represented rather as having to be established than as establishing itself. Throughout, the conception, like indeed to conceptions that prevail still, is that society may be artificially arranged thus or thus. Alleging such likeness between the State and the citizen that from the institutions of the one may be deduced the faculties of the other, Plato, with the belief that the States, growing " out of human characters," are " as the men are," joins the belief that these States, with characters thus determined, can yet determine the characters of their

citizens. Chiefly, however, the erroneous nature of the analogy held by Plato to exist between the individual and the State, he shows by comparing reason, passion or spirit, and desire, in the one, to counsellors, auxiliaries, and traders in the other. Not to the mutually-dependent parts of the bodily organization are the mutually-dependent parts of the political organization supposed to be analogous, but rather to the co-operating powers of the mind. The con
ception of Hobbes in one respect only, approaches nearer to
a rational conception. Like Plato he regards social organization not as natural but as factitious: propounding, as he does, the notion of a social contract as originating governmental institutions, and as endowing the sovereign with irrevocable authority. The analogy as conceived by him is best expressed in his own words. He says: – "For by art is created that great Leviathan called a Commonwealth, or State, in Latin Civitas, which is but an artificial man; though of greater stature and strength than the natural, for whose protection and defence it was intended; and in which the *sovereignty* is an artificial *soul,* as giving life and motion to the whole body; the *magistrates,* and other *officers* of judicature, artificial *joints; reward* and *punishment,* by which fastened to the seat of the sovereignty every joint and member is moved to perform his duty, are the *nerves,* that do the same in the body natural;" etc. Here, in so far as the comparison drawn is in the main between the structures of the two, is it less indefensible than that of Plato; which is a comparison between structures in the one and functions in the other. But the special analogies named are erroneous; as is also, in common with that of Plato, the general analogy; since it is alleged between the organization of a society and the organization of a human being – an analogy far too special. Living at a later time, when biologists
had revealed to some extent the principles of organization, and recognizing social structures as not artificially made but naturally developed, M. Comte avoided these errors; and, not comparing the social organism to an individual organism of any one kind, held simply that the principles of organization are common to societies and animals. He regarded each stage of social progress as a product of preceding stages; and he saw that the evolution of structures advances from the general to the special. He did not, however, entirely escape the early misconception that institutions are artificial arrangements ; for he inconsistently held it possible for societies to be forthwith re-organized in conformity with the principles of his " Positive Philosophy."
Here let it once more be distinctly asserted that there exist no analogies between the body politic and a living body, save those necessitated by that mutual dependence of parts which they display in common. Though, in foregoing chapters, sundry comparisons of social structures and functions to struptures and functions in the human body, have been made, they have been made only because structures and functions in the human body furnish familiar illustrations of structures and functions in general . The social organism, discrete instead of concrete, asymmetrical instead of symmetrical, sensitive in all its units instead of having a single sensitive centre, is not comparable to any particular type of individual organism, animal or vegetal . All kinds of creatures ai'e alike in so far as each exhibits co-operation among its components for the benefit of the whole; and this trait, common to them, is a trait common also to societies. Further, among individual organisms, the degree of co-

operation measures the degree of evolution; and this general truth, too, holds among social organisms. Once more, to effect increasing cooperation, creatures of every order show us increasingly- complex appliances for transfer and mutual influence; and to this general characteristic, societies of every order furnish a corresponding characteristic. These, then are the analogies alleged: community in the fundamental principles of organization is the only commuuity asserted.

§ 270. But now let us drop this alleged parallelism between individual organizations and social organizations. I have used the analogies elaborated, but as a scaffolding tohelp in building up a coherent body of sociological inductions. Let us take away the scaffolding : the inductions will stand by themselves.

This emphatic repudiation of the belief that there is any special analogy between the social organism and the human organism, I have a motive for making. A rude ontline of the general conception elaborated in the preceding eleven chapters, was published by me in the *Westminster Review* for January, 1860. In it I expressly rejected the conception of Plato and Hobbes, that there is a likeness between social organization and the organization 01 *a*   ˎ

"We saw that societies are aggregates which grow ; that in the various types of them there are great varieties in the growths reached; that types of successively larger sizes result from the aggregation and re-aggregation of those of smaller sizes ; and that this increase by coalescence, joined with interstitial increase, is the process through which havo been formed the vast civilized nations.

Along with increase of size in societies goes increase of structure. Primitive hordes are without established distinctions of parts. With growth of them into tribes habitually come some unlikenesses ; both in the powers and occupations of their members. Unions of tribes are followed by more unlikenesses, governmental and industrial – social grades running through the whole mass, and contrasts between the differently- occupied parts in different localities. Such differentiations multiply as the compounding progresses. They proceed from the general to the special . First the broad division between ruling and ruled ; then within the ruling part divisions into political, religions, military, and within the ruled part divisions into food-producing classes and handi-craftsmen ; then within each of these divisions minor ones, and so on.

Passing from the structural aspect to the functional aspect, ve note that so long as all parts of a society have like natures and activities, there is hardly any mutual dependence, and the aggregate scarcely forms a vital whole. As its parts assume different functions they become dependent on one another, so that injury to one hurts others; until, in highly-evolved societies, general perturbation is caused by derangement of any portion. This contrast between undeveloped and developed societies, arises from the fact tliat with increasing specialization of functions comes increasing inability in each part to perform the functions of other parts.

saying that " there is no wjrrant whatever for assuming this." Nevertheless, a criticism on the article in the *Satm-dag Beuieio.* ascribed to mo the idea which I had thus distinct!/ condemned.

The organization of every society begins with a contrast between the division which carries on relations, habitually hostile, with environing societies, and the division which is devoted to procuring necessaries of life; and during the earlier stages of development these two divisions constitute the whole. Eventually there arises an intermediate division serving to transfer products and influences from part to part. And in all subsequent stages, evolution of the two earlier systems of structures depends on evolution of this additional system.

While the society as a whole has the character of its sustaining system determined by the character of its environment, inorganic and organic, the respective parts of this system differentiate in adaptation to local circumstances; and, after primary industries have been thus localized and specialized, secondary industries dependent on them arise in conformity with the same principle. Further, as fast as societies become compounded and re-compounded, and the distributing system develops, the parts devoted to each kind of industry, originally scattered, aggregate in the most favourable localities; and the localized industrial structures, unlike the governmental structures, grow regardless of the original lines of division.

Increase of size, resulting from the massing of groups, necessitates means of communication; both for achieving combined offensive and defensive actions, and for exchange of products. Faint tracks, then paths, rude roads, finished roads, successively arise; and as fast as intercourse is thus facilitated, there is a transition from direct barter to trading carried on by a separate class; out of which evolves a complex mercantile agency of wholesale and retail distributors. The movement of commodities effected by this agency, beginning as a slow flux to and re-flux from certain places atlong intervals, passes into rhythmical, regular, mpid currents; and materials for sustentation distributed hither and thither, from being few and crude become numerous and elaborated. Growing efficiency of transfer with greater variety of transferred products, increases the mutual dependence of parts at the same time that it enables each part to fulfil its function better.

Unlike the sustaining system, evolved by converse with the organic and inorganic environments, the regulating system is evolved by converse, offensive and defensive, with environing societies. In primitive headless groups temporary chieftainship results from temporary war; chronic hostilities generate permanent chieftainship; and gradually from the military control results the civil control. Habitual war, requiring prompt combination in the actions of parts, necessitates subordination. Societies in which there is little subordination disappear, and leave outstanding those in which subordination is great; and so there are produced, societies in which the habit fostered by war and surviving in peace, brings about permanent submission to a government. The centralized regulating system thus evolved, is in early stages the sole regulating system. But in large societies which have become predominantly industrial, there is added a decentralized regulating system for the industrial structures; and this, at first subject in every way to the original system, acquires at length substantial independence. Finally there arises for the distributing structures also, an independent controlling agency.

Societies fall firstly into the classes of simple, compound, doubly-compound, trebly-compound; and from the lowest the transition to the highest is through these stages. Otherwise, though less definitely, societies may be grouped as militant and industrial; of which the one type in its developed form is organized on the principle of compulsory co-operation, while the other in its developed form ia organized on the principle of voluntary co-operation. Theone is characterized not only by a despotic central power, but also by unlimited political control of personal conduct; while the other is characterized not only by a democratic or representative central power, but also by limitation of political control over personal conduct.

Lastly we noted the corollary that change in the predominant social activities brings metamorphosis. If, "where tho militant type has not elaborated into so rigid a form as to prevent change, a considerable industrial system arises, there come mitigations of the coercive restraints characterizing the militant type, and weakening of its structures. Conversely, where an industrial system largely developed has established freer social forms, resumption of offensive and defensive activities causes reversion towards the militant type.

§ 271. And now, summing up the results of this general survey, let us observe the extent to which we are prepared by it for further inquiries.

The many facts contemplated unite in proving that social evolution forms a part of evolution at large. Like evolving aggregates in general, societies show *integration,* both by simple increase of mass and by coalescence and re-coalescence of masses. The change from *homogeneity* to *heterogeneity* is multitudinously exemplified; up from the simple tribe, alike in all its parts, to the civilized nation, full of structural and functional unlikenesses. With progressing integration and heterogeneity goes increasing *coherence.* We see the wandering group dispersing, dividing, held together by no bonds; the tribe with parts made more coherent by subordination to a dominant man; the cluster of tribes united in a political plexus under a chief with sub-chiefs; and so on up to the civilized nation, consolidated enough to hold together for a thousand years or more. Simultaneously conies increasing *definiteness.* Social organization is at first vague; advance brings settled arrangements which grow

slowly more precise; customs pass into laws which, while gaming fixity, also become more specific in their applications to varieties of actions; and all institutions, at first confusedly intermingled, slowly separate, at the same time that each within itself marks off more distinctly its component structures. Thus in all respects is fulfilled the formula of evolution. There is progress towards greater size, coherence, multiformity, and definiteness.

Besides these general truths, a number of special truths have been disclosed by our survey. Comparisons of societies in their ascending grades, have made manifest certain cardinal facts respecting their growths, structures, and functions – facts respecting the systems of structures, sustaining, distributing, regulating, of which they are composed; respecting the relations of these structures to the surrounding conditions and the dominant forms of social activities entailed; and respecting the metamorphoses of types caused by changes in the activities. The inductions arrived at, thus constituting in rude outline an Empirical Sociology, show that in social phenomena there is a general order of co-existence and sequence; and that therefore social phenomena form the subject-matter of a science reducible, in some measure at least, to the deductive form.

Guided, then, by the law of evolution in general, and, in subordination to it, guided by the foregoing inductions, we are now prepared for following out the synthesis of social phenomena. We must begin with those simplest ones presented by the evolution of the family.

POSTSCRIPT TO PART TL

Some remarks made in the *Revue Philnsophiqw* for May, 1877, by an acnte and yet sympathetic critic, M. Henri Marion, show me the need for adding here an explanation which may prevent other readers from being puzzled by a seeming inconsistency.

M. Marion indicates the contrast I have drawn between thoso individual organisms in which, along with a developed nutritive system there ia an undeveloped nervous system, and those in which a developed nervous system enables the organism to co-ordinate its outer actions so as to secure prey and escape enemies : rightly saying that I class the first as relatively low and the second as relatively high. He then points out that I regard as analogous to these types of individual organisms, those types of social organisms which are characterized, the one by a largely-developed sustaining or industrial system with a feeble regulating or governmental system, and the other by a less-developed industrial system joined with a centralized governmental system, enab'ing the society effectually to combine its forces in conflict with other societies. And he proceeds to show that though, in elassing the types of animals, I pnt those with undeveloped nervous systems as low and those with developed nervous systems as high ; in elassing societies I tacitly imply that those with predominant industrial or sustaining systems are superior to those with highly-centralized and powerful regulating systems. He says: – " En naturaliste qu'il est, il regarde visiblement comme sup6rieurs aux autres les 6tats les plus centralists." (Ill, 516.) And then commenting on the dislike which, as "an Englishman of the Liberal school," I show for such centralized societies, and my admiration for the free, less-governed, industrial societies, he emphasizes the incongruity by saying : – " Mais bientGt le moraliste en lui combat le naturaliste ; et la Iibert6 individnelle, principe d'anarchie cependant, trouve en lui un dffenseur aussi chaleureux qu'inattendn." *(ib.)*

I regret that when writing the foregoing chapters I omitted to contrast the lives of individual organisms and of social organisms in such way aa

599

to show the origin of this seeming incongruity. It is this : – Individual organisms, whether low or high, have to maintain thcir lives by offensive or defensive activities, or both : to get food and eseape enemies ever remain the essential requirements. Hence the need for a regulating system by which the actions of senses and limbs may b co-ordinated. Hence the superiority that results from a centralized nervous apparatus to which all the outer organs are completely subordinate. It is otherwise with societies. Doubtless during the militaat stages of social evolution, the lives of societies, like the lives of animals, are largely, or even mainly, dependent on thcir powers of offence and defence; and during these stages, societies having the most centralized regulating systems ean use thcir powers most effectually, and are thus, *relatively to the temporary requiremeats,* the highest . Such requirements, however, are but temporary. Inerense of industrialism and deerense of militancy, gradually bring about a state in which the lives of societies do not depend mainly on thcir powers of dealing offensively and defensively with other societies, but depend mainly on those powers which enable them to hold their own in the struggles of industrial competition. So that, *relatively to thet ultimate requirements,* societies become high in proportion to thfl evolution of thcir industrial systems, and not in proportion to the evolution of those centralized regulating systems fitting them for earrying on wars. In animals, then, the mensure of superiority remains the same throughout, because the ends to be achieved remain the same throughout; but in societies the measure of superiority is entirely changed, beeause the ends to be achieved are entirely changed. This answer prepares the way for an answer to a previous objection M. Marion makes. I have poiuted out that wherens, in the individual organism, the component units, mostly devoid of feeling, eany on thcir activities for the welfare of certain groups of units (forming the nervous ceatres) which monopolize feeling ; in the social organism, all the unita are endowed with feeling. And I have added the corollary that wherens, in the individual organism, the units exist for the benefit of the aggregate, in the social organism the aggregate exists for the benefit of the units. M. Marion, after indieating these views, expresses his astonishment that, having clearly recognized this difference, I afterwards take so little account of it, and do not regard it ns affecting the analogies I draw. The reply is that my recognition of this profound difference between the ends to be subserved by individual organizations and by social organizations, eauses the seemingly-anomalous estimation of social types explained above. Social organization is to be considered high in proportion as it subserves individual welfare,

because in a society the units are sentient and the aggregate insentient ; and the industrial type is the higher because, *in that ttate oj permanent peace to which civilization is tending,* it subserves individual welfare better than the militant type. During the progressive stages of militancy, the welfare of the aggregate takes precedence of individual welfare, because this depends on preservation of the aggregate from destruction by enemies; and hence, under the militant *regime,* the individual, regarded as existing for the benefit of the State, has his personal ends consulted only so far as consists with maintaining the power of the State. But as the necessity for self- preservation of the society in conflict with other societies, decreases, the subordination of individual welfare to corporate welfare becomes less; and finally, when the aggregate has no external dangers to meet, the organization proper to complete industrialism which it acquires, conduces to individual welfare in the greatest degree. The industrial type of society, with its de-centralized structures, is the highest, because it is the one which most subserves that happiness of the units which is to be achieved by social organization, as distinguished from that happiness of the aggregate which is to be achieved by individual organization with its centralized structures.

PART III. DOMESTIC INSTITUTIONS.

8

SECTION 8

CHAPTER I.

THE MAINTENANCE OF SPECIES.

§ 272. As full understanding of the social relations cannot be gained without studying their genesis, so neither can full understanding of the domestic relations; and fully to understand the genesis of the domestic relations, we must go further back than the history of man carries us.

Of every species it is undeniable that individuals which die must be replaced by new individuals, or the species as a whole must die. No less obvious is it that if the death-rate in a species is high, the rate of multiplication must be high, and conversely. This proportioning of reproduction to mortality is requisite for mankind as for every other kind. Hence the facts exhibited by living beings at large must be considered that the facts exhibited by human beings may be clearly comprehended.

§ 273. Regarding the continued life of the species as in, every case the end to which all other ends are secondary (for if the species disappears all other ends disappear), let us look nt the several modes there are of achieving this eud. The requirement that a due number of adults shall arise in successive generations, may be fulfilled in variously-modified ways, which subordinate the existing and next-succeeding members or the species in various degrees.

Low creatures having small powers of meeting the life- destroying activities around, and still smaller powers of protecting progeny, can maintain their kinds only if the mature individual produces the germs of new individuals in immense numbers; so that, unprotected and defenceless though the germs are, one or two may escape destruction. And manifestly, the larger the part of the parental substance transformed *into* germs (and often most of it is so transformed), the smaller the part that can be devoted to individual life.

With each germ is usually laid up some nutritive matter, available for growth before it commences its own struggle for existence. From a given quantity of matter devoted by the parent to reproduction, there may be formed either a larger number of germs with a smaller quantity of nutritive matter each, or a smaller number with a larger quantity each. Hence result differences in the rates of juvenile mortality. Here of a million minute ova left uncared for, the majority are destroyed before they are hatched; multitudes of the remainder, with the feeblest powers of getting food and evading enemies, die or are devoured soon after they are hatched; so that very few have considerable lengths of individual life. Conversely, when the conditions to be met by the species make it advantageous that there should be fewer ova and more nutriment bequeathed to each, the young individuals, beginning life at more advanced stages of development, survive longer. The species is maintained without the sacrifice of so many before arrival at maturity.

All varieties in the proportions of these factors occur. An adult individual, the single survivor from hundreds of thousands of germs, may itself be almost wholly sacrificed individually in the production of germs equally numerous; in which case the species is maintained at enormous cost, both to adults and to young. Or the adult, devoting but a moderate portion of its substance to the production of multitudinous germs, may enjoy a considerable amount of life; in which case the cost of maintaining the species is shown in a great mortality of the young. Or the adult, sacrificing its substance almost entirely, may produce a moderate number of ova severally well provided with nutriment and well protected, among which the mortality is not so great j and in this case the cost of maintaining the species falls more on the adult and less on the young.

§ 274. Thus while, in one sense, the welfare of a species depends on the welfare of its individuals, in another sense, the welfare of the species is at variance with the welfare of its individuals ; and further, the sacrifice of individuals may tell in different proportions on the undeveloped and on the mature.

Already in the *Principles of Biology,* §§ 319 – 51, the antagonism between Individuation and Genesis under ita general aspects has been set forth. Here certain of ita special aspects concern us. To comprehend them clearly, which we shall find it important to do, we must look at them more closely.

CHAPTER IL

THE DIVERSE INTERESTS OF THE SPECIES, OF THE PARENTS, AND OF THE OFFSPRING.

§ 275. Among the microscopic *Protozoa,* there is perpetual spontaneous fission. After a few hours of independent existence, each individual is sacrificed in producing two new individuals, which, severally growing, soon themselves repeat the process. And then from time to time there occurs a still more extreme form of reproductive

dissolution.   After a period of quiescence the entire body breaks up into germs
whence arise a new generation. Here, then, a parental life, extremely brief, disappears
absolutely in the lives of progeny.

Animal aggregates of the second order show us sundry ways in which this direct
transformation of the parental body into the bodies of offspring takes place; though
now, of course, at longer intervals. Among the *Ccdenterata,* there ia the case of certain
Medusae, where the polype-like body of the parent, or jwosi-parent, after reaching a
certnin growth, changes into a series of segments looking like a pile of saucers, each
of which in turn swims away and becomes a medusa. In these and allied cases of
cyclical generation, it may, however, be held that, as the medusa is the adult form, the
body of an unsexual individual is sacrificed in producing these partially-developed
sexual individuals. A

kindred result is achieved in a different manner among some

trematode *Enlozoa.* Evolved far enough to have head, appen-

dages, and alimentary system, a *Cercaria* presently transforms its internal substance
into young *Cerearice* substantially like itself; and, eventually bursting, sets them free,
severally to pursue the same course. Finally, after two or three generations so produced,
complete individuals are formed.

Different in method, but showing ua in an equal degree the dissolution of a parent's
body into portions that are to continue the race, is the mode of reproduction in the
cestoid *Entozoa.*   A segment of a tape-worm, known as a pro- glottis in its adult
and separated state, has then a life shown only by a feeble power of movement. It
has descended from one out of myriads of eggs produced by a preceding tapeworm
; and is itself, at the time of becoming an independent individual, nothing more
than a receptacle for innumerable eggs. Without limbs, without senses, without even
alimentary system, its vitality is scarcely higher than that of a plant; and it dies as
soon as its contained masses of ova are matured. Here we have an extreme instance
of subordination both of adult and young to the interests of the species.

Ascending now to higher types, let us take a few examples from the *Articidata.*
Many kinds of parasitic crustaceans, such as the *Iernea,* pass through a brief early
stage during which the young individual swims about. Nearly always it then dies;
but if it succeeds in fixing itself on a fish, it loses its limbs and senses, and, doing
nothing but absorb nutriment from the fish, evolves enormous ovisaes. Budding out
from the sides of its body, these by and by greatly exceed its body in bulk: the parental
life is lost in producing multitudinous eggs. An instance analogous in result, though
different

in method, occurs even among insects. Having no higher life than is implied
by sucking the juice of the cactus over which it creeps, the female cochineal insect
develops, as it approaches maturity, masses of ova which eventually fill its interior;
and gradually, as its substance is absorbed by the ova, it dies and leaves the shell of
its body as a protective envelope for them: whence issuing, ninety-nine are devoured
for one thatsurvives. Among superior insects, along with perhaps

an equal sacrifice of young, the sacrifice of adults is less. After a larval stage during
which the vital activities are relatively low and the mortality high, there comes, for the

one survivor out of hundreds, an active maturity. This, however, is brief – sometimes lasting but for a few days; and after the eggs are laid, life forthwith ceases.

The *Vertebrata,* furnish such further illustrations as arc needed. In this class the sacrifice of parental life to the maintenance of the species, is in few if any cases direct. A cod produces above a million eggs, and, surviving, does this year after year; but though the life of the parent is preserved, nine hundred and ninety-nine thousand and more of the progeny have their lives cut short at various stages on the way to maturity. In higher types of the class, producing comparatively few eggs that are better provided for, this sacrifice of the rising generation to the interests of the species is much less; and for the like reason it is much less also in the next highest group of vertebrates, the *Amphibia,* Passing to Birds, we find preservation of the race secured at a greatly diminished cost to both parents and offspring. The young are so well fostered that out of a small number most grow up; while here perhaps a half, and there perhaps a fourth, reach the reproductive stage. Further, the lives of parents are but partially subordinated at times when the young are being reared. And then there are long intervals between breeding-seasons, during which the lives of parents arc carried on for their own sakes. In the highest class of vertebrates, the *Mammalia,* regarded as 8 whole, we see a like general advance in this conciliation of the interests of the species, the parents, and the young; and we also see it within the class itself, on ascending from its lower to its higher types. A small rodent reaches maturity in a few months; and, producing large and frequent broods, soon dies. There is but a short early period during which the female lives for herself, and she mostly loses life before the

reproductive age is past: thus having no latter days unburdened by offspring. Turning to the other extreme we find an immense contrast. Between twenty and thirty years of a young elephant's life passes entirely in individual development and activity. The tax of bearing offspring, relatively few and at long intervals, subordinates in but a moderate degree the life of the adult female. And though our knowledge does not enable us to say how long life lasts after the reproductive age is past, yet, considering that the powers remain adequate for sustentatiou and self-defence, we may infer that the female elephant usually enjoys a closing series of many years; while the male is throughout life scarcely at all taxed.

§ 276. In yet another way does evolution decrease the sacrifice of individual life to the life of the species. The material cost of reproduction involves an equivalent subtraction from individual development and activity, for which among low types there is no compensation; but as we ascend through higher types we find an increasing compensation in the shape of parental pleasures.

Limiting our illustrations to vertebrate animals, we see that by most fishes and am-phibians, the spawn, once deposited, is left to its fate: there is great physical expense, and if no subsequent efforts are entailed, there are also none of the accompanying gratifications. It is otherwise with birds and mammals. While the rearing of offspring entails labour on one or both parents, the parental life, though thereby in one way restricted, is in another way extended; since it has become so moulded to the require-ments, that the activities of parenthood are sources of agreeable emotions, just as are the activities which achieve self-sustentation.

When, from the less intelligent of these higher vertebrates which produce many young at short intervals, and have to abandon them at early ages, we ascend to the more intelligent which produce few young at longer intervals, and give themaid for longer periods; we perceive that, while the rate of juvenile mortality is thus diminished, there results both a lessened physical cost of maintaining the species, and an augmented satisfaction of the affections.

§ 277. Here, then, we have definite measures by which to determine what constitutes advance in the relations of parents to offspring and to one another. In proportion as organisms become higher they are individually less sacrificed to the maintenance of the species; and the implication is that in the highest type of man this sacrifice falls to a minimum.

Commonly, when discussing domestic institutions, the welfare of those immediately concerned is almost exclusively regarded. The goodness or badness of given connexions between men and women, is spoken of as though the effects on the existing . adult generation were chiefly to be considered ; and, if the effects on the rising generation are taken into account, little if any thought is given to the effects which future generations will experience. This order has, as we see, to be reversed.

Family organizations of this or that kind have first to be judged by the degrees in which they help to preserve the social aggregates they occur in; for, in relation to its component individuals, each social aggregate stands for the species. Mankind survives not through arrangements which refer to it as a whole, but by survival of its separate societies; each of which struggles to maintain its existence in presence of other societies. And survival of the race, achieved through survival of its constituent societies, being the primary requirement, the domestic arrangements most conducive to survival in each society, must be regarded as relatively appropriate.

In so far as it consists with preservation of the society, the next highest end is raising the largest number of healthy offspring from birth to maturity. The qualification doea not seem needed; but we shall find evidence that it isneeded. Societies, and especially primitive groups, do not always thrive by unchecked increase in their numbers; but, contrariwise, in some cases preserve themselves from extinction at the cost of increased mortality of the young.

After welfare of the social group and welfare of progeny, comes welfare of parents. That form of marital relation must in each case be held the best which, subject to these preceding requirements, furthers most, and burdens least, the lives of adult men and women.

And as a last end to be contemplated comes that furtherance of individual life which we see when the declining years of parents, lengthened and made pleasurable by offspring, also become sources of pleasure to those offspring.

Uniting these propositions, we draw the corollary that tlie highest constitution of the family is reached wlien there is such conciliation between the needs of the society and those of its members, old and young, that the mortality between birth and the reproductive age falls to a minimum, while the lives of adults have their subordination to the rearing of children reduced to the smallest possible. The diminution of this subordination takes place in three ways: first, by elongation of that period which precedes reproduction; second, by decrease in the number of offspring borne, as well as by increase of the pleasures taken in the care of them; and third, by lengthening of the life which follows cessation of reproduction.

This ideal of the family suggested by a survey of the sexual and parental relations throughout the organic world, is also the ideal to which comparisons between the lower and the higher stages of human progress point. In savage tribes we find great juvenile mortality: there is commonly more or less infanticide; or there are many early deaths from unfavourable conditions; or there are both. Again, these inferior races are characterized by early maturity and commencing reproduction; implying shortness of that first period during which the individual life is carried on for its ownsake. While fertility lasts, the tax, especially on the women, who are also exhausted by drudgeries, is great. The marital and parental relations are sources of pleasures neither so high nor so prolonged as in the civilized races. And then after children have been reared, the remaining life of either sex is brief: often being ended by violence; often by deliberate desertion; and otherwise by rapid decay unchecked by filial care.

We are thus furnished with both a relative standard and an absolute standard by which to estimate domestic institutions in each stage of social progress. While, judging them relatively, by their adaptations to the accompanying social requirements, we may be led to regard as needful in their times and places, arrangements that are repugnant to us; we shall, judging them absolutely, in relation to the most developed types of life, individual and national, find good reasons for reprobating them. For this preliminary survey reveals the fact that the domestic relations which are the highest as ethically considered, are also the highest as considered both biologically and sociologically.

This seems the fittest place for naming an important suggestion made by an American adherent of mine, late Lecturer on Philosophy at Harvard University, Mr. John Fiske, respecting the trausition from the gregariousness of anthropoid creatures to the sociality of human beings, caused by the relatious of parents to offspring. (See *Outlines of Cosmic Philosophy,* vol. ii, pp. 342-4.) Postulating the general law that in proportion as organisms are complex they evolve slowly, he infers that the prolongation of infancy which accompanied development of the less intelligent primates into the more intelligent ones, implied greater duration of parental care. Children, not so soon capable of providing for themselves, had to be longer nurtured by female parents, to some extent aided by male parents, individually or jointly; and hence resulted a bond holding together parents and offspring for longer periods, and tending to initiate the family. That this his been a co-operatiug factor in social evolution, is highly probable.

9

SECTION 9

CHAPTER III.
PRIMITIVE RELATIONS OF THE SEXES.

§ 278. Most readers will have thought it strange to begin au account of domestic institutions by suiveying the most general phenomena of race-maintenance. But they may see the propriety of setting out with a purely natural-history view, on being shown that among low savages the relations of the sexes are substantially like those common among inferior creatures.

The males of gregarious mammals usually fight for possession of the females; and primitive men do not in this respect differ from other gregarious mammals. Hearne says of the Chippewayans that " it has ever been the custom, among these people for the men to wrestle for any woman to whom they were attached." According to Hooper, a Slave Indian, desiring another one's wife, fights with her husband. Among the Buslunen, " the stronger man will sometimes take away the wife of the weaker." Narcisse Peltier, who from twelve years of age up to twenty-nine was detained by a tribe of Queensland Australians, states that the men "not infrequently fight with spears for the possession of a woman." And summing up accounts of the Dogrib Indians, Sir John Lubbock says – " In fact, the men fight for the possession of the women, just like stags."

Nor is it on the part of males only, that this practice

exists. Peltier tells us that in the above-named tribe, thewomen, of whom from two to five commonly belong to each man, fig!it among themselves about him: "their weapons being heavy staves with which they beat one another about the head till the blood flows." And the trait of feminine nature thus displayed, is congruous with one indicated by Mitchell, who says that after battle it frequently happens among the native tribes of Australia, that the wives of the vanquished, of their own free will, pass over to the victors: reminding us of a lioness which, quietly watching the fight between two lions, goes off with the conqueror.

We have thus to begin with a state in which the family, as we understand it, does not exist. In the loose groups of men first formed, there is no established order of any kind: everything is indefinite, unsettled. As the relations of men to one another are undetermined, so are the relations of men to women. In either case there are no guides save the passions of the moment, checked only by fears of consequences. Let us glance at the facts which show the relations of the sexes to have been originally unregulated by the institutions and ideas we commonly regard as natural.

§ 279. According to Sparrman, there is no form of union between Bushmen and Bushwomen save " the agreement of the parties and consummation." Keating tells us that the Chippewas have no marriage ceremony. Hall says the samo thing of the Esquimaux, Bancroft of the Aleuts, Brett of the Arawaks, Tennent of the Veddahs; and the Lower Califor- nians, Bancroft says, " have no marriage ceremony, nor any word in their language to express mamage. Like birds or beasts, they pair off according to fancy."

Even where a ceremony is found, it is often nothing more than either a forcible or a voluntary commencement of living together. Very generally there is a violent seizure of the woman by the man – a capture; and the marriage is concluded by the completion of this capture. In some cases the man and woman light a fire and sit by it: in some cases, asamong the Todas, the union is established when the bride performs " some trifling household function;" in some cases, as among the Port Dory people of Kew Guinea, " the female gives her intended some tobacco and betel-leaf." When the Navajos desire to marry, " they sit down on opposite sides of a basket, made to hold water, filled with atole or some other food, and partake of it. This simple proceeding makes them husband and wife." Nay, we have the like in the old Roman form of *confarreatio* – marriage constituted by jointly eating cake. These indications that the earliest marriage-ceremony was merely a formal commencement of living together, imply a preceding time when the living together began informally.

Moreover, such domestic union as results is so loose, and often so transitory as scarcely to constitute an advance. In the Chippewayan tribes divorce " consists of neither more nor less than a good drubbing, and turning the woman out of doors." The Periciii (Lower Californinn) " takes as many women as he pleases, makes them work for him as slaves, and when tired of any one of them turns her away." Similarly, when one of the Tupis "was tired of a wife, he gave her away, and he took as many as he pleased." For Tasmanians not to change their wives, was " novel to their habits, and at variance with their traditions." Among the Kasias, " divorce is so frequent that their unions can hardly be honoured with the name of marriage." Even peoples so advanced as the Malayo-Polynesians furnish kindred facts. In Thomson's *New Zealand* we read that " men were considered to have divorced their wives when they turned them out of doors." And in Tahiti " the marriage tie was dissolved whenever either of the parties desired it." It may be added that this careless breaking of marital bonds is not peculiar to men. "Where women have the power, as among the above-named Kasias, they cavalierly turn their husbands out of doors if they displease them j and the like happened with some of the ancient Nicaraguans.

These facts show us that the marital relations, like the political relations, have gradually evolved; and that there did not at first exist those ideas and feelings which among civilized nations give to marriage its sanctity.

§ 280. Absence of these ideas and feelings is further shown by the prevalence in rude societies of practices which are to us in the highest degree repugnant.

Various of the uncivilized and semi-civilized display hospitality by furnishing guests with temporary wives. Her- rera tells us of the Cumana people, that " the great men. kept as many women as they pleased, and gave the beauti- fullest of them to any stranger they entertained." Savages habitually thus give their wives and daughters. Among such Sir John Lubbock enumerates the Esquimaux, North and South American Indians, Polynesians, Australians, Berbers, Eastern and Western Negroes, Arabs, Abyssinians, Kaffirs, Mongols, Tutski, etc. Of the Bushman's wife Lichtenstein tells us that when the husband gives her permission, she may associate with any other man. Of the Greenland Esquimaux, Egede states that " those are reputed the best and noblest tempered who, without any pain or reluctancy, will lend their friends their wives."

Akin is the feeling shown by placing little or no value on chastity in the young. In Benguela (Congo) poor maidens are led about before marriage, in order to acquire money by prostitution. The Mexicans had an identical custom: " parents used when the maidens were marriageable, to send them to earn their portions, and accordingly they ranged about the country in a shameful manner till they had got enough to marry them off." The ancient people of the Isthmus of Daiian thought " prostitution was not infamous; noble ladies held as a maxim, that it was plebeian to deny anything asked of them " – an idea like that of the Andamanese, among whom "any woman who attempted to resist the marital privileges claimed by any member of the tribe was liable to severe punishment." Equally strange arethe marital sentiments displayed by certain peoples, both extant and extinct. Of the Hassanyeh Arabs, whose marriages are for so many days in the week, usually four, Petheriok says that during a preliminary negotiation the bride's mother protests against " binding her daughter to a due observance of that chastity which matrimony is expected to command, for more than two days in the week;" and there exists on the part of the men an adapted sentiment. The husband, allowing the wife to disregard all marital obligations during the off' days, even considers an intrigue with some other man as a compliment to his own taste. Some of the Chibchas betrayed a kindred feeling. Not simply were they indifferent to virginity in their brides, but if their brides were virgins " thought them unfortunate and without luck, as they had not inspired affection in men: accordingly they disliked them as miserable women."

While lacking the ideas and feelings which regulate the relations of the sexes among advanced peoples, savages often exhibit ideas and feelings no less strong, but of quite contrary characters. The Columbian Indians hold that " to give away a wife without a price is in the highest degree disgraceful to her family ;" and by the Modoes of California " the children of a wife who has cost her husband nothing are considered no better than bastards, and are treated by society with contumely." In Burton's *Abcotuta,* we read that " those familiar with modes of thought in the East well know the horror and loathing with which the people generally look upon the one-wife system" – a statement we might hesitate to receive were it not verified by that of Livingstone concerning the negro women on the Zambesi, who were shocked on hearing that in England a man had only one wife, and by that of Bailey, who describes the disgust of a Kandyan chief when commenting on the monogamy of the Veddahs.

§ 281. Still more are we shown that regular relations ofthe sexes are results of evolution, and that the sentiments upholding them have been gradually established, on finding how little regard is paid by many uncivilized and semi- civilized peoples to those limitations which blood-relationshipa dictate to the civilized.

Among savages, connexions which we condemn as in the highest degree criminal, are not infrequent. The Chippe- wayans "cohabit occasionally with their own mothers, and frequently espouse their sisters and daughters;" and Langs- dorff asserts the like of the Kadiaks. So, too, among the Karens of Tenasserim, " matrimonial alliances between brother and sister, or father and daughter, are not uncommon." To these cases from America and Asia may be added a case from Africa. To keep the royal blood pure, the kings of Cape Gonzalves and Gaboon are accustomed to marry their grown up daughters, and the queens marry the eldest sons.

Incest of the kind that is a degree less shocking is exemplified by more numerous peoples. Marriage between brother and sister was not prohibited by the "barbarous Chechemecas" and "the Panuchese." The pcople of Cali, " married their nieces, and some of the lords their sisters." " In the district of New Spain four or five cases ... of marriage with sisters were found." In Peru, the " Yncas from the first established it as a very stringent law and custom that the heir to the kingdom should marry his eldest sister, legitimate both on the side of the father and the mother." So is it in Polynesia. Among the Sandwich Islanders, near consanguineous marriages are frequent in the royal family – brothers and sisters sometimes marrying; and among the Malagasy, ' the nearest of kin marry, even brother and sister, if they have not the same mother." Nor do ancient pcoples of the old world fail to furnish instances. That the restriction, prohibiting marriage with a uterine sister, was not observed in Egypt, we have sufficient evidence " from the sculptures of Thebes" agreeing " with the accounts of ancient Greek and Roman writers in proving that some of the Ptolomies adopted this ancient custom." Even our own Scandinavian kinsmen allowed incest of this kind. It is stated in the *Ynglinga Saga* that Niord took his own sister in marriage, " for that was allowed by " the Vanaland law.

It may be said that certain of these unions are with half- Bisters (like the union of Abraham and Sarah); that such occurred among the Canaanites, Arabians, Egyptians, Assyrians, Persians ; and that they go along with non-recognition of kinship in the male line. But admitting this to be true in some of the cases, though clearly not in others, we are still shown how little warrant exists for ascribing to primitive instinct the negations of unions between those nearly related; for the very words forbidding marriage to a half- sister having the same mother, though not to one having the same father, clearly imply that the male parenthood is habitually known though disregarded.

As further proving that sentiments such as those which among ourselves restrain the sexual instincts, are not innate, 1 may add the strange fact which Bailey tells us concerning the Veddahs. Their custom " sanctions the marriage of a man with his younger sister. To marry an elder sister or aunt would, in their estimation, be incestuous, a connexion in every respect as revolting to them as it would be to us – as much out of the question and inadmissible as the marriage with the younger sister was proper and natural . It was, in fact, *the* proper marriage."

§ 282. While the facts show us the general association between the rudest forms of social existence and the most degraded relations of the sexes, they do not show us that social progress and progress towards a higher type of family life, are uniformly connected. Various anomalies meet us.

Unenduring unions characterize many of the lowest races; and yet the miserable Veddahs, lower than most in theirsocial state, form very enduring unions. Bailey writes – " Divorce is unknown among them. ... I have heard a Veddah say, ' Death alone separates husband and wife'": a trait in which their Kandyan neighbours, otherwise superior, differ from them widely.

Nor does the diminution of incestuous connexions preserve a constant ratio to social evolution. Those extreme forms of them which we have noted among some of the most degraded races of North America, are paralleled among royal families in African kingdoms of considerable size ; while forms of them a degree less repulsive are common to savage and semi- civilized.

Though that type of family-life in which one wife has several husbands is said to occur among some of the lowest tribes, as the Fuegians, yet it is by no means common among the lowest; while we meet with it among relatively- advanced peoples, in Ceylon, in Malabar, and in Thibet. And the converse arrangement, of many wives to one husband, almost universally allowed and practised by savages, not only survives in semi-civilized societies but has held its ground in societies of considerably-developed types, past and present.

Neither are there connexions so clear as might have been expected, between sexual laxity and general debasement, moral or social; and conversely. The relations between the men and women in the Aleutian Islands are among the most degraded. Nevertheless these islanders are described by Cook as " the most peaceful, inoffensive people I ever met with. And, as to honesty, they might serve as a pattern to the most civilized nation upon earth." On the other hand, while the Thlinkeet men are said to "treat their wives and children with much affection," and the women to show " reserve, modesty, and conjugal fidelity," they are described as thievish, lying, and extremely cruel: maiming their prisoners out of pure wantonness and killing their slaves. Similarly, though the Bachapins (Bechuanas) are reprobatedas lamentably debased, having a universal disregard to truih and indifference to murder, yet the women are modest and " almost universally faithful wives." A kindred anomaly meets us on contrasting societies in higher stages. We have but to read Cook's account of the Tahitians, who were not only advanced in arts and social arrangements, but displayed the kindlier feelings in unusual degrees, to be astonished at their extreme disregard of restraints on the sexual instincts. Conversely, those treacherous, bloodthirsty cannibals the Fijians, whose atrocities Williams said he dared not record, are superior to most in their sexual relations. Erskine states of them that " female virtue may be rated at a high standard for a barbarous people."

Moreover, contrary to what we should expect, we find great sexual laxity in some directions joined with rigidity in others. Among the Koniagas " a young unmarried woman may live uncensured in the freest intercourse with the men ; though, as soon as she belongs to one man, it is her duty to be true to him." In Cumana " the maidens . . . made little account of their virginity. The married women . . . lived chaste." And Pedro Pizarro says of the Peruvians that " the wives of the common people were faithful to their husbands. . . . Before their marriage, their fathers did not care about their being either good or bad, nor was it a disgrace with them" to have loose habits. Even of those Chibcha husbands above referred to as so strangely indifferent, or less than indifferent, to feminine chastity before marriage, it is said that " nevertheless, they were very sensitive to infidelity."

The evidence, then, does not allow us to infer, as we should naturally have done, that advance in the forms of the sexual relations and advance in social evolution, are constantly and uniformly connected.

§ 283. Nevertheless, on contemplating the facts in their *ensemble,* we see that progress towards higher social types isjoined with progress towards higher types of domestic institutions. Comparison of the extremes make this unquestionable. The lowest groups of primitive men, without political organization, are also without anything worthy to be called family organization: the relations between the sexes and the relations between parents and offspring are scarcely above those of brutes. Contrariwise, all civilized nations, characterized by definite, coherent, orderly social arrangements, are also characterized by definite, coherent, orderly domestic arrangements. Hence we cannot doubt that. spite of irregularities, the developments of the vo are associated iu a general way.

Leaving here this preliminary survey, we have now to trace, so far as we can, the successively higher forms of family structure. We may expect to find the genesis of each depending on the circumstances of the society: conducive- ness to social self-preservation under the conditions of the case, being the determining cause. Setting out with wholly- unregulated relations of the sexes, the first customs established must have been those which most favoured social survival; not because this was seen, but because the societies that had customs less fit, disappeared.

But before considering the several kinds of sexual relations, we must consider a previous question – Whence come the united persons ? – Are they of the same tribe or of different tribes ? or are they sometimes one and sometimes the other ?

10

SECTION 10

CHAPTER IV.

EXOGAMY AND ENDOGAMY.

§ 284. In his ingenious and interesting work on *Primitive Marriage* the words " Exogamy " and "Endogamy " are used by Mr. M'Lennan to distinguish the two practices of taking to wife women belonging to other tribes, and taking to wife women belonging to the same tribe. As explained in his preface, his attention was drawn to these diverse customs by an inquiry into " the meaning and origin of the form of capture in marriage ceremonies;" – an inquiry which led him to a general theory of early sexual relations. The following outline of his theory I disentangle, as well as I can, from statements that are not altogether consistent.

Scarcity of food led groups of primitive men to destroy female infants; because, " as braves and hunters were required and valued, it would be the interest of every horde to rear, when possible, its healthy male children. It would be less its interest to rear females, as they would be leas capable of self-support, and of contrili 'iting, by their exei- tious, to the common good." (p. 1G5.)

Mr. M'Lennan next alleges that "the practice in early times of female infanticide," "rendering women scarce, ledat once to polyandry within the tribe, and the capturing of women from without." (p. 138.)

Primitive Marriage. By John F. M'Leunan, Edinburgh, 1865; repub- liihed in *Studies in Ancient History,* London, 1876. As the editions are alike, the references coatinue, as originally made, to the first one.

Joined with a re-statement of the causes we come upon an inferred result, as follows: – " The scarcity of women within the group led to a practice of stealing the women of other groups, and in time it came to be considered improper, because it was unusual, for a man to marry a woman of his own group." (p. 289.) Or, as he says oh p. 140, "usage, induced by necessity, would in time establish a prejudice among the tribes observing it [exogamy] – a prejudice, strong as a principle of religion, as every prejudice relating to marriage is apt to be – against marrying women of their own stock."

To this habitual stealing of wives, and re-stealing of them, as among the Australians (p. 76), he ascribes that doubtful paternity which led to the recognition of kinship through females only. Though elsewhere admitting a more general cause for this primitive form of kinship (p. 159), he regards wife-stealing as its most certain cause: saying that "it must have prevailed wherever exogamy prevailed – exogamy and the consequent practice of capturing wives. Certainty as to fathers is impossible where mothers are stolen from their first lords, and liable to be re-stolen before the birth of children." (p. 226.)

Assuming the members of each tribe which thus grew into the practice of wife-stealing, to have been originally homogeneous in blood, or to have supposed them-selves so, Mr. M'Lennan argues that the introduction of wives who were foreigners in blood, joined with the rise of the first definite conception of relationship (that between mother and child) and consequent system of kinship in the female line, led to recog-nized heterogeneity within the tribe. There came to exist within the tribe, children regarded as belonging by blood to the tribes of their mothers. Hence arose another form of exogamy. The primitive requirement that a wife should be stolen from another tribe, naturally became confounded withthe requirement that a wife should be of the blood of another tribe; and hence girls born within the tribe from mothers belonging to other tribes, became eligible as wives. The original exogamy, carried out by robbing other tribes of their women, gave place, in part, or wholly, to the modified exogamy carried out by marrying from within the tribe, women bearing family names which implied that they were foreign in blood.

In tracing the development of higher forms of the domestic relations, Mr. M'Lennan postulates, as we have seen, that the scarcity of women "led at once to polyandry within the tribe, and the capturing of women from without." (p. 138.) Describing and illustrating the different forms of polyandry, ending in that highest form in which the husbands are brothers, he points out that at this stage there arose recognition not only of descent in the female line, but also of descent in the male line; since the father's blood was known, though not the father.

Then through gradually-established priority of the elder brother, as being the first of the group to marry and the first likely to have children, it became an accepted fiction that all the children were his: " the elder brother was a sort of paterfamilias;" and " the idea of fatherhood " thus caused, was a step towards kinship through males, and a " step away from kinship through females." (pp. 243-4.)

Pointing out that among some polyandrous peoples, an the Kandyans, the chiefs have become monogamists, Mr. M'Lennan argues (p. 245) that their example would be followed, and "thus would arise a practice of monogamy or of polygamy." And he thence traces the genesis of the patriarchial form, the system of agnation, the institution of caste.

Though this outline of Mr. M'Lennan's theory is expressed, wherever regard for brevity permits, in his own words, yet possibly he may take exception to it; for, as already hinted, there are incongruities in his statements, and the order in which they are placed is involved. Unquestionably many of

the phenomena he describes exist. It is undeniable that the stealing of women, still habitual with sundry low races, was practised in past times by races now higher; and that the form of capture in marriage-ceremonies prevails in societies where nc real capture occurs at present . It is undeniable that kinship through females is, among various primitive peoples, the only kinship avowedly recognized; and that it leads to descent of name, rank, and property in the female line. It is undeniable that in many places where wife-stealing is, or has been, the practice, marriage is forbidden between those of the same family name, who are assumed to be of the same stock. But while admitting much of the evidence, and while accepting some of the inferences, we shall find reason for doubting Mr. M'Lennan's theory taken as a whole. Let us consider, first, the minor objections.

r

§ 285. Sundry facts inconsistent with his conclusion, though referred to by Mr. M'Lennan, he passes over as of no weight. He thinks there is warrant for the belief that exogamy and wife-capture have " been practised at a certain stage among every race of mankind" (p. 138): this stage being the one now exemplified by sundry low races. Nevertheless, he admits that "the separate endogamous tribes are nearly as numerous, and they are in some respects as rude, as the separate exogamous tribes." (p. 145.) Now if, as he believes, exogamy and wife-stealing have "been practised at a certain stage among every race of mankind" – that stage being the primitive one; and if, as he seeks to prove, endogamy is a form reached through a long series of social developments; it is difficult to understand how the endogamous tribes can be as rude as the exogamous ones. Again, he names the fact that " in some dis

tricts – as in the hills on the north-eastern frontier of India, in the Caucasus, and the hill ranges of Syria – we find a variety of tribes, proved, by physical characteristics andthe affinities of language, of one and the same original stock, yet in this particular differing *toto ccclo* from one another – some forbidding marriage within the tribe, and some proscribing marriage without it" (pp. 147-8): a faol by no means congruous with his hypothesis.

Should Mr. M'Lennan reply that on pp. 47-8 he has recognized the possibility, or probability, that there were tribes primordially endogamous – should he say that on pp. 144-5 will be found the admission that perhaps exogamy and endogamy " may be equally archaic;" the rejoinder is that besides being inconsistent with his belief that exogamy has " been practised at a certain stage among every race of mankind," this possibility is one which he practically rejects. On pp. 148-50, he sketches out a series of changes by which exoga- mous tribes may eventually become endogamous ; and in subsequent pages on the " Growth of Agnation," and " The Eise of Endogamy," he tacitly asserts that endogamy has thus developed: if not without exception, still, generally. Indeed, the title of one of his chapters – " The Decay of Exogamy in Advancing Communities," clearly implies the belief that exogamy was general, if not universal, with the uncivilized ; and that endogamy grew up along with civilization. Thus the incongruity between the propositions quoted in the lasb paragraph, cannot be escaped.

Sundry other of Mr. M'Lennan's reasonings conflict with one another. Assuming that in the earliest state, tribes were stock-groupg " organized on the principle of exogamy," he speaks of them as having "the primitive instinct of the race against marriage between members of the same stock" (p. 118). Yet, as shown above, he elsewhere speaks of wife- capture as caused by scarcity of women within the tribe and attributes to this " usage induced by necessity " the prejudice against " marrying women of their own stock." Moreover, if, as he says (and I believe rightly says) on p. 145, " men must originally have been iroe of auy prejudice againstmarriage between relations," it seems inconsistent to allege that there was a "primitive instinct" "against marriage between members of the same stock."

Again, while in some places the establishment of the exo- gamous prejudice is ascribed to the practice of wife-stealing (pp. 53-4 and p. 136), it is elsewhere made the antecedent of wife-stealing: interdict against marriage within the tribe was primordial. Now if this last is Mr. M'Lennau's view, I agree with Sir J. Lubbock in thinking it untenable. In the earliest groups of men there cannot have been any established rules about marriage. Unions of the sexes must have preceded all social laws. The rise of a social law implies a certain preceding continuity of social existence; and this preceding continuity of social existence implies the reproduction of successive generations. Hence reproduction entirely unregulated by interdicts, must be taken as initial.

Assuming, however, that of his two views Mr. M'Lennan will abide by the more tenable one, that wife-stealing 1H to exogamy, let us ask how far he is justified in alleging that female infanticide, and consequent scarcity of women, led to wife-stealing. At first sight it appears undeniable that destruction of infant girls, if frequent, must have been accompanied by deficiency of adult l'cmales; and it seems strange to call in question the legitimacy of this inference. But Mr. M'Lennan has overlooked a concomitant. Tribes in a state of chronic hostility are constantly losing their adult males, and the male mortality so caused is often great . Hence the killing many female infants does not necessitate lack of women: it may merely prevent excess. Excess must, indeed, be inevitable if, equal numbers of males and females being reared, some of the males are from time to time slain. The assumption from which Mr. M'Lennan's argument sets out, is, therefore, inadmissible.

How inadmissible it is, becomes conspicuous on finding that where wife-stealing is now practised, it is commonly associated with polygyny. The Fnegians, named by Mr. M'Lennan among wife-stealing peoples, are polygynists. According to Dove, the Tasmanians were polygynists, and Lloyd says that polygyny was universal among them; yet the Tasmanians were wife-stealers. The Australians furnish Mr. M'Lennan with a typical instance of wife-stealing and exogamy ; and though Mr. Oldfield alleges scarcity of women among them, yet other testimony is quite at variance with his. Mitchell says: – " Most of the men appeared to possess two [females], the pair in general consisting of a fat plump gin, and one much younger;" and according to Peltier, named in the last chapter as having lived seventeen years with the Macadama tribe, the women were "more numerous than the men, every man having from two to five women in his suite." The Dakotahs are at once wife-stealers and polygynists, Burton tells us; and the Brazilians similarly unite these traits. Writing of polygyny as practised on the Orinoco, Humboldt says: – " It is most considerable among the Caribs, and all the nations that have preserved the custom of carrying off young girls from the neighbouring tribes." How then can wife-stealing be ascribed to scarcity of women ?

A converse incongruity likewise militates against Mr. M'Lennan's theory. His position is that female infanticide, "rendering women scarce, led at ouce to polyandry within the tribe, and the capturing of women from without." But polyandry does not, so far as I see, distinguish wife- stealing tribes. We do not find it among the above-named Tasmanians, Australians, Dakotahs, Brazilians ; and although it is said to occur among thePuegians, and characterizes some of the Caribs, it is much less marked than their polygyny. Contrariwise, though it is not a trait of peoples who rob ouo another of their women, it is a trait of certain rude peoples who are habitually peaceful. There is polyandry among the Esquimaux, who do not even know what war is. There is polyandry among the Todas, who in no way aggress upou their neighbours.

Other minor difficulties might be dwelt on. There is the fact that in many cases exogamy and endogamy co-exist; as among the Comanches, the New Zealanders, the Lepchas, the Californians. There is the fact that in sundry cases polygyny and polyandry co-exist, as among the Fuegians, the Caribs, the Esquimaux, the Waraus, the Hottentots, the ancient Britons. There is the fact that there are some exogamous tribes who have not the form of capture in marriage; as the Iroquois and the Chippewas. But without dwelling on these, I turn to certain cardinal difficulties, obvious *a priori,* which appear to me insuperable.

§ 286. Setting out with primitive homogeneous groups, Mr. M'Lennan contends that the scarcity of women caused by destruction of female infants, compelled wife-stealing; and he thinks that this happened " at a certain stage among every race of mankind" (p. 138). The implication is, therefore, that a number of adjacent tribes, usually belonging to the same variety of man in the same stage of progress, were simultaneously thus led to rob one another. But immediately we think of wife-stealing as a practice not of one tribe only, but of many tribes forming a cluster, there presents itself the question – How was the scarcity of wives thus remedied ? If each tribe had fewer women than men, how could the tribes get wived by taking one another's women ? The scarcity remained the same : what one tribe got another lost. Supposing there is a chronic deficiency of women and the tribes rob one another equally, the result must be decreasing population in all the tribes. If some, robbing others in excess, get enough wives, and leave certain of the rest with very few, these must tend towards extinction. And if the surviving tribes carry on the process, there appears no limit until the strongest tribe, continuing to supply itself with women from the less strong, finally alone survives and has no tribes to rob.

Should it be replied that female infanticide is usually not carried so far as to make the. aggregate number of wivesinsufficient to maintain the population of all the tribes taken together – should it be said that only exceptional tribes rear so few women as not to have mothers enough to produce the next generation; then we are met by a still greater difficulty. If in each of the exogamous tribes forming the supposed cluster, the men are forbidden to marry women of their own tribe, and must steal women from other tribes; the implication is that each tribe knowingly real's wives for neighbouring tribes, but not for itself. Though each tribe kills many of its female infants that it may not be at the cost of rearing them for its own benefit, yet it deliberately rears the remainder for the benefit of its enemies. Surely this is an inadmissible supposition. Where the interdict against marrying women within the tribe is peremptory, the preservation of girls must be useless – worse than useless, indeed, since adjacent hostile tribes, to whom they must go as wives, will thereby be strengthened. And as all the tribes, living under like interdicts, will have like motives, they will all of them cease to rear female infants.

Manifestly, then, exogamy in its original form, can never have been anything like absolute among the tribes forming a cluster; but can have been the law in some of them only.

§ 287. In his concluding chapter, Mr. M'Lennan says that "on the whole, the account which we have given of the origin of exogamy, appears the only one which will bear examination." (p. 289.) It seems to me, however, that setting out with the postulate laid down by him, that primitive groups of men are habitually hostile, we may, on asking what are the concomitants of war, be led to a dillereut theory, open to none of the objections above raised.

In all times and places, among savage and civilized, victory is followed by pillage. Whatever portable things of worth the conquerors find, they take. The enemies of the Fuegians plunder thorn of their dogs and arms; pastoral tribes in Africa have their cattle driven away by victoriousmarauders; and peoples more advanced are robbed of their money, ornaments, and all valuable things that are not too heavy. The taking of women is but a part of this process of spoiling the vanquished. Women are prized as wives, as concubines, as drudges; and, the men having been killed, the women are carried off along with other moveables. Everywhere among the uncivilized we find this. " In Samoa, in dividing the spoil of a conquered pcople, the women were not killed, but taken as wives." On an Australian being told that certain travellers had shot some natives of another tribo, his only remark was: – " Stupid whitefellows! why did yon not bring away the gins ?" And P. Martyr Anglerius says that among the cannibal Caribs in his day, " to eat women was considered unlawful. . . . Those who were captured young were kept for breeding, as we keep fowl, etc." Early legends of the semi-civilized show us the same thing; as in the *Iliad,* where we read that the Greeks plundered " tha sacred city of Ee'tion," and that part of the spoils " they divided among themselves" were the women. And there need no examples to recall the fact that in later and moie civilized times, successes in battle have been followed by transactions allied in character, if not the same in form. Clearly, from the beginning down to comparatively late stages, women-stealing has been an *incidenl* of successful war.

Observe, next, that the spoils of conquest, some of them prized for themselves, are some of them prized as trophies. Proofs of prowess are above all things treasured by the savage. He brings back his enemy's scalp, like the North American Indian. He dries and preserves his enemy's head, like the New Zealander. He fringes his robe with locks of hair cut from his slain foe. Among other signs of success in battle is the return with a woman of the vanquished tribe. Beyond her intrinsic value she has an extrinsic value. Like n native wife she serves as a slave ; but unlike a native wife ehe serves also as a trophy. As, then, among savages, warriors are the honoured members of the tribe – as, amongwarriors, the most honoured are those whose bravery is best shown by achievements; the possession of a wife taken in war becomes a badge of social distinction. Hence members of the tribe thus married to foreign women, are held to be more honourably married than those married to native women. What must result ?

In a tribe not habitually at war, or not habitually successful in war, no decided effect is likely to be produced on the marriage customs. If the great majority of the men have native wives, the presence of a few whose superiority is shown by having foreign wives, will fail to change the practice of taking native wives: the majority will keep one another in countenance. But if the tribe, becoming successful in war, robs adjacent tribes of their women more frequently, there will grow up the idea that the now-considerable class having foreign wives form the honourable class, and that those who have not proved their bravery by bringing back these living trophies are dishonourable: non- possession of a foreign wife will come to be regarded as a proof of cowardice. An increasing ambition to get foreign wives will therefore arise; and as the number of those who are without them decreases, the brand of disgrace attaching to them will grow more decided; until, in the most warlike tribes, it becomes an imperative requirement that a wife shall be obtained from another tribe – if not in open war, then by private abduction.

A few facts showing that by savages proofs of courage are often required as qualifications for marriage, will carry home this conclusion. Herndon tells us that among the Mahue's, a man cannot take a wife until he has submitted to severe torture. Bates, speaking of the Passes on the Upper Amazons, says that formerly " the young men earned their brides by valiant deeds in war." Before he is allowed to marry, a young Dyak must prove his bravery by bringing back the head of an enemy. When the Apaches warriors return unsuccessful, " the women turn away from them withassured indifference and contempt. They are upbraided as cowards, or for want of skil] ind tact, and are told that such men should not have Tvives." That among other results of sentiments thus exemplified, abduction of women will be one, is obvious; for a man who, denied a wife till he has proved his courage, steals one, satisfies his want and achieves reputation at the same time. If, as we see, the test of deserving a wife is in some cases obtainment of a trophy, what more natural than that the trophy should often be the stolen wife herself? What more natural than that where many warriors of the tribe are distinguished by stolen wives, the stealing of a wife should become the required proof of fitness to have one ? Hence would follow a peremptory law of exogamy.

In so far as it implies that usage grows into law, this interpretation agrees with that of Mr. M'Lennan. It does not, however, like his, assume either that this usage originated in a primordial instinct, or that it resulted from scarcity of women caused by infanticide. Moreover, unlike Mr. M'Lennan's, the explanation *so* reached is consistent with the fact that exogamy and endogamy in many cases coexist ; and with the fact that exogamy often co-exists with polygyny. Further, it does not involve us in the difficulty raised by supposing a peremptory law of exogamy to be obeyed throughout a cluster of tribes.

§ 288. But can the great prevalence of the form of capture in marriage ceremonies be thus accounted for ? Mr. M'Lennan believes that wherever this form is now found, complete exogamy ouce prevailed. Examination will, I think, show that the implication is not necessary. There are several ways in which the form of capture arises; or rather, let us say, it has several conspiring causes.

If, as we have seen, there still exist rude tribes in which men fight for possession of women, the taking possession of a woman naturally comes as a sequence to an act of capture. That monopoly which constitutes her a wife in the only sense known by the primitive man, is a result of successful violence. Thus the form may originate from actual capture within the tribe, instead of originating from actual capture without it.

Beyond that resistance to a man's seizure of a woman, apt to be made by other men within the tribe, there is the resistance of the woman herself. Sir John Lubbock holds that coyness is not an adequate cause for the establishment of the form of capture; and it may be that, taken alone, it does not suffice to account for everything. But there are reasons for thinking it an important factor. Crantz says concerning the Esquimaux, that when a damsel is asked in marriage, she –

" directly falls into the greatest apparent consternation, and rnns out of doors tearing her bunch of hair ; for single women always affect the utmost bnshfulness and aversion to any proposal of marriage, lest they should lose thcir reputation for modesty."

Like behaviour is shown by Bushmen girls. When –

" a girl has grown up to womanhood without having previously been betrothed, her lover must gain her own approbation, ns well ns that of the parents; and on this occnsion his attentions are reccived with an affectation of great alarm and disinclination on her part, and with some squabbling on the part of her friends."

-Again, among the Sinai Arabs, says Burckhardt, a bride –

" defends herself with stones, and often inflicts wounds on the young men, even though she does not dislike the lover ; for, according to custom, the more she strnggles, bites, kicks, eries, and strikes, the more she is applanded ever after by her own companions." . . . During the procession to the husband's eamp, " decency obliges her to cry and sob most bitterly."

Of the Muzos, Piedrahita narrates that after agreement with the parents was made –

" the bridegroom eame to see the bride, and stayed three days caressing her, while she replied by beating him with her fists and with sticks. After these three days she got tamer, and cooked his meals." In these cases, then, coyness, either real or affected for reputation's sake, causes resistance of the woman herself. inother cases there is joined with this the resistance of her female friends. We read of the Sumatran women that the bride and the old matrons make it a point of honour to prevent (or appear to prevent) the bridegroom from obtaining his bride. On the occasion of a marriage among the Mapuchea " the women spring up *en masse,* and arming themselves with clubs, stones, and missiles of all kinds, rush to the defence of the distressed maiden. ... It is a point of honour with the bride to resist and struggle, however willing she may be." And once more, when a Kamschadale " bridegroom obtains the liberty of seizing his bride, he *seeks* every opportunity ot finding her alone, or in company of a few people, for during this time all the women in the village are obliged to protect her."

Here we have proof that one origin of the form of capture is feminine opposition – primarily of the woman herself, and secondarily of female friends who sympathize with her. Though the manners of the inferior races do not imply much coyness, yet we cannot suppose coyness to be wholly absent. Hence that amount of it which exists, joined with that further amount simulated, will make resistance, and consequently an effort to capture, natural phenomena. Morcover, since a savage makes his wife a slave, and treats her brutally, she has an additional motive for resistance.

Nor does forcible opposition proceed only from the girl and her female friends: the male members of her family also are likely to be opponents. A woman is of value not only as a wife, but also as a daughter; and up from the lowest to the highest stages of social progress, we find a tacit or avowed claim to her services by her father. It is so even with the degraded Fuegians: an equivalent in the shape of service rendered, has to be given for her by the youth, " such as helping to make a canoe." It is so with savages of more advanced types all over the world: there is either the like giving of stipulated work, or the giving of a price. And we have evidence that it was originally so among ourselves: iuan action for seduction the deprivation of a daughter's services is the injury alleged. Hence it is inferable that in the rudest states, where claims, parental or other, are but little regarded, the taking away of a daughter becomes the occasion of a fight. *"Facts* support this conclusion. Of the Mapuche's, Smith says that when there is opposition of the parents, " the neighbours are immediately summoned by blowing the horn, and chase is given." Among the Gaudors, a tribe on the southern shores of the Caspian Sea, the bridegroom must run away with his bride, although he thereby exposes himself to the vengeance of her parents, who, if they find him within three days, can lawfully put him to death. A custom with the Gonds is that " a suitor usually carries off the girl that is refused to him by the parents." Thus we find a further natural cause for the practice of capture – a cause which must have been common before social usages were well established. Indeed, on reading that among the Mapuches the man sometimes "Jays violent hands upon the damsel, and carries her off," and that " in all such cases the usual equivalent is afterwards paid to the girl's father," we may suspect that abduction, spite of parents, was the primary form; that there came next the making of compensation to escape vengeance; that this grew into the making of presents beforehand; and that so resulted eventually the system of purchase.

If, then, within a tribe there are three sources of opposition to the appropriation of a woman by a man, it cannot be held that the form of capture is inexplicable unless we assume the abduction of women from other tribes.

But even supposing it to have originated as Mr. M'Lennan thinks, its survival as a marriage-ceremony would not prove exogamy to have been the law. In a tribe containing many warriors who had wives taken from enemies, and who, as having captured their wives, were regarded as more honourably married than the rest, there would result an ambition, if not to capture a wife, still to seem to capture a wife. In every society the inferior ape the superior; and customs thus spread among classes the ancestors of which did not f-illow them. The antique-looking portraits that decorate a modern large house, by no means demonstrate the distinguished lineage of the owner; but often falsely suggest a distinguished lineage. The coat of arms a wealthy man bears, does not necessarily imply descent from men who once had their shields and flags covered by such marks of identity. The plumes on a hearse, do not prove that the dead occupant had forefathers who wore knightly decorations. And similarly, it does not follow that all the members of tribes who go through the form of capturing their wives at marriage, are descendants of men who in earlier days actually captured their wives. Mr. M'Lennan himself points out that, among sundry ancient peoples, captured wives were permitted to the military class though not to other classes. If we suppose a society formed of a ruling group of warriors, originally the conquerors, who practised wife-capture, and their subjects who could not practise it; and if we ask what would happen when such a society fell into more peaceful relations with adjacent like societies, and obtained wives from them no longer by force, but by purchase or other friendly arrangement; we may see that, in the first place, the form of capture would replace the actuality of capture in the marriages of the dominant class; for, as Mr. M'Lennan contends, adherence to ancestral usage would necessitate the simulation of capture after actual capture had ceased. And when, in the dominant class, wife-capture had thus passed into a form, it would be imitated by the subject class as being the most honourable form. Such among the inferior as had risen to superior social positions would first adopt it; and they would gradually be followed by those below them. So that, even were there none of the other probable origins named above, a surviving form of capture in any society would not show that society to have been exogamous; but

would merely show that wife-capture was in early times practised by its leading men.

§ 289. And now, pursuing the argument, let ns see whether exogamy and endogamy are not simultaneously accounted for as correlative results of the same differentiating process. Setting out with a state in which the relations of the sexes were indefinite, variable, and determined by the passions and circumstances of the occasion, we have to explain how exogamy and endogamy became established, the one here, the other there, as consequences of surrounding conditions. The efficient conditions were the relations to other tribes, now peaceful but usually hostile, some of them strong and some of them weak.

Necessarily, a primitive group habitually at peace with neighbouring groups, must be endogamous; for the taking of women from another tribe is either a sequence of open war, or is an act of private war which brings on open war. Pure endogamy, however, resulting in this manner, is probably rare; since the hostility of tribes is almost universal. But endogamy is likely to characterize not peaceful groups alone, but also groups habitually worsted in war. An occasional abducted woman taken in reprisal, will not suffice to establish in a weak tribe any precedent for wife-capture; but, contrariwise, a member of such a tribe who carries off a woman, and so provokes the vengeance of a stronger tribe robbed, is likely to meet with general reprobation. Hence marrying within the tribe will not only be habitual, but

After the above seatence was written, I cnme, by a hnppy joineklence, upon a verifying fact, in *Life in the Southern Islss,* by the Rev. W. VV. Gill (p. 47). A man belonging to one of the tribes in Mangaia stole food from an adjaceat tribe. This adjaceat tribe avenged itself by destroying tlio houses, etc., of the thief's tribe. Thereupon the thief's tribe, angry because of the misehief thus brought on them, killed the thief. If this happened with a stealer of food, still more would it happen with a itealer cf women, when the tribe robbed was the more powerful.

there will arise a prejudice, and eventually a law, against taking wives from other tribes: the needs of self-preservation will make the tribe endogamous. This interpretation harmonizes with the fact, admitted by Mr. M'Lennan, that the endogamons tribes are as numerous as the exogamous; and also with the fact he admits, that in sundry cases the tribes forming a cluster, allied by blood and language, are some of them exogamous and some endogamous.

It is to be inferred that among tribes not differing much in strength, there will be continual aggressions and reprisals, often accompanied by abductions of women. No one of them will be able to supply itself with wives entirely at the expense of adjacent tribes; and hence, in each of them, there will be both native wives and wives taken from other tribes: there will be both exogamy and endogamy. Stealing of wives will not be reprobated, because the tribes robbed are not too strong to be defied; and it will not be insisted on, because the men who have stolen wives will not be numerous enough to determine the average opinion. If, however, in

a cluster of tribes one gains predominance by frequent successes in war – if the men in it who have stolen wives form the larger number – if possession of a stolen wife becomes a mark of that bravery without which a man is not worthy of a wife; then the discreditableness of marrying within the tribe, growing into disgracefulness, will end in a peremptory requirement to get a wife from another tribe – if not in open war, then by private theft: the tribe will become exogamous. A sequence may be traced. The exogamous tribe thus arising, and growing while it causes adjacent tribes to dwindle by robbing them, will presently divide; and its sections, usurping the habitats of adjacent tribes, will carry with them the established exogamous habit. Whon, presently becoming hostile, these diverging sub-tribes begin to rob one another of women, there will arise conditions conducive to that internal exogamy which Mr. M'Lennan supposes, rightly I think, to replace external exogamy. Forunless we assume that in a cluster of tribes, each undertakes to rear women for adjacent tribes to steal, we must conclude that the exogamous requirement will be met in a qualified manner. Wives born within the tribe but foreign by blood, will, under pressure of the difficulty, be considered allowable instead of actually stolen wives. And thus, indeed, that kinship in the female line which primitive irregularity in the relations of the sexes originates, will become established, even though male parenthood is known; since this interpretation of kinship will make possible the conformity to a law of *connubium* that could not otherwise be obeyed.

§ 290. Nothing of much importance is to be said respecting exogamy and endogamy in their bearings on social life.

Exogamy in its primitive form is clearly an accompaniment of the lowest barbarism; and it decreases as the hostility of societies becomes less constant, and the usages of war mitigated. That the implied crossing of tribal stocks, where these tribal stocks are very small, may be advantageous, physiologically, is true; and exogamy may so secure a benefit which at a later stage is secured by the mingling of conquering and conquered tribes; though none who bear in mind the thoughtlessness of savages and their utter ignorance of natural causation even in its simple forms, will suppose such a benefit to have been contemplated. But the exogamous custom as at first established, implies an extremely abject condition of women; a brutal treatment of them; an entire absence of the higher sentiments that accompany the relations of the sexes. Associated with the lowest type of political life, it is also associated with the lowest type of domestic life.

Evidently endogamy, which at the outset must have characterized the more peaceful groups, and which has prevailed as societies have become less hostile, is a concomitant of the higher forms of the family.

[The above chapter, written before the middle of September, 1876, I kept standing in type for several weeks: bcing deterred from printing by the announcement that a second edition of Mr. M'Lennan's work was coming out, and by the thought that perhaps amendments contained in it might entail modifications of my criticisms. In the preface to this new edition he said: –

"Though I am again free to resume the stndies necessary for its revision, it is uncertain whether I could soon revise it in a satisfactory manner – so that I am without an answer to represeutations made to me, that it is better it should be made accessible to stndeuts with its imperfections than that it should remain inaccessible to them. I have done this the more readily that, on the whole, I still adhere to the conclusions I had arrived at more than eleven years ago, on the various matters which are discussed in ' Primitive Marriage.' "

I therefore sent the foregoing pages to press unaltered. The quotations are, as mentioned before, from the first edition, the paging of -which does not correspond with that of the second.] CHAPTER V.

PROMISCUITY.

§ 291. Already, in the chapter on " The Primitive Relations of the Sexes," illus-trations have been given of the in- definiteness and inconstancy of the connexions between men and women in low societies. The wills of the stronger, unchecked by political restraints, unguided by moral sentiments, determine all behaviour. Forcibly taking women from one another, men recognize no tie between the sexes save that which might establishes and liking maintains. To the instances there given others may be added, showing that at first, marriage, as we understand it, hardly exists.

Poole says of the Haidahs that the women " cohabit almost promiscuously with their own tribe, though rarely with other tribes." The Hill-tribes of the Piney Hills, Madura district, have very few restrictions on promiscuous intercourse. Captain Harkness writes: – " They [two Erulars of the Neil- gherry Hills] informed us that the Erulars have no marriage contract, the sexes cohabiting almost indiscriminately; the option of remaining in union or of separating resting principally with the female." Of another Indian people, the Teehurs, it is said that they " live together almost indiscriminately in large communities, and even when two people are regarded as married the tie is but nominal." And according to a Brahmin sepoy who lived more than a year with the

Andamanese, promiscuity is so far sanctioned among them bypublic opinion, that a man who is refused by an unmarried woman " considers himself insulted," and sometimes takes summary vengeance.

As shown by instances before given, this state of things is in many low tribes very little qualified by such form of union as stands for marriage; which sometimes has not even a name. Temporary fancies determine the connexions and mere whims dissolve them. What is said of the Mantras, who marry without acquaintance and divorce for trifles, and among whom some men marry " forty or fifty " times, may bo taken as typical.

§ 292. Facts of this kind are thought by several writers to imply that the primitive condition was one of absolute hetairism. Complete promiscuity is held to have been not simply the practice but in some sort the law. Indeed, the name " communal marriage " has been proposed by Sir John Lubbock for this earliest phase of the sexual relations, as implying recognized rights and bonds. But I do not think the evidence shows that promiscuity ever existed in an unqualified form; and it appears to me that even had it so existed, the name "communal marriage" would not convey a true conception of it.

As before contended, the initial social state must have been one in which there were no social laws. Social laws presuppose continued social existence; and continued social existence presupposes reproduction through successive generations. Hence there could, at first, have been no such social law as that of "communal marriage, where every man and vrcman iu a small community were regarded as equally married to one another " – there could have been no conception of " communal marriage rights." The words " marriage " and " rights " as applied to such a state have, it seems to me, misleading connotations. Each implies a claim and a limitation. If the claim is co-extensive with the members of the tribe, then the only limitation must be one excluding members ofother tribes; and it cannot, I think, be said that the idea of marriage within a tribe is generated by the negation of the claims of those belonging to other tribes. But passing

over the terminology, let us consider the essential question raised – whether what we may call tribal monopoly of its women. regarded as a common possession held against other Iribes, preceded individual monopoly within the tribe. Sir John Lubbock considers that absence of individual marital possession went along with absence of individual possession generally. While the notion of private ownership of other things did not exist, there did not exist the notion of private ownership of women. Just as in the earliest stages tlie tribal territory was common property, so, too, he thinks, were the women of the tribe common property; and he thinks that private ownership of women was established only by stealing them from other tribes : women so obtained being recognized as belonging to their captors. But while admitting that development of the conception of property in general, has had much to do with development of the marital relation, it is quite possible to dissent from the belief that the conception of property was ever so undeveloped as Sir John Lubbock's conclusion implies. It is true that the idea of tribal ownership of territory may be compared to that of many animals, solitary and gregarious, which drive trespassers away from their lairs or habitats: even the swans on each reach of the Thames resist invading swans from other reaches; and the public dogs in each quarter of Constantinople attack dogs from other quarters if they encroach. It is true, also, that generally among savages there is a certain community of property in the game captured; though not an unqualified community. But the reason for all this is clear. Land is jointly held by hunters because it cannot be otherwise held; and joint claims to the food it produces are involved. To infer that there is not in the earliest state a recognition of individual property in other things, is, I think, going further than either the probabilities or the facts warrant. The dog showsus some notion of ownership – will not only fight for the prey he has caught, or for his kennel, but will keep guard over his master's belongings. We cannot suppose that man in his rudest state had less notion of ownership than this. We must suppose he had more; and our snpposition is justified by evidence. Habitually savages individually own their weapons and implements, their decorations, their dresses. Even among the degraded Fuegians there is private property in canoes. Indeed, the very idea of prospective advantage which leads an intelligent being to take possession of, or to make, any useful thing, is an idea which leads him to resist the abstraction of it. Generally, possession is not interfered with, because the thing is not worth the risk of a fight; and even where, after resistance, it is taken by another, still it comes to be held by that other individually. The impulses which lead primitive men thus to monopolize other objects of value, must lead them to monopolize women. There must arise private ownerships of women, ignored only by the stronger, who establish other private ownerships.

And this conclusion seems the one supported by the facts. Everywhere promiscuity, however marked, is qualified by unions having some persistence. If, in the various cases before named, as also among the Aleutian Islanders and the Kutchins of North America, the Badagas, Kurumbahs and Keriahs of India, the Hottentots and various other peoples of Africa, there is no marriage ceremony; we have, in the very statement, an implication that there is something having the nature of marriage. If, as with the North American tribes generally, "nothing more than the personal consent of the parties," unsanctioned and unwitnessed, occurs; still some kind of union is alleged. If, as among the Bushmen and the Indians of California, there is no word signifying this relation between the sexes; still there is evidence that the relation is known. If among such pcoples as the Teehurs of Oude, the promiscuity is such that " even when two people are regarded as married the tie is but nominal;" still, some " are

regarded as married." The very lowest races now existing – Fuegians, Australians, Andamanese – show us that, however informally they may originate, sexual relations of a more or less enduring kind exist; and I do not see reasons for concluding that in social groups lower than these, there was no individual possession of women by men. We must infer that even in prehistoric times, promiscuity was checked by the establishment of individual connexions, prompted by men's likings and maintained against other men by force.

§ 293. Admitting, however, that in the earliest stages promiscuity was but in a small degree thus qualified, let us note, first, the resulting ideas of kinship.

Causes direct and indirect, will conspire to produce recognition of relationship in the female line only. If promiscuity is extensive, and if there are more children born to unknown fathers than to known fathers, then as the connexion between mother and child is obvious in all cases, while that between father and child is inferable only in some cases, there must arise a habit of thinking of maternal kinship rather than of paternal. Hence, even in that minority of cases where paternity is manifest, children will be thought of and spoken of in the same way. Among ourselves common speech habitually indicates a boy as Mr. So-and-so's eon, though descent from his mother is as fully recognized; and a converse usage, caused by prevailing promiscuity among savages, will load to the speaking of a child as the mother's child, even when the father is known.

A further influence helps to establish this practice. Though we conclude that promiscuity is in all cases qualified by unions having some duration, yet we find that in the lowest stages, as among the Andamanese, each of these unions ends when a child is weaned: the result being that thereafter, association of the child with its father ceases, while association with its mother continues. Consequently, even when there is acknowledged paternity, the child will bemostly thought of in connexion with its mother; confirming the habit otherwise caused.

This habit having arisen, the resulting recognition of relationship in the female line only, will, as we have seen, be strengthened by the practice of exogamy when passing from the external to the internal form. The requirement that a wife shall be taken from a foreign tribe, readily becomes confounded with the requirement that a wife shall be of foreign blood. If maternal descent alone is recognized, the daughters of foreign women within the tribe will, as Mr. M'Lennan argues, be rendered available as wives under the law of exogamy; and the custom of so regarding them will be strengthened by making fulfilment of this law possible, when otherwise fulfilment would be impossible. A settled system of kinship through females, and interdict against marriage with those having the same family name, or belonging to the same clan, will result.

Instances collected by Mr. M'Lennan and Sir John Lub- bock, show that this system prevails throughout Western and Eastern Africa, in Circassia, Hindostan, Tartary, Siberia, China, and Australia, as well as in North and South America. For interpreting it in the above manner there are some additional reasons. One is that we are not obliged to make the startling assumption that male parentage was at first entirely unperceived. A second is that we escape an inconsistency. Male parentage is habitually known, though disregarded, where the system of kinship in the female line now obtains; for not only in the lowest races are there unions persistent enough to make male parentage manifest, but the very statement that female kinship is alone counted, cannot be made by these races without implying a consciousness of male kinship: nay, indeed, have not these races, down to the very lowest, always a word for father as well as a word for mother ? And a third is that commonly the names of the clans which are forbidden to intermarry, such as Wolf, Bear, Eagle etc., are names given to me. i; implying, as I have before contended (§ 170-3) descent from distinguished male ancestors bearing those names – descent which, notwithstanding the system of female kinship, was remembered where there was pride in the connexion.

§ 294. From the effects of unregulated relations of the sexes on the system of formally-recognized kinship, in pursuing which I have diverged somewhat from the immediate topic, let us now pass to the effects on the society and its individuals.

In proportion to the prevalence of promiscuity, there must be paucity and feebleness of relationships. Besides having no known male parents, the children of each mother are less connected with one another. They are only half-brothers and half-sisters. Family bonds, therefore, are not only weak but cannot spread far; and this implies defect of cohesion among members of the society. Though they have some common interests, with some vague notion of general kinship, there lacks that element of strength arising from the interests within groups distinctly related by blood. At the same time, establishment of subordination is hindered. Nothing beyond temporary predominance of the stronger is likely to arise ia the absence of definite descent: there can be no settled political control. For the like reason the growth of ancestor-worship, and of the religious bonds resulting from it, are impeded. Thus in several ways indefinite sexual relations hinder social self-preservation and social evolution.

I may add here a conclusive proof that avowed recognition of kinship in the female line only, by no means shows an unconsciousness of male kinship. This proof is furnished by that converse custom which some ancieat Aryans had of recognizing relationship through males, and ignoring relationship through females. When Orestes, after killing his mother for murdering his father, was absolved on the ground urged by him, that a man is related to his father and not to h's mother, undeniable evidence was given that an established doctrine of kinship may disregard a counexion which *ia* obvious to all – more obvious than any other. And if it cannot be supposed that an actual unconsciousness of motherhood was associated with this system of exclusive kinship through males among the Greeks ; then there is no warraat for the supposition that Ml nal unconsciousness of fatherhood is associated with the system of exclusive kinship through females among savages.

Their unfavourableness to the welfare of offspring scarcely needs pointing out. Where paternity is not recognized, children must depend almost wholly on maternal care. Among savages, exposed as they are to great privations, the rearing of children is in all cases difficult; and it must bo more difficult where the mother is unaided by the father. So too is it, if in a smaller degree, with the progeny of brief marriages, such as those of the Audamanese, whose custom it is for a man and wife to part when a child born to them is weaned. Often the child must die from lacking adequate support and protection, which the mother alone cannot give. K"o doubt, under such conditions, miscellaneous help is given. Indeed, the Andamanese women are said to aid one another in suckling; and probably food and other things are furnished by the men : the child becomes, in a measure, the child of the tribe. But indefinite tribal care can but partially replace definite paternal care. How unfavourable to the maintenance of population are these unregulated relations of the sexes, we have, indeed, direct evidence. A recent reporter, Mr. Francis Day, a surgeon, says that the Andamanese appear to be dying out . He saw but one woman who had as many as three living children. During a year, thirty-eight deaths were reported and only fourteen births, among the families living near the European settlements.

Turning from progeny to parents, it is clear that to them also the absence of persistent marital relations is very injurious. Maintenance of the race, in so far as it is effected, is effected at excessive cost to the women; and though the men may not suffer directly, they suffer indirectly. After maturity is past, there come the privations of an early decline unmitigated by domestic assistance. Mr. Day says of the Andamanese that few appear to live to a greater age than forty; and they are subject to various diseases. Absence of those higher gratifications accompanying developed family life, is also to be noted as a concomitant evil.

Irregular relations of the sexes are thus at variance withthe welfare of the society, of the young, and of the adults. We before saw that in all respects the traits of the primitive man – physical, emotional, intellectual – are immense hindrances to social evolution; and here we see that his lack of those sentiments which lead to permanent marriages, constitutes a further hindrance.

§ 295. Out of this lowest state, however, there tend to arise higher states. In two ways do groups thus loose in their sexual relations, evolve into groups having sexual relations of more definite kinds.

If, as we concluded, prevailing promiscuity was from tho first accompanied by unions having some duration – if, as we may infer, the progeny of such unions were more likely to be reared, and more likely to be vigorous, than the rest; then the average result must have been multiplication and predominance of individuals derived from such unions. And bearing in mind that among these there would be inherited, natures leaning towards such unions more than other natures leaned, we must infer that there would, from generation to generation, be an increasing tendency to such unions along certain lines of descent. Where they favoured race-maintenance, survival of the fittest would further the establishment of them. I say advisedly – where they favoured race-maintenance ; because it is conceivable that in very barren habitats they might not do this. Sexual relations conducive to the rearing of many children would be of no advantage: the food would not suflice. It may be, too, that in very inclement habitats more careful nurture would be useless; since where the hardships to be borne in adult life were extreme, the raising of children that could not bear them would not help to preserve the society – nay, by wasting food and effort might prove detrimental. The ability of a child to survive with no care beyond that which its mother can give, may in some circumstances be a test of fitness for the life to be led. But save In such extreme cases, the favourable effects on

offspring must tend to establish in a social group, persistent relations of the sexes.

The struggle for existence between societies conduces to the same effect. Subject to the foregoing limitation, whatever increases the power of a tribe, either in number or in vigour, gives it an advantage in war; so that other things equal, societies characterized by sexual relations which are the least irregular, will be the most likely to conquer. I say other things equal, because co-operating causes interfere. Success in battle does not depend wholly on relative numbers or relative strengths. There come into play courage, endurance, swiftness, agility, skill in the use of weapons. Though otherwise inferior, a tribe may conquer by the quickness of its members in tracking enemies, by cunning in ambush, etc. Moreover, if among a number of adjacent tribes there are no great differences in degrees of promiscuity, conflicts among them cannot tend to establish higher sexual relations. Hence, only an occasional effect can be produced; and we may anticipate that which the facts indicate – a slow and very irregular diminution. In some cases, too, profusion of food and favourable climate, may render less important the advantage which the offspring of regular sexual relations have over those of irregular ones. And this may be the reason why in a place like Tahiti, where life is so easily maintained and children so easily reared, great sexual irregularity was found to co-exist with large population and considerable social advance.

As, however, under ordinary conditions the rearing of more numerous and stronger offspring must have been favoured by more regular sexual relations, there must, on the average, have been a tendency for the societies most characterized by promiscuity to disappear before those less characterized by it.

§ 296. Considering the facts from the evolution point of view, we see that at first the domestic relations are butlittle more developed than the political relations: incoherence and indefiniteness characterize both.

From this primitive stage, domestic evolution takes place in several directions by increase of coherence and definite- ness. Connexions of a more or less enduring kind are ii some cases formed between one woman and several men. In some cases, and very commonly, enduring connexions are formed between one man and several women. Such relations co-exist in the same tribe, or they characterize different tribes; and along with them there usually co-exist relations between individual men and individual women. The evidence implies that all these marital forms by which promiscuity is restricted, have equally early origins.

The different types of the family thus initiated, have now to be considered. We will take them in the above order.

11

SECTION 11

CHAPTER VL

POLYANDItY.

§ 297. Promiscuity may be called indefmite polyandry Joined with indefinite polygyny; and one mode of advance is by a diminution of the indefiniteness.

Concerning the Fuegians, Admiral Fitzroy says: – "We had some reason to think there were parties who lived in a promiscuous manner – a few women being with many men:" a condition which may be regarded as promiscuity to a slight degree limited. But not dwelling on this doubtfully- made statement, let us pass to positive statements concerning what may be described as definite polyandry joined with definite polygyny. Of the Todas, we are told by Shortt that –

" If there be four or five brothers, and one of them, bcing old enough, gets married, his wife claims all the other brothers ns her husbands, and ns they successively attain manhood, she consorts with them ; or if the wife hns one or more younger sisters, they in turn, on attaining a marriageable age, become the wives of thcir sister's husband or husbands, and thus in a family of several brothers, there may be, accoi !- ing to circumstances, only one wife for them all, or many ; but, one or more, they all live under one roof, and cohabit promiscuously."

Akin to this arrangement, though differing in the respect that the husbands are not brothers, is that which exists among the Nairs. From several authorities Mr. M'Lennan takes the statements that –

" It is the custom for one woman ' to have attached to her two males, or four, or perhaps more, and they cohabit according to rules.' Withthis accouut that of Hamilton agrees, excepting that he states that a Nair woman could have no more than twelve husbands, and had to select these under certain restrictions ns to rank and cnste. On the other hand, Buchanan states that the women after marriage are free to cohabit with any number of men, under certain restrictions ns to tribe and cnste. It is consistent with the three accouuts, and is directly stated by Hamilton, that a Nair may be one in several combinations of husbands."

Here then, along with polyandry to some extent defined, there goes polygyny, also to some extent defined. And with the semi-civilized Tahitians, one of the several forms of sexual relations was akin to this. " If the rank of the wife was in any degree superior to that of her husband she was at liberty to take as many other husbands as she pleased;" though still nominally the wife of the first husband.

From these forms of the family, if the word may be extended to them, in which polyandry and polygyny are united, we pass to those forms which come under the head of polyandry proper. In one of them the husbands are not related ; in the other they are akin, and usually brothers.

§ 298. Already we have seen that polyandrous households, apparently of the ruder sort, occur in tribes having also poly- gynous households: the Caribs, the Esquimaux, and the Waraus, having been instanced. Another case is furnished by the Aleutian Islanders, who are polygynists, but among whom, a "woman may enter into a double marriage, inasmuch as she has a right to take " an additional husband. The aborigines of the Canary Islands practised polyandry, probably not fraternal. When the Spaniards arrived at Lance- rota, they found "a very singular custom. ... A woman had several husbands. ... A husband was considered as such only during a lunar revolution." And to these cases of the ruder polyandry which I find among my own data, I may add others given by Mr. M'Lennan. He names the Kasias and the Saporogian Cossaks as exemplifying it.

Of the higher form of polyandry many instances occur;

sometimes co-existing in the same society with the lower form, and sometimes existing alone. Tennent tells us that – - "Polyandry prevails throughout the interior of Ceylon, chiefly amongst the wealthier classes; of whom, one woman has frequently three or four husbands, and sometimes as many as seven. ... As a general rule the husbands are members of the same family, and most frequently brothers."

Of other peoples definitely stated to practise this kind of ptly- andry, Mr. M'Lennan enumerates, in America the Avaroes and the Maypures, and in Asia the inhabitants of Kashmir, Ladak; Kinawer, Kistewar, and Sirmor. In the remote past it existed where it is not known now. Eastian quotes Strabo as saying of the tribes of Arabia Felix that men of the same family married one wife in common. In an ancient Hindu epic, the *Mahdblidrata*, a princess is described as married to five brothers. And, according to Cfesar, there was fraternal polyandry among the ancient Britous.

§ 299. What are we to say about the origin and development of this type of the domestic relations ?

As before contended, facts do not support the belief that it arose from female infanticide and consequent scarcity of women. We saw that it does not prevail where wife-stealing, said also to result from scarcity of women, is habitual; but that in such cases polygyny is more usual. We also saw that its frequent co-existence with polygyny negatives the belief that it is due to excess of males. True, of the Todas we read that owing " to the great scarcity of women in this tribe, it more frequently happens that a single woman is wife to several husbands." But against this may be set such a case as that of Tahiti, where we have no reason to believe that women were scarce, and where the polyandry which was associated M'ith polygyny, went along with other loose sexual relations – where " brothers, or members of the same family, sometimes exchanged their wives, while the wife of every individual was also the wife of his *taio* or friend."

Nor can we, I think, ascribe it to poverty; though povertymay, in some cases, be the cause of its continuance and spread. It is general in some communities which are relatively well off; and though in some cases distinctive of the poorer classes, it is in other cases the reverse. As above quoted, Tennent tells us that in Ceylon polyandry prevails " chiefly among the wealthier classes;" implying that as, among the poorer classes each man has commonly one wife, if not more, the cause there is neither lack of women for wives, nor lack of ability to maintain wives.

We must rather, in pursuance of conclusions already drawn, regard polyandry as one of the kinds of marital relations emerging from the primitive unregulated state; and one which has survived where competing kinds, not favoured by the conditions, have failed to extinguish it.

§ 300. When from that form of polyandry, little above promiscuity, in which one wife has several unrelated husbands and each of the husbands has other unrelated wives, we pass to that form in which the unrelated husbands have but one wife, thence to the form in which the husbands are related, and finally to the form in which they are brothers only; we trace an advance in family structure. Already I have referred to Mr. M'Lennan's indication of the different results.

Where, as among the Nairs, each woman has several unrelated husbands, and each husband has several unrelated wives, not only is the paternal blood of the offspring unknown, but children of each man commonly exist in several households. Besides the fact that the only known kinship is through the woman, there is the fact that each man's domestic interest, not limited to a particular group of children, is lost by dissipation. Maternal parenthood alone being concentrated and paternal parenthood diffused, the family bonds are but little stronger than those accompanying promiscuity. Besides his mother, a man's only known relations are his half-brothers and half-sisters and the children of his half- sisters.

Where the unrelated husbands are limited to one vtfe, and where their children, though they cannot be affiliated upon their fathers individually, form a single domestic group, there is some sphere for the paternal feelings. Each husband has ail interest in the offspring, some of whom may be, and probably are, his own: occasionally, indeed, being severally attributed to each by likeness, or by their mother's statement. Though the positively-known relationships remain the same as in the last case, yet there is some advance in the formation of domestic groups.

And then, as Mr. M'Lennan points out, where the husbands are brothers, the children have a known blood in the male line as well as in the female line. Each boy or girl in the family is known by each husband to be, if not a son or daughter, then a nephew or niece. This fixing of the ancestry on both sides evidently strengthens the family bond. Beyond the closer kinships in each group, there now arise in successive generations, alliances between groups, not on the female side only, but on the male side. And this ramification of connexions becomes an element of social strength.

So that as, in passing from promiscuity to polyandry, we pass to more coherent and definite domestic relations, so do we in passing from the lower forms of polyandry to the higher.

§ 301. What must we say about polyandry in respect of its effects on social self-preservation, on the rearing of offspring, and on the lives of'adults ? Some who have had good

It is proper to poiat out here that the name fraternal polyandry does not exactly represeat the facts, and that in reality there exists no sach institution. A polyandry strictly fraternal, would imply that the husbands had descended from a monogamic union; for only then could they be brothers in the full sense of the word. In a polyandric society the so-ealled brothers who become husbands of one wife, are deseendants of one mother by fathers who were brothers on the maternal side, nnd something less than cousins on the paternal side. The so-called brothers are therefore something more than half-brothers. This qnalification, however, does not uegativc the statement that the male blood of the children is known.

opportunities of judging, contend that in certain places it is advantageous. It would seem that just as there are habitats in which only inferior forms of animals can exist, so in societies physically conditioned in particular ways, the inferior forms of domestic life survive because they alone are practicable.

In his work, *Tfie Abode of Snow,* Mr. Wilson, discussing Thibetan polyandry in its adaptation to the barren Himalayan region, says: –

" There is a tendency on the part of population to inerense at a greater ratio than its power of producing food ; and few more effectual means to check that tendency could well be devised than the system of Tibetan polyandry, taken in conjunction with the Lama monasteries and nuuneries. Very likely it wns never deliberately devised to do so, and eame down from some very rnde state of society; but, at all events, it mint have been found exceedingly serviceable in repressing population among, what Kceppen so well ealls, the snow-lands of Asia. If population had inerensed there at the rate it hns in England during this ceutury, frightful results must have followed cither to the Tibetans or to thcir immediate ncighbours. As it is, almost every one in the Himalaya has cither land and a house of his own, or land and a house in which he has a share, and which provide for his protection and subsistence. ... I wns a little surprised to find that one of the Moravian missionaries defended the polyandry of the Tibetans, not ns a thing to be approved of in the abstract or tolerated among Christians, but ns good for the heathen of so sterile a couatry. In taking this view, he proceeded on the argumeat that superabundant population, in an unfertile country, must be a great ealamity, and produce ' eternal warfare or eternal want.' Turner took also a similar view."

Concerning the effects on the welfare of offspring, I do not meet with definite statements. If, however, it be true that in so very infertile a habitat, a form of marriage which tends to check increase is advantageous; the implication is that the children in each family are better off, physically considered, than they would be were monogamic unions the rule: being better fed and clothed the mortality among them must be less, and the growth more vigorous. As to the accompanying mental influence, we can only suspect that conflict of authority and absence of specific paternity, must entail serious evils.

The lives of adults do not appear to be so injuriously affected as might be anticipated. Mr. Wilson says: –

" In a primitive and not very settled state of society, when the head of a family is often called away on long mercantile journeys, or to attend at court, or for purposes of war, it ia a certain advantage that he should be able to leave a relative in his place whose interests are bound up with his own. Mr. Talbcs Wheeler has suggested that polyandry arose among a pastoral pcople, whose men were away from their families for months at a time, and where the dnty of protecting their families would be undertaken by the brothers in turn. The system certainly answers such an end, and I never knew of a case where a polyaudric wife vas left without the society of one at least of her husbands."

He also quotes Turner as saying : –

"' The influence of this custom on the manners of the people, as far as I could trace, has not been unfavourable. ... To the privilege of unbounded liberty the wife here adds the character of mistress of the family and companion of her husbands.' [And he adds] But, lest so pleasing a picture may delude some of the strong-minded ladies (of America) to get up an agitation for the establishment of polyandry in the West, I must say it struck me that the having many husbands sometimes appeared to be only having many masters and increased toil and trouble."

So, too, in the narrative of Mr. George Bogle's mission to Thibet, in Warren Hastings' time, we read: –

" They elub together in matrimony as merchants do in trade. Nor is this joint concern often productive of jealousy among the partners. They are little addicted to jealousy. Disputes, indeed, sometimes arise abont the children of the marriage ; but they are settled either by a comparison of the features of the child with those of its several fathers, or left to the determination of its mother."

§ 302. If we regard polyandry as one of several marital arrangements independently originating in the earliest societies, we shall not interpret its decline in the same way aa if we consider it a transitional form once passed through by every race, as Mr. M'Lennan apparently does.

To one of the causes he assigns for its decline, we may indeed, assent. He points out that in some cases, as among the Kandyaus, a chief has a wife to himself, though inferior people are polyandrous; and in Horace della Penna's time akindred difference existed in Thibet: he says polyandry " seldom occurs with noble folk, or those in easy circumstances, who take one wife alone, and sometimes, but rarely, more." Hence, with Mr. M'Lennan, we may infer that since in all societies customs spread downwards, imitation tends to make monogamy replace polyandry where circumstances do not hinder. But Mr. M'Lennan, not regarding this dying out of inferior forms in presence of superior forms as the sole cause, argues that the superior forms also arise by transformation of the inferior. Taking as typical the polyandry of Ladak, where the eldest brother has a priority, and where, on his death, " *his property, authority, and widow devolve upon his next In-other,"* (p. 199), he affiliates upon this the arrangement among the early Hebrews, under which " the Levir had no alternative but to take the widow [of his brother]; *indeed, she was his wife without any form of marriage* " (p. 203). And he hence infers that monogamy and polygyny, as existing among the Hebrews, had been preceded by polyandry; saying that –

" It is impossible not to believe that we have here preseuted to *v* successive stages of deeay of one and the same original institution ; impossible not to counect the obligation, in its several phnses, with what we have seen prevailing in Ladak ; impossible not to regard it ns having originally been a right of succession, or the couuterpart of such a right, derived from the practice of polyandry " (pp. 203-4).

It seems to me, however, quite possible to find in the customs of primitive peoples, another explanation which is much more natural. Under early social systems, wives, being regarded as property, are inherited in the same way as other property. When we read that among the " Bella- bollahs (Haidahs), the widow of the deceased is transferred to his brother's harem;" that among the Zulus, " the widow is transferred to the brother of her deceased husband on his death;" that among the Damaras, " when a chief dies, his surviving wives are transferred to his brother or to *his nearest relation;"* the suspicion is raised that taking possession of a brother's wife has nothing to do with poly-

andiy. This suspicion is confirmed on finding that in Congo, "if there be three brothers, and one of them die, the two survivors share his concubines between them;" on finding that in Samoa, " the brother of a deceased husband, considered himself *entitled* to have his brother's wife;" on finding that in ancient Vera Paz, " the brother of the deceased at once took her [the widow] as his wife even if ho was married, and if he did not, *another relation had a right* to her." These facts imply that where wives are classed simply as objects of value (usually purchased), the succession to them by brothers goes along with succession in general. And if there needs further evidence, I may cite this – that in sundry places a father's wives are inherited. Thomson says that among the New Zealanders " fathers' wives descended to their sons, and dead brothers' wives to their surviving brothers." Of the Mishmis, Row- latt states that "when a man dies or becomes old, it is the custom of these people for the wives to be distributed amongst his sons, who take them to wife." Torquemada mentions provinces of Mexico in which the sons inherited those wives of their fathers who had not yet borne sons to the deceased. In his *Abcokuta,* Burton states that among the Egbas "the son inherits all the father's wives save his own mother." We learn from Bosman that on the Slave Coast, " upon the father's death, the eldest son inherits not only all his goods and cattle, but his wives . . . excepting his own mother." And in Dahomey, the king's eldest son " inherits the deceased's wives and makes them his own, excepting, of course, the woman that bare him."

We cannot, then, admit that the practice of marrying a dead brother's widow implies pro-existence of polyandry; and cannot accept the inference that out of decaying polyandry higher forms of marriage grew up.

§ 303. Considering the several forms of polyandry as types of domestic relations which have arisen by successivelimitations of promiscuity, we must say that in this or that society they have evolved, have survived, or have been extinguished, according as the aggregate of conditions lias determined. Probably in some cases the lower polyandry has not been supplanted by the higher, because the two have not so come into competition that the better results of the higher Lavo made themselves felt. In competition with polygyny and monogamy, polyandry may, in certain cases, have had the advantage for reasons above cited : polygyuic and mono- gamic families dying out because the children were relatively ill-fed.

On the other hand, influences like those which in some places made the superior forms of polyandry prevail over the inferior, must, in other places, have tended to extinguish polyandry altogether. Save where great restriction of the food-supply over a considerable area, rendered multiplication disadvantageous, polyandric societies, producing fewer members available for offence and defence, naturally gave way before societies having family-arrangements more favourable to increase. This is probably the chief reason why polyandry, once common, has become comparatively infrequent. Other things equal, this inferior family-type lias yielded to superior family-types; both because of its inferior fertility, and because of the smaller family-cohesion, and consequently smaller social cohesion, resulting from it CHAPTER VII.

POLYGYNY.

J 304. Were it not for the ideas of sacredness associated with that Hebrew history which in childhood familiarized us with examples of polygyny, we should probably feel as much surprise and repugnance on first reading about it as we do on first reading about polyandry. Education has, however, prepared us for learning without astonishment tluit polygyny is common in every part of the world not occupied by the most advanced nations.

It prevails in all climates – in the Arctic regions, in arid burning tracts, in fertile oceanic islands, in steaming tropical continents. All races practise it. We have already noted its occurrence among the lowest tribes of men – the Fuegians, the Australians, the Tasmanians. It is habitual with the Negritos in New Caledonia, in Tanna, in Vate, in Eromanga, in Lifu. Malayo-Polynesian peoples exhibit it everywhere – in Tahiti, the Sandwich Islands, Tonga, New Zealand, Madagascar, Sumatra, Throughout America it is found among the rude tribes of the northern continent, from the Esqui - maux to the Mosquitos of the isthmus, and among the equally rude tribes of the southern continent, from the Caribs to the Putagonians; and it prevailed in the ancient semi-civilized American states of Mexico, Peru, and Central America. It is general with African peoples – with the Hottentots, Damaras, Kaffirs of the south; with the EastAfricans, Congo people, Coast Negroes, Inland Negroes, Dahomans, Ashantis of mid-Africa; with the Fulahs and Abyssinians of the north. In Asia it is common to the settled Cingalese, the semi-nomadic Hill-tribes of India, the wandering Yakutes. And its prevalence in ancient eastern societies needs but naming. Indeed, on counting up all peoples, savage and civilized, past and present, it appears that the polygynous ones far outnumber the rest.

Plurality of wives would be even more general were it not in some cases checked by the conditions. We learn this when told that among the poverty-stricken Bushmen, polygyny, though perfectly allowable, is rare; when Forsyth states that among the Gonds " polygamy is not forbidden, but, women being costly chattels, it is rarely practised;" when Tennent tells us of the Veddahs that " the community is too poor to afford polygamy;" when, concerning the Ostyaks, we read that " polygamy is allowed, but it is not common: for a plurality of wives the country is too poor." And though the occurrence of polygyny among some of the poorest peoples, as the Australians and the Fuegians, shows that poverty does not prevent it if the women can get enough food for self-maintenance, we may understand its exclusion where the mode of life does not permit them to do so.

This natural restriction of polygyny by poverty, is not the only natural restriction. There is another, recognition of which modifies considerably those ideas of polygynous societies conveyed by travellers. Their accounts often imply that plurality of wives is, if not the uniform, still, the most general, arrangement. Yet a little thought makes us hesitate to accept the implication. Turner tells us that in Lifu, " Bula [a chief] has forty wives : common men three or four." How can that be ? we may fitly ask – How come there to be so many women ? Scepticism such as is raised by this statement, is raised in smaller degrees by many other statements. We read in Park that the Mandingoes are poly- gamists, and each of the wives " in rotation is mistress of thehousehold." Andersson says of the Damaras that " polygamy is practised to a great extent . . . each wife builds for herself a hut." We are told by Lesseps that " obliged to make frequent journeys, a Yakout has a wife in every place where he stops." Of the Haidahs, it is alleged that "polygamy is universal, regulated simply by the facilities for subsistence." Acceptance of these statements involves the belief that iii each case there is a great numerical preponderance of women over men. But unless we assume that the number of girls born greatly exceeds the number of boys, which we have no warrant for doing, or else that war causes a mortality of males more enormous than seems credible, we must suspect that the polygynous arrangement is less general than these expressions represent it to be. Examination confirms the suspicion. For habitually it is said, or implied, that t'ne number of wives varies according to the means a man has of purchasing or maintaining them ; and as, in all societies, the majority are comparatively poor, only the minority can afford more wives than one. Such statements as that among the Comanches " every man may have all the wives lie can buy;" that the Nun people " marry as many wives as they are able to purchase; " that " the number of a Fijian's wives is limited only by his means of maintaining them;" that " want of means forms the only limit to the number of wives of a Mishmee;" warrant the inference that the less prosperous men, everywhere likely to form the larger part, have either no wives or but a single wife each.

For this inference we find definite justification on inquiring further. Numerous accounts show that in polygynous societies the polygyny prevails only among the wealthier or the higher in rank. Lichtenstein says " most of the Koossas have but one wife; the kings and chiefs of the kraals only, have four or five." Polygyny is

permitted in Java, says Raffles, but not much practised except by the upper classes, "
The customs of the Sumatrans permit their having as many wives by *jujur* as they can
compass the purchase of, or affordto maintain; but it is extremely rare that an instance
occurs of their having more than one, and that only among a few of the chiefs." In
ancient Mexico " the people were content with one legitimate wife, except the lords,
who had many concubines, some possessing more than 800." The Honduras people
" generally kept but one wife, but their lords as many us they pleased." And Oviedo
says that among the inhabitants of Nicaragua, " few have more than one wife, except
the principal men, and those who can support more."

These statements, joined with others presently to be cited, warn us against the
erroneous impressions likely to be formed of societies described as polygynous. We
may infer that in most cases where polygyny exists, monogamy coexists to a greater
extent.

§ 305. The prevalence of polygyny will not perplex us if, setting out with the
primitive unregulated state, we ask what naturally happened.

The greater strength of body and energy of mind, which gained certain men predominance as warriors and chiefs, also gave them more power of securing women;
either by stealing them from oiher tribes or by wresting them from men of their own
tribe. And in the same way that possession of a stolen wife came to be regarded as a
mark of superiority, so did possession of several wives, foreign or native. Cremony
says the Apache " who can support or keep, or attract by his power to keep, the greatest
number of women, is the man who is deemed entitled to the greatest amount of honour
and respect." This is typical . Plurality of wives has everywhere tended to become a
class-distinction. In ancient Mexico, Ahuitzotl's " predecessors had many wives, from
an opinion that their authority and grandeur would be heightened in proportion to the
number of persons who contributed to their pleasures." A plurality of wives is common
among chiefs and rich people in Madagascar, and " the only law to regulate polygamy
seems to be, that no man may taketwelve wives excepting the sovereign." Among the
East Africans " the chiefs pride themselves upon the number of their wives, varying
from twelve to three hundred." In Ashantee " the number of wives which caboceers
and other persons possess, depends partly on their rank and partly on their ability
to purchase them." Joining which facts with those furnished by the Hebrews, whose
judges and kings – Gideon, David, Solomon – had their greatness so shown; and with
those furnished by extant Eastern peoples, whose potentates, primary and secondary,
are thus distinguished; we may see that the establishment and maintenance of polygyny has been largely due to the honour accorded to it, originally as a mark of strength
and bravery, and afterwards as a mark of social *status*. This conclusion is verified by
European history: witness the statement of Tacitus that the ancient Germans, "almost
alone among barbarians," "are content with one wife," except a very few of noble
birth; and witness the statement of Montesquieu that the polygyny of the Merovingian
kings was an attribute of dignity.

From the beginning, too, except in some regions where the labour of women could
not be utilized for purposes of production, an economic incentive has joined with other
incentives. "We are told that in New Caledonia, "chiefs have ten, twenty, and thirty
wives. The more wives the better plantations, and the more food." A like utilization

of wives prompts to a plurality of them throughout Africa. On reading in Caillie that Mandingo wives " go to distant places for wood and water; their husbands make them sow, weed the cultivated fields, and gather in the harvest;" and on reading in Shooter that among the Kaffirs, "besides her domestic duties, the woman has to perform all the hard work; she is her husband's ox, as a Kaffir once said to me, – she had been bought, he argued, and must therefore labour;" we cannot fail to see that one motive for desiring many wives, ia desiring many slaves.

Since in every society the doings of the powerful and the wealthy furnish the standards of right and wrong, so that even the very words "noble" and "servile," originally expressive of social *status,* have come to be expressive of good and bad in conduct, it results that plurality of wives acquires, in places where it prevails, an ethical sanction. Associated with greatness, polygyny is thought praiseworthy; and associated with poverty, monogamy is thought mean. Hence the reprobation with which, as we have seen, the one-wife system is regarded in polygynous communities. Even the religious sanction is sometimes joined with the ethical sanction. By the Chippewayans " polygamy is held to ba agreeable in the eyes of the Great Spirit, as he that has most children is held in highest estimation " – a belief reminding us of a kindred one current among the Mormons. And that among the Hebrews plurality of wives was not at variance either with the prevailing moral sentiments or with supposed divine injunctions, is proved by the absence of any direct or implied reprobation of it in their laws, and by the special favour said to have been shown by God to sundry rulers who had many wives and many concubines.

It should be added that in societies characterized by it, this form of marital relation is approved by women as well as by men – certainly in some cases, if not generally. Bancroft cites the fact that among the Comanches " as polygamy causes a greater division of labor, the women do not object to it." And of the Makalolo women, Livingstone says: –

" On hearing that a man in England could marry but one wife, several ladies exclaimed that they would not like to live in such a couatry: t hey could not imagine how English ladies could relish our custom; for in thcir way of thinking, every man of respectability should have a number of wives ns a proof of his wealth. Similar idens prevail all down the Zambeai."

Initiated, then, by unrestrained sexual instincts among savage men, polygyny has been fostered by the same causes that have established political control and industrial controlIt has been an incidental element of governmental power in uncivilized and semi-civilized societies.

§ 306, In contrast with the types of marital relations dealt with in the preceding two chapters, polygyny shows some advance. That it is better than promiscuity needs no proof; and that it is better than polyandry we shall find several reasons for concluding.

Under it there arise more definite relationships. "Where the unions of the sexes are entirely unsettled, only the maternal blood is known. On passing from the lower form of polyandry in which the husbands are unrelated, to that higher form in which the husbands are something more than half-brothers, we reach a stage in which the father's blood is known, though not with certainty the father. But in polygyny, fatherhood and motherhood are both manifest. In so far, then, as paternal feeling is fostered by more distinct consciousness of paternity, the connexion between parents and children is strengthened: the bond becomes a double one. A further result is that traceable lines of descent on the male side, from generation to generation, are established. Hence greater family cohesion. Beyond definite union of father and son, there is definite union of successive fathers and sons in a series. But while increased

in a descending direction, family cohesion is little, if at all, increased in a lateral direction. Though some of the children may be brothers and sisters most of them are only half- brothers and half-sisters; and their fraternal feeling is possibly less than in the polyandric household. In a group derived from several unrelated mothers by the same father, the jealousies fostered by the mothers are likely tc be greater than in a group derived from the same mother and indefmitely affiliated on several brothers. In this respect, then, the family remains equally incoherent, or becomes perhaps, more incoherent. Probably to this cause is due the dissension and bloodshed in the households of eastern rulers.

Save, however, where there result among sons struggles for power, we may conclude that by definiteuess of descent the family is made more coherent, admits of more extensive ramifications, and is thus of higher type.

§ 307. The effects of polygyny on the self-preservation of (he society, on the welfare of offspring, and on the lives of adults, have next to be considered.

Barbarous communities surrounded by communities at enmity with them, derive advantages from it. Liehtenstein remarks of the Kaffirs that "there are fewer men than women, on account of the numbers of the former that fall in their frequent wars. Thence comes polygamy, and the women being principally employed in all menial occupations." Now, without accepting the inference that polygyny is initiated by the loss of men in war, we may recognize the *l*'act which Lichtenstein does not name, that where the death-rate of males considerably exceeds that of females, plurality of wives becomes a means of maintaining population. If, while decimation of the men is habitually going on, no survivor lias more than one wife – if, consequently, many women remain without husbands; there will be a deficiency of children: the multiplication will not suffice to make up for the mortality. Food being sufficient and other things equal, it will result that of two conflicting peoples, the one which does not utilize all its women as mothers, will be unable to hold its ground against the other which does thus utilize them: the monogamous will disappear before the poly-gynous. Hence, probably, a chief reason why in rude societies and little-developed societies, polygyny prevails so widely. Another way in which, under early condi

tions, polygyny conduces to social self-preservation, is this. In a barbarous community formed of some wifeless men, others who have one wife each, and other swho have more than one, it must on the average happen that this last class will be the relatively superior – the Btronaer and morecourageous among savages, and among semi-civilized pcoples the wealthier also, who are mostly the more capable. Hence, ordinarily, a greater number of offspring will be left by men having natures of the kind needed. The society will be rendered by polygyny not only numerically stronger, but more of its units will be efficient warriors. There is also

a resulting structural advance. As compared with lower types of the family, polyg-yny, by establishment of descent in the male line, conduces to political stability. It is true that in many polygynous societies succession of rulers is in the female line (the savage system of kinship having survived) ; and here the advantage is not achieved. This may be a reason why in Africa, where this law of descent is common, social consolidation is so incomplete: kingdoms being from time to time formed, and after brief periods dissolved again, as we before saw. But under polygyny, inheritance of power by sons becomes possible; and where it arises, government is better maintained. Not indeed that it is well maintained; for when we read that among the Damaras " the eldest son of the chiefs favourite wife succeeds his father;" and that among the Koossa Kaffirs, the king's son who succeeds is " not always the eldest; it is commonly him whose mother was of the richest and oldest family of any of the king's wives;" we are shown how polygyny introduces an element of uncertainty in the succession of rulers, which is adverse to stable government. Further, this definite

descent in the male line aids the development of ancestor- worship ; and so serves in another way to consolidate society. With subordination to the living there is joined subordination to the dead. Eules, prohibitions, commands, derived from leading men of the past, acquire sacred sanctions; and, as all early civilizations show us, the resulting cult helps to maintain order and increase the efficiency of the offensive and defensive organization.

In regions where food is scarce, the effects on the rearing of offspring are probably not better than, if as good as, those of polyandry; but in warm and productive regions the death- rate of offspring from innutrition is not likely to be higher, and the establishment of positive paternity conduces to protection of them. In some cases, indeed, polygyny tends directly to diminish. the mortality of children: cases, namely, in which a man is allowed, or is called upon, to marry the widow of his brother and adopt his family. For what we have seen to be originally a right, becomes, in many cases, an obligation. Even among inferior races, as the Chippewas, who require a man to marry his dead brother's widow, an ostensible reason is that he has to provide for his brother's children. And on reading that polygyny is not common with the Ostyaks because " the country is too poor," but that " brothers marry the widows of brothers," we may infer that tlie mortality of children is, under such conditions, thereby diminished. Very possibly the Hebrew requirement that a man should raise up seed to his dead brother, may have originally been that he should rear his dead brother's children, though it was afterwards otherwise interpreted; for the demand was made on the surviving brother by the widow, who spat in his face before the elders if he refused. The suspicion that obligation to take care of fatherless nephews and nieces, entailed this kind of polygyny, is confirmed by current facts; as witness the following passage in Lady Dull Gordon's *Letters from Egypt:* – "I met Hasan the janissary of the American Consulate, a very respectable good man. He told me he had married another wife since last year. I asked, What for? It was the widow of his brother, who had always lived in the same house with him, like one family, and who died, leaving two boys. She is neither young nor handsome, but he considered it his duty to provide for her and the children, and not let her marry a stranger." But though in most rude societies poly

gyny may not be unfavourable to the rearing of children and may occasionally check juvenile mortality in societies where philanthropic feeling is undeveloped, yet its moral effects on children can scarcely be better than thoio of still lower marital relations. Where there is but one household, dissensions caused by differences of origin and interest, must be injurious to character. And even where, as happens in many places, the mothers have separate households, there cannot be escaped the evils of jealousies between the groups; and there still remain the evils caused by a too-difiused paternal care.

On the lives of adults in undeveloped societies, the effects of polygyny are not in all respects bad. Where the habitat is such that women cannot support themselves, while the number of men is deficient, it results that, if there is no polygyny, some of them, remaining inicared for, lead miserable lives. The Esquimaux furnish an illustration. Adequate food and clothing being under their conditions obtainable only by men, it happens that widows, when not taken by surviving men as additional wives, soon die of starvation. Even wh? re food is not difficult to procure, if there is much mortality of males in war, there must, iji the absence of polygyny, be many women without that protection which, under primitive conditions, is indispensable. Certain ills to which adult females of rude societies are inevitably exposed, are thus mitigated by polygyny – mitigated in the only way practicable among unsympathetic barbarians. Of course the

evils entailed, especially on women, are great. In Madagascar the name for polyg-yny – " famporai'esana " – signifies " the means of causing enmity;" and that kindred names are commonly applicable to it, we are shown by their use among the Hebrews: in the Mischna, a man's several wives are called "tzaiot," that is, troubles, adversaries, or rivals. Sometimes the dissension is mitigated by separation. Mars- den says of the Battas that " the husband finds it necessary to allot to each of them [his wives] their several ire-places and cooking utensils, Mhere they dress their own victuals sep-arately, and prepare his in turns." Of the wives of a Mishmi chief, Wilcox writes – " The remainder, to avoid

domestic quarrels, Lave separate houses assigned them at some little distance, or live with their relations." Throughout Africa there is usually a like arrangement. But obviously the moral mischief's are thus only in a small degree diminished. Moreover, though polygyny may not

absolutely exclude, still, it greatly represses, those higher emotions fostered by associations of the sexes. Prompted by the instincts of men and disregarding the preferences of women, it can but in exceptional cases, and then only in slight degrees, permit of better relations than exist among animals. Associated as it is with the conception of women as property, to be sold by fathers, bought by husbands, and afterwards treated as slaves, there are negatived those sentiments towards them into which sympathy and respect enter as necessary elements. How profoundly the lives of adults are thus vitiated, may be interred from the characterization -which Monteiro gives of the polygynous peoples of Africa,

" The negro knows not love, affection, or jealousy. ... In all the long years I have been in Africa I have never seen the negro manifest the least tenderness for or to a negress. ... I have never seen a negro pnt his arm round a woman's waist, or give or receive any caress whatever that would indieate the slightest loving regard or affection on either side. They have no woriis or expressions in their language indicative of affection or love."

And this testimony harmonizes with testimonies cited by Sir John Lubbock, to the effect that the Hottentots " are so cold and indifferent to one another that you would think there was no such thing as love between them;" that among the Koossa Kaffirs, there is "no feeling of love in marriage;" and that in Yariba, " a man thinks as little of taking a wife as of cutting an ear of corn – affection is altogether out of the question." Not, indeed, that we can regard polygyny as *causing* this absence of the tender emotion associated among ourselves with the relations of the sexes; for lack of it habitually characterizes men of low types, whether they have only one wife each or have several. We cau say merely thatthe practice of polygyny 13 unfavourable to the development of the emotion.

Beyond this resulting inferiority in the adult life, there is abridgment of the life which remains after the reproductive age is passed. Naturally the women already little regarded, then become utterly unregarded; and the. men, a in a less degree, also suffer from lack of the aid prompted by domestic affection. Hence an early close to a miserable old aga

§ 308. A few words must be added respecting the modifications which polygyny undergoes in progressing societies, and which accompany the spread of monogamy.

Between the two or more wives which the stronger man among savages secures to himself, there tend to arise distinctions. Here he has an older and a younger wife, like the Australian, and occasionally the Bushman. Here he has wives purchased at intervals, of which he makes one or other a favourite; as does the Damara or the Fijian. Here of the several married by him the earliest only is considered legitimate ; as with the Tahitians of rank and with the Chibchas. Here the chief wife is one who has been given by the king. From the beginning the tendency has been to establish differences among them, and for the differences to grow, in course of time, definite. Then there comes also the

contrast between wives who are native women, and wives who are women taken as spoils of war. Hence, probably, the original way in which results the marking off into wives proper and concubines – a way indicated even among the Hebrews, who, in Deuteronomy xxi. 10 – 14, are authorized to appropriate individually the women of conquered enemies – women who, as they may be repudiated without formal divorce, stand in the position of concubines rather than wives. Once made, a difference of this kind was

probably extended by taking account of the ranks from which the women married were derived – wives from the superior class, concubines from the inferior; some exemptfrom labour, some slaves. And then, from the

tendency towards inequality of position among the wives, there at length came in advancing societies the recognized arrangement of a chief wife; and eventually, with rulers, a queen, whose children were the legitimate successors.

Along with the spread of monogamy in ways to be hereafter described, the decay of polygyny may be regarded as in part produced by this modification which more and more elevated one of the wives, and reduced the rest to a relatively servile condition, passing gradually into a condition less and less authorized. Stages in this transformation were exhibited among the Persians, whose king, besides concubines, had three or four wives, one of whom was queen, " regarded as wife in a different sense from the others;" and again among the Assyrians, whose king had one wife only, with a certain number of concubines; and again among the Egyptians, some of whose wall-paintings represent the king with his legitimate wife seated by his side, and his illegitimate wives dancing for their amusement. It was so, too, with the ancient Peruvian rulers and Chibcha rulers; as it is still with the rulers of Abyssinia.

Naturally the polygynic arrangement as it decayed, continued longest in connexion with the governing organization, which everywhere and always displays a more archaic condition than other parts of the social organization. Recognizing which truth we shall not be surprised by the fact that, in modified forms, polygyny survived among monarchs during the earlier stages of European civilization. As implied above, it was practised by Merovingian kings: Clothair and his sons furnishing instances. And after being gradually repressed by the Church throughout other ranks, thia plurality of wives or concubines long survived in the royal usage of having many mistresses, avowed and unavowed : polygyny in this qualified form remaining a tolerated privilege of royalty down to late times.

J 309. To sum up, we must say, firstly, that in degree ofevolution the polygynous type of family is higher than the types we have thus far considered. Its connexions are equally definite in a lateral direction and more definite in a descending direction. There is greater filial and parental cohesion, caused by conscious unity of blood on both male and female sides; and the continuity of this cohesion through successive generations, makes possible a more extensive family integration.

Under most conditions polygyny has prevailed against promiscuity and polyandry, because it has subserved social needs better. It has done this by adding to other causes of social cohesion, more widely ramifying family connexions. It has done it by furthering that political stability which results from established succession of rulers in the same line. It has done it by making possible a developed iorm of ancestor-worship.

While it has spread by supplanting inferior types of the marital relations, it has, in the majority of cases, held its ground against the superior type ; because, under rude conditions, it conduces in a higher degree to social self-preservation by making possible more rapid replacement of men lost in war, and so increasing the chance of social survival.

But while it has this adaptation to certain low stages of social evolution – while in some cases it diminishes juvenile mortality and serves also to diminish the mortality of surplus women; it repeats within the household the barbarism characterizing the life outside the household.

12

SECTION 12

CHAPTER VIIL
MONOGAMY.

§ 310. Already reasons have been given for believing that monogamy dates back as far as any other marital relation. Given a state preceding all social arrangements, and unions of individual men -with individual women must have arisen among other kinds of unions.

Indeed, certain modes of life necessitating wide dispersion, such as are pursued by forest tribes in Brazil and the interior of Borneo – modes of life which in early stages of human evolution must have been commoner than now – hinder other relations of the sexes. The Wood-Veddahs exemplify the connexion between monogamy and great scattering; and, again, the Bushmen, who, having no interdict on polygyny are yet rarely polygynous, show us how separation into very small groups in pursuit of food, tends to produce more or less enduring associations between men and women in pairs. Where the habitat permits larger groups, the unregulated relations of the sexes are qualified by rudimentary monogamic unions as early as by unions ofthe polyandric and polygynic kinds, if not earlier. Tho tendency everywhere shown among the lowest races for men to take possession of women by force, has this implication; since the monopoly established by each act of violence is over one woman, not over several.

Always the state of having two wives must be preceded by the state of hiving one. And the state of having one must in many cases continue, because of the difficulty of getting two where the surplus of women is not great.

Now that the name polyandry has become curreat, it is needful to use polygyny as a name for the converse arrangemeat; and at first it would seem that polygyny implies monogyny as its proper correlative. But monogyny does not fully express the union of one man with one woman, in coatradistinction to the unions of one woman with many men and one man with many women; since the feminine unity is alone indicated by it – not the muscalina unity also. Ifence monogamy, expressing the singleness of the marriage, may be fitly retained.

Of course the union of one man with one woman as it originally exists, shows us but the beginning of monogamic marriage as understood by us. Where, as in cases already given, the wills of the stronger alone initiate and maintain such unions – where, as among the Hudson's Bay Indians, "a weak man, unless he be a good hunter and well beloved, is seldom permitted to keep a wife that a stronger man thinks worth his notice" – where, as among the Copper Indians, Richardson " more than once saw a stronger man assert his right to take the wife of a weaker countryman;" monogamy is very unstable. Its instability thus caused by external actions is made greater by internal actions – by the disruptive forces of unrestrained impulses. When, even in a superior race like the Semitic, we find wives repudiated with extreme frequency, Bo that among some tribes of Bedouins a man will have as many as fifty in succession; we may infer that by slow stages only have enduring monogamic unions been established,

§ 311. There have been several aids to the establishment of them. An important one has been a more developed conception of property, with consequent usages of barter and purchase. The wresting of a woman by one man from another, always checked to some extent by the accompanying danger, was further checked when wives came to be bought, or earned by labour. If he had given to her father a price, or a stipulated length of service, a man would resist with greaterdetermination the abstraction of his wife, than if he had obtained her vithout this sacrifice; and from other men of the tribe who had similarly bought their wives, naturally siding with him, would come reprobation of one who disregarded his claim. From the same cause arises a restraint on divorce. If a wife has been bought or long laboured for, and if another can be had only at like cost, a barrier is raised against desires tending to dissolve the marriage.

Then, too, at later stages, predominance of this higher form of the marital relation is favoured by progress towards equalization of the sexes in numbers. In proportion as war becomes less frequent, and in proportion as an increasing part of the male population is industrially occupied, the mortality of males diminishes, and monogamy spreads. For polygyny now meets with positive resistance. Where there is an approximate balance of men and women, plurality of wives cannot be common without leaving many men wifeless; and from them must come a public opinion adverse to polygyny, tending to restrain and diminish it. That public opinion thut acts even on rulers after a certain stage, is shown by Low's remark concerning the rarity of polygyny among the Land l)yaks: chiefs sometimes indulge in it, but they are apt to lose their influence over their followers by so doing.

To these negative causes for the spread of monogamy, have to be added positive causes. But before turning to them we must contrast the monogamic type of family with the types already discussed.

§ 312. Evidently, as tested by the definiteness and strength of the links among its members, the monogamic family is the most evolved. In polyandry the maternal connexion is alone distinct, and the children are but partially related to one another. In polygyny both the maternal and paternal connexions are distinct; but while some of the children are fully related, others are related on the paternal side only. In monogamy not only are the maternal and paternal connexions both distinct, hut all the children are related on both sides. The family cluster is thus held together by more numerous ties; and beyond the greater cohesion so caused, there is an absence of those repulsions caused by the jealousies inevitable in the polygynic family.

This greater integration characterizes the family as it ramifies through successive generations. Definiteness of descent from the same father, grand-father, great grand-father, etc., it has in common with polygyny ; but it has also defiuiteness of descent from the same mother, grand-mother, great grand-mother, eta Hence its diverging branches aro joined by additional bonds. Where, as with the Romans, there is a legally-recognized descent in the male line only, so that out of the *cognates* constituting the whole body of descendants, only the *aynatesnre* held to be definitely related, the ramifying family-stock is incompletely held together; but where, as with ourselves, descendants of female members of the family are included, it is completely held together.

§ 313. How the" interests of the society, of the offspring, and of the parents, are severally better subserved by monogamy during those later stages of social evolution characterized by it, needs pointing out only for form's sake.

Though, while habitual war and mortality of males leaves constantly a large surplus of females, polygyny favours maintenance of population; yet, when the surplus of females ceases to be large, monogamy becomes superior in productiveness. For, taking the number of females as measuring the possible number of children to be born in each generation, more children are likely to be born if each man has a wife, than if some men have many wives while others have none. So that after passing a certain point in the decrease of male mortality, the monogamic society begins to have an advantage over the polygynic in respect of fertility; and social survival, in so far as it depends on multiplication, is aided by monogamy. The stronger and morowidely ramified family-bonds indicated above, aid in binding the monogamic society together more firmly than any other. The multiplied relationships traced along both lines of descent in all families, which, intermarrying, are ever initiating other double sets of relationships, produce a close net-work of connexions increasing the social cohesion otherwise caused. Political stability is also furthered in a greater degree. Polygyny shares with monogamy the advantage that inheritance of power in the male line becomes possible; but under polygyny the advantage is partially destroyed by the competition for power liable to arise between the children of different mothers. In monogamy this element of dissension disappears, and settled rule is less frequently endangered. For kindred reasons ancestor-worship has its development aided. Whatever favours stability in the dynasties of early rulers, tends to establish permanent dynasties of deities, with the resulting sacred sanctions for codes of conduct.

Decreased mortality of offspring is a manifest result of monogamy in societies that have outgrown barbarism. It is true that in a barren region like the snow-lands of Asia, the children of a polyandric household, fed and protected by several men, may be better off than those of a monogamic household. Probably, too, among savages whose slave-wives, brutally treated, have their strength overtaxed, as well as among such more advanced peoples as those of Africa, where the women do the field-work as well as the domestic drudgeries, a wife who is one of several, is better able to rear her children than a wife who has no one to share the multifarious labours with her. But as fast as we rise to social stages in which the men, no longer often away in war aud idle during peace, are more and more of them occupied in industry – as fast as the women, less taxed by work, are able to pay greater attention to their families, while the men become the bread-winners; the monogamic union subserves better in two ways the rearing of children. Beyond thebenefit of constant maternal care, the children get the benefit of concentrated paternal interest.

Still greater are the advantageous effects on the lives of adults, physical and moral. Though in early societies monogamic unions do not beget any higher feelings towards women, or any ameliorations of their lot; yet in later societies they are the necessary concomitants of such higher feelings and such ameliorations. Especially as the system of purchase declines and choice by women becomes a factor, there evolve the sentiments which characterize the relations of the sexes among civilized peoples. These sentiments have far wider effects than at first appear. How by their influence on the domestic relations they tend to raise the quality of adult life, materially and mentally, is obvious. But they tend in no small degree otherwise to raise the quality of adult life: they create a permanent and deep source of aesthetic interest. On recalling the many and keen pleasures derived from music, poetry, fiction, the drama, etc., all of them having for their predominant theme the passion of love, we shall see that to monogamy, which has developed this passion, we owe a large part of the gratifications which fill our leisure hours.

Nor must we forget, as a further result of the monogamio relation, that in a high degree it favours preservation of life after the reproductive period is passed. Both by the prolonged marital affection which it fosters, and by the greater filial affection evoked under it, declining years are lengthened and their evils mitigated.

§ 314 May we, in ending the discussions occupying this nnd preceding chapters, conclude that monogamy is the natural form of sexual relation for the human race ? If so, how happens it that during the earlier stages of human progress the relations of the sexes have been so indeterminate ?

Among inferior creatures, inherited instinct settles the fit arrangement – the arrangement most conducive to thewelfare of the species. In one case there is no continuous association of male and female ; in another there is a poly- gynous group; in a third there is monogamy lasting for a season. A good deal of evidence may be given that among primates inferior to man, there are monogamic relations of the sexes having some persistence. Why, then, in groups of primitive men did there come divergences from this arrangement prompted by innate tendencies ? Possibly with association into larger groups than are formed by inferior primates, there came into play disrupting influences which did not before exist; and perhaps these were not cheeked because the resulting marital forms furthered survival of the groups. It may be that during certain transitional stages between the first extremely scattered, or little gregarious, stage, and the extremely aggregated, or highly gregarious, stage, there have arisen various conditions favouring various forms of union: so causing temporary deviations from the primitive tendency.

Be this as it may, however, it is clear that monogamy has long been growing innate in the civilized man. For all the ideas and sentiments now associated with marriage, have, as their implication, the singleness of the union.

13

SECTION 13

CHAPTER IX.

  THE FAMILY.

  § 315. Let us now look at the connexions between types of family and social types. Do societies of different degrees of composition habitually present different forms of domestic arrangement ? Are different forms of domestic arrangement associated with the militant system of organization and the industrial system of organization ?

  To the first of these questions no satisfactory answer can be given. The same marital relation occurs in the simplest groups and in the most compound groups. A strict monogamy is observed by the miserable Wood Veddahs, living so widely scattered that they can scarcely be said to have reached the social state; and the wandering Bushmen, similarly low, though not debarred from polygyny, are usually monogamic. Certain settled and more advanced peoples, too, are monogamic; as instance those of Port Dory (New Guinea), and as instance also the Dyaks, who have reached a stage passing from simple into compound. And then we find monogamy habitual with nations which have become vast by aggregation and re-aggregation. Polyandry, again, is not restricted to societies of one order of composition. It occurs in simple groups, as among the Fuegians, the Aleutians, and the Todas; and it occurs in compound groups in Ceylon, in Malabar, in Thibet. Similarly with the distribution of polygyny. It is common to simple, compound, doubly-compound, and even

trebly-compound societies. One kind of connexionbetween the type of family and the degree of social composition may, however, be alleged. Formation of compound groups, implying greater co-ordination and the strengthening of restraints, implies more settled arrangements, public and private. Growth of custom into law, which goes along with an extending governmental organization holding larger masses together, affects the domestic relations along with the political relations; and thus renders the family arrangements, be they polyandric, polygynic, or monogamic, more definite.

Can we, then, allege special connexions between the different types of family and the different social types classed as militant and industrial ? None are revealed by a cursory inspection. Looking first at simple tribes, we see among the unwarlike Todas, a mixed polyandry and polygyny ; and among the Esquimaux, so peaceful as not even to understand the meaning of war, we see, along with monogamic unions, others that are polyandric and polygynic. At the same time the warlike Caribs show us a certain amount of polyandry and a greater amount of polygyny. If, turning to the opposite extreme, we compare with one another large nations, ancient and modern, it seems that the militant character in some cases co-exists with a prevalent polygyny and in other cases with a prevalent or universal monogamy. Nevertheless we shall, on examining the facts more closely, discern general connexions between the militant type and polygyny, and between the industrial type and monogamy.

But first we must recognize the truth that a predominant militancy is not so much shown by armies and the conquests they achieve, as by constancy of predatory activities. The contrast between militant and industrial, is properly between a state in which life is occupied in conflict with other beings, brute and human, and a state in which life is occupied in peaceful labour – energies spent in destruction instead of energies spent in production. So conceiving militancy, we find polygyny to be its habitual accompaniment.

To trace the co-existence of the two from Australians and Tasmanians on through the more developed simple societies up to the compound and doubly compound, would be tedious and is needless; for observing, as we have already done (§ 304), the prevalence of polygyny in the less advanced societies, and admitting, as we must, their state of chronic hostility to their neighbours, the co-existence of these traits is a corollary. That this co-existence results from causal connexion, is suggested by certain converse cases. Among the natives of Port Dory, New Guinea, there is a strict monogamy, with forbidding of divorce, in a primitive community comparatively unwarlike and comparatively industrial. Another instance is furnished by the Land Dyaks, who are monogamic to the extent that polygyny is an offence; while, though given to tribal quarrels about their lands and to the taking of heads as trophies, they have such industrial development that the men, instead of making war and the chase habitual occupations, do much of the heavy work, and there is division of trades with some commercial intercourse. The Hill-tribes of India furnish other instances. There are the amiable Bodo and Dhimals, without military arrangements and having no weapons but their agricultural implements, who are industrially advanced to the extent that there is exchange of services and that the men do all the out-of-door work;

and they are monogamous. Similarly the monogamous Lepchas are wholly unwarlike. Such, too, is the relation of traits in certain societies of the New World distinguished from the rest by being partially or entirely industrial . Whereas most of the aborigines of North America, habitually polygynous, live solely to hunt and fight, the Iroquois had permanent villages and cultivated lauds; and each of them had but one wife. More marked still is the case of the Pueblos, who, " walling out black barbarm" by their ingeniously conglomerated houses, fight only in self-defence, and when let alone engage exclusively in agricultural and other industries, and whose marital relations are strictly

monogamic. This connexion of traits in the simpler

societies, where not directly implied by the inadequate descriptions of travellers, is often traceable indirectly. We have seen (§ 250), that there is a natural relation between constant fighting and development of chiefly power: the implication being that where, in settled tribes, the chiefly power is small the militancy is not great. And this is the fact in those above-named communities characterized by monogamy. In Dalrymple Island (Torres Strait) there are no chiefs; among the Hill-Dyaks subordination to chiefs is feeble; the headman of each Bodo and Dhimal village has but nominal authority; the Lepcha flees from coercion; and the governor of a Pueblo town is annually elected. Conversely, the polygyny which prevails in simple predatory tribes, persists in aggregates of them welded together by war into small nations under established rulers; and in these frequently acquires large extensions. In Polynesia it characterizes in a marked way the warlike and tyrannically- governed Fijians. All through the African kingdoms there goes polygyny along with developed chieftainship, rising to great heights in Ashanti and Dahomey, where the governments are coercive in extreme degrees. The like may be said of the extinct American societies: polygyny was an attribute of dignity among the rigorously-ruled Peruvians, Mexicans, Chibchas, Xicaraguans. And the old despotisms of the East were also characterized by polygyny. Allied with

this evidence is the evidence that in a simple tribe all the men of which are warriors, polygyny is generally diffused; but in a society compounded of such tribes, polygyny continues to characterize the militant part while monogamy begins to characterize the industrial part. This differentiation is foreshadowed even in the primitive militant tribe; since the least militant men fail to obtain more than one wife each. And it becomes marked when, in the growing population formed by compounding of tribes, there arises a division between warriors and workers. But there are moredirect connexions between militancy and polygyny, which we shall recognize on recalling two facts named in the chapter on "Exogamy and Endogamy." By members of savage communities, captured women are habitually taken as additional wives or concubines, and the reputations of warriors are enhanced in proportion to the numbers thus obtained (§ 305). As Mr. M'Lennan points out, certain early peoples permitted foreign wives (presumably along with other wives) to the military class, though such wives were forbidden to other classes. Even among the Hebrew.? the laws authorized private appropriations of women taken in war (§ 308). The further direct connexion is the one implied in §307; namely, that where loss of men in frequent battles leaves a great surplus of women, the possession of more wives than one by each man conduces to maintenance of population and preservation of the society. Hence continuance of polygyny is, under these circumstances, insured by those habitual conflicts, which, other things equal, entail the disappearance of societies not practising it. To which must be added the converse fact, that as fast as decreasing militancy and increasing devotion to industry cause an approximate equalization of the sexes in numbers, there results a growing resistance to polygyny; since it cannot lie practised by many of the men without leaving many ot the rest wifeless, and causing an antagonism inconsistent with social stability. Monogamy is thus to a great extent compelled by that balance of the sexes which industrialism brings about. Once more, the natural relation

between polygyny and predominant militancy, and between monogamy and predominant industrialism, is shown by the fact that these two domestic forms harmonize in principle with the two associated political forms. We have seen that the militant type of social structure is based on the principle of compulsory co-operation, while the industrial type of social structure is based on the principle of voluntary cooperation. Now it is clear that plurality of wives, whetheithe wives are captured in war or purchased from their fathers regardless of their own wills, implies domestic rule of the compulsory type: the husband is tyrant and the wives are slaves. Conversely, the establishment of monogamy where fewer women are taken in war and fewer men lost in war, is accompanied by increased value of the individual woman; who, even when purchased, is therefore likely to be better treated. And when, with further advance, some power of choice is acquired by the woman, there is an approach to the voluntary co-operation which characterizes this marital relation in its highest form. The domestic despotism which polygyny involves, is congruous with the political despotism proper to predominant militancy; and the diminishing political coercion which naturally follows development of the industrial type, is congruous with the diminishing domestic coercion which naturally follows the accompanying development of monogamy. Probably

the histories of European peoples will be cited against this view: the allegation being that, from Greek and Eoman times downwards, these peoples, though militant, have been monogamic. The reply is that ancient European societies, though often engaged in wars, had large parts of their populations otherwise engaged, and had industrial systems characterized by much division of labour and commercial intercourse. Further, there must be remembered the fact that in northern Europe, during and after Roman times, while warfare was constant, monogamy was not universal. Tacitus admits the occurrence of polygyny among the German chiefs. Already we have seen, too, that the Merovingian kings were polygynists. Even the Carolingian period yields such facta as that –

The confidence of Conan II, duke of Britauny, " was kept up by the incredible number of men-at-arms which his kingdom furnished ; for you must know that here, besides that the kingdom is extensive ns well, each warrior will beget fifty, since, bound by the laws ncither of decency nor of religion, each lins ten wives or more even." – *(Ouil. Pict. ap. Banquet, Recneil de llistoriens,* xi. p. 88.)

And Kcenigswarter says that " such was the persistence of legal concubinage in the customs of the people that traces of it are found at Toulouse even in the thirteenth century." To which let me add the startling fact that after the thirty years' war had produced in Germany so immense a mortality of males, bigamy was for a time tolerated by law!

Thus, considering the many factors which have co-operated in modifying marital arrangements – considering also that some societies, becoming relatively peaceful, have long retained in large measure the structures acquired during previous greater militancy, while other societies which have considerably developed their industrial structures have again become predominantly militant, causing mixtures of traits; the alleged relations are, I think, as clear as can be expected. That advance from the primitive predatory type to the highest industrial type, has gone along with advance from prevalent polygyny to exclusive monogamy, is unquestionable; and that decline of militancy and rise of industrialism have been the essential causes of this change in the type of family, is shown by the fact that this change has occurred where such other supposable causes as culture, religious creed, etc., have not come into play.

§ 310. The domestic relations thus far dealt with mainly under their private aspects, have now to be dealt with under their public aspects. For, on the structure of the family, considered as a component of a society, depend various social phenomena.

The facts grouped in foregoing chapters show that no true conception of the higher types of family in their relations to the higher social types, can be obtained without previous study of the lower types of family in their relations to the lower social types. In this case, as in all other cases, error results when conclusions are drawn from the more complex products of evolution, in ignorance of the simpler products from which they have been derived. Already an instancehas been furnished by the interpretations of primitive religions given by the reigning school of mythologists. Possessed by the ideas which civilization lias evolved, and looking back on the ideas which prevailed among progenitors of the civilized races, they have used the more. complex to interpret the less complex; and when forced to recognize the entire unlikeness between the inferred early religious ideas and the religious ideas found among the uncivilized who now exist, have assumed a fundamental difference in mode of action between the minds of the superior races and the minds of the inferior races: classing with the inferior, in pursuance of this assumption, such ancient races as the Accadians, to which the modern world is largely indebted for its present advance.

All who accept the conclusions set forth in the first part of this work, will see in this instance the error caused by analysis of the phenomena from above downwards, instead of synthesis of them from below upwards. They will see that in search of explanations we must go beneath the stage at v hich men had learnt to domesticate cattle and till the ground.

§ 317. These remarks are introductory to a criticism on the doctrines of Sir Henry Maine. While greatly valuing his works, and accepting as true within limits the views he has set forth respecting the family in its developed form, and respecting the part played by it in the evolution of European nations, it is possible to dissent from his assumptions concerning the earliest social states, and from the derived conceptions.

As leading to error, Sir Henry Maine censures " the lofty contempt which a civilized people entertains for barbarous ncighbours," which, he says, " has caused a remarkable negligence in observing them." But he has not himself wholly escaped from the effects of this sentiment. While utilizing the evidence furnished by barbarous peoples belonging to tha higher types of man, and while in some cases citing confirmatory evidence furnished by barbarous peoples of lower types, he has ignored the great mass of the uncivilized, and disregarded the multitudinous facts they present at variance with his theory. Though criticisms have led him somewhat to qualify the sweeping generalizations set forth in his *Ancient Law* – though, in the preface to its later editions, he refers to his subsequent work on *Village Communities,* as indicating some qualifications; yet the qualifications are but small, and in great measure hypothetical. He makes light of such adverse evidence as Mr. M'Lennan and Sir John Lubbock give, on the ground that the part of it he deems most trustworthy is supplied by Indian Hill-tribes, which have, he thinks, been led into abnormal usages by the influences invading races have subjected them to. And though, in his *Early Institutions,* he says that " all branches of human society may or may not have been developed from joint families which arose out of an original patriarchal cell," he clearly, by this form of expression, declines to admit that iu many cases they have *not* been thus developed.

He rightly blames earlier writers for not exploring a sufficiently wide area of induction. But he has himself not made the area of induction wide enough; and that substitution of hypothesis for observed fact which he ascribes to his predecessors, is, as a consequence, to be noticed in his own work. Respecting the evidence available for framing generalizations, he says: –

" The rndiments of the social sta e, so far as they are known to ua at all, are known through testimony of three Boris – accoxmts by contemporary observers of civilizations less advanced than thcir own, the records which particular races have preserved concerning thcir primitive history, and ancient law."

And since, as exemplifying the " accounts by contemporary observers of civilizations less advanced than their own," he names the account Tacitus gives of the Germans, and does not name the accounts modern travellers give of uncivilized races at large, he clearly does not include as evidence thestatements made by these. Let me name here two instances of the way in which this limitation leads to the substitution of hypothesis for observation.

Assuming that the patriarchal state is the earliest, Sir Henry Maine says that " the implicit obedience of rude men to their parent is doubtless a primary fact." Now though among lower races, sons, while young, may be subordinate, from lack of ability to resist; yet thab they remain subordinate when they become men, cannot be asserted *t. s* a uniform, and therefore as a primary, fact. On turning to § 35, it will be seen that obedience does not ch, i. racterize all types of men. When we read that the Mantra " lives as if theie were no other person in the world but himself;" that the Carib " is impatient under the least infringement" of his independence ; that the Mapuche" " brooks no command," that the Brazilian Indian begins to display impatience of all restraint at puberty; we cannot concludw that filial submission is an original trait. When we are told that by the Gallinomeros, " old people are treated with contumely, both men and women," and that by Shoshor. es and Araucanians, boys are not corrected for fear of destroying their spirit; we cannot suppose that subjection of adult sons to their fathers characterizes all types of men. When we learn that by the Navajos, "born and bred with the idf-a of perfect personal freedom, all restraint is unendurable," and that among them " every father holds undisputed sway over his children uniil the age of puberty" – whe. i we learn that among some

At page 17 of his *Village Communities,* he deliberately discredits this evidence – speaking of it as " the slippery testimony concerning savaies which is gathered from travellers' tales." I am aware that in the eyes of most, aatiquity gives sacredness to testimony ; and that so, what were " travellers' tales " when they were written in Roman days, have come, in our davs, to be regarded as of higher authority than like tales written by receat or living travellers. I see, however, no reason to ascribe to the second-band statements of Taciti. s a trustworthiness which I do not ascribe to the firsthand statemeats of modern explorers ; many of them scientifically edacated – Barrow, Earth, Gallon, Burton, Livingstone, Secmnn, Darwin, Wallace, Humboldt, Burekhardt, and others too numerous ki set down.

Californians, children after puberty " were subject only to tlie chief," that among the lower Californians, "as soon as children are able to get food for themselves they are left to their own devices," and that among the Comanches maJe children " are even privileged to rebel against their parents, who are not entitled to chastise them but by consent of the tribe;" we are shown that iu some races the parental and filial relation early comes to an end. Even the wilder members of the very race which has familiarized us with patriarchal government, yield like facts. Burckhardt says that " the young Bedouin" pays his father " some deference as long as he continues in his tent; " but "whenever he can become master of a teat himself ... he listens to no advice, nor obeys any earthly command but that of his own will." So far from showing that filial obedience is innate, and the patriarchal type a natural consequence, the evidence points rather to the inference that the two have evolved hand in hand under favouring conditions.

Again, referring to the way in which originally, common ancestral origin was the only ground for united social action, Sir Henry Maine says: – -

" Of this we may at least be certain, that all ancient societies regarded themselves as having proceeded from one original stock, and even laboured under an incapacity for comprchending any reason except this for their holding together iu politieal union. The history of politieal ideas begius, in fact, with the assumption that kinship in blood ia the sole possible ground of community in politieal functions."

Now if by " ancient societies " is meant those only of which records have come down to us, and if the "history of politi- fcil ideas " is to include only the ideas of such societies, this may bo true; but if we are to take account of societies more archaic than these, and to include other political ideas than those of Aryans and Semites, it cannot be sustained. Proof has been given ($\S\S$ 230 – 252) that political co-operation arises from the conflicts of social groups with one another. Though establishment of it may be facilitated where " the commonwealth is a collection of persons united by a commondescent from the progenitor of an original family;" yet, in hosts of cases, it takes place where no connexion of this kind exists among the persons. The members of an Australian tribe which, under a temporary chief, join in battle against those of another tribe, have not a common descent, but are alien in blood. If it be said that political functions can here scarcely be alleged, then tako tr. e case of the Creeks of North America, whose men have various totems implying varous ancestries, and whose twenty thousand people living in seventy villages havo nevertheless evolved for th mselves a government of considerable complexity. Or still better take the Iroquois, who, similar in their formation of tribes out of intermingled clans of different stocks, were welded by combined action in war into a league of five (afterwards six) nations under a republican government. Indeed arly systems of kinship put relations in political antagonism; so that, as we read in Bancroft concerning the Kutchins, " there can never be inter-tribal war without ranging fathers and sons against each other." Even apart from the results of mixed clanships, that instability which characterizes primitive relations of the sexes, negatives the belief that political co-operation everywhere originates from family co-operation : instance the above-named Creeks, of whom " a large portion of the old and middle-aged men, by frequently changing, have had many different wives, and their children, scattered around the country, are unknown to them."

Thus finding reason to suspect that Sir Henry Maine's theory of the family is not applicable to all societies, let us proceed to consider it more closely.

§ 318. He implies that in the earliest stages there were definite marital relations. That which he calls " the infancy of society " – " the situation in which mankind disclose themselves at the dawn of their history;" is a situation in which '"every one exercises jurisdiction over his wives and his children, and they pay no regard to one another.'" But inthe chapters on " The Primitive Relations of the Sexes," on " Promiscuity," and on " Polyandry," I have cited numerous facts showing that defmite coherent marital relations are preceded by indefinite incoherent ones; and also that among the types of family evolving out of these, there are some composed not of a man with wife and children, but of a wife with men and children: such being found not alone in societies of embryonic and infantine forms, but also in considerably advanced societies.

A further assumption is that descent has always and everywhere been in the male line. That it has from the recorded times of those pcoples with whom Sir Henry Maine deals, may be true; and it is true that male descent occurs among some rude peoples of other types, as the Rookies of India, the Beluchis, the New Zealanders, the Hottentots. It is by no means the rule, however, among the uncivilized. Mr. M'Lennan, who has pointed out the incongruity between this assumption and a great mass of evidence, shows that all over the world descent in the female line is common ; and the many examples given by him I might, were it needful, enforce by others. This system is not limited to groups so little organized that they might be set aside as pre- infautiue (were that permissible); nor to groups which stand on a level with the patriarchal, or so-called infantine, societies in point of organization; but it occurs in groups, or rather nations, which have evolved complex structures. Kinship was through females in the two higher ranks of the Tahitians; and among the Tongans " nobility has always descended by the female line." It was so with the ancient Chibchas, who had made no insignificant strides in civilization. Among the Iroquois, again, titles, as well as property, descended through women. and were hereditary in the woman's tribe: the son could never succeed to his father's title of sachem, nor inherit even his tomahawk ; and these Iroquois had advanced far beyond the infantine stage – were governed by a representative assembly of fifty sachems, had a separata military organization, a separate ecclesiastical organization' definite laws, culti-vated lauds individually possessed, permanent fortified villages. So, too, in Africa, succession to rank and property follows the female line among the Coast- negroes, Inland-negroes, Congo people, etc.; who have distinct industrial systems, four and five gradations in rank, settled agricultures, considerable commerce, towns in streets. How misleading is the observation of a few societies only, ia shown by Marsden's remark respecting the Sumatrans of the Batta district. He says that "the succession to the chief- ships does not go, in the first instance, to the son of the deceased, but to the nephew by a sister;" and adds " that the same extraordinary rule, with respect to property in general, prevails also amongst the Malays of that part of the island:" the rule which he considers " extraordinary," being really, among the uncivilized and little civilized, the ordinary rule.

Again, Sir Henry Maine postulates the existence of government from the beginning – patriarchal authority over wife, children, slaves, and all who are included in the primitive Bocial group. But in the chapters on " The Regulating System" and " Social Types," I have shown that in various parts of the world there are social groups without heads; as the Fuegians, some Australians, most Esquimaux, the Ara- furas, the Land Dyaks of the Upper Sarawak river; others with headships that are but occasional, as Tasmanians, some Australians, some Caribs, some Uaupes; and many with vague and unstable headships, as the Andamanese, Abipones, Snakes, Chippewayans, Chinooks, Chippewas, some Kam- schadales, Guiana tribes, Mandans, Coroados, New Guinea people, Tanuese. Though in some of these cases the communities are of the lowest, I see no adequate reason for excluding them from our conception of the "infancy of society." And even saying nothing of these, we cannot regard as lower than infantine in their stages, those communities which, like the Upper Sarawak Dyaks, the Arafuras the New Guinea people, carry on their peaceful lives without other government than that of public opinion and custom. Morcover, *aa* we saw in § 250, the head ship which exists in many simple groups is not patriarchal. Such chieftainship as arose among the Tasmanians in time of war, was determined by personal fitness. So, too, according to Edwards, with the Caribs, and according to Swan, with the Creeks. Then, still further showing that political authority does not always begin with patriarchal authority, we have the Iroquois, whose system of kinship negatived the genesis of patriarchs, and who yet developed a complex republican government; and we have the Pueblos, who, living in well- organized communities under elected governors and councils, show no signs of patriarchal rule in the past.

Another component of the doctrine is that originally, property is held by the family as a corporate body. According to Sir Henry Maine, " one peculiarity invariably distinguishing the infancy of society," is that " men are regarded and treated not as individuals but always as members of the particular group." The man was not" regarded as himself, as a distinct individual. His individuality was swallowed up in his family." And this alleged primitive submergence of the individual, affected even the absolute ruler of the group. " Though the patriarch, for we must not yet call him the paterfamilias, had rights thus extensive, it is impossible to doubt that he lay under an equal amplitude of obligations. If he governed the family it was for its behoof. If he was lord of its possessions, he held them as trustee for his children and kindred .

. . the l'amily in fact was a corporation j and he was its representative." Here, after expressing

a doubt whether there exist in the primitive mind ideas so abstract as those of trusteeship and representation, I go on to remark that this hypothesis involves a conception difficult to frame. For while the patriarch is said to hold his possessions "in a representative rather than a proprietary character," he is said to have unqualified dominion over children, as over slaves, extending to life and death; which implies that though he possesses the greater right of owning subordinate individuals absolutely, he does not possess the smaller right of owning absolutely the property used by them and himself. I may add that besides being difficult to frame, this conception is not easily reconcilable with Sir Henry Maine's description of the Patria Potestas of the Romans, which he says is " our type of the primeval paternal authority," and of which he remarks that while, during its decline, the father's power over the son's *person* became nominal, his "rights over the son's *property* were always exercised without scruple." And I may also name its seeming incongruity with the fact that political rulers who have unlimited powers over their subjects, are usually also regarded as in theory owners of their property: instance at the present time the kings of Dahomey, Ashanti, Congo, Cayor on the Gold Coast. Passing to the essential

question, however, I find myself here at issue not with Sir Henry Maine only, but with other writers on primitive social states, who hold that all ownership is originally tribal, that family-ownership comes later, and ownership by individuals last. As already implied in § 292, the evidence leads me to believe that from the beginning there has been individual ownership of such things as could without difficulty be appropriated. True though it is that in early stages rights of property are indefinite – certain though it may be that among primitive men the moral sanction which property equitably obtained has among ourselves, is lacking – obvious as we find it that possession is often established by right oi the strongest; the facts prove that in the rudest communities there is a private holding of useful movables, maintained by each man to the best of his ability. A personal monopoly extends itself to such things as can readily be monopolized. The Tinneh who, " regarding all property, including wives, as belonging to the strongest," show in a typical way the primitive form of appropriation, also show that this ap-

propriation is completely personal; since they "burn with the deceased all his effects." Indeed, even apart from evidence, it seems to me an inadmissiblo supposition that in '-' the infancy of society " the egoistic savage, utterly without idea of justice or sense of responsibility, consciously held his belongings on behalf of those depending upon him.

One more element, indirectly if not directly involved in the doctrine of Sir Henry Maine, is that " the infancy of society" is characterized by the perpetual tutelage of women. While each male descendant has a capacity " to become himself the head of a new family and the root of a new set of parental powers," " a woman of course has no capacity of the kind, and no title accordingly to the liberation which it confers. There is therefore a peculiar contrivance of archaic jurisprudence for retaining her in the bondage of the family for life." And the implication appears to be that this slavery of women, derived from the patriarchal state, and naturally accompanied by inability to hold property, has been slowly mitigated, and the right of private possession acquired, as the primitive family has decayed. But when we pass from the progenitors of the civilized races to existing uncivilized races, we meet with facts requiring us to qualify this proposition. Though in rude societies entire subjection of women is the rule, yet there are exceptions; both in societies lower than the patriarchal in organization, and in higher societies which bear no traces of a past patriarchal state. Among the Kocch, who are mainly governed by "juries of elders," " when a woman dies the family property goes to her daughters." In tribes of the Karens, whose chiefs, of little authority, are generally elective and often wanting, " the father wills his property to his children. . . . Nothing is given to the widow, but she is entitled to the use of the propertytill her death." Of the Khasias, Steel says that " the house belongs to the woman; and in case of the husband dying or being separated from her, it remains her jropeity." Among the Sea-Dyaks, whose law of inheritanceis not that of primogeniture, and whose chieftainships, where they exist, are acquired by merit, as the wife does au equal share of work with her husband, " at a divorce she is entitled to half the wealth created by their mutual [joint] labours ;" and Brooke writes of certain Land-Dyaks, that " the most powerful of the people in the place were two old ladies, who often told me that all the land and inhabitants belonged to them." North America furnishes kindred facts. In the Aleutian Islands " rich women are permitted to indulge in two husbands-," ownership of property by females being implied. Among the JSTootkas, in case of divorce there is " a strict division of property" – the wife taking both what she brought and what she has made; and similarly among the Spokanes, " all household goods are considered as the wife's property," and there is an equitable division of property on dissolution of marriage. Again, of the Iroquois, who, considerably advanced as we have seen, were showa by their still-surviving system of descent in the female line, never to have passed through the patriarchal stage, we read that the proprietary rights of husband and wife remained distinct; and further, that in case of separation the children went with the mother. Still more striking is the instance supplied by the peaceable, industrious, freely-governed Pueblos; whose women, otherwise occupying good positions, not only inherit property, but, in some cases, make exclusive claims to it. Africa, too, where the condition of women is in most respects low, but where descent in the female line continues, furnishes examples. In Timbuctoo a son's share of the father's property is double that of a daughter. Above the Yellala falls on the Congo, fowls, eggs, manioc, and fruits, " seem all to belong to the women, the men never disposing of them without first consulting their wives, to whom the beads are given,"

Thus many things are at variance with the theory which assumes that " the infancy of society" is exhibited in the patriarchal group. As was implied in the chapters on the "Primitive Eolations of the Sexes," on "Promiscuity," on" Polyandry," the earliest societies were without domestic organization as they were without political organization. Instead of a paternally-governed cluster, at once family and rndimentary State, there was at first an aggregate of males and females without settled arrangements, and having no relations save those established by force and changed when the stronger willed.

§ 319. And here we come in face of the fact before obliquely glanced at, that Sir Henry Maine's hypothesis takes account of no stages in human progress earlier than the pastoral or agricultural. The groups he describes *as* severally formed of the patriarch, his wife, descendants, slaves, flocks, and herds, are groups implying domesticated animals of several kinds. But before the domestication of animals was achieved, there passed long stages stretching back through pro-historic times. To understand the patriarchal group, we must inquire how it grew out of the less-organized groups which preceded it.

The answer is not difficult to fmd if we ask what kind of life the domestication of herbivorous animals entail?. Where pasture is abundant and covers large areas, the keeping of flocks and herds does not necessitate separation of their owners into very small clusters: instance the Comanches, who, with their hunting, join the keeping of cattle, which the members of the tribe combine to guard. But where pasture is not abundant, or is distributed in patches, many cattle cannot be kept together; and their owners consequently have to part. Naturally, division of the owners will be into such clusters as are already vaguely maiked off in the oiiginal aggregate. Individual men with such women as they have taken possession of, such animals as they have acquired by force or otherwise, and all their other belongings, will wander hither and thither in search of food for their sheep and oxen. As already pointed out, we have, in pre-pastoral stages, as among the Bushmen, cases where scarcityof wild food necessitates parting into very small groups, usually single families; and clearly when, instead of game and vermin to be caught, cattle have to be fed, the distribution of pasturage, here in larger oases and there in smaller ones, will determine the numbers of animals, and consequently of human beings, which can keep together. In the separation of Abraham and Lot we have a traditional illustration.

Thus recognizing the natural origin of the wandering family-group, let us ask what are likely to become its traits. We have seen that the regulating system of a society is evolved by conflicts with environing societies. Between pastoral hordes which have become separate, and in course of time alien, there must arise, as between other groups, antagonisms: caused sometimes by appropriations of strayed cattle, sometimes by encroachments upon grazing areas monopolized. But now mark a difference. In a tribe of archaic type, such ascendancy as war from time to time gives to a man who is superior in strength, will, or cunning, commonly fails to become a permanent headship (§ 250); since his power is regarded with jealousy by men who are in other respects his equals. It is otherwise in the pastoral horde. The tendency which war between groups has to evolve a head in each group, here finds a member prepared for the place. Already there is the father, who at the outset was by right of the strong hand, leader, owner, master, of wife, children, and all he carried with him. In the preceding stage his actions were to some extent kept in check by other men of the tribe; now they are not . His sous could early become hunters and carry on their lives independently; now they cannot.

Note a second difference. Separation from other men brings into greater clearness the fact that the children are not only his wife's children, but his children; and further, since among its neighbours his group is distinguished by his name, the children spoken of as members of his group are otherwise spoken of as his children. The establishment ofmale descent is thus facilitated. Simultaneously there is apt to come acknowledged supremacy of the eldest son. The first to give aid to the father; the first to reach manhood; the irst likely to marry and have children; he is usually the one on whom the powers of the father devolve as he declines and dies. Hence the average tendency through successive generations will be for the eldest male to become head of the increasing group; alike as family ruler and political ruler – the patriarch.

At the same time industrial co-operation is fostered. Savages of the lowest types get roots and berries, shell-fish, vermin, small animals, etc., without joint action. Among those who have reached the advanced hunting stage and capture large animals, a considerable combination is implied, though of an irregular kind. But on rising to the stage in which flocks and herds have to be daily pastured and guarded, and their products daily utilized, combined actions of many kinds are necessitated; and under the patriarchal rule these become regularized by apportionment of duties. Tins co-ordinacion of functions and consequent mutual dependence of parts, conduces to consolidation of the group as an organic whole. Gradually it becomes impracticable for any member to live by himself: deprived not only of the family aid and protection, but of the food and clothing yielded by the domesticated animals. So that the industrial arrangements conspire with the governmental arrangements to produce a well-compacted aggregate, internally coherent and externally marked off definitely from other aggregates.

This process is furthered by disappearance of the less- developed. Other things equal, those groups which are most subordinate to their leaders will succeed best in battle. Other things equal, those which, submitting to commands longer, have grown into larger groups, will also thus benefit. And other things equal, advantages will be gained by those in which, under dictation of the patriarch, industrial cooperation has been rendered efficient. So that by survivalof the fittest among pastoral groups struggling for existence with one another, those which obedience to their heads and mutual dependence of parts have made the strongest, will be those to spread; and in course of time the patriarchal type will thus become well marked. Not, indeed, that entire disappearance of less-organized groups must result; since regions favourable to the process described, facilitate survival of a few smaller hordes, pursuing lives more predatory and less pastoral.

Mark next how, under these circumstances, there arise certain arrangements respecting ownership. That division of goods which is pre-supposed by individualization of property, caunot be carried far without appliances unknown to savage life. Measures of time, measures of quantity, measures of value, are required. When, from the primitive appropriation of things found, caught, or made, we pass to the acquisition of things by barter and by service, we see that approximate equality of value between the exchanged things is implied; and in the absence of recognized equivalence, which must be exceptional, there will be great resistance to barter. Among savages, therefore, property extends but little beyond the things a man can procure for himself. Kindred obstacles occur in the pastoral group. How can the value of the labour contributed by each to the common weal bs measured ? To-day the cowherd can feed his cattle close at hand; to-morrow he must drive them far and get back late. Here the shepherd tends his flock in rich pasture; and in a region next visited the sheep disperse in search of scanty food, and he has great trouble in getting in the strayed ones. No accounts of labour spent by either can be kept; nor are there current rates of wages to give ideas of their respective claims to shares of produce. The work of the daughter or the bond-woman, who milks and who fetches water, now from a well at hand and now from one further off, varies from day to day ; and its worth, as compared with the worths of other works, cannot be known

So with the preparation of skins, the making of clothing, the setting up of tents. All these miscellaneous services, differing in arduousness, duration, skill, cannot be paid for in money or produce while there exists neither currency noi market in which the relative values of articles and labours may be established by competition. Doubtless a bargain for eeivices rudely estimated as worth so many cattle or sheep, may be entered into. But beyond the fact that this form of payment, admitting of but very rough equivalence, cannot conveniently be carried out with all members of the group, there is the fact that even supposing it to be carried out, the members of the group cannot separately utilize their respective portions. The sheep have to be herded together: it would never do to send them out in small divisions, each requiring its attendant. Milk must be dealt with in the mass – could not without great loss of labour be taken by so many separate milkmaids and treated afterwards in separate portions. So is it throughout. The members of the group naturally fall into the system of giving their respective labours and satisfying from the produce their respective wants. The patriarch, at once family-head, director of industry, owner of the group and its belongings, regulates the labour of his dependents; and, maintaining them out of the common stock which results, is restrained in his distribution, as in his conduct at large, only by custom and by the prospect of resistance and secession if he disregards too far the average opinion.

The mention of secession introduces a remaining trait of the patriarchal group. Small societies, mostly at enmity with surrounding societies, are anxious to increase the numbers of their men that they may be stronger for war. Hence not infrequently female infanticide, to facilitate the rearmg of males; hence in some places, as in parts of Africa, a woman is forgiven any amount of irregularity if she bears many children; hence the fact that among the Hebrews barrenness was a reproach. This wish to strengthen itself byadding to its fighting members, leads each group to welcome fugitives from other groups. Everywhere and in all times, there goes on desertion – sometimes of rebels, sometimes of criminals. Stories of feudal ages, telling of knights and men- at-arms who, being ill-treated or in danger of punishment, escape and take service with other princes or nobles, remind us of what goes on at the present day in various parts of Africa, where the dependents of a chief who treats them too harshly leave him and join some neighbouring chief, and of what goes on among such wandering tribes as the Coroados, members of which join now one horde and now another as impulse prompts. And that with pastoral peoples the like occurs, we have direct evidence. Pallas tells us of the Kalmucks and Mongols that men oppressed by their chief, desert and go to other chiefs. Occasionally occurring

everywhere, this fleeing from tribe to tribe entails ceremonies of incorporation if the stranger is of fit rank and worth – exchange of names, mingling of portions of blood, etc, – by which he is supposed to be made one in nature with those he has joined. What happens when the group. instead of being of the hunting type, is of the patriarchal type ? Adoption into the tribe now becomes adoption into the family. The two being one – the family being otherwise called, as in Hebrew, " the tent" – political incorporation is the same thing as domestic incorporation. And adoption into the family, thus established as a sequence of primitive adoption into the tribe, long persists in the derived societies when its original meaning is lost.

And now to test this interpretation. Distinct in nature as are sundry races leading pastoral lives, we find that they have evolved this social type when subject to these particular conditions. That it was the type among early Semites does not need saying: they, in fact, having largely served to exemplify its traits. That the Aryans during their nomadic Btage displayed it, is implied by the account given above of Sir Henry Maine's investigations and inferences. We find itagain among the Mongolian peoples of Asia; and again among wholly alien peoples inhabiting South Africa. Of the Hottentots, who, exclusively pastoral, differ from the neighbouring Bechuanas and Kaffirs in not cultivating the soil at all, we learn that all estates " descend to the eldest son, cr, where a son is wanting, to the next male relation;" and an eldest son may after his father's death retain his brothers and sisters in a sort of slavery. Note, too, that among the neighbouring Damaras, who, also exclusively pastoral, are unlike in the respect that kinship in the female line still partially survives, patriarchal organization, whether of the family or the tribe, is but little developed, and the subordination small; and further, that among the Kaffirs, who though in large measure pastoral are partly agricultural, patriarchal rule, private and public, is qualified.

It would be unsafe to say that under no other conditions than those of the pastoral state, does this family-type occur. We have no proof that it may not arise along with a direct transition from the hunting life to the agricultural life. But it seems that usually this direct transition is accompanied by a different set of changes. "Where, as in Polynesia, pastoral life has been impossible, or where, as in Peru and Mexico, we have no reason to suppose that it ever existed, the political and domestic arrangements, still characterized much or little by the primitive system of descent in the female line, have acquired qualified forms of male descent and its concomitant arrangements; but they appear to have done so under pressure of the influences which habitual militancy maintains. We have an indication of this in Gomara's statement respecting the Peruvians, that " nephews inherit, and not sons, except in the case of the Yncas." Still better are we shown it by sundry African states. Among the Coast Negroes, whose kinships are ordinarily through females, and whose various societies, variously governed, are most of them very unstable, male descent has been established in some of the kingdoms. The Inland Negroes, too, similarly

retaining as a rule descent in the female line, alike in the State and in the family, have acquired in their public and private arrangements, some traits akin to those derived from the patriarchal system; and the like is the case in Congo. Further, in the powerful kingdom of Dahomey, where the monarchy has become stable and absolute, male succession and primogeniture are completely established, and in the less-despotically governed Ashanti, partially established.

But whether the patriarchal type of family does or does not arise under other conditions, we may safely say that the pastoral life is most favourable to development of it. From the general laws of evolution it is a corollary that there goes on integration of any group of like units, simultaneously exposed to forces that are like in kind, amount, and direction *(First Principles,* §§ 163, 168); and obviously, the members of a wandering family, kept together by joint interests and jointly in antagonism with other such families, will become more integrated than the members of a family associated with other families in a primitive tribe; since in this the joint interests are largely tribal. Just as a larger social aggregate becomes coherent by the co-operation of its members in conflict with neighbouring like aggregates; so does this smallest social aggregate constituted by the nomadic horde. Of the differentiations which simultaneously arise, the same may be said. As the government of a larger society is evolved during its struggles with other such societies; so is the government of this smallest society. And as here the society and the family are one, the development of the regulative structure of the society becomes the development of the regulative family-structure. Moreover, analogy suggests that the higher organization given by this discipline to the family-group, makes it a better component of societies afterwards formed, than are family-groups which have not passed through this discipline. Already we have seen that great nations arise only by aggregation and reaggregation. Small communities have first to acquire some consolidation and structure; then they admit of union into compound communities, which, when well integrated, may again be compounded into still larger communities; and so on. It now appears that social evolution is most favoured when this process begins with the smallest groups – the families : such groups, made coherent and definite in the way described, and afterwards compounded and re-compounded, having originated the highest societies.

An analogy between social organisms and individual organisms supports this infer- ence. In a passage from which I have already quoted a clause, Sir Henry Maine, using a metaphor which biology furnishes, says: – " All branches of human society may or may not have been developed from joint families which arose out of an original patriarchal cell; but, wherever the Joint Family is an institution of an Aryan race, we see it springing from such a cell, and, when it dissolves, we see it dissolving into a number of such cells:" thus implying that as the cell is the proximate component of the individual organism, so the family is the proximate component of the social organism. In either case, however, this, though generally true, is not entirely true ; and the qualification required is extremely suggestive. Low down in the animal kingdom exist creatures not possessing definite cell-structure – small portions of liv- ing protoplasm without limiting membranes and even without nuclei. There are also certain types produced by aggregation of these; and though it is now alleged that the individual components of one of the compound *Foraminifcra-* have nuclei, yet they have none of the definiteness of developed cells. In types above these, however, it is otherwise: every ccelente- rate, molluscous, annulose, or vertebrate animal, begins as a cluster of distinct, nucleated cells. Whence it would seem that the tmdifferentiated portion of protoplasm constituting the lowest animal, cannot, by union with others such, furnish the basis fur a higher animal; and that the simplest aggregateshave to become definitely developed before they can form by combination larger aggregates capable of much development. Similarly with societies. Tribes in which the family is vague and unsettled remain politically rude. Sundry partially- civilized peoples characterized by some definiteness and coherence of family structure, have attained corresponding heights of social structure. And the highest organizations have been reached by nations compounded out of family groups which had previously become well organized.

§ 320. And now, limiting our attention to these highest societies, we have to thank Sir Henry Maine for showing us the ways in which many of their ideas, customs, laws, and arrangements, have been derived from those which characterized the patriarchal group.

In all cases habits of life, when continued for many generations, mould the nature; and the resulting traditional beliefs and usages with the accompanying sentiments, become difficult to change. Hence, on passing from the wandering pastoral life to the settled agricultural life, the patriarchal type of family with its established traits, persisted, and gave its stomp to the social structures which gradually arose. As Sir Henry Maine says – " All the larger groups which make up the primitive societies in which the patriarchal family occurs, are seen to be multiplications of it, and to be, in fact, themselves more or less formed on its model:" The divisions which result become distinct in various degrees. " In the joint undivided family of the Hindoos, the stirpes, or stocks, which are only known to European law as branches of inheritors, are actual divisions of the family, and live together in distinct parts of the common dwelling ;" and similarly in some parts of Europe. In the words of another writer – " The Bulgarians, like the Russian peasantry, adhere to the old patriarchal method, and fathers and married sons, with their children and children's children, live under the same roof until the grandfather dieaAs each son in his turn gets married, a new room is added to the old building, until with the new generation there will often be twenty or thirty people living under the same roof, all paying obedience and respect to the head of the family." Further multiplication produces the village community; in which the households, and in part the landed properties, have become distinct. And then where larger populations arise, and different stocks are locally mingled, there are formed such groups within groups as those constituting, among the Romans, the family, the house, and the tribe: common ancestry being in all cases the bond.

Along with persistence of patriarchal structures under new conditions, goes persistence of patriarchal principles. There is supremacy of the eldest male; sometimes continuing, as in Roman Law, to the extent of life and death power over wife and children. There long survives, too, the general idea that the offences of the individual are the offences of the group to which he belongs; and, as a consequence, there survives the practice of holding the group responsible and inflicting punishment upon it. There come the system of agnatic kinship, and the adapted laws of inheritance. And there develops the ancestor-worship in which there join groups of family, house, tribe, etc., that are large in proportion as the ancestor is remote. These results, however, here briefly indicated, do not now concern us: they have to be treated of more as social phenomena than as domestic phenomena.

But with one further general truth which Sir Henry Maine brings into view, we are concerned – the disintegration of the family. " The *unit* of an ancient society was the Family," he says, and "of a modern society the Individual." Now excluding those archaic types of society in which, as we have seen, the family is undeveloped, this generalization appears to be amply supported by facts; and it is one of profound importance. If, recalling the above suggestions respecting the genesis of the patriarchal family, we ask what musthappen when the causes which joined in forming it are replaced by causes working in an opposite way, we shall understand why this change has taken place. In the lowest groups, while there continues co-operation in war and the chase among individuals belonging to different stocks, the family remains vague aud incoherent, and the individual ia the unit. But when the imperfectly-formed families with their domestic animals severally become distinct groups – when the co-operations carried on are between individuals domestically related es well as socially related, then the family becomes denned, compact, organized; and its controlling agency gains strength because it is at once parental and political. This organization which the pastoral group gets by being at once family and society, and which is gradually perfected by conflict and survival of the fittest, it carries into settled life. But settled life entails multiplication into numerous such groups adjacent to one another; and in these changed circumstances, each of the groups is sheltered from some of the actions which originated its organization, and exposed to other actions which tend to disorganize it. Though there still arise quarrels among the multiplying families, yet, as their blood-relationship is now a familiar thought, which persists longer than it would have done had they wandered away from one another generation after generation, the check to antagonism is greater. i'uither, the worship of a common ancestor, in which they can now more readily join at settled intervals, acts as a restraint on their hatreds, and so holds them together. Again, the family is no longer liable to be separately attacked by enemies, but a number of adjacent families arc simultaneously invaded and simultaneously resist: co-operation among them is induced. Throughout subsequent stages of social growth this co-operation increases; and the families jointly exposed to like external forces tend to integrate. Already we have seen that by a kindred process such communities as tribes, as feudal lordships, as small kingdoms, become united inln

larger communities; and that along with the union caused by co-operation, primarily for offence and defence and subsequently for other purposes, there goes a gradual obliteration of the divisions between them, and a substantial fusion. Here we recognize the like process as taking place with these smallest groups. Quite harmonizing with this

general interpretation are the special interpretations which Sir Henry Maine gives of the decline of the Patria Potestas among the Romans. He points out how father and sou had to perform their civil and military functions on a footing of equality wholly unlike their domestic footing; and how the consequent separate acquisition of authority, power, spoils, etc., by the son, gradually undermined the paternal despotism. Individuals of the family, no longer working together only in their unlike relations to one another, and coming to work together under like relations to State-authority and to enemies, the public co-operation and subordination grew at the expense of the private co-operation and subordination. And in the large aggregates eventually formed, industrial activities as well as militant activities conduced to this result. In his work *Throvgh Bosnia and the Herzcgdvina,* Mr. Evans, describing the Sclavonic house-communities, which are dissolving under the stress of industrial competition, says – " The truth is, that the incentives to labour and economy are weakened by the sense of personal interest in their results being sub-divided."

And now let us note the marvellous parallel between this change in the structure of the social organism and a change in the structure of the individual organism. We saw that definite nucleated cells are the components which, by aggregation, lay the foundations of the higher organisms; in the same way that the well-developed simple patriarchal groups are those out of which, by composition, the higher societies are eventually evolved. Here let me add that as, in the higher individual organisms, the aggregated cells which form the embryo, and for some time retain their separateness, gradually give place to structures in which the cell-form is

masked and almost lost; so in the social organism, the family groups and compound family groups which were the original components, eventually lose their distinguish-ableness, and there arise structures formed of mingled individuals belonging to many different stocks.

§ 321. A question of great interest, which has immediate bearings on policy, remains – Is there auy limit to this disintegration of the family ?

Already in the more advanced nations, that process which dissolved the larger family-aggregates, dissipating the tribe and the gens and leaving only the family proper, has long been completed; and already there have taken place partial disintegrations of the family proper. Along with changes which substituted individual responsibility for family responsibility in respect of offences, have gone changes which, in some degree, have absolved the family from responsibility for its members in other respects. When by Poor Laws public provision was made for children whom their parents did not or could not adequately support, society in so far assumed family-functions; as also when undertaking, in a measure, the charge of parents not supported by their children. Legislation has of late further relaxed family-bonds by relieving parents from the care of their children's minds, and replacing education under parental direction by education under governmental direction ; and where the appointed authorities have found it needful partially to clothe neglected children before they could be taught, and even to whip children by police agency for not going to school, they havo still further substituted national responsibility for the responsibility of parents. This recognition of the individual, rather than the family, as the social unit, has indeed now gone so far that by many the paternal duty of the State is assumed as self-evident; and criminals are called " our failures."

See *Times,* 28tb Feb., 1877.

Are these disintegrations of the family parts of a normal progress? Are we on our way to a condition like that reached by sundry Socialist bodies in America and elsewhere? In these, along with community of property, and along with something approaching to community of wives, there goes community in the care of offspring: the family is entirely disintegrated. We have made sundry steps towards such an organization. Is the taking of those which remain only a matter of time ?

To this question a distinct answer is furnished by those biological generalizations with which we set out. In Chap. II were indicated the facts that, with advance towards the highest nnimal types, there goes increase of the period during which offspring are cared for by parents; that in the human race parental care, extending throughout childhood, becomes elaborate as well as prolonged ; and that among the highest members of the highest races, it continues into early manhood : providing numerous aids to material welfare, taking precautions for moral discipline, and employing complex agencies for intellectual culture. Moreover, we saw that along with this lengthening and strengthening of the solicitude of parent for child, there grows up a reciprocal solicitude of child for parent. Among even the highest animals of sub-human types, this aid and protection of parents by offspring is absolutely wanting. In the lower human races it is but feebly marked – aged fathers and mothers being here killed and there left to die of starvation; and it becomes gradually more marked as we advance to the highest civilized races. Are we in the course of further evolution to reverse all this ? Have those parental and filial bonds which have been growing closer and stronger during the latter stages of organic development, become untrustworthy ? and is the social bond to be trusted in place of them ? Are the intense feelings which have made the fulfilment of parental duties a source of high pleasure, to be now regarded as valueless; and is the sense of public duty to children at large, to be culti-vated by each man and woman as a sentiment better and more efficient than the parental instincts and sympathies ? Possibly Father Noyes and his disciples at Oneida Creek, will say Yes, to each of these questions; but probably fnv ethers will join in the Yes – even of the many who are in consistency bound to join.

So far from expecting disintegration of the family to go further, we have reason to suspect that it has already gone too far. Probably the rhythm of change, conforming to ita usual law, has carried us from the one extreme a long way towards the other extreme; and a return movement is to be looked for. A suggestive parallel may be named. In early stages the only parental and filial kinship formally recognized was that of mother and child; after which, in the slow course of progress was reached the doctrine of exclusive mala kinship – the kinship of child to mother being ignored; after which there came, in another long period, the establishment of kinship to both. Similarly, from a state in which family- groups were alone recognized and individuals ignored, we are moving towards an opposite state in which ignoring of the family and recognition of the individual goes to the extreme of making, not the mature individual only, the social unit, but also the immature individual; from which extreme we may expect a recoil towards that medinm state in which there has been finally lost the compound family-group, while there is a renovation of the family-group proper, composed of parents and offspring.

§ 322. And here we come in sight of a truth on which politicians and philanthropists would do well to ponder. The salvation of every society, as of every species, depends on the maintenance of an absolute opposition between the regime of the family and the regime of the State.

To survive, every species of creature must fulfil two conflicting requirements. During a certain period each member must receive benefits in proportion to its incapacity. Afterthat period, it must receive benefits in proportion to its capacity. Observe the bird fostering its young or the mammal rearing its litter, and you see that imperfection and inability are rewarded; and that as ability increases, the aid given in food and warmth becomes less. Obviously this Li w that the least worthy shall receive most aid, is essential as a law for the immature: the species would disappear in a generation did not parents conform to it. Now mark what is, contrariwise, the law for the mature. Here individuals gain benefits proportionate to their merits. The strong, the swift, the keen-sighted, the sagacious, profit by their respective superiorities – catch prey or escape enemies as the case may be. The less capable thrive less, and on the average of cases rear fewer offspring. The least capable disappear by failure to get food or from inability to escape. And by this process is maintained that quality of the species which enables it to survive in the struggle for existence with other species. There is thus, during mature life, a reversal of the principle that ruled during immature life.

Already we have seen that a society stands to its citizens in the same relation as a species to its members (§ 277); and the truth which we have just seen holds of the one holds of the other. The law for the undeveloped is that there shall be most aid wjiere there is least merit. The helpless, useless infant, extremely *exigeant,* must from hour to hour be fed, kept warm, amused, exercised. As fast as, during childhood and boyhood, the powers of self-preservation increase, the attentions required and given become less perpetual, but still have to be great. Only with approach to maturity, when some value and efficiency have been acquired, is this policy considerably qualified. But when the young man enters into the battle of life, he is dealt with after a contrary system. The general principle now is that his reward shall be proportioned to his value. Though parental aid, not abruptly ending, may soften the effects of this social law, yet the mitigation of them is but slight; and, apart from parentalaid, this social law is but in a small degree traversed by private generosity. Then in subsequent years when parental aid has ceased, the stress of the struggle becomes greater, and the adjustment of prosperity to efficiency more rigorous. Clearly with a society, as with a species, survival depends on conformity to both of these antagonist principles. Import into the family the law of the society, and let children from infancy upwards have life-sustaining supplies proportioned to their life-sustaining labours, and the society disappears forthwith by death of all its young. Import into the society the law of the family, and let the life-sustaining supplies be great in proportion as the life-sustaining labours are small, and the society decays from increase of its least worthy members and decrease of its most worthy members. It fails to hold its own in the struggle with other societies, which allow play to the natural law that prosperity shall vary as efficiency.

Hence the necessity of maintaining this cardinal distinction between the ethies of the Family and the ethies of the State. Hence the fatal result if family disintegration goes so far that family-policy and state-policy become confused. Unqualified generosity must remain the principle of the family while offspring are passing through their early stages ; and generosity increasingly qualified by justice, must remain its principle as offspring are approaching maturity. Conversely, the principle of the society, guiding the acts of citizens to one another, must ever be, justice, qualified by such generosity as their several natures prompt; joined with unqualified justice in the corporate acts of the society to *its* members. However fitly in the battle of life among adults, the proportioning of rewards to merits may be tempered by private sympathy in favour of the inferior; nothing but evil can result if this proportioning is so interfered with by public arrangements, that demerit profits at the expense of merit.

§ 323. And now to sum up the several conclusions, relatedthough heterogeneous, to which our survey of the family haa brought us.

That there are connexions between polygyny and the militant type and between monogamy and the industrial type, we found good evidence. Partly the relation between militancy and polygyny is entailed by the stealing of women in v. ai ; and partly it is entailed by the mortality of males and resulting surplus of females where war is constant. In societies advanced enough to have some industrial organization, the militant classes remain polygynous, while the industrial classes become generally monogamous ; and an ordinary trait of the despotic ruler, evolved by habitual militancy, is the possession of many wives. Further, we found that even in European history this relation, at first not manifest, is to be traced. Conversely, it was shown that ith development of industrialism and consequent approach to equality of the sexes in numbers, monogamy becomes more general, because extensive polygyny is rendered impracticable. "We saw, too, that there is a congruity between that compulsory co-operation which is the organi/ing principle of the militant type of society, and that compulsory co-operation characterizing the polygynous household ; while with the industrial type of society, organized on the principle of voluntary co-operation, there harmonizes that monogamic union which voluntary domestic co-operation presupposes. Lastly, these relationships were clearly shown by the remarkable fact that in different parts of the world, among different races, there are simple societies in other respects unadvanced, which, quite exceptional in being peaceful, are also exceptional in being monogamic.

Passing to the social aspects of the family, we examined certain current theories. These imply that in the beginning there were settled marital relations, which we have seen is not the fact; that there was at first descent in the male line, which the evidence disproves ; that in the earliest groups there was definite subordination to a head, which is not asustainable proposition. Further, the contained assumptions that originally there was an innate sentiment of filial obedience, giving a root for patriarchal authority, and that originally family connexion afforded the only reason for political combination, are at variance with accounts given us of the uncivilized. Eecognizing the fact that to understand the higher forms of the family we must trace them up from those lowest forms accompanying the lowest social state, we saw how, in a small separated group of persons old and young, held together by some kinship, there was, under the circumstances of pastoral life, an establishing of male descent, an increasing of cohesion, of subordination, of co-operation, industrial and defensive ; and that acquirement of structure became relatively easy, because domestic government and social government became identical. Hence the genesis of a simple society more developed than all preceding simple societies, and better fitted for the composition of higher societies.

Thus originated under special conditions, the patriarchal group with its adapted ideas, sentiments, customs, arrangements, dividing in successive generations into subgroups which, held together in larger or smaller clusters according as the environment favoured, carried its organization with it into the settled state ; and the efficient co-ordination evolved within it, favoured efficient co-ordination of the larger societies formed by aggregation. Though, as we are shown by partially-civilized kingdoms existing in Africa and by extinct American kingdoms, primitive groups of less evolved structures and characterized by another type of family, may form compound societies of considerable she and complexity ; yet the patriarchal group with its higher family-type is inductively proved to be that out of which the largest and most advanced societies arise.

Into communities produced by multiplication of it, the patriarchal group, carrying its supremacy of the eldest male, its system of inheritance, its laws of property, its jointworship of the common ancestor, its blood-feud, its complete subjection of women and children, long retains its individuality. But with these communities as with communities otherwise constituted, combined action slowly leads to fusion; the lines of division become gradually less marked; and at length, as Sir Henry Maine shows, societies which have the family for their unit of composition pass into societies which have the individual for their unit of composition.

This disintegration, first separating compound family groups into simpler ones, eventually affects the simplest: the members of the family proper, more and more acquire individual claims and individual responsibilities. . And this wave of change, conforming to the general law of rhythm, has in modern nations partially dissolved the relations of domestic life and substituted for them the relations of social life. Not simply have the individual claims and responsibilities of young adults in each family, come to be recognized by the State; but the State has, to a considerable degree, usurped the parental functions in respect of children, and, assuming their claims upon it, exercises coercion over them.

On looking back to the general laws of life, however, and observing the essential contrast between the principle of family life and the principle of social life, we conclude that this degree of family disintegration is in excess, and hereafter be followed by partial re-integration.

14

SECTION 14

CHAPTER X.

THE *STATUS* OF WOMEN.

§ 324. Perhaps in no way is the moral progress of mankind more clearly shown, than by contrasting the position of women among savages with their position among the most advanced of the civilized. At the one extreme a treatment of them cruel to the utmost degree bearable; and at the other extreme a treatment which, in some directions, gives them precedence over men.

The only limit to the brutality women are subjected to by men of the lowest races, is their inability to live and propagate under greater. Clearly, ill-usage, under-feeding, and over-working, may be pushed to an extent -which, if not immediately fatal to the women, incapacitates them for rearing children enough to maintain the population; and disappearance of the society follows. Botli directly and indirectly such excess of harshness disables a tribe from holding its own against other tribes; since, besides greatly augmenting tie mortality of children, it causes inadequate nutrition, and therefore imperfect development, of those which survive. But short of this, there is at first no check to the tyranny which the stronger sex exercises over the weaker. Stolen from another tribe, and perhaps stunned by a blow that she may not resist; not simply beaten, but speared about the limbs, when she displeases her savage owner; forced to do all the drudgery and bear all the burdens,

while she has to care for and carry about her children; andfeeding on what is left after the man has done; the woman's sufferings are carried as far as consists with survival of herself and her offspring.

It seems not improbable that by its actions and reactions, this treatment makes these relations of the sexes difficult to change; since chronic ill-usage produces physical inferiority, and physical inferiority tends to exclude those feelings which might check ill-usage. Very generally among the lower races, the females are even more unattractive in aspect than the males. It is remarked of the Puttooahs, whose men are diminutive and whose women are still more so, that" the men are far from being handsome, but the palm of ugliness must be awarded to the women. The latter are hard-worked and apparently ill-fed." Of the inhabitants of the Corea, Giitzlaff says – " the females are very ugly, whilst the male sex is one of the best formed of Asia . . . women are treated like beasts of burden." And for the kindred contrast habitually found, a kindred cause may habitually be assigned: the antithetical cases furnished by such uncivilized peoples as the Kalmucks and Khirghiz, whose women, less hardly used, are better looking, yielding additional evidence.

We must not, however, conclude that this low *status* of vomen among the rudest peoples, is caused by a callous selfishness existing in the males and not equally existing in the females. When we learn that where torture of enemies is the custom, the women out-do the men – when we read of the cruelties perpetrated by the two female Dyak chiefs described by Brooke, or of the horrible deeds which Winwood Eeade narrates of a blood-thirsty African queen; we are shown that it is not lack of will but lack of power which prevents primitive women from displaying natures equally brutal with those of primitive men. A savageness common to the two, necessarily works out the results we see under the conditions. Let us look at these results more closely.

§ 325. Certain anomalies may first be noticed. Even

among the rudest men, whose ordinary behaviour to their women is of the worst, predominance of women is not unknown. Snow says of the Fuegians that he has "seen one of the oldest women exercising authority over the rest of her people;" and of the Australians Mitchell says that old men and even old women exercise great authority. Then we have the fact that among various peoples who hold their women in degraded positions, there nevertheless occur female rulers; as among the Battas in Sumatra, as in Madagascar, and as in the above-named African kingdom. Possibly this anomaly results from the system of descent in the female line. For though under that system, property and power usually devolve on a sister's male children; yet as, occasionally, there is only one sister and she has no male children, the elevation of a daughter may sometimes result. Even as 1 write, I find, on looking into the evidence, a significant example. Describing the Haidahs, Bancroft says : – " Among nearly all of them rank is nominally hereditary, for the most part by the female line. . . . Females often possess the right of chieftainship."

But leaving exceptional facts, and looking at the average facts, we find these to be just such as the greater strength of men must produce, during stages in which the race has not yet acquired the higher sentiments. Numerous examples already cited, show that at first women are regarded by men simply as property, and continue to be so regarded througli several later stages: they are valued as domestic cattle. A Chippewayan chief said to Hearne: –

" Women were made for labour ; one of them can earry, or haul, as much ns two men ean do. They also piteh our teats, make and mend our clothing, keop us warm at night; and, in fact, there is no such thing ns travelling any considerable distance, in this country, without thcir nssistance."

And this is the conception usual not only among peoples so low as these, but among peoples considerably advanced. To repeat an illustration quoted from Barrow, the woman "is

her husband's ox, as a Kalh'r once said to me – she has been bought, he argued, and must therefore labour;" and to the like effect is Shooter's statement that a Kaffir who kills his wife " can defend himself by saying – ' I have bought her once for all.'"

As implied in such a defence, the getting of wives by abduction or by purchase, maintains this relation of the sexes. A woman of a conquered tribe, not killed but brought back alive, is naturally regarded as an absolute possession; as is also one for whom a price has been paid. Commenting on the position of women among the Chibchas, Simon writes – " I think the fact that the Indians treat thcir wives so badly and like slaves, is to be explained by their having bought them." Fully to express the truth, however, we must rather say that the state of things, moral and social, implied by the traffic in women, is the original cause; since the will and welfare of a daughter are as much disregarded by the father who sells her as by the husband who buys her. The accounts of these transactions, in whatever society occurring, show this. Sale of his daughter by a Mandan, is "conducted on his part as a mercenary contract entirely, where he stands out for the highest price he can possibly command for her." Among the ancient Yucatanese, "if a wife had no children, the husband might sell her, unless her father agreed to return the price he had paid." In East Africa, a girl's " father demands for her as many cows, cloths, and brass-wire bracelets as the suitor can afford. . . . The husband may sell his wife, or, if she be taken from him by another man, he claims her value, which is ruled by what she would fetch in the slave-market." Of course where women are exchangeable for oxen or other beasts, they are regarded as equally without personal rights.

The degradation they are subject to during phases of human evolution in which egoism is unchecked by altruism, is, however, most vividly shown by the transfer of a deceased man's wives to his relatives along with other property. Alracdy, in § 302, sundry examples of this have been given 'and many others might be added. Among the Mapuche's " a widow, by the death of her husband, becomes her own mistress, unless he may have left grown-up sons by another wife, in which case she becomes their common concubine, being regarded as a chattel naturally belonging to the heiu of the estate."

Thus recognizing the truth that as long as women continue to be stolen or bought, their human individualities are ignored, let us observe the division of labour that results between the sexes; determined partly by this unqualified despotism of men and partly by the limitations which certain incapacities of women entail.

§ 326. The slave-class in a primitive society consists of the women; and the earliest division of labour is that which arises between them and their masters. Of course nothing more is to be expected among such low peoples as Tas- manians, Australians, Fuegians, Andamanese, Bushmen. Nor do we find any advance in this respect made by the higher hunting races, such as the Comanches, Chippewas, Dacotahs.

Of the occupations thus divided, the males put upon the females whatever these are not disabled from doing by inadequate strength, or agility, or skill. While the men among the now-extinct Tasmanians added to the food only that furnished by the kangaroos they chased, the women climbed trees for opossums, dug up roots with sticks, groped for shell-fish, dived for oysters, and fished, in addition to looking after their children; and there now exists a kindred apportionment among the Fuegians, Andamanese, Australians. Where the food consists mainly of the greater mammals, the men catch and the women carry. We read of the Chippewayans that "when the men kill any large beast, the women are always sent to bring it to the tent;" of the Comanches, that the women " often accompany their husbands in hunting. He kills the game, they butcher andtransport the meat, dress the skins, etc.;" of the Esquimaux, that when the man has " brought his booty to laud, ho troubles himself no further about it; for it would be a stigma on bis character, if he so much as drew a seal out of the water." Though, in these cases, an excuse made is that the exhaustion caused by the chase is great; yet, when we read that the Esquimaux women, excepting the wood-work, " build the houses and tents, and though they have to carry stones almost heavy enough to break their backs, the men look on with the greatest insensibility, not stirring a finger to assist them," we cannot accept the excuse as adequate. Further, it is the custom with these low races, nomadic or semi-nomadic in their habits, to give the females the task of transporting the baggage. A Tasmanian woman often had piled on the other burdens she carried when tramping, " sundry spears and waddies not required for present service;" and the like happens with races considerably higher, both semi-agricultural and pastoral. A Damara's wife " carries his things when he moves from place to place." AVhen the Tupis migrate, all the household stock is taken to the new abode by the females: " the husband only took his weapons, and the wife ... is loaded like a mule." Enumerating their labours among the aborigines of South Brazil, Spix and Martins say the wives " load themselves . . . like beasts of burden;" and Dobrizhoffer writes – " the luggage being all committed to the women, the Abipones travel armed with a spear alone, that they may be disengaged to fight or hunt, if occasion require." Doubtless the reason indicated in the last extract, is a partial defence for this practice, so general with savages when travelling; since, if surprised by ambushed enemies, fatal results would happen were the men not ready to fight on the instant. And possibly knowledge of this may join with the force of custom in making the women themselves uphold the practice, as they do.

On ascending to societies partially or wholly settled, and

a little more complex, we begin to find considerable diversities in the divisions of labour between the sexes. Usually the men are the builders, but not always: the women erect the huts among the Bechuanas, Kaffirs, Damaras, as also do the women of the Outanatas, New Guinea; and sometimes it is the task of women to cut down trees, though nearly always this business falls to the men. Anomalous as it seems, we are told of the Coroados, that " the cooking of the dinner, as well as keeping in the fire, is the business of the men;" and the like happens in Samoa : " the duties of cooking devolve on the men " – not excepting the chiefs. Mostly among the uncivilized and semi-civilized, tra'ding is done by the men, but not always. In Java, " the women alone attend the markets and conduct all the business of buying and selling." So, too, in Angola the women " buy, sell, and do all other things which the men do in other countries, whilst their husbands stay at home, and employ themselves in spinning, weaving cotton, and such like effeminate business." In ancient Peru there was a like division: men did the spinning and weaving, and women the field-work. Again, in Abyssinia " it is infamy for a man to go to market to buy anything. He cannot carry water or bake bread; but he must wash the clothes belonging to both sexes, and, in this function, the women cannot help him." Once more, among certain Arabs "the females repudiate needlework entirely, the little they require being performed by their husbands and brothers."

From a general survey of the facts, multitudinous and heterogeneous, thus briefly indicated, the only definite conclusion appears to be that men monopolize the occupations requiring both strength and agility always available – war and the chase. Leaving undiscussed the relative fitness of women at other times for fighting enemies and pursuing wild animals, it is clear that during the child-bearing period, their ability to do either of these things is so far interfered with, both by pregnancy and by the suckling of infants.

that they are practically excluded from them. Though the Dahomans with their army of amazons, show us that women may be warriors; yet the instance proves that women can be warriors only by being practically unsexed; for, nominally wives of the king, they are celibate, and any unchastity is fatal. But omitting those activities for which women are, during large parts of their lives, physically incapacitated, or into which they cannot enter in considerable numbers without fatally diminishing population, we cannot defme the division of labour between the sexes, further than by saying that, before civilization begins, the stronger sex forces the weaker to do all the drudgery; and that along with social advance the apportionment, somewhat mitigated in character, becomes variously specialized under varying conditions.

As bearing on the causes of the mitigation, presently to be dealt with, we may here note that 'women are better treated where circumstances lead to likeness of occupations between the sexes. Schoolcraft says of the Chippewayans that " they are not remarkable for their activity as hunters; which is owing to the ease with which they snare deer and spear fish ; and these occupations are not beyond the strength of their old men, women, and boys;" and then he also says that "though the women are as much in the power of the men as other articles of their property, they are always consulted, and possess a very considerable influence in the traffic with Europeans, and other important concerns." We read, too, that " among the Clatsops and Chinooks, who live upon fish and roots, which the women are equally expert with the men in procuring, the former have a rank and inflnence very rarely found among Indians. The females are permitted to speak freely before the men, to whom, indeed, they sometimes address themselves in a tone of authority." Then, again, " in the province of Cueba, women accompany the men, fighting by their side and sometimes even leading the van;" and of this same people Wafer says " their husbands are very kind and loving to them. I never knew an

Indian beat his wife, or give her any hard words." A kindred meaning is traceable in a fact supplied by the Dahomans, among whom, sanguinary and utterly unfeeling as they are, the participation of women with men in war goes along with a social *status* much higher than usual; for Burton remarks that in Dahomey " the woman is officially superior, but under other conditions she still suffers from male arrogance."

A probable further cause of improvement in the treatment of women may here be noted. I refer to the obtaining of wives by services rendered, instead of by property paid. The practice which Hebrew tradition acquaints us with in the case of Jacob, proves to be a widely diffused practice. It is general with the Bliils, Gonds, and Hill-tribes of Nepaul; it obtained in Java before Mahometanism was introduced; it was common in ancient Peru and Central America; and among sundry existing American races it still occurs. Obviously, a wife long laboured for is likely to be more valued than one stolen or bought. Obviously, too, the period of service, during which the betrothed girl is looked upon as a future spouse, affords room for the growth of some feeling higher than the merely instinctive – initiates something approaching to the courtship and engagement of civilized peoples. But the facts chiefly to be noted are – first, that this modification, practicable with difficulty among rude predatory tribes, becomes more practicable as there arise established industries affording spheres in which services may be rendered; and, second, that it is the poorer members of the community, occupied in labour and unable to buy their wives, among whom the substitution of service for purchase will most prevail: the implication being that this higher form of marriage into which the industrial class is led, develops along with the industrial type.

And now we are introduced to the general question – What connexion is there between the *status* of women and the type of social organization ?

§ 327. A partial answer was reached when we concluded that there are natural associations between militancy and polygyny and between industrialism and monogamy. For as polygyny implies a low position of women, while monogamy is a pre-requisite to a high position; it follows that decrease of militancy and increase of industrialism, are general concomitants of a rise in their position. This conclusion appears also to be congruous with the fact just observed. The truth that among peoples otherwise inferior, the position of women is relatively good where their occupations are nearly the same as those of men, seems allied to the wider truth that their position becomes good in proportion as warlike activities are replaced by industrial activities ; since, when the men fight while the women work, the difference of occupation is greater than when both are engaged in productive labours, however unlike such labours may be in kind. From general reasons for alleging this connexion, let us now pass to special reasons.

As it needed no marshalling of evidence to prove that the chronic militancy characterizing low simple tribes, habitually goes with polygyny; so, it needs no marshalling of evidence to prove that along with this chronic militancy there goes brutal treatment of women. It will suffice if we glance at the converse cases of simple tribes which are exceptional in their industrialism and at the same time exceptional in the higher positions held by women among them. Even the rude Todas, low as are the sexual relations implied by theii combined polyandry and polygyny, and little developed as is the industry implied by their semi-settled cow-keeping life, furnish evidence. To the men and boys are left all the harder kinds of work, while the wives " do not even step out of doors to fetch water or wood, which ... is brought to them by one of their husbands;" and this trait goes along with thetrait of peacefulness fmd entire absence of the militant type of social structure. Striking evidence is furnished by another of the Hill-tribes – the Bodo and Dhimals. We have seen that among peoples in low stages of culture, these furnish a marked case of non-militancy, absence of the political orga- nization which militancy develops, absence of class-distinctions, and presence of that voluntary exchange of services implied by industrialism ; and of them, monogamous as alriady shown, we read – " The Bodo and Dhimals use their wives and daughters well; treating them with confidence and kindness. They are free from all out-door work whatever." Take, again, the Dyaks, who though not without tribal feuds and their consequences, are yet without stable chieftainships and military organization, are predominantly industrial, and have rights of individual property well developed. Though among the varieties of them the customs differ somewhat, yet the general fact is that the heavy out-door work is mainly done by the men, while the women are well treated and have considerable privileges. With their monogamy goes courtship, and the girls choose their mates. St. John says of the Sea Dyaks that " husbands and wives appear to pass their lives very agreeably together;" and Brooke names Mukah as a part of Borneo where the wives close their doors, and will not receive their husbands, unless they procure fish. Then, as a marked case of a simple community having relatively high industrial organization, with elected head, representative council, and the other concomitants of the type, and who are described as " industrious, honest, and peace-loving," we have the Pueblos, who, with that monogamy which characterizes them, also show us a remarkably high *status* of women. For among them not simply is there courtship with exercise of choice by girls – not simply do we read that " no girl is forced to marry against her will, however eligible her parents may consider the match;" but sometimes "the usual order of courtship is reversed: when a girl is disposed to marry she does not wait for a young man to propose to hei, hut selects one to her own liking and consults her father, who visits the parents of the youth and acquaints them with his daughter's wishes."

On turning from simple societies to compound societies, we find two adjacent ones in Polynesia exhibiting a strong contrast between their social types as militant and industrial, and an equally strong contrast between the positions they respectively give to women. I refer to Fijians and Samoans. The Fijians show us the militant structure, actions, and sentiments, in extreme forms. Under an unmitigated despotism there are fixed ranks, obedience the most profound, marks of subordination amounting to worship; there is well organized army with its grades of officers; the lower classes exist only to supply necessaries to the warrior classes, whose sole business is war, merciless in its character and accompanied by cannibalism. And here, along with prevalent polygyny, carried among the chiefs to the extent of from ten to a hundred wives, we find the position of women such that, not only are they, as among the lowest savages, "little better than beasts of burden," and not only may they be sold at pleasure,

but a man may kill and eat his wife if he pleases. Contrariwise, in Samoa the type of the regulating system has become in a considerable degree industrial. There is representative government; chieftains, exercising authority under considerable restraint, are partly elective j the organization of industry is so far developed that there are journeymen and apprentices, payment for labour, and even strikes with a rudimentary trades-unionism. And here, beyond that improvement of women's *status* implied by limitation of their labours to the lighter kinds, there is the improvement implied by the fact that "the husband has to provide a dowry, as well as the wife, and the dowry of each must be pretty nearly of equal value," and by the fact that a couple who have lived together for years, make, at separation, a fair division of the property. Of other
  compound societies fit for comparison, I may name two in
America – the Iroquois and the Araucanians. Though these, alike in degree of composition, were both formed by combination in war against civilized invaders; yet, in their social structures, they differed in the respect that the Araucanians became decidedly militant in their regulative organization, while the Iroquois did not give their regulative organization the militant form; for the governing agencies, general and local, were in the one personal and hereditary and in the other representative. Now though these two peoples were much upon a par in the division of labour between the sexes – the men limiting themselves to war, the chase, and fishing, leaving to the women the labours of the field and the house; yet along with the freer political type of the Iroquois there went a freer domestic type; as shown by the facts that the women had separate proprietary rights, that they took with them the children in cases of separation, and that marriages were arranged by the mothers.

The highest societies, ancient and modern, are many of them rendered in one way or other unfit for comparisons. In some cases the evidence is inadequate; in some oases we know not what the antecedents have been; in some cases the facts have been confused by agglomeration of different societies; and in all cases the co-operating influences have increased in number. Concerning the most ancient ones, of which we know least, we can do no more than say that the traits presented by them are not inconsistent with the view here set forth. The Accadians, who before reaching
  that height of civilization at which phonetic writing was achieved, must have existed in a settled populous state for a vast period, must have therefore had for a vast period a considerable industrial organization ; and it is probable that during such period, being powerful in comparison with wandering tribes around, their social life, little perturbed by enemies, was substantially peaceful. Hence there is no incongruity in the fact that they are shown by their records to have given their women a relatively high *status*. Wivesowned property, and the honouring of mothers was especially enjoined by their laws. Of the Egyptians some
  thing similar may be said Their earliest wall-paintings show us a people far advanced in arts, industry, observances, mode of life. The implication is irresistible that before the stage thus exhibited, there must have been a Ion"' era of risin
  civilization ; and their pictorial records prove that they had long led a life largely industrial. So that though the militant type of social structure evolved during the time of their consolidation, and made sacred by their form of religion, continued; yet industrialism had become an important factor, influencing greatly their social

arrangements, and diffusing its appropriate sentiments and ideas. Coucomitantly the position of women was relatively good. Though polygyny existed it was unusual; matrimonial regulations were strict and divorce difficult; " married couples lived in full community ;" women shared in social gatherings as they do in our own societies; in sundry respects they had precedence over men; and, in the words of Ebers, " many other facts might be added to prove the high state of married life."

Ancient Aryan societies illustrate well the relationship between the domestic *rAjime* and the political *rdyime*. The despotism of an irresponsible head, which characterizes the militant type of structure, characterized alike the original patriarchal family, the cluster of families having a common ancestor, and the united clusters of families forming the early Aryan community. As Mommsen describes him, the early Roman ruler once in office, stood towards the citizens in the same relation that the father of the family did to wife, children, and slaves. " The regal power had not, and could not have, any external checks imposed upon it by law: the master of the community had no judge of his acts within the community, any more than the house-father had a judge within his household. Death alone terminated his power." I'rom this first stage, in which the political head was absolute, and absoluteness of the domestic head went to theextent of life-and-death power over his wife, the advance towards a higher *status* of women was doubtless, as Sir H. Maine contends, largely caused hy that disintegration of the family which went along with the progressing union of smaller societies into larger ones effected by conquest. But though successful militancy thus furthered female emancipation, it did so only by thereafter reducing the relative amount of militancy; and the emancipation was really associated with an average increase of industrial structures and activities. As before pointed out, militancy is to be measured not so much by success in war as by the extent to which war occupies the male population. Where all men are warriors and the work is done entirely by women, militancy is the greatest. The introduction of a class of males who, joining in productive labour, lay the basis for an industrial organization, qualifies the militancy. And as fast as the ratio of the free industrial class to the militant class increases, the total activities of the society must be regarded as more industrial and less militant. Otherwise, this truth is made manifest on observing that when many small hostile societies are consolidated by trinmph of the strongest, the amount of fighting throughout the area occupied becomes less, though the conflicts now from time to time arising with neighbouring larger aggregates may be on a greater scale. This is clearly seen on comparing the ratio of fighting men to population among the early Romans, with the ratio between the armies of the Empire and the number of people included in the Empire. And there is the further fact that the holding together of these compound and doubly-compound societies eventually formed by conquest, and the efficient co-operation of their parts for military purposes, itself implies an increased development of the industrial organization. Vast armies carrying on operations at the periphery of an extensive territory, imply a large working population, a considerable division of labour, and good appliances for transferring supplies : the sustaining and distributing systems must be well elaboratedbefore great militant sttuctures can be worked. So that this disintegration of the patriarchal family, and consequent emancipation of women, which went along with growth of the Roman Empire, really had for its concomitant a development of the industrial organization.

§ 328. In other ways a like relation of cause and effect is shown us during the progress of European societies since Roman times.

Respecting the *statu-s* of women in mediaeval Europe, Sir Henry Maine says : –

" There ean be no serious question that, in its ultimate result, the disruption of the Roman Empire wns very unfavourable to the personal and proprietary liberty of women. I purposely say ' in its ultimate result," in order to avoid a learned controversy ns to thcir position under purely Teutonic customs. "

Now leaving open the question whether this conclusion applies beyond those parts of Europe in which institutions of Roman origin were least affected by those of Germanic origin, we may, I think, on contrasting the condition of things before the fall of the Empire and the condition after, infer a connexion between this decline in the *status* of women and a return to greater militancy. For while Rome dominated over the populations of large areas, there existed throughout them a state of comparative internal peace; whereas its failure to maintain subordination was followed by universal warfare. And then, after that decline in the position of women which accompanied this retrograde increase of militancy, the subsequent improvement in their position went along with aggregation of small feudal governments into larger ones; which had the result that within the consolidated territories the amount of diffused fighting decreased.

Comparisons between the chief civilized nations as now existing, yield verifications. Note, first, the fact, significant of the relation between political despotism and domestic despotism, that, according to Legouve, the first Napoleonsaid to the Council of State "un mari doit avoir un empire absolu sur les actions de sa femme;" and sundry provisions of the Code, as interpreted by Pothier, cany out this dictum. Further, note that, according to the Vicomte de Se'gur, the position of women in France declined under the Empire; and " it was not only in the higher ranks that this nullity of women existed. . . . The habit of fighting filled men with a kind of pride and asperity which made them often forget even the regard which they owed to weakness." Passing over less essential contrasts now presented by the leading European peoples, and considering chiefly the *status* as displayed in the daily lives of the poor rather than tho rich, it is manifest that the mass of women have harder lots where militant organization and activity predominate, than they have where there is a predominance of industrial organization and activity. The sequence observed by travellers in Africa, that in proportion as the men are occupied in war more labour falls on the women, is a sequence which both France and Germany show us. Social sustentation has to be achieved in some way; and the more males are drafted off for military service, the more females must be called on to fill their places as workers. Hence the extent to which in Germany women are occupied in rough out-of-door tasks – digging, wheeling, carrying burdens; hence the extent to which in France heavy field-operations are shared in by women. That the English housewife is less a drudge than her German sister, that among shopkeepers in England she is not required to take so large a share in the business as she is among shopkeepers in France, and that in England the out-of-door work done by women is both smaller in quantity and lighter in kind than on the Continent, is clear; as it is clear that this difference is associated with a lessened demand on the male population for purposes of offence and defence. And then there may be added the fact of kindred meaning, that in the United States, where till the late war the degree of militancy had been so small, and tha

industrial type of social structure and action so predominant, women have reached a higher *status* than anywhere else.

Evidence furnished by existing Eastern nations supports this view. China, with its long history of wars causing consolidations, dissolutions, re-consolidations, etc., going back more than 2,000 years B. C., and continuing during Tatar and Mongol conquests to be militant in its activities, has, notwithstanding industrial growth, retained the militant type of structure; and absolutism in the State has been accompanied by absolutism in the family, qualified in the one as in the other, only by the customs and sentiments which industrialism has fostered: wives are bought; concubinage is common among the rich; widows are sometimes sold as concubines by fathers-in-law ; and women join in hard work, sometimes to the extent of being harnessed to the plough; while, nevertheless, this low *status* is practically raised by a public opinion which checks the harsh treatment legally allowable. Japan, too, after passing through long periods of internal conflict, acquired an organization completely militant, under which political freedom was unknown, and then showed a simultaneous absence of freedom in the household – buying of wives, concubinage, divorce at mere will of the husband, crucifixion or decapitation for wife's adultery; while, along with the growth of industrialism characterizing the later days of Japan, there went such improvement in tho legal *status* of women that the husband was no longer allowed to take the law into his own hands in case of adultery; and now, though women are occasionally seea using the flail, yet mostly the men "leave their women to the lighter work of the house, and perform themselves the harder out-door labour."

§ 329. It is of course difficult to generalize phenomena into the production of which enter factors so numerous and involved – character of race, religious beliefs, surviving customs and traditions, degree of culture, etc.; and doubtlessthe many co-operating causes give rise to incongruities which qualify somewhat the conclusion drawn. But, on summing up, we shall I think see it to be substantially true.

The least entangled evidence is that which most distinctly presents this conclusion to us. Remembering that nearly all simple uncivilized societies, having chronic feuds with their neighbours, are militant in their activities, and that their women are extremely degraded in position, the fact that in the exceptional simple societies which are peaceful and industrial, there is an exceptional elevation of women, almost alone suffices as proof: neither race, nor creed, nor culture, being in these cases an assignable cause.

The connexions which we have seen exist between militancy and polygyny and between industrialism and monogamy, exhibit the same truth under another aspect; since polygyny necessarily implies a low *status* of women, and monogamy, if it does not necessarily imply a high *status,* is an essential condition to a high *status.*

Further, that approximate equalization of the sexes in numbers which results from diminishing militancy and increasing industrialism, conduces to the elevation of women; since, in proportion as the supply of males available for carrying on social sustentation increases, the labour of social sustentation falls less heavily on the females. And it may be added that the societies in which these available males undertake the harder labours, and so, relieving the females from undue physical tax, enable them to produce more and better offspring, will, other things equal, gain in the struggle for existence with societies in which the women are not thus relieved. Whence an average tendency to the spread of societies in which the *status* of yomen is improved.

There is the fact, too, that the despotism distinguishing a community organized for war, is essentially connected with despotism in the household; while, conversely, the freedom which characterizes public life in an industrial community, naturally characterizes also the accompanying private life. In the one case compulsory co-operation prevails in both; in the other case voluntary co-operation prevails in both.

By the moral contrast we are shown another face of the same fact. Habitual antagonism with, and destruction of, foes, sears the sympathies; while daily exchange of products and services among citizens, puts no obstacle to increase of fellow-feeling. And the altruism which grows with peaceful co-operation, ameliorates at once the life without the household and the life within the household.

Since this chapter was written, I have met with a striking verification in the work of Mr. W. Mattieu Williams, – *Through Norwag with Lidies.* He says, " there are no people in the world, however refined, among whom the relative position of man and woman is more favourable to the latter than among the Lapps." After giving evidence from personal observation, he asks the reason, saving: – -" *is* it beeause the men are not warriors ? . . . They hove no soldiers, fight no battles, either with outside foreigners, or between the various tribes and families among themselves. ... In spite of their wretched huts, their dirty faces, their primitive clothing, their ignorance of literature, art, and science, they rank above us in the highest nlement of true civilization, the moral element; and all the military nations of tho world may stand uncovered beforo them " (pp. 163-3).

15

SECTION 15

CHAPTER XL

THE *STATUS* OF CHILDREN.

§ 330. That brutes, however ferocious, treat their offspring tenderly, is a familiar fact; and that tenderness to offspring is shown by the most brutal of mankind, is a fact quite congruous with it . An obvious explanation of this seeming anomaly exists. As we saw that the treatment of women by men cannot pass a certain degree of harshness without causing extinction of the tribe; so here, we may see that the tribe must disappear unless the love of progeny is strong. Hence we need not be surprised when Mouat, describing the Andaman Islanders, says " Mincopie parents show their children the utmost tenderness and affection ;" or when Snow says of the Fuegians that both sexes are much attached to their offspring ; or when Sturt describes Australian fathers and mothers as behaving to their little ones with much fondness. Affection intense enough to prompt great self-sacrifice, is, indeed, especially requisite under the conditions of savage life, which render the rearing of young difficult; and maintenance of such affection is insured by the dying out of families in which it is deficient.

But this strong parental love is, like the parental love of animals, very irregularly displayed. As among brutes the philoprogenitive instinct is occasionally suppressed by the desire to kill, and even to devour, their young ones ; so among primitive men this instinct is now and again over-ridden byimpulses temporarily excited. Though attached to their offspring, Australian mothers, when in danger, sometimes desert them; and if we may believe Angas, men have been known to bait their hooks with the flesh of boys they have killed Notwithstanding their marked parental affection, Fuegians sell their children for slaves. Among the Chonos Indians, a father, though doting on his boy, will kill him in a fit of auger for an accidental offence. Everywhere among the lower races we meet with like incongruities. Falkner, while describing the paternal feelings of Patagonians as very strong, says they often pawn and sell their wives and little ones to the Spaniards for brandy. Speaking of the Sound Indians and their children, Bancroft says they " sell or gamble them away." The Pi-Edes " barter their children to the Utes proper, for a few trinkets or bits of clothing." And among the Macusi, " the price of a child is the same as the Indian asks for his dog."

This seemingly-heartless conduct to offspring, often arises from the difficulty experienced in rearing them. To it the infanticide Bo common among the uncivilized and semi- civilized, is mainly due – the burial of living infants with mothers who have died in childbirth; the putting to death one out of twins; the destruction of younger children when there are already several. For these acts there is an excuse like that commonly to be made for killing the sick and old. When, concerning the desertion of their aged members by wandering prairie tribes, Catlin says – " it often becomes absolutely necessary in such cases that they should be left, and they uniformly insist upon it, saying, as this old man did, that they are old and of no further use, that they left their fathers Jn the same manner, that they wish to die, and their children must not mourn for them " – when, of the " inhabitants bordering on Hudson's Bay," Heriot tells us that in his old age " the father usually employed as his executioner, the son who is most dear to him " – when, in Kane, we read of the Assiniboine chief who " killed his own mother," because, being " old and feeble," she " asked him to take pity oil her and end. her misery ;" there is suggested the conclusion that as destruction of the ill and infirm may lessen the total amount of suffering to be borne under the conditions of savage life, so may infanticide, when the region is barren or the mode of life hard. And a like plea may be urged in mitigation of judgment on savages who sell or barter away their children.

Generally, then, among uncivilized peoples, as among animals, instincts and impulses are the sole incentives and deterrents. The *status* of a primitive man's child is like that of a bear's cub. There is neither moral obligation nor moral restraint; but there exists the unchecked power to ioster, to desert, to destroy, as love or anger moves.

§ 331. To the yearnings of natural affection are added in early stages of progress, certain motives, partly personal, partly social, which help to secure the lives of children ; but which, at the same time, initiate differences of *status* between children of different sexes. There is the desire to strengthen the tribe in war; there is the wish to have a future avenger on individual enemies ; there is the anxiety to leave behind, one who shall perform the funeral rites and continue the periodic oblations at the grave.

Inevitably the urgent need to augment the number of warriors leads to preference for male children. On reading Of such a militant race as the Chechemecas, that they " like much their male children, who are brought up by their fathers, but they despise and hate the daughters;" or of the Panches, that when " a wife bore her first girl child, they killed the child, and thus they did with all the girls born before a male child ;" we are shown the effect of this desire for sons ; and everywhere we find it leading either to destruction of daughters, or to low estimation and ill-usage of them. Through long ascending stages ot' progress the desire thus arising persists; as witness the statement of Herodotus, thatevery Persian prided himself on the number of his sons, and that an annual prize was given by the monarch to the one who could show most sons living. Obviously the social motive, thus coming in aid of the parental motive, served to raise the *status* of male children above that of female.

A reason for the care of sons implied in the passage of *Ecdesiasticus* which says, " he left behind him an avenger against his enemies," is a reason which has weighed with all races in barbarous and semi-civilized states. The sacred duty of blood-revenge, earliest of recognized obligations among men, survives so long as societies remain predominantly warlike; and it generates an anxiety to have a male representative who shall retaliate upon those from whom injuries have been received. This bequest of quarrels to be fought out, traceable down to recent times among so-called Christians, as in the will of Brantome, has of course all along raised the value of sons, and has put upon the harsh treatment of them, a check not put upon the harsh treatment of daughters : whence a further differentiation of *status.*

The development of ancestor-worship, which, requiring each man to make sacrifices at the tombs of his immediate and more remote male progenitors, implies anticipation of like sacrifices to his own ghost by his son, initiates yet another motive for cherishing male children rather than females. The effects of this motive are at the present time Bhown us by the Chinese ; among whom the death of an only son is especially lamented, because there will be no one to make offerings at the grave, and among whom the peremptory need for a son, hence arising, justifies the taking of a concubine, though, if a person has sons by his wife (for daughters never enter into the account) it is considered derogatory to take a handmaid at alL On recalling Egyptian wall-paintings and papyri, and the like evidence furnished by Assyrian records, showing that sacrifices to ancestors were made by their male descendants – on remembering, too, that among ancient Aryans, whether Hindu, Greek, or Eoman, thu

daughter was incapable of performing such rites; we are shown how this developed form of the primitive religion, while it strengthened filial subordination, added an incentive to parental care – of sons but not of daughters.

In brief, then, the relations of adults to young among human beings, originally like those among animals, began to assume higher forms under the influence of the several desires – first to obtain an aider in fighting enemies, second to provide an avenger for injuries received, and third to leave behind one who should administer to welfare after death: motives which, strengthening as societies passed through their early stages, enforced the claims of male children, but not those of female children. And thus we again see how intimate is the connexion between militancy of the men and degradation of the women.

§ 332. Here we are introduced to the question – what relation exists between the *status* of children and the form of social organization ? To this the reply is akin to one given in the last chapter; namely that mitigation of the treatment of children accompanies transition from the militant type to the industrial type.

Those lowest social states in which offspring are now idolized, now killed, now sold, as the dominant feeling prompts, are states in which hostilities with surrounding tribes are chronic. This absolute dependence of progeny on parental will, is shown whether the militancy is that of archaic groups or that of groups higher in structure. In the latter as in the former, there exists that life-and-death power over children which is the negation of all rights and claims On comparing children's *status* in the rudest militant tribes, with their *status* in militant tribes which are patriarchal and compounded of the patriarchal, all we can say to the advantage of the last is that the still-surviving theory becomes qualified in practice, and that qualification of it increases as industrialism grows. Note the evidence.

The Fijians, intensely despotic in government and ferocious in war, furnish an instance of extreme abjectness in the position of children. Infanticide, especially of females, reaches nearer two-thirds than one-half; they " destroy their infants from mere whim, expediency, anger, or indolence;" and " children have been offered by the pcople of their own tribe to propitiate a powerful chief," not for slaves but fur food. A sanguinary warrior-race of Mexico, the Chichimees, yield another example of excessive parental power: sons " cannot marry without the consent of parents; if a young man violates this law . . . the penalty is death." By this instance we are reminded of the domestic condition among the ancient Mexicans (largely composed of conquering cannibal Chichimees), whose social organization was highly militant in type, and of whom Clavigero says – "their children were bred to stand so much in awe of their parents, that even when grown up and married, they hardly durst speak before them." In ancient Central America family-rule was similar; and in ancient Peru it was the law "that sons should obey and serve their fathers until they reached the age of twenty-five."

If we now turn to the few uncivilized and semi-civilized societies which are wholly industrial, or predominantly industrial, we find children, as we found women, occupying much higher positions. Among the peaceful Bodo and Dhimals, "infanticide is utterly unknown;" daughters are treated "with confidence and kindness:" to which add the reciprocal trait that "it ia deemed shameful to leave old parents entirely alone." With the nearly-allied Kocch, similarly peaceful, when marriages are being arranged there is a "consulting the destined bride." The Dyaks, again, largely industrial and having an unmilitant social structure, yield the fact that " infanticide is rarely heard of," as well as the facts before named under another head, that children have the freedom implied by regular courtship, and that girls choose their mates. We are told of the Samoans, wholire more industrial in social type than neighbouring Malayo-Polynesiuns, that infanticide after birth is unknown, and that children have the degree of independence implied by elopements, when they cannot obtain parental assent to their marriage. Similarly of the Negritos inhabiting the island of Tanna, where militancy is slight and there are no pronounced chieftainships, Turner writes: – " the Tannese are fond of their children. No infanticide there. They allow them every indulgence, girls as well as boys." Lastly, there is the case of the industrial Pueblos, whose children were unrestrained in marriage, and by whom, as we have seen, daughters were especially privileged.

Thus with a highly militant type there goes extreme subjection of children, and the *status* of girls is still lower than that of boys; while in proportion as the type becomes iion-militant, there is not only more recognition of children's claims, but the recognized claims of boys and girls approach towards equality.

§ 333.   Kindred evidence is supplied by those societies which, passing through the patriarchal forms of domestic and political government, have evolved into large nations. Be the race Turanian, Semitic, or Aryan, it shows us the same connexion between political absolutism over subjects and domestic absolutism over children.

In China destruction of female infants is common ; parents sell their children to be slaves; in marriage " the parents of the girl always demand for their child a price." " A union prompted solely by love would be a monstrous infraction of the duty of filial obedience, and a predilection on the part of a female as heinous a crime as infidelity." Their maxim is that, as the Emperor should have the care of a father for his people, a father should have the power of a sovereign over his family. Meanwhile it is observable that this legally-unlimited paternal power descending from militant times, and persisting along with the militant type of socialstructure, has come to be qualified in practice by sentiments which the industrial type fosters. Infanticide, reprobated by proclamation, is excused only on the plea of poverty, joined with the need for rearing a male child; and public opinion puts checks on the actions of those who buy children. "With that militant organization which,

during early wars, became highly developed among the Japanese, similarly goes great filial subjection. Mitford admits that needy people " sell their children to be waitresses, singers, or prostitutes;" and Sir Rutherford Alcock, too, says that parents " have undoubtedly in some cases, if not in all, the power to sell their children." It may be added that the subordination of young to old irrespective of sex, is greater than the subordination of females to males ; for abject as is the slavery of wife to husband, yet, after his death, the widow's power " over the son restores the balance and redresses the wrong, by placing woman, as the mother, far above man, as the son, whatever his age or rank." And the like holds among the Chinese.

How among primitive Semites the father exercised capital jurisdiction, and how along with this there went a lower *status* of girls than of boys, needs no proof. But as further indicating the parental and filial relation, I may name the fact that children were considered so much the property of the father, that they were seized for his debts (2 *A'inys* iv. 1; *Job* xxiv. 9); also the fact that selling of daughters was authorized *(Exodus* xxi. 7); also the fact that injunctions respecting the treatment of children referred exclusively to their father's benefit: instance the reasons given in *Hcclesias- ticus,* chap, xxx., for chastising sons. Though some qualification of paternal absolutism arose during the later settled stages of the Hebrews, yet along with persistence of the militant type of government there continued extreme filial subordination.

Already in the chapter on the Family, when treating of the Romans as illustrating both the social and domesticorganization possessed by the Aryans when conquering Europe, something has been implied respecting the *status* of children among them. In the words of Mommsen, relatively to the father, " all in the household were destitute of legal rights – the wife and child no less than the bullock or the slave." He might expose his children. The religious prohibition which forbade it, "so far as concerned all the sons – deformed births excepted – and at least the first daughter," was without civil sanction. He "had the right and duty of exercising over them judicial powers, and of punishing them as he deemed fit, in life and limb." He might also sell his child. And then mark that the same industrial development which we saw went along with improvement in the position of women during growth of the Roman Empire, went along with improvement in the position of children. I may add that in Greece there were allied manifestations of paternal absolutism. A man could bequeath his daughter, as he could also his wife.

§ 334. If, again, we compare the early states of existing European peoples, characterized by chronic militancy, with their later states, characterized by a militancy less constant and diffused, and an increased industrialism, differences of like significance meet us.

We have the statement of C; esar concerning the Celts of Gaul, that fathers " do not permit their children to approach them openly until they have grown to manhood." In the Merovingian period a father could sell his child, as could also a widowed mother – a power which continued down to the ninth century or later. Under the decayed feudalism which preceded the French Revolution, domestic subordination especially among the aristocracy, was stiJl such that, Chateaubriand says – "my mother, my sister, and myself, transformed into statnes by my father's presence, used only to recover ourselves after he left the room;" and Taine, quoting Beaumarchais and Restif de la Bretonne, indicaiesthat this rigidity of paternal authority wag general. Then, after the Revolution, the Vicomte de Segur writes: – " Among our good forefathers a man of thirty was more in subjection to the head of the family than a child of eighteen is now."

Our own history furnishes kindred evidence. Describing manners in the fifteenth century, Wright says: – " Young ladies, even of great families, were brought up not only strictly, but even tyrannically. . . . The parental authority was indeed carried to an almost extravagant extent." Down to the seventeenth century, " children stood or knelt in trembling silence in the presence of their fathers and mothers, and might not sit without permission." The literature of even the last century, alike by the use of " sir " and "madam" in addressing parents, by the authority pnients assumed in arranging marriages for their children, and by the extent to which sons and still more daughters, recognized the duty of accepting the spouses chosen, shows us a persistence of filial subordination proportionate to the political subordination. And then, during this century, along with immense development of industrialism and the correlative progress towards a freer type of social organization, there has gone a marked increase of juvenile freedom ; as shown by a greatly moderated parental dictation, by a mitigation of punishments, and by that decreased formality of domestic intercourse which has accompanied the changing of fathers from masters into friends.

Differences having like meanings are traceable between the more militant and the less militant European societies as now existing. The relatively-developed industrial type of political organization in England, is associated with a treatment of children less coercive than in France and Germany, where industrialism has modified the political organizations less. Joined to great fondness for, and much indulgence of, the young, there is in France a closer supervision of them, and the restraints on their actions are both stronger and morenumerous : girls at home are never from under maternal control, and boys at school are subject to military discipline. Moreover parental oversight of marriageable children still goes so far that little opportunity is afforded for choice by the young people themselves. In Germany, again, there is a stringency of rule in education allied to the political stringency of rule. As writes to me a German lady long resident in England, and experienced as a teacher, – " English children are not tyrannized over – they are *guided* by their parents. The spirit of independence and personal rights is fostered. I can therefore understand the teacher who said he would rather teach twenty German [children] than one English child – I uuderstand him, but I do not sympathize with him. The German child is nearly a slave compared to the English child ; it is therefore more easily subdued by the one in authority."

Lastly come the facts that in the United States, long characterized by great development of the industrial organization little qualified by the militant, parental government has become extremely lax, and girls and boys are nearly on a par in their positions: the independence reached being such that young ladies form their own circles of acquaintances and carry on their intimacies without let or hindrance from their fathers and mothers.

§ 335. As was to be anticipated, we thus find a series of changes in the *status* of children parallel to the series of changes in the *status* of women.

In archaic societies, without laws and having customs extending over but some parts of life, there are no limits to the powers of parents; and the passions, daily exercised in conflict with brutes or men, are restrained in the relations to offspring only by the philoprogenitive instinct.

Early the needs for a companion in arms, for an avenger, and for a performer of sacrifices, add to the fatherly feeling other motives, personal and social, tending to give somethinglike *a. status* to male children ; but leaving female children still in the same position as are the young of brutes.

These relations of father to son and daughter, arising in advanced groups of the archaic type, and becoming more settled where pastoral life originates the patriarchal group, continue to characterize societies that remain predominantly militant, whether evolved from the patriarchal group or otherwise. Victory and defeat, which express the outcome of militant activity, have for their correlatives despotism and slavery in military organization, in political organization, and in domestic organization.

The *status* of children, in common with that of women, rises in proportion as the compulsory co-operation characterizing militant activities, becomes qualified by the voluntary co-operation characterizing industrial activities. We see this on comparing the militant uncivilized peoples "with others that are not militant; we see it on comparing the early militant states of civilized nations with their later more industrial states ; we see it on comparing civilized nations that are now relatively militant with those that are now relatively industrial.

Most conclusively, however, is the connexion shown on grouping the facts antithetically thus : – On the one hand, savage tribes in general, chronically militant, have, ir common with the predominantly militant great nations of antiquity, the trait that a father has life-and-death power over his children. On the other hand, the few uncivilized tribes which are peaceful and industrial, have, in common with the most advanced civilized nations, the traits that children's lives are sacred and that large measures of freedom are accorded to both boys and girls.

16

SECTION 16

CIIAPTEK XIL
JWMKSTIC RETROSPECT AND PROSPECT.

§ 336. Induction has greatly predominated over deduction throughout the foregoing chapters; and readers who have borne in mind that Part II closes with a proposal to interpret social phenomena deductively, may infer either that this intention has been lost sight of or that it has proved impracticable to deal with the facts of domestic life otherwise than by empirical generalization. On gathering together the threads of the argument, however, we shall find that the chief conclusions forced on us by the evidence are those which Evolution implies.

We have first the fact that the genesis of the family fulfils the law of Evolution under its leading aspects. In the rudest social groups nothing to be called marriage exists: the unions are extremely incoherent. Family-groups, each consisting of a mother and such children as can be reared without permanent paternal assistance, are necessarily small and soon dissolve: integration is slight. Within each group the relationships are less definite ; since the children are mostly half-brothers or half-sisters, and the paternity is often uncertain. From such primitive families, thus small, incoherent, and indefinite, there arise, in conformity with the law of Evolution, divergent and redivergent types of families – some characterized by a mixed polyandry and polygny; some that are polyandrous, differentiating into the fraternal and non-

fraternal , some that are polygynous, differentiating into those composed of wives and those composed of a legitimate wife and concubines; some that are monogamous, among which, besides the ordinary form, there is the aberrant form distinguished by a wife married only for a part of each week. Of these genera and species of families, those which are found in advanced societies are the most coherent, most definite, most complex. Not to dwell on intermediate types, we see on contrasting the primitive kind of family-group with that highest kind of family-group which civilized peoples present, how relatively great is the evolution of the last. The marital relation has become quite definite ; it has become extremely coherent – commonly lasting for life; in its initial form of parents and children it has grown larger (the number of children reared by savages being comparatively small); in its derived form, comprehending grandchildren, great grand-children, etc., all so connected as to form a definable cluster, it has grown relatively very large ; and this large cluster consists of members whose relationships are very heterogencous.

Again, the developing human family fulfils, in increasing degrees, those traits which we saw at the outset are traits of the successively-higher reproductive arrangements throughout the animal kingdom. Maintenance of species being the end to which maintenance of individual lives is necessarily subordinated, we find, as we ascend in the scale of being, a diminishing sacrifice of individual lives in the achievement of this end; and as we ascend through the successive grades of societies with their successive forms of family, we find a further progress in the same direction. Human races of the lower types as compared with those of the higher, show us ' l greater sacrifice of the adult individual to the species; ahLe in the brevity of that stage which precedes reproduction, in the relatively-heavy tax entailed by the rearing of children under the conditions of savage life, and in the abridgment of the period that follows: women especially, early bearingchildren and exhausted by the toils of maternity, having a premature old age soon cut short. In superior types of family, juvenile life is also less sacrificed: infanticide, which in the poverty-stricken groups of primitive men is dictated by the necessities of social self-preservation, becomes rarer ; and mortality of offspring otherwise caused, lessens at the same time. Further, along with decreasing sacrifice of adult life there goes increasing compensation for the sacrifice that has to be made: more prolonged and higher pleasures are taken in rearing progeny. Instead of states in which children are early left to provide for themselves, or in which, as among Bushmen, fathers and sous who quarrel try to kill one another, or in which, as Burton says of the East Africans, " when childhood is past, the father and son become natural enemies, after the manner of wild beasts;" there comes a state in which keen interest in the welfare of sons and daughters extends throughout parental life. And then to this pleasurable care of offspring, increasing in duration as the family develops, has to be added an entirely new factor – the pleasurable care of parents by offspring: a factor which, feeble where the family is rudimentary and gaining strength as the family develops, serves in another way to lessen the sacrifice of the individual to the species, and begins, contrariwise, to make the species conduce to the more prolonged life, as well as to the higher life, of the individual.

A fact not yet named remains. Evolution of the higher types of family, like evolution of the higher types of society, lias gone hand in hand with evolution of human intelligence and feeling. The general truth that there exists a necessary connexion between the nature of the social unit and the nature of the social aggregate, and that each continually moulds and is moulded by, the other, is a truth which holds of domestic organization as well as of political organization. The ideas and sentiments which make possible any more advanced phase of associated life, whether in the Family 01 in the State, imply a preceding phase by the experiences anddiscipline of which they were acquired ; and these, again, a next preceding phase ; and so from the beginning. On turning to the *Principles of Psychology* (edition of 1872), containing chapters on " Development of Conceptions," " Sociality and Sympathy," " Ego-Altruistic Sentiments," " Altruistic Sentiments," the reader will find it shown how the higher mental faculties, made possible only iy an environment such as social life furnishes, evolve as this environment evolves – each increment of advance in the one being followed by an increment of advance in the other. And he will see the implication to be that since altruism plays an important part in developed family life, the superior domestic relations have become possible only as the adaptation of man to the social state has progressed.

§ 337. In considering deductively the connexions between the forms of domestic life and the forms of social life ; and in showing how these are in each type of society related to one another because jointly related to the same type of individual character; it will be convenient to deal simultaneously with the marital arrangement, the family structure, the *status* of women, and the *status* of children.

Primitive life, cultivating antagonism to prey and enemies, brute or human – daily yielding the egoistic satisfaction of conquest over alien beings – daily gaining pleasure from acts which entail pain; maintains a type of nature which generates coercive rule, social and domestic. Brute strength glorying in the predominance which brings honour, and unchecked by regard for other's welfare, seizes whatever women fancy prompts and abandons them at will. And children, at the mercy of this utter selfishness, are preserved only when, and as far as, the instinct of parenthood predominates. Clearly, then, weakness of the marital relation, indefinite incoherent forms of family, harsh treatment of women, and infanticide, are naturally concomitants of militancy in its extreme form.

As included in the general thcory of the adaptation of organic beings to their circumstances, this doctrine that the human mind, especially in its moral traits, is moulded by the social state, pervades *Social Staties;* and it especially insisted upon in the chapter entitled " General Cousiderations."

Advance from these lowest social groups, hardly to be called societies, to groups that are larger, or have more sti uc ture, or both, implies increased co-operation. This co-operation may be compulsory or voluntary, or it may be, and usually is, partly the one and partly the other. We have seen that militancy implies predominance of compulsory co-operation, and that industrialism implies predominance of voluntary co-operation. Here we have to observe that it is deductivc-ly manifest, as we have found it inductively true, that the accompanying domestic relations are in each case congruous with the necessitated social relations. The individual nature which, exercising that despotic control, and submitting to that extreme subjection, implied by pronounced militancy in developing societies, – an individual nature at the same time continually hard ened by a life devoted to war, inevitably determines the arrangements within the household as it does the arrangements without it . Hence the disregard of women's claims shown in stealing and buying them; hence the inequality of *status* between the sexes entailed by polygyny; hence the use of women as labouring slaves; hence the life-and-death power over wife and child; and hence that constitution of the family which subjects all its members to the eldest male. Conversely, the type of individual nature developed by voluntary co-operation in societies that are predominantly industrial, whether they be peaceful, simple tribes, or nations that have in great measure outgrown militancy, is a relatively-altruistic nature. The daily habit of exchanging services, or giving products representing work done for money representing work done, is a habit of seeking such egoistic satisfactions only as allow like egoistic satisfactions to those dealt with. There is an enforced respect forothers' claims; there is an accompanying mental representation of their claims, implying, in so far, fellow-feeling; and there is an absence of those repreisions of fellow-feeling involved by coercion. Necessarily, the type of character thus cultivated, while it modifies social actions and arrangements, modifies also domestic actions and arrangements. The discipline which brings greater recognition of the claims of fellow-men, brings greater recognition of the claims of women and children. The practice of consulting the wills of those with whom there is co-operation outside the household, brings with it the practice of consulting the wills of those with whom there is co-operation inside the household. The. marital relation becomes changed from one of master and subject into one of approximately-equal partnership; while the bond becomes less that of legal authority and more that of affection. The parental and filial relation ceases to be a tyranny which sacrifices child to parent, and becomes one in which, rather, the will of the parent subordinates itself to the welfare of the child.

Thus the results deducible from the natures of militancy and industrialism, correspond with those which we have found are, as a matter of fact, exhibited. And, as implying the directness of the alleged connexions, I may here add an instance showing that in the same society the domestic relations in the militant part retain the militant character, while the domestic relations in the industrial part are assuming the industrial character. Commenting on the laws of inheritance in ancient France, as affecting children of different sexes and different ages, Kceuigswarter remarks that "it is always the feudal and noble families which cling to the principle of inequality, while the ideas of equality penetrate everywhere into the *roturier* and *bourgeois* families." Similarly Thierry, speaking of a new law of the thirteenth century, equalizing rights of property between the sexes and among children, says: – " This law of the *bourgeoisie,* opposed to that of thenobles, was distinguished from it by its very essence. It had for its basis natural equity."

§ 338. And now we come to the interesting question – What may be inferred respecting the future of the domestic relations ? We have seen how the law of evolution iu general, has been thus far fulfilled in the genesis of the family. We have also seen how, during civilization, there has been carried still further that conciliation of the interests of the species, of the parents, and of the offspring, which has been going on throughout organic evolution at large. Moreover, we have noted that these higher traits in the relations of the sexes to one another and to children, which have accompanied social evolution, have been made possible by those higher traits of intelligence and feeling produced by the experiences and disciplines of progressing social states. And we have lastly observed the connexions between special traits so acquired and special types of social structure and activity. Assuming, then, that evolution will continue along the same lines, let us consider what further changes may be anticipated.

It is first inferable that throughout times to come, the domestic relations of different peoples inhabiting different parts of the Earth, will continue to be unlike. We must beware of supposing that developed societies will become universal. As with organic evolution, so with super-organic evolution, the production of higher forms does not involve extinction of all lower forms. As superior species of animals, while displacing certain inferior species which compete with them, leave many other inferior species in possession of inferior habitats; so the superior types of societies, while displacing those inferior types occupying localities they can utilize, will not displace inferior types inhabiting barren or inclement localities. Civilized peoples are unlikely to expel the Esquimaux. The Fuegians will probably survive, because their island cannot support a civilized population. It isquestionable whether the groups of wandering Semites who have for these thousands of years occupied Eastern deserts, will be extruded by nations of higher kinds. And perhaps many steaming malarious regions in the Tropies will remain unavailable by races capable of much culture. Hence tho domestic, as well *as* the social, relations proper to the lower varieties of man, are not likely to become extinct. Polyandry may survive in Thibet; polygyny may prevail throughout the future in parts of Africa; and among the remotest groups of Hyperboreans, mixed and irregular relations of the sexes will probably continue.

It is possible, too, that in certain regions militancy may persist; and that along with the political relations natural to it there may survive the domestic relations natural to it . Wide tracts, such as those of North-Eastern Asia, unable to support populations dense enough to form industrial societies of advanced types, will perhaps remain the habitats of societies having those imperfect forms of State and Family which go along with offensive and defensive activities.

Omitting such surviving inferior types, let us limit ourselves to types carrying further the evolution which civilized nations now show. Assuming that among these industrialism will increase and militancy decrease, we have to ask what are the domestic relations likely to co-exist with complete industrialism.

§ 339. The monogfimic form of the sexual relation ia manifestly the ultimate form; and any changes to be anticipated must be in the direction oi' completion and extension of it. By observing what possibilities there are of greater divergence from the arrangements and habits of the padt we shtill see what modifications are probable.

Many acts that are normal with the uncivilized, are, witn the civilized; transgressions and crimes. Promiscuity, once unchecked, has been more and more reprobated as societies have progressed; abduction of women, originally honourable. is now criminal; the marrying of two or more wives, allowable and creditable in inferior societies, has become in superior societies felonious. Hence, future evolution along lines thus far followed, m. iy be expected to extend the monogamic relation by extinguishing promiscuity, and by suppressing such crimes as bigamy and adultery. Dying out of the mercantile element in marriage may also be inferred. -After wife-stealing came wife-purchase; and then followed the usages which made, and continue to make, considerations of property predominate over considerations of personal preference. Clearly, wife-purchase and husband-purchase (which exists in some semi-civilized societies), though they have lost their original gross forms, persist in disguised forms. Already some disapproval of those who marry for money or position is expressed; and this, growing stronger, may be expected to purify the monogamic union by making it in all cases real instead of being in many cases nominal.

As monogamy is likely to be raised in character by a public sentiment requiring that the legal bond shall not be entered into unless it represents the natural bond; so, perhaps, it may be that maintenance of the legal bond will come to be held improper if the natural bond ceases. Already increased facilities for divorce point to the probability that whereas, while permanent monogamy was being evolved, the union by law (originally the act of purchase) was regarded as the essential part of marriage and the union by affection as non-essential; and whereas at present the union by law is thought the more important and the union by affection the less important; there will come a time when the union by affection will be held of primary moment and the union by law as of secondary moment: whence reprobation of marital relations in which the union by affection has dissolved. That this conclusion will be at present unacceptable is likely – I may say, certain. In passing judgment on any arrangement suggested as likely to arise hereafter, nearly all err by considering what would result from the supposed change

other things remaining unchanged. But other things must be assumed to have changed *pari passu*. Those higher sentiments accompanying union of the sexes, which do not exist among primitive men, and were less developed in early European times than now (as is shown in the contrast between ancient and modern literatures), may be expected to develop still more as decline of militancy and growth of industrialism foster altruism; for sympathy, which is the root of altruism, is a chief element in these sentiments. Moreover, with an increase of altruism must go a decrease of domestic dissension. Whence, simultaneously, a strengthening of the moral bond and a weakening of the forces tending to destroy it. So that the changes which may further facilitate divorce under certain conditions, are changes which will make those conditions more and more rare.

There may, too, be anticipated a strengthening of that ancillary bond constituted by joint interest in children. In all societies this is an important factor, which has sometimes great effect among even rude peoples. Falkner remarks that though the Patagonian marriages " are at will, yet when once the parties are agreed, and have children, they seldom forsake each other, even in extreme old age." And this factor must become more efficient in proportion as the solicitude for children becomes greater aud more prolonged; as we have seen that it does with progressing civilization, and will doubtless continue to do.

But leaving opsn the question what modifications of monogamy conducing to increase of real cohesion rather than nominal cohesion, are likely to arise, there is one conclusion we may draw with certainty. Eecurring to the three ends to be subserved in the order of their importance – welfare of species, welfare of offspring, welfare of parents ; and seeing that in the stages now reached by civilized peoples, welfare of species is effectually secured in so far as maintenance of numbers is concerned; the implication is that welfare of offspring must hereafter determine thecourse of domestic evolution. Societies which from generation to generation produce in due abundance individuals who, relatively to the requirements, are the best physically, morally, and intellectually, must become the predominant societies; and must tend through the quiet process of industrial competition to replace other societies.   Consequently, marital relations which favour this result in the greatest degree, must spread; while the prevailing sentiments and ideas must become so moulded into harmony with them that other relations will be condemned as immoral.

§ 340. If, still guiding ourselves by observing the course of past evolution, we ask what changes in the *status* of women may be anticipated, the answer must be that a further approach towards equality of position between the sexes will take place. With decline of militancy and rise of industrialism – with decrease of compulsory co-operation and increase of voluntary co-operation – with strengthening sense of personal rights and accompanying sympathetic regard for the personal rights of others; must go a diminution of the political and domestic disabilities of women, until there remain only such as differences of constitution entail.

To draw inferences more specific is hazardous: probabilities and possibilities only can be indicated. While in some directions the emancipation of women has to be carried further, we may suspect that in other directions their claims have already been pushed beyond the normal limits. If from that stage of primitive degradation in which they were habitually stolen, bought and sold, made beasts of burden, inherited as property, and killed at will, we pass to the stage America shows us, in which a lady wanting a seat stares at a gentleman occupying one until he surrenders it, and then takes it without thanking him; we may infer that the rhythm traceable throughout all changes has carried this to an extreme from which there will be a recoil. The like may be said of some other cases: what were originally concessionshave come to be claimed as rights, and in gaining the character of assumed rights, have lost much of the grace they had as concessions. Doubtless, however, there will remain in the social relations of men and women, not only observances of a kind called forth by sympathy of the strong for the weak irrespective of sex, and still more called forth by sympathy of the stronger sex for the weaker sex; but also observances which originate in the wish, not consciously formulated but felt, to compensate women for certain disadvantages entailed by their constitutions, and so to equalize the lives of the sexes as far as possible.

In domestic life, the relative position of women will doubtless rise; but it seems improbable that absolute equality with men will be reached. Legal decisions from time to time demanded by marital differences, involving the question which shall yield, are not likely to reverse all past decisions. Evenly though law may balance claims, it will, as the least evil, continue to give, in case of need, supremacy to the husband, as being the more judicially-minded. And, similarly, in the moral relations of married life, the preponderance of power, resulting from greater massiveness of nature, must, however unobtrusive it may become, continue with the man.

When we remember that up from the lowest savagery, civilization has, among other results, caused an increasing exemption of women from bread-winning labour, and that in the highest societies they have become most restricted to domestic duties and the rearing of children; ve may be struck by the anomaly that in our days restriction to indoor occupations has come to be regarded as a grievance, and a claim is made to free competition with men in all outdoor occupations. This anomaly is traceable in part to the abnormal excess of women; and obviously a state of things which excludes many women from those natural careers in which they are dependent on men for subsistence, justifies the demand for freedom to pursue independent careers. That hindrances standing in their way should be, and will be, abolished must be admitted. At the same time it must be concluded that no considerable alteration in the careers of women in general, can be, or should be, so produced; and further, that any extensive change in the education of women, made with the view of fitting them for businesses and professions, would be mischievous. If women comprehended all that is contained in the domestic sphere, they would ask no other. If they could see everything which is implied in the right education of children, to a full conception of which no man has yet risen, much less any woman, they would seek no higher function.

That in time to come the political *status* of women may bo raised to something like equality with that of men, seems a deduction naturally accompanying the preceding ones. But such an approximate equalization, normally accompanying a social structure of the completely industrial type, is not a normal accompaniment of social types still partially militant. Just noting that giving to men and women equal amounts of political power, while the political responsibilities entailed by war fell on men only, would involve a serious inequality, and that the desired equality is therefore impracticable while wars continue; it may be contended that though the possession of political power by women might improve a society in which State-regulation had been brought within the limits proper to pure industrialism, it would injure a society in which State-regulation has the wider range characterizing a more or less militant type. Several influences would conduce to retrogression. The greater respect for authority and weaker sentiment of individual freedom characterizing the feminine nature, would tend towards the maintenance and multiplication of restraints. Eagerness for special and immediate results, joined with inability to appreciate general and remote results, characterizing the majority of men and still more characterizing women, would, if women had power, entail increase of coercive measures for achieving present good, at the cost of future evil caused by excess of control.

But there is a more direct reason for anticipating mischief from the exercise of political power by women, while the industrial form of political regulation is incomplete. We have seen that the welfare of a society requires that the ethies of the Family and the ethies of the State shall be kept distinct. Under the one the greatest benefits must be given where the merits are the smallest; under the other the benefits must be proportioned to the merits. For the infant unqualified generosity; for the adult citizen absolute justice. Now the ethies of the family are upheld by the parental instincts and sentiments, which, in the female, are qualified in a smaller degree by other feelings than in the male. Already these emotions proper to parenthood as they exit in men, lead them to carry the ethies of the Family into the policy of the State; and the mischief resulting would be increased were these emotions as existing in women, directly to influence that policy. The progress towards justice in social arrangements would be retarded; and demerit would be fostered at the expense of merit still more than now.

But in proportion as the conceptions of pure equity become clearer – as fast as the *regime* of voluntary co-operation develops to the full the sentiment of personal freedom, with a correlative regard for the like freedom of others – as fast as there is approached a state under which no restrictions on individual liberty will be tolerated, save those which the equal liberties of fellow-citizens entail – as fast as industrialism evolves its appropriate political agency, which, while commissioned to maintain equitable relations among citizens, is shorn of all those powers of further regulation characterizing the militant type; so fast may the extension of political power to women go on without evil. The moral evolution which leads to concession of it, will be the same moral evolution which renders ; t harmless and probably beneficial.

§ 341. No very specific conclusions are to be drawn respecting future changes in the *status* of children.

While an average increase of juvenile freedom may be anticipated, we may suspect that in some cases the increase has already gone too far. I refer to the United States. Besides often unduly subordinating the lives of adults, the independence there allowed to the young, appears to have the effect of bringing them forward prematurely, giving them too early the excitements proper to maturity, and so tending to exhaust the interests of life before it is half spent. Such regulation of childhood as conduces to full utilization of childish activities and pleasures before the activities and pleasures of manhood and womanhood are entered upon, is better for offspring at the same time that it ia better for parents.

How far is parental authority to go? and at what point shall political authority check it ? are questions to be answered in no satisfactory way. Already I have given reasons for thinking that the powers and functions of parents have been too far assumed by the State; and that probably a re-integration of the family will follow its present undue disintegration. Still there remain the theoretical difficulties of deciding how far the powers of parents over children may be carried; to what extent disregard of parental responsibilities is to be tolerated; when does the child cease to be a unit of the family and become a unit of the State. Practically, however, these questions will need no solving; since the same changes of character which bring about the highest form of family, will almost universally prevent the rise of those conflicts between authorities and between obligations, which habitually result from characters of lower types belonging to lower societies.

Moreover, there always remains a security. Whatever conduces to the highest welfare of offspring must more and more establish itself; since children of inferior parents reared in inferior ways, will ever be replaced by children of better parents reared in better ways. As lower creatures at large have been preserved and advanced through the instrumentality of parental instincts; and as in the course of human evolution the domestic relations originating from the need for prolonged care of offspring have been assuming higher forms; and as the care taken of offspring has beell becoming greater and more enduring; we need not doubt that in the future, along with the more altruistic nature accompanymg a higher social type, there will come relations of parents and children needing no external control to ensure their well-working.

§ 342. One further possibility of domestic evolution remains. The last to show itself among the bonds which hold the family together – the care of parents by offspring – is the one which has most room for increase. Absent among brutes, small among primitive men, considerable among the partially civilized, and tolerably strong among the best of those around us, filial affection is a feeling that admits of much further growth; and this is needed to make the cycle of domestic life complete. At present the latter days of the old whose married children live away from them, are made dreary by the lack of those pleasures yielded by the constant society of descendants; but a time may be expected wlien this evil will be met by an attachment of adults to their aged parents, which, if not as strong as that of parents to children, approaches it in strength.

Further development in this direction will not, however, occur under social arrangements which partially absolve parents from the care of offspring. A stronger affection to be displayed by child for parent in later life, must be established by a closer intimacy between parent and child in early life. *No* such higher stage is to be reached by walking in the ways followed by the Chinese for these two thousand years. We shall not rise to it by imitating, even partially, the sanguinary Mexicans, whose children at the age of four, or sometimes later, were delivered over to be educated by the priests. Family-feeling will not be improved by approaching towards the arrangements of the Koossa-Kaffirs, among whom "all children above ten or eleven years old are publicly instructed under the inspection of the chief." This latest of the domestic affections will not be fostered by retrograding towards customs like those of the Andamanese, and, as early as possible, changing the child of the family into the child of the tribe. Contrariwise, such a progress will be achieved only in proportion as mental and physical culture are carried on by parents to an extent now rarely attempted. "When the minds of children are no longer stunted and deformed by the mechanical lessons of stupid teachers – when instruction, instead of giving mutual pain gives mutual pleasure, by ministering in proper order to faculties which are eager to appropriate n't conceptions presented in fit forms – when among adults wide-spread knowledge is joined with rational ideas of teaching, at the same time that in the young there is an easy unfolding of the mind such as is even now shown by exceptional facility of acquisition – when the earlier stages of education passed through in the domestic circle have come to yield, as they will in ways scarcely dreamed of at present, daily occasions for the strengthening of sympathy, intellectual and moral, then will the latter days of life be smoothed by a greater filial care, reciprocating the greater parental care bestowed in earlier life.

17

SECTION 17

APPENDICES APPENDIX A.

FURTHER ILLUSTRATIONS OP PRIMITIVE THOUGHT.

[To *avoid over-burdening the text with illustrations – even now, perhaps, too numerous – I suppressed many that I migh t have added: tome because they seemed superfluous; some because they were too long. Partly to give the more striking of these, I make this Appendix ; bnt chiefy to add evidence which has since come to liijht, verifying certain of the conelusions not adequately supported.*

The foregning paragraph stands as it did in the first edition. I have now to add that in this revised third edition, I have largely increased this Appendix by ineluding many further illustrations which reading and inquiri) have brought to my knowledge. Joined with thosebefore given, tiieseadditional illustrations, as now arranged, form so coherent a body of evidence, that even ly themsulces they would go far to establish the general doctrine set forth in the preceding volume.]

Primitive Credulity. – In tTie genesis of superstitions, a factor difficult to appreciate sufficiently, is the unqnestioning faith with which statements are accepted. Here are some cases.

Of the Coast Negroes, Winterbottom says (vol. i, p. 255) – " So strongly are they persuaded of the effieacy of these meaus of protection [amulets, etc.], that an Afriean, a man of very superior mind, offered to allow a friend of mine, whose accuracy he had just beeu praising, to lire at him with a pistol, charged with ball."

Laird and Oldficld tell us of the Inland Negroes (vol. ii, pp. 10, 11), that a Nuffi woman –

" imagined that she possessed a *maijhong* (charm), which rendered her invulnerable to all edge tools an. i cutting instruments. So positive and convinced was she of the cllicacy of her charm, that she voluntarily assented to hold her leg while some person should strike it with an nxe. The king (or chief) of her town, on hearing this, determined to try the power of her charm, and desired a man to take an axe, and see whether this wonderful *mai)hong* would protect her from its effects. . . . Her leg was laid upon a block, anil a powerful blow given below the knee. . . . To the poor woman's great horivr and the terror of all present, her leg flew to the other side of tha room."

To this absolute confidence in dogmas impressed by seniors during early life, must be ascribed the readiness with whichattendants, wires, and even friends, kill themselves at a funeral that they mav join the deceased in thi; other world. The instance named by Bancroft (vol. i, p. 28) of the Walla Walla chieftain who "caused himself to be buried alive in the grave with the last of his five sons," reminding us of the Fijians and Taunese who go cheerfully to their voluntary deaths, vividly illustrates this trait which makes monstrous creeds possible.

No evidence shakes such beliefs. Disproofs are evaded by- asserting beliefs equally absurd. Speaking of a distant stump mistaken for a man, an Australian said to Mr. Cameron – " That fellow was a gumateh !"ghost], only when you came up he made himself like a stump " *(Anthropol. lust. Juur.,* vol. xiv, p. 863).

Natural Hlvsiuns. – Tn § 53, I argued that these probably aid in strengthening those conceptions of things which the primitive man forms. How they thus play a part is shown in Vauibery's *Sketches of Central Asia,* pp. 72, 73: –

"As we wore crossing the high plateau of Kaflan Kir, which forms part of TTstyort, ruuning towards the north-enst, the horizon was often adorned with the most beantiful Fata Morgana. This phenomenon is undoubtedly to be seen in the greatest perfection in the hot, but dry, atmosphere of the deserts of Central Asia, and affords th most splendid optieal illusious which one ean imagine. 1 was always enchanted with these pictures of cities, towers, and castles dancing in the air, of vast earavans, horsemen engaged in combat, and individual gigantic forms which continually disappeared from one place to reappear in another. As for my nomad companions, they regarded the neigh- bourhoods where these

phenomenaareobservedwitit no little awe. According to their opinion these ure ghosts of men and cities which formerly existed there, und uow at certain times roll abont in the air."

This account recalls the descriptions given by the nneultnrcd among ourselves of the northern aurora: similarly showinar, as it does, that an excited imagination gives definiteness to indefinite forms ; for it does not seem possible that in the remote regions indicated by Vambery, there can have been any such thing as a Fata Morgana derived from an actual city. Among ourselves, especially in troubled times, unusual displays of the Aurora Borealis are described by superstitious people as the conflicts of armies in the heavens.

Not only has hypothesis an effect conspicuous to all in perverting judgment, but it has an effect, less manifest but still decided, in perverting perception. Elsewhere I have given examples of this effect *(Essags,* first series, original edition, p. 412), and doubtless they have been observed by many. If hypothesis thus perturbs perception during states of mental calm, still more does it perturb it during states of mental excitement – especially those produced by fear. The faintest suggestion proceeding either from within or from without, then impostsitself so strongly on the mind tliat trne perception becomes scarcely possible. It needs but to remember that recognition of a thing as such or such, is a mental act in which imagination always plays a large part, by adding to the mere visual impressions those many ideas which constitute a conception of the thing giving the impressions, to see that when, in a state of fright, imagination is put on a wrong track, association readily furnishes all those attributes which are needful to fill up the framework which the appearance yields ; and consciousness once filled with the alarming conception, can with difficulty be brought back to that relatively passive state required for receiving the actual impressions, and rightly interpreting them.

Hence where there exists that primitive credulity exemplified above, the rectifying of a pereeption thus distorted by imagination cannot be expected. Minds having those traits set forth in the chapter entitled " The Primitive Man, Intellectual " – minds which have had no culture giving them tendencies towards criticism and scepticism – minds which have no notion of a natural order, of law, of cause ; are minds which can make no resistance to any suggested idea or interpretation. There is no organized experience to produce hesitation. There is no doubt taking the shape – " This cannot be," or – " That is impossible." Con- Bequeutly, a fancy once having got possession, retains possession, and becomes an accepted fact. If we always carry with us the remembrance of this attitude of mind, we shall see how apparently rensonable to savages are explanations of things which they muke.

Some Early Iuterpretations. – Tf we set out with the truth that the laws of mind are the same throughout the animal kingdom, we shall see that from the behaviour of animals in presence of unfamiliar phenomena, we may obtain some clue to the interpretations which primitive men make of such phenomenn. A brute, even of great power and courage, betrays alarm in presence of a moving object the like of which it has never seen before. The assertion that a tiger has been known to show fear of a mouse in his cage, is made more credible than it would else be by watching a dog when there is placed before him some such creature ns a small crab. Dread of the unknown appears to be a universal emotion – even when the unknown is not at all portentous in character.

Stranger and enemy are almost synonymous in the minds of brutes and of primitive men. By inherited effects of experiences the connexion of ideas haa been made organic ; as an infant in arms shows us when an unfamiliar face makes it cry, though in its own life no evil has ever followed the sight of an unfamiliar lace. While " familiarity breeds contempt" even ofthe vast or of the powerful, nnusualness breeds fear even ol that which is relatively small or feeble.

On the Oyio hand, then, a periodic event which, is intrinsically very imposing, excites but little attention if no mischief has ever been joined with it; while, on the other hand, an event not intrinsically imposing, if it has never before been witnessed, and especially if it seems to show the spontaneity indicative of life, arouses a sense of insecurity. As was shown in Chapter IX of Part I, it is by the spontaneity of their acts that living objects are conspicuously distinguished from dead objects; and hence this trait becomes the sign of an ability to do various things besides that which is witnessed – to do, therefore, something which may prove injurious or fatal.

Carrying with us this conception of the attitnde common to animal intelligence and uninstructed human intelligence, vo shall see why certain regularly recurring phenomena of an astonishing kind, such as the daily appearance and disappearance of the Sun, excite in the primitive man neither surprise nor speculation; at the same time that a phenomenon which unexpectedly breaks tho ordinary course of things by a sound or motion, produces dismay, followed by some vague suggestion of an agent: the agent thought of being one having some likeness to agents diselosed by past experiences. Hence the tendency to ascribe any irregularly recurring phenomenon to a living creature (the actions of living creatures being irregular), and, primarily, to a living creature differing in the least degree possible from living creatures of known kinds. Observe some samples of these early interpretations. Of a place in the Chippevay country, Catlin says –

" Near this spot, also, on a high mound, is the ' *Thunder's nett' (niiJ-du- tounere),* where 'a very small bird sits upon her eggs during fair weather, and the ekies are rent with bolts of thunder at the approach of a storm, which is oceasioned by the hatching of her brood!' " (Geo. CatUn, /':'.— -.-..- *tiont, etc., of the North Ameriean Indians,* Vo!, ii, p. 164.)

Of an allied race, the Ojibways, we read: –

" No one seemed fortunate enough to discover the resort of these great birds, which were ealled *Ah-ne-me-keefl* (Thunders)." . . . "These birdj are seldom seen, but are often heard in the skies, where they fly higher than they once did. . . . They wink, and the (Ire flashes from their eyes." (O. Copwuy, *The Traditional History and Characteristic Skelvket of the Ojibwag Nation,* pp. 110, 113.)

So, too, concerning the Western Indians of North America, Mr. H. A. Boiler tells us that his companion, " the Bob-tiil-

Wolf " –

"said that there was, high in air, far ont of sight, flying continually and never resting, an enirlo of terrible size. . . . He flnps his wings, and loud peals of thunder roll over the prairie; when he winks his eyes, it lighteus." *(Among the Indians,* p. 257.)

By a distant nnallied people, the Karens, the cause of storms iri said to be an animal "with bat-like wings." "When it utters its voice, it thunders, and when it flaps its wings, fire is produced, and it lightens." (Mason, *Jour. Asiatic Socy. Bengal,* xxxiv, Part 2, p. 217.)

Now a thunderstorm bcing one of those incidents characterized by an apparent spontancity suggestive of living ngeney, the question which naturally arises is – "What is the living agent ? " The sky is the region in which this sudden action is witnessed. The living agent is therefore inferred to bo some creature which frequents the sky – a flying creature, bird-like or bat-like. Here let us note two things. First there is formed in the mind a simple association between this incident which by its character suggests living agency, and a living agent such as is commonly seen in the ncighbourhood of its occurrence. Second, the conccived agent is not of the kind we call super, natural – does not belong to a supposed spiritual world; but is a purely natural agent. And the obvious course of thought is one that brings the actions observed into the sarae category with the actions of the living ereatures supposed to be instrnmental : wind bcing ascribed to the flapping of wings, sound to this cause or to a voice, and lightning to the flnshing of eyes.

In a different though allied clnss, stand the interpretations of eclipses. Among uncultured peoples, animals are generally the assigned agents ; and though they are not flying animals, yet they are animals supposed to be in the heavens. Remembering that various savages, as instance the Esquimaux, believe beasts as well as men have access to the sky from the mountain-tops – remembering the Cahroc story given in § 189, of the coyote who thus got among the stars ; we may see how it happens that when imagining some living agent which produces this sudden change in the Sun by taking out a piece from hia side, savages should think of a beast as the cause. Naturally enough "the Ehthoniaus say the sun or moon ' ia bcing eaten'" (Grimm, *Teutonic Myth.,* vol. ii, p. *70") ;* since the bcing eaten accounts alike for the gradual disappearance, and for the sharp outline of the increasing gap made. Wo find kindred interpretations in many places. By the Guaranis "eclipses were held to be occasioned by a jaguar and a great dog, who pursued the sun and moon to devour them " (Southey, *History of Hrazil,* vol. ii, pp. 3/1-2). The Norse mythology tells of " Managarmr (moon- dog); "and on the occasion of an eclipse the Norse "fancied the monster had already got a part of the shining orb between his jaws" (Grimm, *Teutonic Myth.,* vol. ii, p. 7U6). We read of the remote Chiquitos of South America, that " during an eclipse [of the moon] they shoot arrows upward, and cry alond to drive away the dogs, who, they believe, hunt her throughheaven; and when they overtake her, the darkness of the orb 1b caused, by the blood which runs from her wounds" (Sonthey, *History of Brazil.* vol. i, p. 335). Evidently, then, this explanation arises naturally in primitive minds. The kindred, and yet different, explanation of the Iootka-Sound people, who, on the occasion of an eelipse " pointed to the moon, and said that a great cod-fish was endeavouring to swallow her" (Jewitt, *Narrative of Captivity among lie Savages of NoolJia- Sound,* p. 166), and the similar belief current among the Arabs, that a huge fish pursnes the planet which is eelipsed (Niebuhr, *Deseription de I'Arahie,* p. 106), may possibly result from the conception of waters above the firmament in which great fish reside. But, in any case, we see in these interpretations, as in those of thunderstorms, that there is as near an assimilation as may be to the natural actions of natural agents. There is neither any thought of a deity as the cause, nor of anything to be elassed as spiritual power.

Take next the interpretations given in different places of earthquakes. Kaempfer says the Japanese "are of opinion, that the cause of earthquakes is a huge whale's creeping underground" *(Hislori) of Japan, Piuker)on's Voyages,* vol. vii, pp. 6845). Now whether or not it is true that, as Dr. Tlor suggests, the finding of large fossil bones, implying the occasional presence of great animals underground, led to this interpretation, and similarly in Siberia, led to the interpretation of earthquakes as due to motions of underground mammoths – creatures whose bones, and even undecayed bodies, are found imbedded in ice below the surface; it is elear that the same mode of thought is exhibited. This sudden and seemingly- spontaneous motion of the Earth is ascribed to an agent of the elass which habitually exhibits sudden spontancous motions – an animal. And the qnestion – What animal r" being raised, the conclusion is that it must be an animal which exists down below. Explanations elsewhere given betray like trains of ideas. Bancroft says " the Southern California-as believed that when the Creator made the world he fixed it on the back of seven giants, whose movements . . . caused earthquakes" *(Nutira Races of tlie Pacific States,* vol. iii, p. 122). As given by John Bell, a conception of the Lamas was that the Eurth rests on a golden frog; " and whenever this prodigious frog had occasion to scratch its head, or streteh out its foot, that part of the earth immediately above was shaken " *(A Journey from St. PetersbuTyTi to Pekin in the year* 1719. *Pivkerton's Voi). iges,* vol. vii, p. 30y). So, too, by the Norse belief that earthquakes are caused "by the struggles of chained Loki" (Grimm, *Teutonic Myth.,* vol. ii, p. 816) ; as well as by the Fijiim belief that when Dcngeh " turns about or trembles in his cave theearth stages and quakes exceedingly " *(Loliima, or Two Years in Cannibal-land,* by H. Britten, p. 195-6); we are shown that the hypothesis is of the naturalistic elass rather than of the super- naturalistic elass. The effect is ascribed to a living agent conceived as existing where the effect is produced, and operating after the same mechanical manner with known, living agents. The only case I have met with in which agency of this kind is not assigned, serves still better to stow that the phenomenon is elassed with known natural phenomena. Concerning the Esquimaux interpretation of earthquakes, Crantz says – " they imagine that the globe of the earth rests upon pillars, which are now mouldering away by age, so that they frequentlT crack " *(History of Greenland,* i, 211).

From earthquakes we may pass to volcanic eruptions without finding any wider divergence from this form of explanation than is to be expected from the nature of the appearances. Two low races, remote in habitat and type, yield illustrations. In North America " the Koniagas, for example, held that the craters of Alaska were inhabited hy beings mightier than men, and that these sent forth fire and smoke when they heated their sweat-houses, or cooked their food" (B; mcroft, *Native Races, etc.,* vol. iii, p. 122). And among the aborigines of Westein Australia, it is a tradition that " 'once on a time, the In-gnas, who live underground, being very sulky, to spito the poor black fellows, who seem to have the good-will of no one, made great fires and threw up red-hot stones, fire, etc., and thus burned the whole of that country' " *(The Aborigines of Australia.* A. Oldfield, in *Tr. Eth. tiocy.,* N. S., vol. iii, p. 23'2). The only noteworthy uulikeness here, is that beings of the human type are assumed : probably for the reason that they are the only known kinds of beings who can produce fire or make use of it.

For collecting together these interpretations of thunderstorms, eelipses, earth-quakes, and eruptions, my motive has been to show that in primitive thought, events which are of irregular occurrence, snd by this, as well as by their apparent spontaneity, suggest living agents, are ascribed to living agents deviating as little from ordinary ones as may be ; and are devoid of anything like religious idea or sentiment. The beliefs held concerning these events yield no signs of that Nutnre-worship supposed to be innate in the uncivilized; though the portentousuess of the events might be expected to arouse it, did it exist. Nor do they betray the conception of one or many invisible powers of the kind called supernatural among advanced peoples. Though we carelessly group together all absurd ideas of savages under the general name of superstitions, yet, afi we here see, there *is* a significant distinction between these which show norecognition of alleged spiritual beings and those in which such recognition is shown. But now, how does there result transition from the one to the other ? Some interpretations of intermediate kinds will prepare the way for an answer.

The ancient Peruvians fancied Thunder "to bee a man in heaven, with a sling and a mace, and that it is in his power to cause raine, haile, thunder " *(Jos. de Acosta,* vol. ii, p. 304). In Samoa "the chiefs were supposed to go to the heavens and send down lightning, thunder, and rain" (Turner, *Samoa a Hundred Years Ago,* p. 277). And describing the beliefs of the Veddahs (whose gods are the ghosts of relatives), Bailey writes: – "Of thunder they say 'a spirit or a god has cried out'" *(Traus. Eth. Socy. ion.,* N. S., ii, p. 302, and note §). In these cases, then, the living agent conceived is a man who either retains in the heavens his original character, or is in some way transfigured. Concerning eelipses we read that "the Tlascaltees, regarding the sun and the moon as husband and wife, believed eelipses to be domestic quarrels " (Bancroft, *Native Races, etc.,* vol. iii, p. 111). Marsden says of the Sumatraus, that " during an eelipse they made a loud noise with sounding instruments, to prevent one luminary from devouring the other" *(History of Sumatra,* p. l94,). And then among the Polynesians, " some imagined that on an eelipse, the sun and moon rere swallowed by the god which they had by neglect offended. Liberal presents were offered, which were supposed to induce the god to abate his anger, and eject the luminaries of day and night from his stomach." (Ellis, *Polynesian Researches,* 1859, vol. i, pp. 331-2).

Here then, while the appearances are explained as caused by unknown living beings acting in ways allied to those of known living beings, we have, in the introduction here of a transfigured man, and there of a god, as instrumental, a recourse to explanations no longer of the purely natural kind.

Whence comes this new order of supposed beings ? How does there arise in men's minds the idea ot a species of animate power unlike the animate powers they see around them iu beasts and men ? What originates the conception of this supernatural agency which, once adopted, develops so largely as nearly to exelude all other agency ? There is a simple answei. By transition from the dream to the ghost, and from the ghost to the god, there is reached a conceived kind of cause capable of indefinite espnnsion and admitting of all adjustments; and hence serving for explanations of every kind.

Confusion of Dreams with Realities during Ohtidliund. – Occasionally we hear it remarked of dreams that their seeming actuality affected the feelings for some time after awaking: animpression like that, say, of eseape from real danger, continuing after recognition of the fact that the danger wns ideal. The tendency of an extremely vivid dream thus to generate an emotion such as accompanies reality, is one factor in producing' belief in its reality. I have lately met with striking proofs of this. In a company of less than a dozen persons, three testified to having in childhood hnd such vivid dreams of flying down stairs, and bcing impressed so strongly with the experiences as real, that they actually tried to fly down stairs ; and one of them. suffered from an injured ankle consequent on the attempt.

On writing subsequently to the lady in whose family these statements were made, to verify my recollections of them, she gave mo a stoiy which one of her daughters had subseqncntly narrated, showing how literally this daughter had accepted her visions in childhood. Brought up amid much talk about nnimals, she, on one occasion, dreamed that a gorilla, who lived near at hand, gave her something; and, she added – "When I walked up the lane, I used to wonder where the gorilla lived."

Now if dream-experiences and waking experiences are thus confounded by the children of the civilized, notwithstanding the discriminations which they have heard made by adults, and notwithstanding the conception that hns been given to them of mind as an indwelling entity distinct from body; it is obvious that primitive men, lacking this theory of mind, lacking words in which to express many perceivable distinctions, and lacking, too, instruction from the more cultivated, will inevitably confuse dream-thoughts and the thoughts of the waking state. Hence on reading of savages, as for instance the Kamschadales, that the idens of sleeping and waking life are apt to be confounded by them, we shall see that, so far from bcing anomalous, a confounding of them. to a greater or less extent is at first inevitable.

Especially shall we see no difficulty in recognizing the interpretations of primitive conceptions thus yielded, when wo remember that even still, in some of the educated among ourselves, there survives a belief in the reality of bcings seen in dreams ; and that at the present moment there exists a group of highly-cultivated men having for one of thcir objects to collect the narratives of supernatural visitations during sleep.

Drrnms as literally accepted by Savages. – Already in §§ 70, 71, I have variously illustrated the truth that adults among savages, like many children among ourselves, regard as real the adventures gone through, and persons seen, in dreams. The Zulus furnished sundry instances, which will be recalled by this additional one: –

" Why did not our ancestral spirits tell me in a dream that there wassomething which they wsntl, iustead of revealing themselves by coming to kill the child in this way?" (Bp. Callaway, *Tke Religions Systent of the Amazulu,* pp. 371-2.)

And I may add another somewhat different in kind furnished by the mythology of the Mungaians. They say thut " Vatea, the father of gods and men ... in his dreams several times saw a beautiful woman. On one happy occasion he succeeded in elutehing her in his sleep, and thus detained the fair sprite as his wife" (W. W. Gill, *Myths and Songs,* ifcc., pp. 3, 7). But among the most specific and instructive facts exhibiting these primitive conceptions, are those recently given by Mr. Everard F. Im Thurn, concerning the Indians of British Guiana. I quote from the *Journal of the Anthrupological Iustitnte,* vol. xi : –

" One morning when it was important to get away from a enmp on the Essequibo River, at which I had been detained for some days by the illness of some of my Indian companions, I found that one of the invalids, a young Mneusi Indian, though better in health, was Bo earaged uguinst me that he refused to stir; for he declared that, with great want of consideration for his weak health, I had taken him out during the night, and had made him drag the canoe up a scries of difficult cataracts. Nothing would persuade him of the fact that this was but a dream." (p. 364.)

" At that time we were all suffering from a great searcity of food

Morning after morning the Indiaus declared that some absent man, whom they named, had visited their hammocks during the night, und had beaten or otherwise maltreated them ; and they always insisted upon much rubbing of the supposed bruised parts of their bodies. (p. 364.)

" In the middle of one night I was awakened by an Arawak, named Sam, the eaptain or headman of my Indians, only to be told the bewildering words, ' George speak me very bad, boss ; you cut his bits.' It was some time before I could sufficiently collect my senses to remember that ' bits,' or fourpeuny pieces, are the units in which, among Crcoles and semi-civilized Indiaus, calculations of money, and cousequently of wages, are made; that 'to cut bits' means to reduce the number of bits, or the wages given ; and to understand that Sam, as eaptain, having dreamed that Gcorge, his subordinate, had spoken impudenily to him, the former with a fine sense of the dignity of his position, now insisted that the culprit should be punished in real life." (pp. 3o4-5.)

Experiences of this kind led Mr. Im Thurn to the conelusion expressed in another paragraph, that " the dreams which come in sleep to the Indian are to him as real as any of the events of his waking life." (p. 36-1.)

WuJflng Vlainns. – In illustration of these, and the acceptance of them as real by the Guiana Indians, Mr. Im. Thurn writes, in the above-named paper in the *Journal of the Anthropological Institute,* as follows: –

" One morning in 1878, when I was living in a Maousi village, a party of Indians of the same tribe with whom I lmd had some dealings, came from their neighbouring village with the extraordinary request that I would lend them guus and would go with them to attack the Areeuna Indians of a some twenty miles dijtuut. Though there 13 au unusually strongfeeling of hostility between the facusi and the Areeuna Indians, this request, remembering how peaceful the Indians now generally are, seemed to me very trange. It wos explained that *a.* certain man, named Tori, one of the suppliants, had a day or two previously been silting alone on the savannah outside his house, when looking up from the arrow-head which he was fashioning, he found some Arecunas, whom he knew by sight, belonging to the village against which war was now to be waged, standing over him with uplifted war-clubs as if to strike him down. Tori coatinued to explain that his shouts bringing his own people *out* of thcir houses, the Arecunas vanished without doing any harm. The etory was utterly incredible, but after mach eross-examination, it was evident that Tori himself believed it, and I ean only suppose that it was a case in which a natural vision was believed as a reality." (p. 366.)

Respecting phenomena of tins kind Mr. Im Thnm says of the Indian that "visions are to him, when awake, what dreams are to him when asleep ; and the creatures of his visions seem in no way different from those of his dreams." (p. 3C5.) And he then contrnsts visions of two kinds: –

" A distinction may here bo drawn . . . between natural visions – those which appear to a man in consequence of the abnormal condition in which liis body accidentally happens to be at the moment – and artificial visions, which appear to a man in consequence of the abnormal condition into which he has brought himself by such means as fasting and the use of stimulaats or narcoties for the express purpose of experiencing visions." (p. 365.)

These last, which he distinguishes as artificial visions, he remarks are "mach more freqncnt in Indian life, especially in one particular connection – the *peaiman,* or medicine man, the priest, doctor, sorcerer, and prophet of Indian society." (p. 3GG.)

Wuling Visions among the Civilized. – How naturally savages, accepting as real thcir visions during sleep, may be misled by waking visions, will be made clear by reading accouats of illusions which occur during abnormal nervous excitements among ourselves. In support of the interpretations given in the first part of thin work, I reccived, in 1877, an account of liis experiences from Mr. F. G. Fleay, the Shakspearean scholar. He kindly allows me to publish them ; which I do after making some abridgmeuts: –

" About IS-tl, when 13 years old, after a lengthened experience of somnambulism and sleep talking, indaced by nervous excitement caused bv i'-ju- dicious legends told me by a nurse in order to secure silence through fright as to her connexion with a policeman, I read a vast amount of ghost-literature, old witch-trials, German tales of horror, etc. This produced an exalted nervous excitemeat, whence disease of optic nerves. The first illusion was seeing my bedroom tilled with stars at night, and the fluur covered with oyster-shells in the morning. I always weat to bed without candle in order to get rid of a fear of the dark. This was followed by a number of more complex illusions, the most remarkable of which was a shower of human heads passing in through the window in a caseade.

" About 1815, I woke up at midnight, and saw my brother (then living) lying on the beil. 1 attempted to take hold of him but my uria passed through him. His subsequent death convinced me that this was no illusion, but that lie had actually visited me in his sleep. I mean tlmt his ' soul' had *been* with me. . . . My belief, previously pure materialistic (2nd stage, 1st being pagan) became a sort of spirilnalislic Christianity.

" In 1851-2, when an undergradnate, I woke up one morning, and on opening my eyes (not having been dreaming of the tiling), I saw Raphael's Madonna 'in the chair' on the ceiling in full colours. I had often seen """ engravings of this picture, but no coloured copy as I supposed. I thereupon noted the colours carefully, and was surprised on enquiry to find them accurate. By chance, some weeks afier, I was told of Baiier's oleograph, and found that I had passed one in a shop-window in Trinity Street, Cambridge, i the night before my vision.

"In 1854, I had been playing whist late. Mr. "VV hod lost a few shillings, perhaps five. I woke up in the night, and saw him standing in his nightshirt demanding compensation audiblv, and stating that be liad committed suicide. He pul lns cold hand on my chest, then I tried to move it, and found it my own, which had become numb and cold from being exposed. There is a case of ' ghosts demanding revenge.' Had he really been a great loser and I a gainer, he might have killed himself, and a strong ease for actnal appearance have been made out.

" In 1853-4, I had my most singular experiences. Over-reading for triposes (I got two firsts and two seconds) caused independeat action of the two halves of the brain, and I held conversation with myself, one-half of me assuming the personality of John Gedge of my year.

" About 1856, I was staying in Bloomsbury street. . . . The house had been used as a lunatic asylum. 1 slept in the room formerly used for lunaties. I saw at 1 a. m. a man cutting his throat at the bed-foo. On rising up he vanished, lying down he reappeared. I drank water, he disappeared altogether. I found that moonlight on white drapery of the bed exactly represeuted a shirt-sleeve – the rest of the figure was prodaced by association.

" About 1859, I dreamed at Leeds that I was in my father's kitchen at Clapham, calling out to my brother, ' Gus, come down.' A few days after, I had a letter from him stating that he had a singular dream that I wns ealling out to him on the same night, or the night after; he had made no nnte, and could not tell which when I saw him. But the dates of the letters left no doubt it was same night. Case of singular coincidence which would suggest theory of actual separation of sold from body, eases of non- coincidence bcing explained by forgetfulness, or Swedenborgiau self-evolve-mont ol scenerv.

" About 1855,1 dreamed that I had received a letter containing some importaat statemeat about me, I did not know whut (compare Lie Quincey, Opinm), on which all my future depended. The delusion lasted all the next day, which I spent in looking for the imaginary letter. Case of over-smokmg. *Use of stimulants* (wrongly called narcoties) *a most important factor in later development of superstitions.*

"Later, before 186 (.. – Sleeping at Mr. Henry Wallis' (Death of Chatterton Vallis): in semi-waking state could produce at will panorama of towns, historical eveats, &c., in full colour. But the figures had no motion, only the canvas so to say moved as in a diorama. Smoking again with arUsls till 2 n. m., and talking of pictures.

" In 1S71, at Hipperholme. – My predecessor committed suicide in the room I slept in, by hanging. I saw him in cap and gown lyiirr n my bed at midday. Found it was my own gown; cap, head, &c., supplied by association. Tin's was my last experience."

The part which mere coincidence plays in causing apparent supernatural agency is fur greater than is supposed. Tlie instance given above by Mr. Fleay, which he thus aceouuts for, is less remnrkable than two perfectly natural coincidences, and quite meaningless ones, which have occurred within my own personal experience.

Wandering of the Soul during Life. – Such illusions as those above described, which, among cultured peoples, are no regarded ns subjective, are naturally, by the primitive man, regarded aa objective: his iaterpretation of them being that they are things seen and done by his soul when it leaves his. body while he is awake. Says Mr. Im Thurn respecting such illusions among the Guiana Indians – "Not only in death and in s dreams, bat in yet a third way the Indian sees the spirit separate from the body." (p. 365.) The following extracts show among other peoples, partially-different forms of this primitive belief: – " At Uea, one of the Loyalty Islands, it was tlie custom formerly when a person was very ill to send for a man whose employmeat it was ' *to restore souls to forsaken bodies.'* The soul-docior would at once collect his friends and assistants, to the number of twenty men and as many women, and start off to the place where the family of the sick man was accustomed to bury their dead. Upon arriving there, the soul-doctor and his male companions commenced playing the *nasal* flutes witli which they had come provided, in order to entice back the spirit to its old tenemeat. The women assisted by a low whisiling, supposed to be irresistibly attractive to exile spirits. After a time the eatire procession proceeded towards the dwelling of the sick person, tluten plaving and the women whistling all the time, *leading back the truant spiril !* To preveat its possible eseape, with thcir palms open, they seemingly di ove it along with gentle violence aad coaxing. . . . On entering tlw dwelling of the patient, the vaaraat spirit was ordered in loud tones at once to ente the body of the eick man." (Gill, Rev. W. W., *Myths and Songs from the Sovth Pacific,* pp. 171-2.)

Among- the Hervey Islanders –

"The philosophy of sneezing is, that the spirit having gone travelling ftbout – perch:mrc on a v:sit to the homes or burying-places of its ancestors – its return to the body is naturally attended with some ditficulty and excitemeat, occasioning a tingling and enlivening sensation all over the body. Hence the various customary remarks addressed to the returned spirit in ditferent islands. At Rarotonga, when a person sneezes, the bystanders exclaim, as though addressing a spiri . . . 'Ha! yoa have come back.'" (Gill, *Myths and Hongs from the South Pacific,* p. 177.)

The belief held by the Karens is that –

" The ' Wi' has the power of reviving the dead or dying, but he must first eatch the spirit of some perse. n silive and divert it to the dead one." (DalLou, *J. lescripl!. ve ELhnology of Bengal,* p. 117.)

By tLe Samoans –

"The eoul of man is ealled his angfmga, or that which goes or comes. It *is* said to be the daughier of Taufanuu, or *raponr of l'intls,* which forms clouds, and as the dark cloudy covering of night comes on, man feels sleepy, because the soul wishes to go and visit its mother." (Turner, *Samoa a Hundred Years Ago,* p. 8.)

Concerning the Andamancse we read : – " When appealed to in serious illness the *oko-paiad [lit.* a dreamer] firstexamines the patient and presses the limbs, muttering and making sundry strange noises as if invoking and kissing some invisible person; he then mforms the sufferer and his friends that lie is about to search for the spirit. which, at such times, is believed to be wandering in or towards . . . Hades." (E. H. Man, *Journal of the Anthropological Institule,* li, 289).

Dcntli and Re-Animnti'on. – Placed in the foregoing order, the extracts show the natural transition from the belief that the soul wanders away in dreams and during waking hours, to the belief that at death it takes its departure for a longer period, but will eventually come hack. In his account of the Guiana Italians, Mr. Ini Thurn recoguizes this connexion of ideas. lie Bays –

"When a man dies something goes, something is left. The survivors necessarily distiaguish in thought between these two parts, and they call them respectively by some sach mimes as spirit and body. A curious illustration of this is affonlel by a saying of the Maeusi Indians of Guiana, u they point out that at death the small human figure disappears from ihe pupil of n man's eye, that tlie spirit, the *emmitnarri,* as they rail it, has go-:o from out of him. . . . But it is not only in death that the Indian sees tlu two separate. It is n platitude among civilized people to remark on the similarity between ' death and his brother sleep.' But great as (be similarity is to us it seems far greater to the Indian. To us the similarity lies merely in the fact that in both there is rest from the work of this life : but to tho Indian it lies in the fact that in both t'ie spirit departs from the hoily only to coatinue its labours under hardly altered cireumstances." (pp. 363-1.)

How little the state after death is supposed to differ from tho state during life, is shown by the extent to which bodily comforts are cared for. Many instances were given in Part I, and here are some further instructive ones. In his elaborate work on the Australians, Mr. Brongh Smyth quotes Senior Constable James concerning the Dieyerie tribe, as follows: –

" Every night for one moon (four weeks) two old men went to the grave about dusk, and carefullv swept all round it ; each morning. for the same period, they visited it, to see if there were any tracks of the dead man on the swept space. They told me that if they were to find tracks they would have to remove the body and bury it elsewhere, as the foot-marks would denoto that the dead man was ' walking" and dizeoateated with his preseat grave." *(Aboriginet of Victoria, i,* 11U.)

Mr. Smyth precedes this by another case. He gives it on the authority of Mr. W. H. Wright to the effect that a native having been buried with the usnal implements and comforts, his friends came back to the spot after " a great storm of wind and rain and dug up " that poor fellow ' Georgey,'" because he " was too much cold and wet and miserable whore he wns buried." They exhumed the body, "wrapped an additional blanket and comforter round it," and " placed it in a hollow tree." *(Ibid.,* i, 108.)

Similar idens are implied by certain customs in Humphrey's Island, as described by Turner.

" At the grave the priest prayed, called out the name of tha persou whohad died, handed over to the corpse some sceated oil, and ? id it liad been made specially for him. In filling up the grave they put in first of all a qnantity of small coral stones ami told the dead man to cover himself well." (Turner, *Samoa a Hundred Years Ago,* p. 277.)

Among the Coreans, too, there is an observance betraying a like belief that the dead retain thcir senses and desires.

" During this first mourning, a serving person takes a garmeat, formerly worn by the deceased, and goes with it to the highest point on the top of the house, where – holding the garmeat, the neck in liis left hand, the hem in his right, and looking northwards, whither the spirits *(Yin)* flee – ho thrice calls loudly the name of the deceased. . . . This is the last effort to bring back the spirit to the body." (Rev. John Ross, *HMory of Corea,* p. 321.)

And similar in thcir implications are sundry of the other funeral ceremonies, which Ross describes thus: –

" At the ordinary hours of the day at which he used to take his food, dishes are prepared and offered, and then wailing and weeping follow." (p. 318.) Food and precious stones are put iato the deceased's mouth. (pp. 324 – 5.) The mourners bow twice and mourn; and then the things are removed. "During the removal, the Shangjoo, [principal mourner] leaning on his staff, weeps bitterly because liis father cannot eat." (p. 332.)

With these may fitly be named the observances by which the ancient Scythians betrayed a kindred conception.

" When any one dies, his nearest of kin lay him upon a wagon and take him round to all his friends in saccession: each reccives them in turn and entertains them with a banquet, whereat the dead man is served with a portion of all that is set before the others; this is done for forty days, at the end of which time the burial takes place." (Herodotus, Bk. iv, 73.)

Reviving Corpses. – Of course as a sequence of the belief that death is a suspended animation, there naturally goes the belief that buried persons are from time to time resuscitated. The Eyrbyggja-Saga shows that among our Scandinavian kinsmen there prevailed the primitive notion that the material body, reanimated by its wandering double, can leave its burial-place and work mischief. Here is a note appended to the abstract of the Saga compiled by Sir W. S. cott. (Alallet, *Northern Autiquities,* 1847, pp. 530-1.)

" After the death of Arnkill, Ba-gifot became again troublesome, and walked forth from his tomb to the great terror and damage of the neighbourhood, slaying b"th herds aml domesties, and driving the inhabitaats from the eanton. It was, therefore, resolved to consume his carcase with (ire ; for . . . he, or some evil demon in his stead, made use of his mortal reliques as u vehicle during commission of these enormities. The body" was burat.

Noting the implied belief, like that which wo have found prevalent among the savage and semi-civilized, that destruction of the body preveuts this kind of resurrection, wo may also note the implied belief, illustrated in other cnses, that one who gets part of a dead body thereby gets power over the decensed person; for if destruction of the whole paralyzes the ghost entirely, injury of a part must be detrimental to the ghost.

The Vampire-stories of the Russians illustrate the same belief in excursions made by the corpse. Here is one : –

" A peasant was driving past a grave-yard, after it had grown dark. After him eame running a stranger, dressed in a red sbirt and a new jacket, who crie. l, – 'Stop! take me as jour companion.' ' Pray take a seat.' They enter a village, drive up to tins and that house. . . . They drive on to the very last house. . . . They go into the house ; there on the bench lie two sleepers – an old man and a lad. The stranger takes a pail, places it near the youth, and strikes him on the back; immediatelv the back opens, and forth dowa rosy blood. The stranger fills the pail full, and drinks it dry. Then he tills another pail with blood from the old man, slakes his brutal thirst, and says to the peasant, – 'It begins to grow light ! let us go back to my dwelling." In a twinkling they found themselves at the grave yard. The vampire woutd Imve clasped the peasant in its arms, but luckily for him the coeks began to crow, and the corpse disappeared. The next morning, when folks eame and looked, the old mau and the lad were both dead." (itjlstou, *Souys of tke Muisiau Peoltle,* pp. 411-2.)

Sorrenj. – The relation of the foregoingr beliefs to those practices by which magicians are supposed to mise the dead and control demons, was suggested iu § 133. Further proofs that the more developed forms of sorcery thus originate, have since come to me. The following passage from Sir George Grey'a *Polynesian Mi)tholnyi),* pp. 114-5, implies the anxiety of a sou to rescue relies of his father from enchanters.

" Eata, without stopping, crept directly towards the fire, and hid himself behind some thick bushes of the llarakeke ; he then saw that ihere were some priests upon the other side of the same bushes, serving at the sacred place, and, to assist themselves in their magieal arts, they were making use of the bones of Wahieroa, knocking them together to beat time while they were repeating a powerful ineantation, . . . he rushed suddenly upon the priests. . . . The bones of his father, Wahieroa, were theu eagerly snatched up by Lim ; he hastened with them back to the eanoe."

From pp. 34-5 of the same work, I quote another passage, similarly implying the power which possession of a relio gives : –

" When the stonmeh of Jfuri-ranga-whenua had quietly sunk down to its usual size, her voice was again heard saying, ' Art thou Muui ? ' and he auswered, ' Even so.' Then she asked him, 'Wherefore hast thou seried thy old ancestress in this deceitful way?' and Muui answered, 'I was anxious that thy jawbone, by which the great enchamments ean be wrought, should be given to me.' She answered, ' Take it, it has been reserved tor thoe.' And Mnui took it, and having done so returned to the place where he and his brethren dwelt."

When with these, and other such illustrations given in § 133, we join the fact that even still in Italy the people tell of the child that is "kidnapped and buried up to the chin, while the witches torment him to dettb to make *lull-broth of his liver," (Furtnightly Review,* Feb., 1874, p. 220), we caunot doubt the origin of necromancy. Starting with tho primitive belief that the spirit of the living person, inhering in all parts of *his* body, is affected by acting on a detached part of it, there is reached the belief that the spirit of the dead person is similarly affected by maltreating a relic; and with this goes the belief that all parts of the body will eventually be needed by the deceased, and that therefore his spirit can be commanded by one who has any part.

Evidence even more strongly confirming this view ia contained in *Tales and Traditions of the Eskimo,* by Dr. Henry Rink. The following extracts I place in au order which shows their bearings : –

" Some tales seem to hint at a belief that the mauner in which the body of the deceased ia treated by the survivors iniluences the condition of his soul." (p. 43.) " But a slain man is said to have power to avenge himself upon the murderer by *rushing into him,* which can only be preveated by euting a piece of his liver." (p. 45.) And then, among the materials necessary for sorcery, are named, *first,* "parts of human bodies, or objects that had been in some way connected with dead bodies." (p. 49.)

Here we have the three concurrent ideas – effect on the ghost by action on the body belonging to it; protection against the ghost by incorporating part of the body, and so establishing community ; and coercion of the ghost by treating part of the body injuriously.

That in the higher forms of sorcery the medicine-man, now more properly to be regarded as a priest, is supposed to get knowledge and work miraculous effects by the help of a superior spirit, might be illustrated by many cases besides those given in the text. Here is one concerning the people of Mangain.

"Priests were significantly named *'god-boxen?* – generally abbreviated to *'gods,'* i. e.,* living embodiments of these divinities. Whenever consulted, a preseat of the best food, accompanied with a bowl of intoxicating ' piper mythisticum,' was indispensable. The priest, throwing himself iato a frenzy, delivered a response in langnage iatelligible only to the initiated. A favouriie subject of inquiry was ' the sin why so and so was ill;' no one being supposed to die a natural death unless decrepit with extreme old age. If a priest cherished a spite against somebody, he had only to declare it to be the will of the divinity that the victim should be put to death or be laid on the altar for some offence against the gods." (Gill, *JUyl&s and Hongs from thn South Pacifie*, p. 35.) -

Saered Places, Temples, S, c. – Further illustrations of the genesis of these are yielded by the following extracts.

In the New Hebrides " places where remarkable men have been buried, whether recently or in times beyond preseat memory, are saered, not to be approached but by their owners, who make prayers there to the *Tamate"* [gliosls]. *(Journal of the Anthropological Institute,* x, 292.)

Among the Blantyre negroes the decensed's house becomes his temple.

"The man may be buriod in his own dwelling. In this case the house ia not taken down [as it otherwise would bej, but in generally covered withcloth, and the rerandah beeomes the place for preseating offerings. His oM house thus becomes a kind of temple. There may be cases also where tho deceased is buried in the village, although not in Ms own house. In such cases a new house wii be raised above the remains." (Maedonald, *Africana, i,* p. 109.)

" Over some of the graves a small roof is built, three or sis feet high, the gables of which are filled in with siunot. wrought into differeat sized square-;, arranged diagonally." The Queen's " body was further protected with large roof, made of a kind of mahogany, and ornameated with pure whiia cowries." (Williams, *Fiji and the Fijians,* i, 192.)

Concerning the inhabitants of the Corea, we read : – The "graves are ornamented ot great cost. A small temple is built, where the deceased is mourned ; the froat of the grave is paved with cut flagstones, which are often anarded by upright stones earved iato human and other figures." (Ross, *History of Corea,* p. 320.)

In Humphrey's Island –

"The dead were usnally buried, but chiefs and others much lameated were Inid on a small raised platform over which a house was erected." (Turner, *Samoa a Hundred Years Ago,* 277.)

Immolations and Sacrifices at Graves. – The instances given in § 104, showing that the motive for sacrificing wives at funerals ; imong existing barharous peoples, is that they may accompany thcir dead husbands to the other world, prove how erroneous have been the interpretations given by Europeans of suttee among the Hindus : one of the statements being that it was adopted as a remedy for the practice of poisoning thcir husbands, which had become common among Hindu women (!). If there needs a further illustration of the origin of wife-sacrifice, here is one.

" The Thraeians who live nhove the Crestonneans observe the following iustoms. Each man among them has seveial wives, and no sooner does A man die than a sharp oontest ensues among the wives upon the question, which of them all the husband loved most tenderly; the friends of each eagerly plead on her behalf. and she to whom the honour is adjudged, alter receiving the praises both of men and women, is slain over the grave bv the hand of her next of kin, and then buried with her husband. The others are sorely grieved, tor nothing j considered suck a disgrace." (Herodotus, Uk. v, 5;.

That human victims are immolated at the tombs of great men, as well as at the altars of gods, and, indeed, sometimes on a far more extensive scale, is proved in. the cnse of Hamilkar.

"The Carthaginians erected funereal monumeats to him, graced with periodical sacrifice!, both in Carthage and in their principal colonies ; on the field of battle itself [Uimcni] also, a monument was raised to bim by tho Greeks. On that monument, seveuty years afterwards, his victorious grandson, fresh from the plunder of this same city of Uimera, offered the bloody sacrifice of 3,000 Grecian prisoners." (Groto, *History of Greece,* v, 297-S.)

How the primitive practice of sacrificing animals at graves sometimes revives after having died out, and how it then formspnrt of a worship of the dead person, is exemplified among Christians by the case of St. Agnes.

" About eight days after her execution [a. d. 306], her pareats going to lameat and pray at her tomb, where they coatinued watching all night, it is reported that there appeared uato them a vision of angels . . . among whom they saw their own daughter . . . and a lamb standing by her as white as snow . . . Ever after which time the Roman ladies weat every vear (as they still do) to offer and preseat to her on this day [St. Agues' Day) the two best and purest white lambs they could procure. These they offered at St. Agnes's altar (ns they call it)." (Wheatly's *Common Praiter,* p. 56.)

Nor is this cnse occurring among Catholics without parallel among Protostants. Here are cases from Wales and frum Scotland : –

" There are many . . . instances of saerifice performed in comparatively modern times either to a local god distinguished as a saiat or to some real person whose memory has become confused with a pagan leaend. There are records, for example, of bulls bcing kilhd at Kirkcudbrigh ' as an alma and oblation to St. C'uthbirt,' of bullocks offered to St. Beuno, 'the saint of the Parish nf Clynnog' in Wales." (Charles Elton, *Onrtins of English Mistorit,* pp. 21'5-6.)

" Less tnnn two hundred rears ago it was customary in the group of parishes which surrounded Applecross to sacrifice a bull on a particular day of the year – tin- 25th of August – that is, the day of St. Mourie, who is the well-known pitron-saint of Applecross. an i who wa. and is to this day, sometimes spoken of in the district as the CroJ Mourie." (Arthur Mitchell, *The Past in the Preseat,* p. 147.)

Demons and Demon-worship. – At the outset, the ghost-theory gives origin to beliefs in ghosts that are friendly and ghosts that are malicious ; of which the last, usually not ancestral, are feared more than the first, and often in a greater degree propitiated. Good illustrations occur in an essay by Mr. M. J. VValhouse, on the belief in Bhutns among the people in Western India. Here are some extracts.

"But the last three classes, of whom more particularly it is now iatended to speak, are of exclusively human origin, being malignant, diseontented beings, wandering in an intermediate state between Heaven and IJell, mtent upon misehief and annoyance to mortals ; chiefly by means of possession and wicked inspiration, every aspect of which ancient ideas, as well as of the old doctrine of transmigration, they exemplify and illustrate. They are known by the names of Bhula, I'retn, and l'uacha ; the first name being ordinarily applied to all three, and even vulgarly to the seven superior classes. These beings, always evil, originate from the souls of those who have died untimely or violeat deaths, or been deformed, idiotic, or insane ; afflicted with fits or unusnal ailments ; or drunken, dissolute, or wicked during life. . . . The death of any well-known bad character is a source of terror to all his neiahbourhood, as he is sure io become a Bhuta or demon, as powerful anJ malignaat as he was in life. Some of the BhQfns now most dreaded were celebrated personages of old duM. . . . In their haunls and modes of nppr. irance Bhfltas repeat the beliefs ot many countries. They wander borne upon the air, especially in uninhabited, dry, and desert places ; and tall trees am a favourite abode. ... As the ancieat Jews would speak to none whom they met after midnight, for fear ttu-y might be addressmg a devil, so Hinduvillagers will speak to no one they may meet at that time, lest lie should be a Bhflt, nor, indeed, willingly then stir out of their houses. The eddies of wind that career Over plaius in the hot weather, whirling up leaves and columus of dust, and nickering lights seen gliding over marshes, are regarded as Bhuts passing by. . . . The before-mentioned classes are believed more particularly to afflict human beings by entering into and possessing them. Gaping or drawing deep breaths arc supposed to give them opportunities for this, and no Brahman ever gapes without snapping his lingers before his mouth, as a charm to prevent an evil spirit entering. . . . AH this closely tallies with the beliefs regarding possession current amongst the Jews and early Christians ; the former in particular believing that unclean spirits, by reason of their tenuity, were inhaled and insinuated themselves into the human body, injuring: health through the viscera, and forcing the patients to fulfil their evil desires. . . . The edifices and observances counected with Bhflta worship arc both domestic and public. In villages, and very generally in towns, there is in every house a wooden cot or cradle, placed on the ground or suspended by ropes or chaius, and dedieated to the Bhilta of the spot. . . . Should a member of the family be stricken with any unusual attack, such as apoplexy, paralysis, cholera, &c., or should diseiso break out amongst the eattle, it is at once ascribed to the anger of the Bhut, and a propitiatory sacrifice is offered. . . The general buildings dedieated to these demous are called Bhutastaus, and when dedieated to one of the superior, or very popular Bhutns, sometimes of considerable size. . . . The Bhiitas themselves are usually represented by mere rough stones. . . . Various disputes and litigated matters, especially when evidence and ordinary means of adjustment fail, are then brought forward and submitted to the decision of the Bhuta, and his award, pronounced through the Uher, is generally, though not always, submitted to. ... In the days of the Kajahs of Coorg, a principality bordering on Canara, it was customary for the Amildars, or native heads of divisious, to issue notices and orders to the Bhutas, in the name of the Rajah, not to molest any particular individual, to quit any tree they haunted, which was required to bo felled, and to desist from any particular act or aunoyance. It is stated that these behests of the Government were never disobeyed, which, indeed, is not unlikely, as the last Coorg Rajah was not a man who understood being trifled with, either by man or demon. After his deposition, the native officials continued the same style of orders, in the name of the British Government, for some time before the authorities were aware of it!" *(On the Belief in Bhiltas – Devil and*

Ghost Worship in Western India. By M. J. Walhouto. *Journal of the Anthropologieal Iustitute* vol. v, pp. 40S-122.)

Of like nature are the beliefs of the Kanjars, as narrated in a pamphlet which Sir Alfred Lyall has been kind enough to forward me from India.

" The religion of the Kanjara, as far as we have been able to learn it, is quite what we should expect to find among a primitive and uncultivated pcople. It is a religion without idols, without temples, and without a priesthood. They live in the coustant dread of evil spirits, the souls of the departed, who aro said to enter into the bodies of the living as a punishment for past misdeeds or neglect of burial rites, and to produce most of the ills to which flesh is heir. In this creed they stand on the same intellectual level with their more civilized kiusfolk, the Hindus, amongst whom it is universally believed that the air is peopled with *bhuts,* malignant spirits, who haunt graveyards, lurk in trees, re-animate corpses, devour living men, or altnck them with madness, epilepsy, cramp, etc." (J. C. Neslield, *An An-onut of the Kanjaei of Upper Iiulia* [from *Calcutta liecitie;* Oct. 16S3J, p. 11.)

And in Africa there are propitiations of demons obviously in like manuer conceived as the ghosts of the malicious dc:ul. Cameron tells us that while cruising on Lake Tanganyika, they passed a haunted headland, whereupon –

" The [native] pilota stood together in the how of Hie eanoe to mnke nn offering to these evil spirits [the devil and his wife]. One hold out a paddle on the blade of which a few common beads h; ul been placed, and both said together, as nearly as it can be translated, ' You big man, *you* big devil, you great king, you take ail men, you kill all men, you now let us go all right,' and after a little bowing und gesticulation the beads were dropped into the watar and the dreaded devil propitiated. There is a kind of double cape at this place, one being the supposed residence of the male devil and the other that of his wife, and the spot is therefore believed to be doubly dangerous." (Cameron's *Acrosi Africa,* i, 253-4.)

Worshipped Ghosts of Rollers in India. – Writing under date, August 1, 1884, from the N. W. Provinces of India, Sir Alfred Lyall has obliged me with some instructive instances of apotheosis in Indin. He says – "I enclose you herewith part of a memo. upon the religious practices of the Doms or L)omras, who live on the edge of the forests under the Himalayas, and who are the most utterly degraded and irreclaimablo tribe, or relic of a tribe, in all these parts. You will observe that they propitiate ghosts and worship notable thieves of bygone days, and there canuot be the slightest doubt that this practice is characteristic of all the lowest and most barbarous Indian societies." The memorandum he encloses, from the magistrate of Gorakhpur, is as follows : –

" The Maghia Domras have two special divinities of their own ; the chief is Gimdak, whose grave is to be found in Karmani Garhi, two days' journey to the east of Motihari, in Bengal. According to their traditions, Gandak was hanged for theft' a long time ago,' and when dying he promised always to help Maghias in trouble. He is worshipped by the whole clan, and is invoked ou all importaat occasions, but ho is pre-eminently the patron god of thefts. A successful theft is always celebrated by a sa-.-riflce and feast in his honour. They also worship Samaya, a female divinity ; she is without any special history, and there is no sharp distinction between her sphere and ijandak's. Iler functions apparently relate chiefly to birth and illness, etc.

"The Maghias sacrifice young pigs and wine with sugar and spices to these two deities. Every Maghin is capable of performing the sacrifice, and tiie remains are divided among the company. . . . The Mnghias have neither altars nor idol, nor do they erect any Ohabutras for worship. A spot is cleared and leeped in the middle of a field, and the sacrifice is then offered.

"The Maghias niturally believe in ghosts and spirits. When a man dies, my informant told me, ho turns into a 'Shaitan.' The 'dcotas,' also he added, were innumerable. In most villages of this district there is a special altar for all the local ghosts and dcities, which may reside within tlie village boundaries, and the Maghiaa are always ready to share in the sacritico of tha villagers to them. They also reverence trees and Chabutrus, consecrated by Hindus, in passing, but pay no further homage."

Wurship of BiMejlcent Spitits – Ancestors and others. – Heraare examples furnished by five unallied races. The first concerns the Laplanders.

" They worshipped the ghosts of departed persous, but especially of thei kindred, for they thought there was some diviuity in them, and thnt they were able to do hann : just such as the Romans fancied their manes to be ; therefore it was that they offered sacrifice to them." (Professor John Scheffer, *Hislory of Lipldnd,* Oxford, 1674, p. 36.)

In an early account of an African people, the Qnoians, tve find illustrations of their necrolatry. Saying that the Quoians believe the spirits of the dead to be omniscient, and that they make offerings of rice or wine at their graves, we are told that they " hold familiar colloquies with them, telling them all troubles and adversities under which they labour. . . . The King calls upon the souls of his father and mother almost in every matter of difficulty." (0. Dapper, *Africa by J. Oyilby,* 1670, pp. 402-4.)

Concerning the Kanjnrs we read : –

"In the wide range of human history, it is difficult to find an example of ii primitive horde or nation, which has not had its inspired prophet or deified uncestor. The man-god whom Konjars worship is Mdmi, – A iame which does not appear in any of the lists of the Hindu divinities. While he lived amongst men, he was the model fighter, the great hunter, the wise artificer, and the unconqucred chief. He was not only the teacher and the guide, hut also the founder and ancestor of the tribe. He is therefore to the Kanjur what Hcllen was to the Greeks, Romulus to the Romaus, Abraham to the Jews, or Ishmael to the Arabs, . . . Maua is worshipped with more ceremony in the rainy season, when the tribe is less migratory, than in the dry months of the year. On such oceasions, if sufficient notice is circulated, several eneampments unite temporarily to pay honour to their common ancestor. No altar is raised. No image is erected. The worshippers collect ncur a tree, under which they sacrifice a pig or goat, or sheep, or fowl, and make an offering of roasted flesh and spirituous liquor. Formerly (it U said) they used to sacrifice a child, having first made it insensible with fermented palm-juice or toddy. They dance round the tree in honour of Man6, and sing the customary songs in commemoration of his wisdom and deeds of valour. At the close of the ceremony there is a general feast, in which most of tiie banqueters get drunk. On these oceasions, – but before the drunken stage has been reached, – a man sometimes comes forward, and declares himself to be especially filled with the divine presence. He abstaius from the flesh and wine of which others partake, and remains standing before the tree with his eves closed as in a trance. If he is seized with a fit of trembling, the spirit of Maua is thought to have possessed him, and while the inspiration lasts he is consulted as an oracle by any man or woman of the assembly who desires to be helped out of a difficulty." (J. C. Nesfield, *An Account of the Kunjan of Up)ier India,* pp. 12-13.)

That this god M:in:l was originally a man, as he is said to have been by the Kanjars, cannot well be doubted when we find cases in India of historical persons being deified, not by these inferior races only, but by the Aryans. Pivmisiug that the Portugnese were extremely crnel to the Hindus during the trne that they had a monopoly of the trade in India, Hunter tells us that –

" Albuquerque alone endeavoured to win the pood will of the natives, and to live in friendship with the Hindu princes. In such veneration was his memory held, that the)Iindus of Goa, and even the Muhammadaus, were wont to repair to his tomb, and there to utter their complaints, as if in the presence of his spirit, and call upon God to deliver them from the tyranny of hia successors." (Hunter's *Brief History of the Indian People,* 150-1.)

Russia, too, supplies us with an instance of kindred nature, in so f:ir as that the worship is of an historical personage, who was reverenced during his life.

Alexander Nevski, governor of Novgorood at the time of the Mongol invasion, and who died in 1263, was " deeply mourned bT a grateful pcople, who count him ever since amongst the saints. . . . and there is not one of the Russian emperors who has not knelt before the shrine of Alexander Nevski. Many great generals have implored him for his support and intercession, whenever theT departed for a great battle or an important eam- piign." (O. V. Wahl, *The Land of the Czar,* 2u-i.)

Gtncsls rf New Culls among Hindus. – Along with the account of robber-worship among the Uomras given above, Sir Alfred Lyall transmitted, from the same source, the following: –

"It mny perhaps be interesting to know that a weekly pilgrimage has been instituted within the last year to the tomb of a Fakir in the compound next my own. The Fakir died two centuries ago, it is said. A'jlumdi was struck over his grave – somebody got cured there last year, and a concourse of pe'ople now visit it every Thursday, with drums beating, etc. I counted once seven gr. ives within a mile or 10 of mT house, at which offerings are presented by the Hindu public, on fixed days. The tombs aro generally those of Mahomedans, but this is immaterial. As my Hon. Magistrate liahu Durga l'ershad explained one day, when pointing out a tree frequented by a *'Jin,'* a ' bhut,' is generally a Hindu, ruthcr harmless and indistinct, hut a ' Jin' is always a wicked old Mahoniedan, and there *is* no appeasing him. The number of 'Devia' is also innumerable, new ones nre alwavs springing up. and the most fashionable shrines ure generally very recent. The principal Mahadro on this side the town was discovered by two herd boys, some years ago, in the Ramgarh Tal. One boy struck it, it began to bleed, and the boy fell dead. There is a famous Kali at the corner of my compound, another Devi lives in the judges' compound, and her image is carried home every evening by the mali who olliciates." (Letter from the magistrate of Gorakhpur to Sir Alfred Lyall.)

These statements harmonize entirely with those given by Sir Alfred Lyall himself in his *Asiatic Ktiulius.* To the instances be names, he adds the remark –

" The suint or hero is admitted into the upper circles of divinity, much as successful soldier or millionaire is recognized bT fashionable societT, tnkes a new title, and is welcomed by a judiciously liberal aristocracy." (p. 20.)

Fftichism. – I believe M. Comte expressed the opinion that fetichistio conceptions are formed by the higher animals. Holding, for reasons already given, that fetichism is not original but derived, I cannot, of course, coincide in tins view. Nevertheless, the behaviour of intelligent animals elucidates tliegenesis of it. I have myself witnessed in dogs two illustrative actions.

One of these was that of a formidable beast, half mastiff, half blood-hound, belonging to friends of mine. While playing on the lawn with a walking-stick, which he had seized by the lower end, it happened that in his gambols he thrust the handle against the ground : the result being that the end he had in his mouth was forced against his palate. Giving a yelp, he dropped the stick, rushed to some distance from it, and betrayed a consternation which was particularly laughable in so large and ferocious-looking a creature. Only after cantious approaches and much hesitation was he induced again to pick it up. This behaviour showed very elearly that the stick, while displaying none but properties he was familiar with, was not regarded by him as an active agent; but when it suddenly inflicted a pain in a way never before experienced from an inanimate object, he was led for the moment to elass it with animate objects, and to regard it as capable of again doing him injury. Similarly to the mind of the primitive man, the anomalous behaviour of an object previously elassed as inanimate, suggests animation. The idea of voluntary action is made nascent; and there arises a tendency to regard the object with alarm lest it should act in some other unexpected and perhaps mischievous way. Obviously the vague notion of animation thus aroused, becomes a more definite notion as fast as development of the ghost- theory furnishes a specific agency to which the anomalous behaviour can be ascribed.

A very intelligent and good-tempered retriever, much pelted in the house of certain other friends, had a habit which yields the second hint I have alluded to. On meeting in the morning one with whom she was on friendly terras, she joined with tho usual wagging of the tail, an unusual kind of salute, made by drawing apart tho lips so as to produce a sort of smile or grin ; and she then, if out of doors, proceeded to make a further demonstration of loyalty. Being by her duties as a retriever led to associate the fetching of game with the pleasing of the person to whom she brought it, this had become in her mind an act of propitiation; and so, after wagging her tail and griuning, she would perform this act of propitiation as nearly as was practicable in the absence of a dead bird. Seeking about, she would pick up a dead leaf, a bit of paper, a twig, or other small object, and would bring it with renewed manifestations of friendliness. Some kindred stale of mind it is which, I believe, prompts the savage to certain fetichistic observances. Occasion ally, when seeking supernatural did, the savage will pick up perhaps the first stone he sees, paint it red, and make offerings to it. Anxious to please some ghostly agent, he feels the need for displaying his anxiety; and he adopts this as the nearest fulfilment of a propitiatory act winch circumstances permit. Ghosts are all about, and one may be present in anything – perhaps in this stone – very likely in this stone. And so the primitive man, with whom fancy passes easily into belief, adopts this method of expressing his subordination. Daily occurrences among ourselves prove that the desire *to do something* in presence of an emergency, leads to the most irrelevant actions. " It may do good, and it can't harm,"is the plea for many proceedings which have scarcely more rationality than worship of a painted stone.

The Fetich-ghost. – *The* evidence given in §§ 159-163, that the supernatural agent supposed to be contained in an inanimate object, was originally a human ghost, is, I think, tolerably conelusive. I have, however, met with still more conelusive evidence, in the work of Dr. Rink on the Eskimo. In the passage which I here extract, the two are identified by name.

" The whole visible world is ruled by supernatural powers, or ' owner',' taken in a higher seuse, each of whom holds his sway within certain limits, and is ealled *inua* (viz., its or his, *inuk,* which word signifies ' *man,*' and also *owner* or *inhabitant).* " (p. 37.)

The supposed possessing agent to which the powers of an object are ascribed, is thus called *its man;* the man in it – that is, the man's ghost in it. The *"iiiue"* of certain celestial objects were persons known byname; and the implication is that the " *inue"* of other objects are thought of as persons, but not individually identified.

And now observe that in a work published since that of Dr. Rink, concerning an unallied people in the remote region of Polynesia, we find a kindred conception joined with an interpretation of it. Describing the superstitions of the Hurvey Islanders, Mr. Gill says: –

" Thus it is evident that many of their cods were orifrinully men. whoso spirits were supposed to enter into various birds, fish, reptile-, and iusects ; and into inanimate objects, such as the triton shell, particular trees, cinet, sandstone, bits of basalt, etc." (Eev. Wm. W. Gill, *KJylhi and Suuyt Jnm the South Pacifie,* p. 32.)

Ghosts in Stones. – The genesis of that form of fetichism which uscribes supernat-ural powers to shapeless inanimate objects, is very elearly exhibited in the following passages from a letter, for which I am indebted to Commander W. H. Henderson, R. N., who dates from H. M. S. " Nelson," Australian Station, October 9th, 1881 : –

" While on the eastern side of the Island of Tauna, New Hebrides, in July last year, I was told by the Rev. J. Gray, Presbyterian Missionary, stationed tt Wnisisi, near to the voleano, in auswer to an inquiry of mine relative to the invonveuient position of his house, that in order to gain a footing he wna obliged to build where the natives allowed him to. That the sae he wouldhave chosen included the piece of sacred ground on which were deposited the stones in which they suppiised the spirits of their departed relatives to reside, that lie had nut been able to get them removed, though he hoped to be able to do so, and to purchase the ground. He stilted that these stones were common ones of various sizes ; that after being deposited they were not again touched ; and that they seldom retained any sacredness as the abode of the departed spirit for any length of time – a generation at the utmost – most were soon forgotten. Soon after this, while at Vela Harbour. Sandwich, or Vati Island, in the same group, the Rev. J. Mackenzie, also of the Presbyterian Mission, showed me without reference to what I had heard :tt auna, a collection of stones and rudely cut shells and stones, which he said when he arrived there some years previously, were the only form of goda the natives possessed, and into which they supposed the spirits of their departed friends or relatives to enter; though the recollection of them did not often last long.

" Some of the stones were ordinary smooth water-worn boulders, three to four inches long and from two to three inches in diameter. Others, one of which I have in my possession, were similar, but had a small piece chipped out on one side, by meaus of which the indwelling ghost or spirit was sup- pjsed to have ingress or egress. A third and higher form were rudely fashioned shells or stones ; the former being cut out as large rings. These it seen. ed lo me Here the begiunings of a graven imae – a common stone sacred u the dwelling-place of an ancestral ghost."

With such evidence before us, we can scarcely doubt that in other places where stones are worshipped, or regarded as sacred, human ghosts nre or were believed to bo present in them ; and, that the stones supposed to be possessed by powerful ghosts, thus became the shrines of gods. Hence the interpretation of such facts as this told us about the Karens: –

"Many keep stones in their houses that they suppose possess mirneulous powers and which seem to represent the household gods of the ancients." (*At. Soc. of Beayal, Journal*, xxxiv, pt. 2, p. 223.)

And this told us about the Buwditeli Islanders: –

" Their great god was ealled Tui Tokelau, or King of Tokelan. He was supposed to be embodied in a stone, which was carefully wrapped up with fine mats." (Turner, *Samoa a Hundred Years Ago,* p. 2U8.)

And this told us about the Fijians : –

"The Fijiaus are unacquainted with idols properly so-called; but they reverence certain stones as shrines of gods, and regard some clubs with superstitious respect. . . . Rude consecrated stones are to be seen near Vuna, where offerings of food are sometimes made." *(Fiji and the Ft jinn I,* t jl. i, by T. Williams, pp. 219 and 220.)

And hero we arc once more shown how baseless is the belief of those who, in aid of their theories, thcological or mythological, assert that the noble types of man – the Aryan and Semitic – displayed from the beginning, higher religious ideas than men of inferior types. For besides having various other beliefs and rites like those of existing savages, both of them agreed with savages in exhibiting this lowest form of fetichism. In their early days, tho Greeks believed that ghosts dwelt iustones; and stones wore the shrines of their gods. Pausanias gives various instances ; and shows that these inhabited stones, anointed with oil in propitiation, continned even in late (Jays to be regarded ns sacred and to be occasionally honoured. So was it, too, with the Hebrews ; as witness this passage : –

"The large smooth stones referred to above were the fetishes of *fh* primitive Semitic races, and anointed with oil, according to a widely eprend custom (cnmp. Aitfoi Xiiraeoi, lapides uncti, lubrieati). It was such a stone which Jacob took for a pillow, and afterwards cousecrated by pouring oil upon it (Gen. xxviii, 11, 18). The early Semites and reactionary, idolatrous Israclites called such stones Bethels, . . . i. e., houses of El (the early Seniitie word for God). . . . In spite of the efforts of the 'Jehovisr,' who desired to convert these ancient fetished into memorials of patriarchal history (comp. Gen. xxxi, 45-52), the old heathenish use of them si'ems to have continued, especially in secluded places." (Rev. T. K. Cheyre, *The Prophecio of Isaiah: a Reio Translation with Commentary and Appendices,* 1882, vol. ii, p. 70).

Let us observe, too, bow comptely Jacob's conception of his dream as caused by a god in the stone, corresponds with the conceptions of existing savages. In his account of the lilautyre negroes, the Rev. Duff Macdonald writes: –

" Very frequently a man presents an offering at the top of his own bed beside his head. He wishes his god to come to him aud whisper in his ear as he sleeps." *(Afeieana,* vol. i, p. 6O.)

I may add that Jacob's act of pouring oil on the stone in propitiation of the indwelling spirit (thus employing an established mode of honouring living persons) points the way to an interpretation of another usage of stone-worshippers. A Dakotah, before praying to a stone lor succour, paints it with some red pigment, such as red ochre. Now when we read that along with offerings of milk, honey, eggs, fruit, flour, etc., the Bodo and Dhimals offer "red lead or cochineal," we may suspect that these three colouring matters, having red as their common character, are substitutes for blood. The supposed resident ghost was at first propitiated by anointing the stone with, human blood ; and then, in defanlt of this, red pigment was nsed: ghosts and gods being supposed, by primitive men to be easily deceived by shams.

Anfmat-naming among the Semites. – In vol. i, p. 126, Palgrave, referring to an Arab, writes : – " 'Obeyd, 'the wolf,' to give him the name by which he is commonly known, a name well earned by his unrelenting cruelty and deep deceit." Now read the following from the *Vook of Jvdyes,* vii, "5: – "And they took two princes of the Midianites, Oreb [raven] and Zecb [wolf], and they slew Oreb upon the rock Oreb, and Zeeb they slew at the wine-press of Zeeb, and pursued Midian, and brought the heads of Oreb and Zi'eu to Gideon on the other side Jordan."Thus we have proof that Semitic chiefs boro animal names; doubtless given, as wo see they are still given, as nicknames. With this we may join the fact that at the present time "the Cabyles are said to distinguish their different tribes by figures of animals tatooed on forehead, nose, temples, or cheeks :" implying descent from founders identified by name with these animals *(L. Gdger, Zcitsehr. D.* if. (?., 1869, p. 169). When we put this evidence side by side with that given in §§ 170-4, showing how animal-naming among savages leads to belief in animal- ancestors and to the propitiation of animals, it becomes still more manifest that among Mesopotamian peoples, animal- gods and gods half-man half-brute, originated in the way alleged.

Since tho above was published ia the first edition of this work, there has appeared an interesting essay on " Animal Worship and Animal Tribes," by Professor Robertson Smith (see *Journal of Philology,* vol. ix), in which he shows how extensive is animal-naming, and the consequent rise of animal- tribes, among existing Arabs. Here is a part of a list given by him : –

" *Amd,* lion ; 'a number of tribes. *Au's,* wolf ; ' a tribe of the Ancar,' or Defenders. *Budan,* ibex; a tribe of the Kalb and others. ' *Tha'taba,* ehe-fox; 'name of tribes.' *Gan'td,* loeusts; 'a sub-tribe of the Tamtin. *lieni flnmama,* sous of the dove; 'a sub-tribe of, tbe Azd.' *TJiawr,* bull; ' a sub-tribe of Uamdan and of 'Abd Manah.' *tjahsh,* ealf uf an ass; ' a ub-tribe of the Arabs.' *Ilith'i,* kite ; ' a sub-tribe of Murad.' *Dhfb,* wolf ; 'son of 'Amr, a sub-tribe of the Azd.' *Jjubey'u,* little hyama ; 'bob of Qaya, a sub-tribe of Bekr bin Wiil.' " (p. 79.)

And continuing the list, Professor Smith gives as other animal-names of tribes, lizard, eagle, she-goat, raven, hedgehog, dog, whelp, jerboa, panthers, little panther, etc. He goes on to Bay that –

" The origin of all these names is referred in the genealogieal system of the Arabs to an ancestor wlio bore the tribal or gentile name. Thus the *Kalb,* or dog-tribe, consists of the Beni Kalb – sons of Kalb (the dog), who is in turn son of Wabru (the female rockbadgei')," etc. (p. 80.)

Rejecting this interpretation in favour of the interpretation of Mr. M'Lennan, Professor Smith says –

" A conclusive argument against the genealogical system is that it is built on the patriarchal theory. Kvery notion and every tribe must have an ancestor of the same name from whom kiuahip U reckoned exclusively in the male line." (p. 81.)

And he thereupon contends th:it since kinship through females is the primitive form, the system of tribal naming could not have thus arisen. But, ns I have elsewhere shown (j 293), this is not a necessary implication. Remarking that thu system of kinship through females evidently does not exclude the knowledge of male paren'age (since in the rudest tribu tneru is aname for fatter as well as for mother) I have poiuted out that in the same way among ourselves, the tracing of kinship through males does not exclude a perfect recognition of motherhood. And here I have to add that descent from a distinguished man will naturally survive in tradition, notwithstanding the system of kinship through females, and the male genealogy, regarded with pride, will supplant the female ; just as among ourselves the posterity of a woman of rank who married a man of low degree, will preserve the record of thcir ancestress while dropping that of thcir ancestor, notwithstanding the system of descent through males. [On considering, after writing the above, where l should be likely to fa'nd proof, there occurred to me the case of Lord Clyde, of whom I had heard that his mother, a woman of good family, had married a man of inferior origin. Whether the name Campbell was that of his father or his mother, I did not know ; but inquiry proved my suspicion to be well founded. His father's name was John Macliver, and his mother's Agnes Campbell. By successive steps the maternal name displaced the paternal mime; and his daughter is now called Miss Campbell. This, I think, makes it clear that notwithstanding descent in the female line, the name of a distinguished chief, usurping the place of the previous name, will readily become a tribal name.]

But there is a co-operative cause. A tribe from time to time divides, and the migrating part attaches itself to some leader: a man of strength, or courage, or cunning, or resource. How are members of the migrating part to be distinguished by the remainder, and by adjacent tribes ? Evidently by the name of thcir leader or chief. They become known ns followers of the Snake, the Wolf, or the Bear, as the case may be. It needs but to recall the cnse of a Highland clan, all members of which habitually acquired the clan-name, whether related by blood to its head or not. to show how the tendency to speak generally of the followers of the Snake as Snakes will conflict with recognition of thcir maternally-derived relationships. Especially when there grows up a new generation, having individual names unknown to adjacent tribes, there will arise an established practice of calling them Snakes – a practice ending in the story of descent from an ancestral snake who wns the founder of the tribe. Hence the origin of the Snake Indians of North America, or the Nagas (snakes) of the Indian Hills, who are worshippers of the snake.

Animal-naming in Great Britain. – Anyone who upon occasion Bpeaks of a keen and merciless man as " a hawk," or of another as " a pig " because of his dirtiness, ought to have no difficulty in understanding how in rnde times animal-names are acquired.

While recognizing the exceptional cnses of birth-naming ftfter some animal visible at the time of birth, he will the less doubt that animal-names nsunlly result from nicknaming, on finding among ourselves cases in which the animal nickname becomes substituted for the conventional surname previously current. Two cases, one dating some centuries back, and the other belonging to our own time, may be here given. Doubtless there still exists, ns there existed some years since when I saw it, the remnant of an old castle built on an island in Loch-an-Eilean in Rothietnurelms, which was, according to tradition, a stronghold of the "Wolf of Badenoch." Who was he ? Mr. Cosmo limes, in his *Sketches of Early Scotch History* (p. 424), speaks of " the harrying of the country and burning of the church by the Wolf of Badenoch ; " and in his *Scotland in the Middle Ayes* (p. 297), says: – "The magnificent cathedral of Elgin [was] .... so roughly handled by the Wolf of Badenoch in the end of the fourteenth century, that the bishops called their restoration a rebuilding." Mr. Innes doer. Mot give the Christian name or surname of this robber-chief. Further inquiry, however, diselosed it. In Burton's *llitiirjf of Scotland* (vol. iii, p. 97), he is referred to as " King Robert's brother, Alexander." Evidently, then, the original proper name had become less familiar than the substituted nickname; which sup. planted it not only in popular speech, but partially in literature. We have but to suppose times still ruder than those in which he lived, and times in which Christianity had in no degree undermined primitive superstitions, to see that just as Earl Siward, of Northumbria, was said to be the ; randson of an actual bear, so the descendants of the Wolf of Badenoch would have been described in tradition as derived from an aetual wolf. A further significant fact remains. It is stated in Jervise's *Land of the Lindsags* (p. 350) that Countess Isabella " was the wife of the Wolf of Badenoch." Here, in this very statement, the nickname has replaced the pre-established name of the man, while the name of the woman remains unchanged. It needs but that this statement should be accepted literally, as such statements are among the uneivili/ed, to understand how it happens that here and there a family traces back its origin to a woman identified by name, who was married to an animal; as in " the story of the origin of the Dikokameuni Kirghiz . . . from a red greyhound and a certain queen with her forty handmaidens," quoted by Mr. M'Leunau from the Miehells.

The other instance comes from the Forest of Dean, a region little visited, and retaining old usages. There the surname " James " is so common that nicknames are required to distinguish among thoe bearing it. A gentleman known to me. Mr. Keeling, C. E., of Cheltenham, having to find a man thus named,

diseovered that lie was nicknamed " *Jinout,* " that is " mole." Moreover he was one of a number who had inherited the nickname, and who had thcir respective Christian names – John Hoont, Henry Hoont, etc. Clearly, among savages a few generations would have established the tradition of descent from an actual mole : memory of the original bearer of the nickname having died out. When we find that even where there are established surnames of the civilized kind, nicknames derived from animals usurp thcir places and become inherited, it seems to me scarcely questionable that in the absence of established surnames, animal-names will eventually becomes the names of *genius* and tribes, supposed to be descended from the animals they are named after – supposed, that is, by the uncivilized man, who is without our general ideas of law, order, cause ; who has no notions of possible and impossible; who, without capacity fop criticizing, accepts blindly the statemeuts made to him by his seniors; and who, indeed, were he critical, might reasonably conclude that these metamorphoses of animals into men were of the same nature as those animal metamorphoses which really take place, and which he has observed. Strong renson should be given before rejecting this interpretation in face of the fact that savages themselves thus explain thcir tribal names ; as instance the Arawaks, most of whom " assert that each family is descended – thcir fathers knew how, but they themselves have forgotten – from its eponymous animal, bird, or plant." Once more, if it be admitted that the conception of an animal-ancestor thus originates, it can hardly be doubted that, going along with the idens and feelings respecting ancestors entertained by primitive men, it will originate a special regard for the animal which gives the tribal name – a regard which here results in making the animal a sacred totem, and here in producing worship of it.

That our relatives the Scandinavians exemplified in thcir ideas of the alliance between men and animals, certain further results of animal-naming, is made tolerably clear by the following passage: –

"Brutes were included in the social compact, and dealt with as if they had been rational creatures'. If a beaver was killed, by tlie laws of Hnkon the Oood a fine of three marks was paid to the owner of tho ground, ' botli for bloodwite aml liamesuckcn,' thus recognizing the animal's rights us an inhabitaat of the soil. The old Norwegian statutes decreed that ' tho bear and wolf shall be outlaws in every place.' . . . Yet even Bruin was eatitled to hid judicial privileges ; for if he had robbed or injured his two-legged couatrymen, it was necessary to summon a Tinwald court, and pronounce him liable to punishment in due form. In the Saga of Finboga hinom Rama, the grizzly offender is challenged to a duel, and slain by Finbog with all 'he courtesies of chivalry. Werlauff, the editor of this saun (Copenhagen, 1812), ',-; , the opinion that bears hare u reasonable knowledge of Dauuh is siill prevalent in Norway. (Crichton and Wheaton, *Scandinavia, Ancient and Modern,* i, 192-3 (uote).)

Animal-worship. – One of the catisps assigned in the text (§ 168) for the worship of animals, wns the belief, illustrate! in sundry ways, that a creature found in the ncighbourhood *r* the dead body is a new form assumed by the double, or otherwise a re-incarnation of the ghost. Here are further exampleS of this belief: the first of them supplied by the people of Bank's Island.

" A woman knowing tliat a neiahbour wns at the point of death, heard a rustling of something in her house,'as if it were a muth fluttering, just as the sound of eries and wailinga showed her that the soul was flown. She eaught the fluttering thing between her hands, and run with it, erymg out that she hod eaught the *atai [i. e.,* that which a ' man believer' to ' be a kind of reflection of his own personality; the man and his *atai* lire, flourish, suffer, and die (?) together,' 280-1]. But though she opened her ban-is above the mouth of the corpse there was no recovery." (Codrington, *Journal of the Anthropological Institute,* x, 2S1.)

Here is another which the Samoans fnrnish.

"On the beach, nenr where a person had been drowned. and whose body was supposed to have become a porpoise, or on the battlefield, where another fell, might have been seen, titting in silence, a group of fire or six, and Dim a few yards before them with a sheet of native clot h spread out on the ground in front of him. Addressing some god of the family lie said, ' Oh, be kind to us; let us obtain without difficulty the spirit of the young man !' The first thing that happened to light upon the sheet was supposed to be the spirit . . . grasshopper, butterfly, aat. or whatever else it might be, it was earefully wrapped up, taken to the family, the friends assembled, and the bundle buried with all due ceremony, as if it contained the real spirit of the departed." (Turner, *Samoa a Hundred Yearj Ago,* pp. 150-1.)

Along with this belief respecting ordinary ghosts, the Samoans have an allied, and to all appearance resulting, belief, respecting extraordinary ghosts.

" The village gods, like those of the household, had all some particular incarnation : one was upuosed to appear as a bat, another as a heron, another as an owl. ... A dead owl found under a tree in the settlemeat was the signal for all the village to assemble at the place, burn their bodies with firebrands, and beat thcir foreheads with stones till the blood tlowel, and so they expressed their sympathy and condolence with the god over the ealamity ' by an offering of blood.' He still lived, however, and moved about in all the other existing owls of the couniry. (Turner, *Samoa a Hundred Years Ago,* pp. 21 and 26.)

Concerning these same people I may add that they furnish a striking example of the way in which unlimited credulity causes that literal acceptance of traditions, which in many cases ends in the belief in animal-ancestors and resulting worship of them. Turner tells us that the Samonns have traditions of battles between trees, birds, fish, and beasts; and after giving sen no examples, he says : –

" I tell them tliut tuti shark, red finh, etc., *must* have been mere fif uratJynames for chiefs and districts, and the fiuny troops under them were doubtless living *men,* but in all those stories the Samoans are rigid literalists, and belicvs in the very words of the tradition. And yet at the present day they have towus and districts bearing figurative names, distinct from the real names, such as the sword fish, the stinging ray, the dog, the wild boar, the lougan cock, the frigate bird, etc." *(Samoa a Hundred Years Ago,* pp. 213 4.)

ors in North America.   – A recently published work, *The Snake-Diince of the Maquis of Arizona,* by John (I. Bonrke, gives some interesting facts illustrative of the belief in snake-ancestors. Giving his inferences from the evidence, the writer says –

"My own suspicion is that one of the minor objects of the snake-dance has been the perpetuation in dramatic form of the legend of the origin and growth of the Moqui family (p. 178). ... In the religious dances of such peoples as the Zunis, Moquis, and Qnerez, suggestions of their history and previous environment will crop ont ia features which from any other point of yiew would be without import. The fact that the snake-dance rellects in some mauner the worship of ancestors has already been indieated, but beyond learning Hmt the willow wands standing around the altars commemorated their dead, nothing was elicited at Hualpi. . . . Should it be shown 'positively, as I think ean be done, that snake worship and ancestor or spirit worship are combined in the same rite, we may . . . with a little more patient work determine whether or not the Moquis have ever believed in the transmigration of souls (p. 179)." . . . Nanahe persistently " spoke of the snakes as his ' fathers,' a reverential expression which of itself would go far towards establishing a connexion between the rattlesnake- dance and ancestor worship " (p. 195).

These conelusions were based, upon statements elicited from one of the Indians who took part in the snake-dance, of which the following are the most significant ones : –

" Nanahe continued : ' The members of the order always carry these medicines with them, and when they meet with a rattlesnake they first pray to their father, the sun, and then say : ' Father, make him to be tame ; nmke him that nothing shall happen that he bring evil unto mo. Verily, make him to bo tame.' Then they address the rattlesnake and say : ' Father, be good' *(i. e.* kind or tamo) 'unto me, for here I niako my prayers. This being done, the rattlesnake is eaptured . . . and taken home (p. 189) . . .' "

Nahi-vehma (the Peacemaker) said, "Many years ago the Moquis used to live upon the other side of a high mountain, beyond the San Juan River. . . . The chief of those who lived there thought he would take a trip down thf big river to see where it went to. . . . The stream carried him to the seashore. . . . When he arrived on the beach he saw on top of a cliff a number of houoes, in which lived many men and women. . . . That night he took unto himself one of the women as his wife. Shortly after his return to lu's home the woman gave birth to snakes, and this was the origin of the snake family (gens or clan) which manages this dance. When she gave birth to these snakes they bit a number of the children of the Moquis. The Moquia then moved in a body to their present villages, and they have this dance to conciliate the snakes, so that they won't bite their children " (p. 177).

In another chapter the writer refers to a large amount of con- firmatory evidence showing the prevalence elsewhere of kindred ideas.

The Snake-Spirit among the Ancinnts. – A verification of the view set forth in §§ 167-8, is furnished by the following passage from the *jEneid,* Bk. v, 75.

. iEneas " was already on his way from the council to the tomb [of Anehisto, his father] . . . Here in due libation, he pours on the ground two bowls uf the wine-god's pure juice, two of new milk, two of sacrificial blood ; he flings bright flowers, and makes this utterance : – ' Hail to thee, blessed sire, once more! Hail to you, ashes of one rescued in vhin, spirit and shade of niv father !' . . . He had said this, when from the depth of the grave a smooth shining serpent trailed along . . . coiling peacefully round the tomb, and gliding between the altars. . . . tineas stood wonderstruck : the creature . . . tasted of the viands, and then, iunocent of harm, re-entered the tomb at its base, leaving the altars where its mouth had been. Quickened by tins, the hero resumes the work of homage to his sire, not knowing whether to think this the genius of the spot or his father's menial spirit."

Though here, along with the conceptions of a higher stage than that described in §§ 167-8, there is not distinct identification of the snake with the ancestral ghost, some connexion between them is assumed. That among the possible relations between the tomb-haunting animal and the deceased person, metamorphosis will be supposed by early peoples, is elear. And that henco results the identification of owls and bats (and possibly *scarabcei)* with souls, can no longer be doubted.

A striking verification of the foregoing inference has come to me quite recently (188-1) in an essay entitled *A Sepulchral Relief from Tarentum,* by Mr. Percy Gardner (reprinted from the *Journal of Hellenic Studies,* vol. v). Discussing the reasons assigned for the not infrequent presence of sculptured snakes on sepulchral tablets, representing ministrations to deceased persons, Mr. Gardner says: –

" We know that it was by no meaus unusual among the Qreeks to have tame snakes, and to allow them the range of the house." . . . The inference of some is "that his [the snake's] presence in these reliefs muet have reference to the widely-spread belief of ancient limes, that snakes were either the companions or even the representatives of dead heroes. I need not surely bring forward proofs of this statement, bnt I may for a moment pause to point out how ancient science explained the fact. Plutarch tells us, that when the dead body of Clcomenes was hanging on the cross in Egypt, a largo serpent was seen wound abont it, repelling the attacks of the birds of pn-y who would have fed on it. This phenomenon, he says, terrified some of tho Alexandriaus, as proving that Cleomenes wus a hero of semi-divine nature, until it was pointed out, that as the dead hotly of a butl produces bees and that of a horse wasps, so the dead body of a man pioduces in the natural course of its deeay, snakes."

Hero then we find further support for the conclusion drawn in § 167, that a house-haunting animal is liable to be identified with a returned ancestor; at the same time that we geb an illustration of the supposed mode of metamorphosis – a mode supposed in sundry cases of kindred superstitions; as in the belief that gods take the shape of flies – a belief of the Accadiana, of the Philistines, and of some extant North Amer-ica. ii Indians.

T may add that certain incidents attending the worship of Asklepios, while they serve in one way to verify the above inferences, serve to show how, under somc circumstances, snake- worship arises in a partially-different way. Originally referred to by Homer as a physician *(i. e.,* a medicine-man), among whose sourees of influence, skill as a snake-charmer may naturally have been one (giving origin to the habitual representation of him as holding a staff round which a serpent is coiled), Asklepios, in the later periods of his worship, is himself represented as a serpent. Speaking of certain Roman coins, Mr. Warwick Wroth, of the British Museum, says: –

"On the reverse of this specimen Caracalla is represeated in military dress, with his right Imnd upraised to salute a serpent eatwined around a tree, its head towards the Emperor. . . . That the serpeat who is here receiving alor. ition is Asklepios is rendered certain both by the presence of Tele- ephoros, and by a comparison of this piece with another of Caracalla's Per-

§mene coins, . . . Although the serpeat is an attribute of the God of ealing, which is almost inrariably preseat, it is not usual to finl the god represented as on the coin n. under diseussion. Serpeats, however, were kept in many of his temples, and, indeed, were sometimes considered as the incarnation of the deity himself, especially in the transmission of his worship from one city to another. Thus, the people of Sikyon traced the origin of their Asklepios cultus to a Sikyoniau woman who had brought the god from Epidaurus in the form of a serpent. In the form of a serpent also the god was brought from Epidaurus to Rome. On a famous medallion of Antoninus Pms we see the serpeat – that is, Asklepios – about to plunge from the vessel which has conveyed him iato the waves of Father Tiber, who welcomes him with outstretched hand, imd upon whose island the first Roman temple of the new divinity was afterwards erected. This medallion hears the inscription, scvlapivs." *(Axklepios and the Coins of Prrytnnon* [republislied from *The Eumismatic Chronicle,* 3rd series, vol. ii], by Warwick Wroth, Esq., pp. 47-8.)

Lotus-wnrsJtip. – I have not included in the chapter on plant- worship, the case of the lotus; because I did not wish to endanger the general argument by a doubtful support. The evidence is, however, sufficient to raise the suspicion that lotus- worship arose in the same way ns did soma-worship.

Clearly some plant, or the product of some plant, called lotns, was eaten as a nervous stimulant, producing a state of blissful indifference; though among sundry plaats which have gone by the name, it is not decided which was the one. Further, there was in the Enst the belief in a divinity residing in a vater-plant known as the lotus; and at present in Thibet, worship of this divinity in the lotus is the dominant religion. As is stated in Mr. Wilson's *Abode of Snow,* pp. 304-6, the daily and hourly prayer is " Om mani padmo haun," which literally rendered means, "O God! the jewel in the lotus. Amen." The word *mani,* here translated jewel, and meaning more generally a precious thing. is variously applied to sacred objects – to the long stone tumuli, to the prayer-mills, etc. So thatreading through the figurative expression to the original thought, it would seem to be – " Oh. God ! the precious or sacred power in the lotus." Difficulties in exphiining the ancient legend about lotus-eating, as well as this existing superstition, arise from the fact that the plant now known ns the lotus has no toxic qualities. There is, however, a possible solution. The lotus has a sveet root; and at the present time in Cashmere, this root is hooked up from the bottoms of the lakes and nscd as food. But a sweet root contains fermentable matters – both, the saccharine and the amylaceous : even now, alcohol is made from beet-root. Possibly, then, in early times the juice and starch of the lotus-root were used, just as the sap of the palm is in some places used still, for making an intoxicating beverage; and the beliefs concerning the lotus may have survived in times when this beverage was replaced by others more easily produced. The fact that in the early days of soma-worship the juice was fermented, while in later days it was not (other kinds of intoxicating liquors having come into use), yields additional reason for thinking so. Be this as it may, however, we have this evidence: – some plant yielding a product causing a pleasurable mental state, was identical in name with a plant regarded as sacred because of an indwelling god.

It is, indeed, alleged that in Egypt the lotus was sacred as a symbol of the Nile, and that the Indian lotus stood in like relation to the Ganges. I notice this interpretation for the purpose of remarking that I do not believe any early usage aroso through symbolization. This is one of the many erroneous interpretations which result from ascribing developed ideas to undeveloped minds. No one who, instead of fancying how primitive usages could have arisen, observes how they do arise, will believe that the primitive man. ever *deliberately* adopted a symbol, or ever even conceived of a symbol as such. All symbolic actions are modifications of actions which originally had practical ends – were not invented but grew. The case of mutilations sufficiently exemplifies the process.

OtJier-Worlds. – The speculation ventured in § 113, that conquest of one race by another introduces beliefs in different other worlds, to which the superior and inferior go, is supported by this passage which I have since met with: –

"If there are strong easte-distinctions, the souls of the noble and chief men are said to go to a better country than those of the rest. ... It is tor this reason that in Cochin Chins, common people do not entertain the souls of tlieir friends on the same day of the All-Souls' feast as that on which the. nobility ha. ve invited theirs ; heeause otherwise those souls when returning would have their former servants to earry the gifts received." – *Hiiian, l'ergl. Ptycholugie,* p. 8W.

Snpersiitinm of the Russians. – Under foregoing heads the examples of each form of superstition resulting from the ghost- tlieorj, ore taken from divers societies. Here it will be instructive to present an eutire series of these several forms of such superstitions as exhibited in the same society. This is done in the following extracts from Mr. Ralston's *Hongs of the Russian People.*

Because they believe one of the forms of the soul to be the shadow " (here are persons there who object to having their silhouettes taken, fearing that if the) do so they will die before the ycur is out." (p. 117.)

" A man's reflected imago is supposed to be in communion with his inner elf." (p. 117.)

" The Servians believe that the soul of a witch oflen leaves her body while she is asleep, and tlies abroad in the shape of a butterfly." (pp. 117-8.)

"After death the soul at first remains in the ncighbourhood of the body, and then follows i to iho tomb. The Bulgarians hold that it assumes the form of a bird or a butterfly, and sits on the nearest tree waiting till the funeral is over." (p. 115.)

"A common belief among the Russian peasantry is that the spirits of the departed haaut their old homes for the space ot six weeks, during which they eat and drink, and watch the sorrowing of the mourners." (p. 118.)

" Great care is taken to provide the dead man with what ho requires on bis long journey, especially with a handkerchief aml towel, . . . and with a coin . . . for the purpose of buying *a.* place in the other world . . . The custom of providing money for the corpse has always been universal among the Slavonians." (pp. 315-6.)

Mourning "was Jormcrly attended by laceration of the faces of the mourners, a custom still preserved among some of the inhabitants of Dal- Uiatia and Moatenegro." (p. 31U.)

Among the old Slavonians " in some cases at least, human sacrifices were offered on the occasion of a burial." (p. .321.)

"in addition to being accompanied by his widow, the heathen Slavonian, if a mun of means and distinctiou, was solaced by the saerifice of some of Hm slaves." (p. 328.)

On Dmitry's Saturday " the peasaats attend a church service, and after- wards they go out to the graves of thcir friends, and there mstitute a feast, lauding . . . the virtues and good qualities of the deaJ, and then drinking to their eternal rest." (p. 260.)

" In olden days a memorial banquet was held in his [the departed one's] honour on the third, sixth, ninth, and fortieth day after his death, and ou its anniversary, and he was remembered also in the feasts celebrated . . . in memory of the Fathers. ... To these feasts it was customary to invito the dead. . . . Sileatly the living . . . threw portions of the food under tho table for their spirit-guests." (pp. 320-1.)

"Among the (non-Slavonic) Mordvins in the Penza and Saratof Governmeats, a dead man's relations offer the corpse eggs, butter, and money, saying : ' Here is something for you: Marfa has brought you this. Watchover her corn and cattle.'" (p. 121.)

"The festival called *Riidunitsa* ... is chiefly devoted to the memory of the dead. In certain districts ihe women and iria still take food and drink to the cemeteries, and there 'howl' over the grave of thcir dead friends and relatives. When they have ' howled' long enough, they . . . proceed to eat, drink, and be merry, deeming ihat the dead can 'rejoiee' with them." (". 22.)

" Here is a specimen of a *Prichitanie,* intended to be recited over a graT on the twentieih of April . . .

'0 ye, our own lathers and mothers! in what have we angered you, our own, that vou have no welcome for us, no joy, no parental charm ? . . .'

And here ... is a specimen of an orphan's wailing above her motLer's grove : –

'O mother dear that bare me, O with sadness longed-for one! To whom hast thou left us, on whom are we orphans to rest our hopes ? . . . Have a care for us, mother, dear, give us a word of kindness! No, thou hast hardened thy h. art harder than stone, and hast folded thy uncaressiug hands over thy heart.' " (pp. 343-4.)

There is trood evidence that "the Domovoy or house-spirit (p. 119) is an ancestor. " The Ruthenians reverence in the person of the Domovoy the original constructor of the family hearth." (p. 122.) " In some districts tradition expressly refors to the spirits of the dead the functions which are generally attributed to the Domovoy, and they are supposed to keep wateh over the house of a descendant who honours thorn and provides them with due offerings." (p. 121.)

" The Russian peasant draws a clear line between his own Domovoy and his neighbour's. The former is a benignant spirit, who will do him good, even at the expense of others ; the latter is a malevolent being, who will very likely steal his hav, drive away his poultry, and so forth, for his neighbour's benefit." (pp. 129-130.)

" The domestic spirits of different households often engage in contests with one another." (p. 130.)

" In Bohemia lishermen are afraid of assisting a drowning man, thinking the Vodyany [water-sprite] will be offended, aud will drive away the fish from their nets." (p. 152.)

" According to some traditious she [the witch Baba Taga] even feeds on the souls of the dead. The White-Russians, for instance, atlirm that '. . . . the Baba Yaga and her subordinate witches feed on the souls of people.' " (p. 163.)

During a drought some peasants " dng up the body of a Raskolnik, or Dissenter, who had died in the previous December, and had been buried in the village graveyard. Some of the party then beat it about the head, exclaiming, ' Give us rain!'" (pp. 425-6.)

"In White-Russia the Domovoy is ealled *TsmoTc,* a snake, . . . This House Snake brings nil sorts of good to the master who treats it well, and gives it omelettes, which should be placed on tke roof of the house or on the throhiug-floor." (pp. 124-5.)

" By the conimou people of the present day snakes are there [in Russia] looked upon with much respect . and even affection. 'Our peasants,' says Afanasief, 'consider it a happy omen if a snake takes up its quarters in cottage, and they gladly set out milk for it. To kill such a snake would be a very great sin. ('p. 175.)

" Some traces of tree-worship may be found in the song wtch the girli ing as they go into the woods to fetch the birch-tree . . . " Rejoice, Birch-tree, rejoice green ones! . . . To you the maideus ! To you they bring pies, Cukes, omelettes.

"The eatables here mentioned seem to refer to sacrifices offered in oldeu to the b rch, the tree of the sp. ing." (p. 238.)

" They [Hie old heathen Slavonians] appear to have looked upon the life beyond the grave as a mere prolongation of that led on earth – the rich man retained ai leust some of his possessions ; the slave remained a slave." (p. 1U.)

Many instructive passages might be added. The dead are paid to complain of the pressure of the earth on them ; describe themselves as cold; and at festivals to which they are invited, are sympathized with ns tired and hungry. Ancestral . spirits are carried to new homes ; diseases are evil spirits often with bodily shapes ; there are wizards who control tho weather; they ride in dust-whirlwinds. But the above suffice to show how completely the ghost-theory has developed into an ancestor- worship, betraying, notwithstanding the repressive influences of Christianity, all the essentials of a religion – sacrifices, prayers, praises, festivals.

Apotheosi in Polynesia. – The more the evidence furnished by every race is looked into, the more irresistible becomes the conclusion that gods were originally men: sometimes even ordinary men, but usually men in some way superior, belonging either to the tribe or to a conquering tribe. That which the traditions of the Egyptians tell us, namely, that Egypt was originally ruled by a dynasty of gods; that which we see in Greek beliefs as set down by Herodotus, who distinguishes Minos as preceding the generations of men, and belonging to the dynasty of the gods; that which is implied by the Japanese story that Jimmu, " the fifth ruler in descent from the sun goddess," was " considered to have been the first *mortal* ruler" (Adams' *History of Japan,* vol. i, p. 7) ; is shown us by the uncivilized. These now entertain idiyxs like those entertained by the progenitors of the civilized. Here are a few instances: –

" Rangi requested the invincible warrior Tangiia to send him one of hij eons as a god." (Gill, *Myths and Songs from the South Pacific,* p. 25.)

"And yet, strangely enough, associated with these original gods are the deified heroes of antiquity, in no wise inferior to thcir fellow divinities. *(Ibid,* p. 20.)

"The proper denizens of Avaiki [Hades = an underground world] arc the major and lesser divinities, witli their dependeats. These marry, multiply, and quarrel like mortals. They wear clothing, plaat, cook, fish, build, and inhabit dwellings of exactly the same sort as exist on earth. The food of immortals is no better than that eaten by mankmd. . . . Murder, adultery, drunkenness, theft, and lying arc practised by them. The arts of this world are fac-similes of what primarily belonged to nether-land, and were taught to mankind by the gods." *(Ibid.,* p. 154.)

There is a tradition of a council of gods to determine as to man's immortality. " VVhile the diseussion was proceeding a pouring ruin came on and broke up the meeting. The gods ran to the housed for shelter." (Turner, *Samoa a Hundred Years Ago,* pp. 8-9.)

Concerning the natives of San Christovnl, Solomon Islands, we ire tolJ that: –

" The bodies of common pcople arc thrown into the sea, but mrn of eonre- quence arc buried. After a time they take up the skull or some part of the skeleton, and put it in a small building in the village, when- upon oceasious they pray or sacrifice to obtain help from the spirit." (Codrington, *Journal of the Anthropoluyival Institute,* x, 300.)

But perhaps the elearest evidence, as well as the most abundant, is that furnished by the Fijians. Since writing the comparison made in § 201, between the Greek pantheon and the pantheon of the Fijiaus, an unknown friend has beeu good enough to forward me a statement which bears, in an interesting way, on the question. It is contained iu a parliamentary paper, *Correspondence respecting the Cession of Fiji,* presented February 6, 1875, p. 57. This document concerns the native ownership of land ; and the passage I refer to appears to be appended for the purpose of showing how the native idea of ownership is affected by the associated creed : –

" Note. – Their fathers or their Gods. – It may not be out of place in connection with the above memorandum to advance one or two facts with the object of showing that the head of the tribo, *i. e.,* its highest living male ascendant, was regarded as its father. He held absolute authority over the persous, property, and lives of his people, and both before and. after death, hud the same reverence shown to him as to a God.

" The Fijiau language makes no distinction, in terms, between the marks of respect and reverence rendered to a Chief and those rendered to a God, I will select a few words, with their meanings, from Hazelwood's Fijian Dictionary. ' 1. Tama – a father. 2. Tama-ka – to reverence, to elap hands, or to make somo expression of a God or Chief. 3. Cabora – lo offer or present property to a God or to a Chief. 4. Ai sevu – the first dug vams, the first fruits, which arc generally offered to the Gods aml given to a Chief of a place. 5. Tauvu, and Vcitaimi – Literally, to have the same root, or sprung from the same uourue ; used of people who worship the same God.' ...

" The swearing of Fijiaus is like that of the High Asiatic peoples. Two men quarrelling never swear at each other personally, nor even utter their respective names ; they will curse their fathers, their grandfathers, and their most remote ancestry. The reason being that to curse a Fijian's father is to curse his God. . . . The successive stages of authority among the Fijian pcople is first, that of the individual family ; secondly, the association of many families, which constitute the Q. ali; and thirdly, the union of these Ijalis under their recognized hereditary Chief, which constitutes the Mata- nitn. It is the Famity, Gens, and Tribe of early history found extant, and as a system still closely observed in Polynesia at the present day."

This account agrees completely with the indications given by earlier voyagers and missionaries; as witness the following ei tracts: –

" It is impossible to aseertain with any degree of probability how many gods the Feejeeans have, as anv man who ean distinguish himself in murdering his fellow-men may ceriainly secure to himself deification after his death." (Erskine's *Western. Pacific,* p. 246.)

The lower order of Fijian gods "generally described as men of superior mould and earriage," " bear a close analogy to the *lares, lemures,* and genii of the Romans." "Admission into their number is easy, and any one maysecure his own apotheosis who can insure the service of some one as his representative and priest after his decease." (Williams, *Fiji, etc.,* pp. 218-9.)

Natare-Gnds. – Here arc a few further facts supporting tl'o conclusion that after the rise of the ghost-theory, the various kinds of objects which irregularly appear, disappear, and reappear, in the heavens, are frequently regarded ns ghosts. Says Gill, concerning the fates of the Mangaians after death : –

" Not so warriors slain on the field of battle. The spirits of these lucky foflows for a while wander about amongst the rocks and trees in the neighbourhood of which their bodies were thrown. . . . At length the first shun on eacli battle-field would collect his brother ghosts," and lead them to the summit of a mountain, whence " they leap inlo the blue expanse, thus becoming the peculiar clouds of the winter." [Compare with North American Indians among whom the name " Cloud" is frequeat. in Callin's list.] (Gill, *Myths and Sonffifrom the South Pacific,* pp. 162-3.)

" It was supposed that in these lower regions there were heavens, earth and eca, fruits and flowers, plauting, fishing and cooking, marrying and giving in marriage – all very mach as in the world from which they had gone. Their new bodies, however, wereVingalarly volatile, could aseend at night, become luminous sparks [stars] or vapour, revisit their former homes and retire again at early dawn to the bush or to the Polotu hades. These visits were dreaded, as they were supposed to be errands of destruction to the living, especially to any with whom the departed had reason to be angry. Hy means of preseats and peniteatial confession all injurers were anxious to part on good terms with the dying whom they had ill-used." (Turner, *Samoa a Hundred Years Ago,* p. 259.)

. . . . " Others saw their vilhige-god in the rainbow, others saw him in the shooting-star ; and in time of war the position of a rainbow and the direction of a shooting-star were always ominous." *(Heid.,* p. 21.)

Mountain Deities. – In § 114, I suggested two ways in which ancestor-worship originates beliefs in gods who reside on the highest peaks and have access to the heavens. Burfal of the dead on mountain crags, I indicated as one origin; and the occupation of mountain strongholds by conquering races, as probably another origin. I have since met with verifications of both suggestions.

The first of them is contained in the *Travels in the Philippines,* by F. Jagor. Giving proof that before the Spanish settlement the people had the ordinary ideas and customs of ancestor- worshippers, ho describes the sacred burial caves; and shows tho survival of the religious awe with which these caves were originally regarded. Ho visited some of these caves at Nipa- Nipa; and snys (p. 259) that " the numerous coffins, implements, arms, and trinkets, protected by superstitious terrors, continncd to be undisturbed for centuries. No boat ventured to cross over without the observance of a religious ceremony, derived frum heathen times, to propitiate the spirits of the caverns, who were believed to punish tho omission of it with storm and shipwreck." Moreover he tells us that the boatmen who went wilhthe pastor of Bascy to the cave to get remains, re-garded a thunderstorm which broke on thcir way back, as " a punishment for thoir outrage." After thus exhibiting the popular beliefs as they still exist, notwithstanding Catholic teaching:, he proves, from early writers, what these beliefs originally were. It appeai-s that men when dying often chose thoir burial-places ; nnd he quotes one authority to the effect that " those who were of note" sometimes had thcir coffins deposited " on an elevated place or rock on the bank of a river, where they might be venerated by the pious." (p. 262.) He says that Thevenot describes them as worshipping " those of their ancestors who had most distinguished themselves by courage and genins, whom they regarded as dcities. . . . Even the aged died under this conccit, choosing particular places, such us one on the island of Ley to, which allowed of thcir bcing interred at the edge of the sea, in order tliat the mariners who crossed over might acknowledge them as dcities, and pay them respect." (p. 263.) And he also quotes Gemelli Careri, who says that " the oldest of them chose. some remarkable spot in the mouatains, and particularly on headlands projecting into the sea, in order to be worshipped by the sailors." (p. 2ti3.) This combination of facts is, I think, amply significant. We have distinguished persons becoming gods after death; wo see them providing for this apotheosis, and in a sense demanding worship ; we find them choosing high and conspicuous burial-places to facilitate the worship ; we see that approach to burial-places is regarded as saerilege; and we see that the ghosts of the dead have Iveome dcified to the extent that they are supposed to vent thcir anger in thunderstorms. LI ere are all the elements from which might result a Philippine Sinai.

The instance to which I refer ns showing that invaders, or dominant men, scizing a high stronghold (see § 114), may give origin to a celestial hierarchy, whose residence is a mountain top, I take from Bancroft's version of the Quiche legend. It begins with a time when as yet there was no Sun (possibly a fragment of some still more ancient story brought southwards by dwellers in the Arctic regions); and iu the first place narrates a migration in search of the Sun.

" So the four men nnd their people set out for Tulan-Zuiva, otherwise ealled the Seven-caves or Seven-ravines, and there they received gods, eacli man as head of a family, a god; though inasmach as the fourth man, Iqi- Balam, had no children, and founded no family, his god is not usnally taken into the accouat. . . . Many other trials also they underweat in Tulan, famines and such things, and a general dampness and cold, – for the earth was moist, there being as yet no sun. . . . They determined to leave Tulan ; and the greater part of them, nnder the guardianship and directiu. i of Tohil, set out to see where they should take up their uboile. They continued on thcir wuy nmid the must extreme hardships for wiuit oi Jood. ... At lostthey came to a mountain that they named Hooavitz, after one of their gods, and here they rested, – for here they were by some means given to understand that they should st-e the sun. . . . And the sun, and the moon, and the itars were now all established. Yet was not the Buq then in the beginning the same as now; his heat waated force, and he was but as a reflection in a mirror. [This is explained if we suppose migration from the far north.] . . . Another wonder when the sun rose! The three tribal gods, Tohil, Avilix, and Hacavitz, were turned into stone, as were also the gods connected with the lion, the tiger, the viper, and other fierce and dangerous animals. . . . And the people multiplied on this Mouat Hacavitz, and hero they built their city. . . . And they worshipped the gods that had become stone, Tohil, Avilix, and Hacavitz. . . . They began to wet their altars with the heart's blood of human victims. From thcir mouatain hold they watched for lonely travelers belonging to the surrounding tribes, seized, overpowered, and slew them for a sacrifice. . . . The hearts of the villagers were thus fatigued within them, pursuing unknown enemies. At last, however, it became plain that the gods Tohil, Avilix, and Hacavitz, and thcir worship, were in some way or other this cause of this bereavemeat: so the people of the villnges conspired against them. Many attacks, both openly and by ruses, did they make on the gods, and on the four men, and on the children and people connected with them; but not once did they succeed, so great was the wisdom, and power, and courage of the four men and of their dcities. . . . At last the war was finished. . . . And the tribes humiliated themselves before the face of Balam-Quitze, of Balam-Agab, and of Mahu- cutah. . . . Now it eame to pass that the time of the death of Balam-Quitze,

Balam-Agab, Muhacutah, and Iqi-Balam drew near ind they said :

we return to our people. . . . Ko the old men took leave of thcir sons and thcir wives. . . . Then instaatly the four old men were not; but in theii place was a great bundle. . . . o it was ealled the Majesty Enveloped . . . and they burned incense before it." [Such a bundle was said "to contain the remains of Cmmvxtli, the chief god of TIaseala."J *Jfaltci Maces, etc.,* vol. iii, pp. 49-54.

Men in ihe Sky. – Already the Esquimaux have furnished in the text an illustration of the primitive belief that stars, etc., were originally men and animals who lived on the Earth (§ 190). In the work of Dr. Rink, I find a detailed account of Esquimaux ideas concerning the physical connexion between the upper and lower worlds, and the routes joining them : –

" The earth, with the sea supported by it, rests upon pillars, and covers an under world, accessib. e by various entrances from the sea, as well as from mouatain clefts. Above the earth an upper world is found, beyond which the blue sky, bcing of a solid consistence, vaults itself like an outer shell, and, as some say, revolves around some high mouatain-top in the far north. The upper world exhibits a real land with mouatains, valleys, and lakes. After death, human souls either go to the upper or to the under world. The Iftttcr is decidedly to be preferred, as being warm and rich in food. There are the dwellings of the happy dead called *arsissut* – *viz.,* those who live in abundance. On the coatrary, those who go to the upper world will suffer from cold and famine ; and these are ealled *arssartut,* or ball-players, on accouat of thcir playing at ball with a walrus-head, which gives rise to the aurora borealis, or northern lights. Further, the upper world must be eon- eidereil a coutinnation of the earth in the direction of hcight, although those individnals, or at least those souls temporarily delivered from the body, that re said to have visited it, for the most part pasted through the aur. The upueiworld, it would seem, may be cousidered identical with the mountain round the top of which the vaulted sky is for everctrHing – ttie proper road l? a; ling to it from the foot of the mountain upwards being itself either too far off or too steep. One of the tales also mentions a man going in his kayak [boat] to the border of the ocean, where the sky comes down to meet it." (pp. 37-S.) " The upper world is also inhabited by several rulers besides the souls of the' deceased. Among these are the owners or inhabitants of celestial bodies, who, having been once men, were removed in their lifetime from the earth, but are still attac'icd to it in different ways, and pay occasional visits to it. They have also been represented as the celestial bodies themselves, and not their *inue* only, the tales mentioning them in both ways. The owner uf the moon originally was a man, ealled Aningaut, and the *inua* of the sun was hia sister. . . . The *erdlaveersissok* – viz., tho entrail-seizer – is a woman residing on the way to the moon, who takes out the entrails of every person whom she can tempt to laughter. The *siaglut,* or the three stars in Orion's belt, were men who were lost in going out to hunt on the ice." (pp. 48-9.)

There could scarcely be better proof that the personalization of heavenly bodies has resulted from the supposed translation of terrestrial beings – men and animals – to the sky. Here wo have the upper world regarded as physically continuous with the lower world as well as like it in character; and the migration to it af I or death parallels those migrations to distant parts of tho Earth's surface after death, which primitive races in general show us. While we have no evidence of Nature-worship, we have elear evidence of identification of celestial bodies with traditional persons. That is to say, personalization of the heavenly bodies, *precedes* worship of them, instead of *succeeding* it, as inythologists allege. Joining these facts with those given in the text, the origin of names for constellations and the genesis of astrology, are made, I think, sufficiently clear.

Star-Oods. – While the proofs of these pages are under Cop- rection [this refers to the first edition], I am enabled to add an important piece of evidence, harmonizing with the above, and supporting sundry of tho conelusions drawn in the text. It is furnished by a Babylonian inscription (Rawlinson's *Cuneiform Inseriptions, etc.,* iii, 53, No. 2, lines 36, ete.), which, as translated by Prof. Schrader, runs thus : –

" The star Venus at sunrise is Ishtar among the gods,
Tho star Venus at sunset is Boaltis among the gods."

We have thus another case of multiple personality in a heavenly body, analogous to the cases of the Sun and Moon before pointed out (§ I'. H), but differing in definiteness. For whereas, before, the belief in two or more personalities was inferred, *wo* here have it directly stated. This belief, inexplicable on any current theory, we see to be perfectly explicable as a result of birth-naming.

Rrligiou of the Iranians. – Dr. Seheppig has translated for meBOTne important passages from the work of Fr. Spiegel, *1Uranifche Alterthumskuwlc,* vol. ii (1873), pp. 91, etc. While this work brings clearly into view the many and various indications of ancestor-worship in the *Zend-Avesla,* it contains highly significant evidence concerning the ideas of ghosts *(fravashis)* and of ghost-mechanism throughout creation, which were held by the Persian branch of the Aryans.

Nature of the Fravashi. – (p. 92.) " The *fravashi* is in the first place a part ... of the human sonl. In this sense the word is used in the *Acexta.* . . . Later works of the Parsees give us more exact information about the activity of *the fravashi.* The *frohar* or *fravnshi* – so it is stated in one of those works, the *Sadder liundeltesh*

– hns the tnsk of making useful what a man eats, and removing the heavier parts. Accordingly, the *fravnshi* is the part intermediating between body and soul; bnt it is conccived ns a person, independent in general, and particularly from the body. The *Sudder Bundehesh* recognizes other psychic powers besides : the vital power *(jdn)*, the conscience *(akho)*, the eonl *(revan)*, the consciousness *(Ji6i)*. [This recalls the theory of the Egyptians, by whom also each man was supposed to unite within himself four or five different entities. These seemingly-strange beliefs are not difficult to account for. As shown in §§ 56, 57, 94, 95, shadow, reflexion, breath, and heart are all regarded as partially-independent components of the individual, sometimes spoken of as separable during life, and as going to different places after death.] Of these the vital power is so intimately connected with the body that the latter perishes as Booh as the former has vanished. In a body thus doomed to perish the other psychic powers caunot stay cither : they leave it; the conscience, because it has not done anything wrong, makes straightway for heaven, while soul, consciousness, and *fravnshi* remaining together, have to answer for tLb deeds of the man, and are rewarded or punished."

Fravashis of Gods and Men. – (p. 94.) "Every living being has a *fravnshi*, not only in the terrestrial but in the spiritual world. Not even Ahura-Mnzda [the chief god] *la* exceptcd ; his *fravaahi* is frequently alluded to (Vd. 19, 46, Yt. 13, 80) as well as the *fracnshis* of tlfe Amesha-cpentns and the other Yazatas (Ye. 23, 3, Yt. 13, 82). Most frequently the *fravasltis* of the Paoiryo-tkaesbas are invoked, *i. e.,* those of the pious men who lived before the appearance of the law. To them, gem-rally, the *fravnshis* of the nearest relations, and the *fravaslii* of the person himself, are added. ... It may appear surprising that the/ra- *i-nsltis* of the ' born and unborn ' are invoked (Yc. 26, 20). The clue may be found in Yt. 13, 17, where it is stated that the *frarnshis* of the pious who lived before the law, and of the bcings who will appear in future, are more powerful than those of otherpeople, living or dead. Here worship of manes and of heroes is mixed up. Among these *fraonsJiis* the ancestors of the particular family, and of the particular elan or tribe, were worshipped."

Powers of the Fravashis. – (p. 95.) " The *fravashis* were not deficient in power. Their chief task was the protection of living beings. It is by their splendour and majestv that Ahum-Mazda is enabled to protect the Ardvicura Anahita (Tt. 13,4) [a certain spring and a goddess], and the earth on which the water runs and the trees grow. *The fravashis* protect, as well, the children in the womb. . . . They are very important for the right distribution of terrestrial benefits. It is by their assistance that cattle and draught beasts can walk on the earth; and bat for their help sun, moon, and star, as well as the water, would not find their way, nor would the trees grow (Yt. 13, 53, etc.)." (p. 95-6.) "Accordingly, the peasant will do well to secure the assistance of these important deities. The same holds trne for the warrior; for the *fravasliis*are helpers in battles, . . . Mithra, Itashun, and the victorious wind are in their company. ... It is of great importance that *the fravashis* remain in elose connection with their families. They demand water for their elans, each one for his kin, when it is taken out of the Lake Vonru- kasha; . . . each of them fights on the spot where he has got to defend a homestead, and kings and generals who want their help against tormenting enemies, must specially call on them; they then come and render assistance, provided they have been satisfied and not offended (Yt. 13, 69-72). The *fravaxhis* give assistance not only as warriors; they may bo invoked against any thing alarming, . . . against bad men and bad spirits." . . . Fravashis and Stars. – (p. 94.) We read in the Min6-khired : " 'All the innumerable stars which are visible are called the *fravashis* of the terrestrial ones [men ?] ; because for the whole creation created by the creator Ormuzd, for the born and the unborn, a fravashi of the same essence is manifest.' Hence it appears that the *fravashis,* or the stars, form the host that . . . fights against the demons." . . .

Worship of the Fravashis. – (p. 97.) " As in the case of other genii of the Zoroastrian religion, much depends on the satisfactory propitiation of the *fravashis;* for their power, and consequent activity, depends on the sacrifices. Probably they were worshipped upon the 19th day of each month : their chief feasts, however, were on the . . . intercalatory days added to the year at its termination. About that time *the frarashis* descend to the earth, and stay therefor 10 nights, expecting to be met with appropriate sacrifices of meat and elothes. (Yt. 13, 49.) [Compare with the German and Selavonian superstitions.] . . . There cannot be any doubt that the worship of the *fraea'his* played an important part with the Iranians, though perhaps more in privatethan in public. It would appear that there were two different sorts of it. General, certainlv, was the hero-worship – the veneration of the Paoiryo-tkaeshas [pious men before the law]. With this, in some ages perhaps, the worship of *fravnshis* of the royal family wns combined. The ancestor-worship, on the other hand, was of a strictly private character."

Parallelisms. – (p. 98.) " The custom of honouring tho memory of ancestors by sacrifices would appear to have been characteristic of the Indo-Germans from the very first. It is for this renson that quite striking similarities are found in tho cult, which no doubt refer to vei'y old times. ... It has been justly poiuted out that, as the *fravashis* are conccived as stars, so, in the opinion of the ancient Hindoos, the blessed men beam in form of stars (see *Jusli, Handbuch, s. v., frnvashi,* p. 200). Nor should it be overlooked that this star-worship is very like the worship of the heavenly host mentioned in the Old Testament."

Here, then, concerning these ancient Aryans of Persia, we have, on high authority, statements proving a dominant ancestor- worship ; and also yielding support to various of the doctrines set foiili in Part I. While it is only one of several souls possessed by each individual, the *fravashi* is the predominant and propitiated sonl. It is supposed to need food, like the other-self of the dead savage. Not ordinary men only, but dcities, up to the supreme one, have each his ghost; implying that he was originally a man. We see, too, that these *fravusMs* which are ancestral ghosts, become the agents to whom the powers of surrounding objects are ascribed – fetich ghosts. We see that they have peopled the heavens – have become the in-dwelling spirits of sun, moon, and stars. And we see that worship of them, beginuing with worship of those of the family and the clan, originates in time tho worship of conspicuous traditional persons, ns ancient heroes and gods; just as among the Fijians and others at the present day.

Aryan Ancestor-vrirsltip. – The more I have looked into tho evidence, the more I have marvelled at those who, in the interests of the mythological theory, assert that the Aryans have been distinguished from inferior races by not being ancestor-worshippers ; and who ascribe such ancestor-worship as cannot be overlooked, to imitation of inferior races. If the Americun fillibuster Ward, now apotheosized in

China, has a temple erected to him there, the fact is accepted as not unuatural among the ancestor-worshipping Chinese. But in India, among Aryans, we must nscribe to the bad example of lower peoples, the erection of a temple at Benares to tho English fillibuster Warren Hastings. *(Parl. Hist.,* xxvi, pp. 773-7.)

1 find nothing but such unwarranted assumption to place against the elear evidence that ancestor-worship was dominant among primitive Aryans, long remained dominant among civilized Aryans, survived in considerable strength in mediaeval Christendom, and has not yet died away. When we learn that the *Acesta* describes sacrifices for the dead, and contains prayers calling upon them – when we read in the *Institntes of M, nn* (Sir W. Jones's translation, vol. iii, p. 147) that "an oblation by *Itrdhmcns* to their ancestors transcends an oblation to the deities ; because that to the deities is considered as the opening and completion of that to ancestors" – when, turning to the Aryans who migrated West, we remember how active was their propitiation of the dead, calling from Grote the words " sepulchral duties, sacred beyond all others in the eyes of a Greek" – when we are reminded how the early Romans, ascribing to their manes-gods a love of human blood, duly administered to it; our boldness of assumption must be great if we can say that Aryan ancestor- worship was not indigenous but adopted.

Were it true that necrolatry was not rooted in the primitive Aryan mind, as in other primitive minds (a marvellous difference, did it exist), it would be strange that though superficial it was so difficult to extirpate. Christianity spread without extinguishing, it. In a capitulary of 742, Karloman prohibits "sacrifices to the dead " *(lialazius,* i, 148). Nor has it been extinguished by modern Christianity, as was shown in § 152. Here is further evidence from Hanusch, *Die Wissenschaftdet Slawisehen Milthus,* p. 408 : –

"According to GeMmrdi . . . the Misniaus, Tausitziaus, Bohemians, Silesians, und Poles, upon the first of Mareh, early in the morning, w.-nt forth with torches, going to the cemeterT and offering up food to their ancestors. [According to Grimm] the Esthonians leave food for the dead in the night of the second of November, and are glad if in the morning something is found to be cousumed. . . . With all Slaves it was a custom to havo a meal for the dead, not only upon the day of funeral but annually; the fornii r was intended for the particular dead, the latter for the dead in general. . . . At the latter they believed the souls to be present personally. Silently little bits of food were thrown for them under the table. People believed they heard them rustle, and saw them feed upon the smell and vapour of the food."

I may elose with the conclusive testimony of one who has had nunsual opportunities of studying Aryan superstitions as now being generated, and whose papers in the *Fortnightly Reviiio* show how competent he is both as observer and reasoner – Sir A. C. Lyall. In a letter to me he says: – "1 do not know who may be the author of the statement which you quote [in § 1-0], that 'No Indo-Kuropcnn nation seems to have made a religion of tho worship of the dead;' but it is a generalization entirely untenable. Here in Rajputana, among the purest Aryan tribes, the worship of famous ancestors is most prevalent; and all thcii heroes are more or less duilied."

among the Greeks. – The foregoing evidence, published in the first edition, I can now re-inforce. The already- quoted essay *A Sepulchral Relief from Tarentwn,* by Mr. Percy Gardner, contains elear proofs, brought to light by recent investigations, that ancestor-worship was no less dominant among the Greeks than among inferior peoples. The first two of the following extracts, concerning Lycians and Etrurians, I prefix to ehow that the Greeks had identical conceptions and usages: –

"Thus so far as Lyeia is concerned there can be no doubt that as early as the fourth century B. c. dead heroes were represented on their tombs as receiving homage from the living." (pp. 14-15.)

"And that the feast here [on a sarcophagus] is a feast after death, is shown by the analogy of the wall paintings of several of the large tombs of Utruria, in which the occupant of the tomb is seen eating, drinking, and muking merry, as if fee had but to continue in the tomb the life which while he was in the flesh he had found so pleasant." (p. 15.)

" These reliefs readily attach themselves to the more archaic class of Spartan monuments, ami throw a fresh light on their character, so that after seeing them Milchhocfer retracted his previously expressed opinion, and no longer hesitated to believe that in all alike dead mortals held the post of honour, and that all referred to the cult us of ancestors." (p. 18.)

"The worship of the dead did not occupy among the *ehte* of Greece the tame spare in men's minds which at an earlier time it had held, and which is still held in the more conservative districts."

" Nevertheless, a careful search will disclose many passages even in the Attic writers which illustrate this form of religion. The opening passage of the *Chotphori,* for example, tells of cultus kept up at the tombs of deceased worthies. In the *Alcestis,* the heroine of the play is searcely dead before she is invoked by the chorua as a spiritual power, able to give and to withhold favours." (p. 21.)

" At a lower level than that of poetry, in the laws and the customs, more especially the burial-customs, of the Greeks, wo find ampie prcof of the tenacity with which they clung to the belief that the dead desired offerings of food and incense, and were willing in return to furnish protection and aid." (p. 22.)

" The dead man, living in his tomb as he had lived in his house, requires frequent supplies of food and drink, rejoices in the presence of armour and ornaments, such as he loved in life, and is very seusitive to discourteous treatment. These ideas were part of the mental furniture of the whole Aryan race, before it separated into branches, and are found in all tho countries oier which it spread." (p. 22.)

" It is well known with what care the early Greeks provided in the chamber in which they placed a corpse, all that was necessary for its comfort, I had almost said its life. Wine and food of various kinus were there laid up in a little store, a lamp was provided full of oil, frequently even kept burning to relieve the darkness ; and around were strewn the clothes and the armour in which the dead hero had delighted ; sometimes even, by a refinement of realism, a whetstone to sharpen the edge of sword and spear in case they should grow blunt with use. The horse of a warrior was sometimes slain and buried with him that he might not in another world endure the indignity of having to walk. Even in Homeric days the custom survived of slaying at the tomlj of a noted warrior some of a hostile race to be his slaves thereafter." (p. 23)

" If a body was leit unhuried. or if the tomb in which it was luid was nolfrom time to time supplied with food and drink, then the ghost inhatnttn!" such body beeame a wretched wanderer on the face of the earth, and neither had peace itself nor allowed survivors to be at pence." (p. 24.)

"The lect isternia of the Romans, in which they spread feasts for certain of the gods, and laid their images by the tables that they might enjoy wlmt was provided are well known, and most people fancy that tite custom was of Latin origin, but it is certain that the Romans in this matter were mere imitators of the Greeks. We shoidd naturally suppose that the cmslom nf feasting the gods arose from that of feasting deceased ancestors. And this view receives fresh confirmation when we consider that these banquets were, among the Greeks, bestowed not upon all the gods, but nearly always on those of mortal birth, such as the Dioscuri, Aselepius and Dionysus. They are bestowed indeed upon Zeus and Apollo, and this may seem strange, unless we remember how commonly Zeus Palroins or Herceius, and Apollo were confused in cultus walt the traditional family ancestor." (pp. 32-33.)

Origin of Egyptian Gods. – Amid incongruities, the general meaning of the passages which follow is sufficiently clear. Brugsoh writes : –

"In ... the primeval history of their land " the Egyptiaus " supposed three ages which followed one another, till Mena placed the double crown upon his head. During the first age, a dynasty of the Gods reigned in the land ; this wus followed by the age of the Demi-gods, and the dynasty of the mysterious Manes closed the prehistoric time. ... It is to be regreited that the fragments of the Turin papyrus (once containing the most complete list of the kings of Kgypt in their chronological order) have preserved not the slightest intelligible information about those fabulous sncee.-surs of the God-Kings. A single shred allows us to make out with tolerable certainty the names of sacred animals, such as the Apis of Memphis and the Mncvisof Heliopolis, so that it would appear ns if these aUo had contrihuted to the number of the prehistoric rulers of Egypt." *(History of Egypt,* i, 33, 39.)

The continuity of the series from these early divine personages, some of them figured as animals and half-animals, down to gods who were unquestionably deified men, is implied by the fact that to the worship of those earliest rulers whose vagne personalities, surviving from remote times, had become gods proper, there was joined a worship of early historic kings, which, similar in nature, similarly lasted through many ages. Here is a passage from Maspero's *line Enqucte Judiciaire a Thiles* (3/e' m. *de l'Acadt'mie dus Inscriptions,* t. viii), pp. 62-3: –

" A Memphis on trouve, jusque sous les Ptolemies, des pr$tres de Meres, d'Ata, de Sahura et d'autres pharaons appartenant aux plus anoicnnes dvnaa- ties (Do Rouge, *$lade sur Ins monuments gu'on peut aitribacr aux six premieres ilynuxties de Man-clhon,* pp. 31, 53, 83) ; a Thebes, lo culte des Usortesen, des Ahmes, des Amenophis (voir au *Papgrus Abbott,* pi. i, 1. 13, la mention d'un pretre d'Amenophis), ou de certaines reines comme la reino *Nefer-t-ari* (Liehlein, *Deux papgrus, etc.,* p. 31, pi. iii. 1. 6 ; Sharpe, *Eff. Iasc.* ii), fut florissant pendant des siecles. Si nous no saisissous pas chet les particuliers les indices d'une veneration aussi vivace, c'est que, dans Ka tomhes prives, lea ceremonies etaient aceomplies non par des pretres spe'ciaux, mais par Irs fils ou les descendants du def unt. Souvent, au bout de quelqm a ginirations, soit negligerce, soit doplacement, mine, ou extinction de ! t'amille, le culte etait tuspeiulu et la memoire di s morts se perdait."

To which passage, showing that the permanent worship of the dead kings was a more developed form of the ordinary ancestor- worship, I may add a confirmatory passage from E. de Rouge : – " Each pyramid had by its side a funeral building, a sort of temple, where were perforn. ed the ceremonies of a cult dedicated to tbe dcified sovercigns. 1 have no doubt that this cult commenced during thcir lifetime." – *Mem. d I'Ac. des Inser.,* pt. xxv, 2, p. 254.)

And yet in face of such evidence, harmonizing with all the Other evidences we have found, it is alleged that the earlj Egyptian gods were personalized powers of nature!

"Gods and men" in Hebrew Legend. – Further grounds for taking the view expressed in § 200, respecting the " gods and men " of the Hebrew legend, have since been disclosed in the *Chaldean Accouut of Genesis,* by George Smith. Here is a passage from the new edition edited by Prof. Sayce, published in 1880: –

" One of the most curious statements made in these hymns is that the raeo of men created *by* tlie deity was black-headed. The same race of men is mentioned elsewhere in the ancient literature of the Accndians. ... In tho bilingnal tablets Uie black race is rendered in Assyrian by the word *Adamalu* or ' red-skins." A popular etymology connected this word *Adamalu* with the word *Adamu,* or *Adam,* ' man,' partly on accouat of the similarity of sound, partly because in the age of Accadian supremacy and literature, the men *par excellence,* the special human bcings made by the Creator, were the dark-skinned race of Accad. The Accadian Adam or ' man' was dark ; it was only when the culture of the Aceadians had been handed down to their Semitic successors that he became fair. The discovery that the Biblical Adam is identical with the Assyrian *Adamu* or ' man/ and that the Assyrian *Adamu* goes back to the first created man of Accadian tradition who belonged to the black, that is, to the Accadian race, is due to Sir Heury Rawlinson. He has also suggested that the coatrast between the black and the white races, between the Accadian and the Semite, is indicated in tiie sixth chapter of Genesis, where a coatrast is drawn between the daughters of men or *Adamu,* and the sons of (iod." (pp. 81-83.)

Verification is also hereby afforded of the suggestion made in §] 78 (note), that the forbidden fruit was the inspiriting and illuminating product of a plant which the conquering race forbade the subject race to consume. The objection, not unlikely to be raised, that the words "fruit" and "eating" do not countenance this interpretation, would be sufficiently met by cases of our own metaphorical uses of these words (" fruit of the womb," "opinm-eating"); but it may be met more directly. Of the Zulus, Bp. Callaway says – " The natives speak of beer as food – and of eating it. They also eall snuff food, and speak of eating it."

Theology of the Aceadians. – The distinguished Assyriologist, Prof. A. H. Sayce, in his article on " Babylonia" in the newedition of the *Encyelopedia Eritaunica* (iii, 192-3), writes aa follows; –

"The earliest religion of Aeead was a Shamanism resembling that of the Siberian or Samoyed tribes of to-day. Every object had i's spirit, good of bad ; and the power of controlling these spirits was in the hands of priests and sorcerers. The world swarmed with them, especially with the demous, and there was tearcely un action which did not risk demoniac possession. Diseases were regarded as eaused in this way. ... In course of time certain spirit! (or-rathor deified powers of Nature) were elevated above the rest into the position of gods. . . . The old Shamanism gradually became trausformed into a religion, with a host of subordinate semi-divine beings ; but so strong a hold had it upon the mind, that the new gods were still addressed by their spirits. The religion now entered upon a new phase ; the various epithets applied to the same deity were crystallized into fresh divinities, and the sun- god under a multitude of forms became the central object of worship."

This account of Accadian beliefs harmonizes with the numerous foregoing facts illustrating the genesis of religion from the ghost- theory. The first stage above described is one in which spirits, originally human, have become identified with, or inhabitants of, BuiTounding objects, as we saw they everywhere tend to do. Just as among the Esquimaux and others, Sun and Moon thus come to be residences of particular ghosts, so with the Accadians. Prof. Sayce has just pointed out to me (June, 1885) that he had in 1874 expressed the belief that "the worship of dead ancestors" is the primitive form of religion.

As given *by* JVI. Lenormant, in his *La Mayfe chez les Chaldecns,* the following is part of an incantation against pestilence: –

" De la fievre, esprit da ciel, souvieus-t'en! Esprit de la terre, couvienn- t'enl . . . Esprits males et fcmelles, seigneurs des e"toiles, souvenez-voua en! ... Esprits miles et femelles de la montagne sublime, souvenez-voiu en! Esprits males et femelles de la lumicre de vie, souvenez-voua en! ... Esprits femelles du perc et de la mere de Moul-ge [the Assyrian

god Bel] souvenez-vouz en! ... Eeprit de la Diesee-onde, mere de Ea,

souvieus-t'en! Esprit de Ninouab, fille de Ea (Nouah). souvieus-t'en! . . . i"-l n it du dieu Feu, pontife supreme But In surface de la terre, eouvieus-t'en! " (p. 128.)

Here, then, the address is uniformly made to ghosts; and these are the ghosts of beings allied by name to traditional Luman beings – the ghosts of beings who have come to be called gods and goddesses : ghosts regarded as lords and spirits of e, tars, mountains, fire. And this too, as we saw above, was the creed of the Iranians. The *fravashis* were the ghosts or spirits possesstd alike by men and by gods – even by the chief god.

Morcover, little as the fact is recognized, the Hebrew god is habitually spoken of in a parallel way and with the same implication. "The Spirit of the Lord" is a consistent expression if, as in the Accadian belief, and in the beliefs of existing Bedouins, the original conception of a god was that of a powerfulterrestrial raler – a ruler such as the one hospitably entertained by Abraham, with whom he covenanted to yield allegiance in return for territory. But the expression " Spirit of the Lord," reasonably applied to the double of a potentate after his death, is nonsense if otherwise applied ; since, as every critical reader must have observed, if the Lord was originally conceived as a Spirit, then the Spirit of the Lord must have been conceived Bs the spirit of a spirit. Such an expression as that in Isaiah rlviii, 16, "the Lord God, and His Spirit, hath sent me," which, is reconcilable with the primitive idea that every human being', whether king or subject, ineludes at least two individualities, is irreconcilable with the current theology; for the word spirit, whether interpreted in the sense accepted alike by savage and civilized, or whether referred back to its derivation as meaning breath (which it does in Hebrew as in various other languages), inevitably connotes a body of which it is the spirit.

Thus all three of the widely unlike types of men inhabiting these eastern regions – the so-called Turanians, the Aryans, and the Semites – had the same theory of supernatural beings. However otherwise different, deities, like men, were conceived by them as having doubles. The notion is perfectly congruous with the conelusion everywhere else forced upon us, that deities are the expanded ghosts of dead men, aad is utterly incongruous with a:iy other theory.

It was pointed out in § 202 that in various essential respects the Hebrew conception of god was at one with all other conceptions of gods; and hero we see this unity implied even in the descriptive phrases used by the Hebrews in speaking of their god.

Note. – I am indebted to the RiiOiop of Gloucester, und more recently to Prof. St. George Mirart, for Ixiinting out that the statement on p'ige 783, concerning the sacrifice of lambs to St. *Asnea* at Home is incorrect. It appears that the lambs are not actually sarrifiml, but only offered. "We mny regjrJ the usage, Ikjreiore, as u forai substitnted tor whui was ouco u rculitjr.

18

SECTION 18

APPENDIX B.

THE MYTHOLOGICAL THEORY.

[Though in the text, while setting forth that negative criticism on the mythological thcory which is constituted by an opposed theory, I have incidentalli) made some positive criticisms, I have preferred not to encumber the argument with many of these; nor can I here afford space for a lengthened exposition of reasons for rejecting the mythological thcory. What follow must be regarded as merely the heads of an argument, the elaboration of which must be left to the reader.]

An inquiry carried on in a way properly called scientific may, according to the mrturc of the case, proceed either inductively or deductively. Without making any assumptions, tho inquirer may, and in some cases must, begin by collecting together numerous cases; and then, after testing by the method of difference the result yielded by the method of agreement, cr subjecting it to others of the tests needful to exelude error, he may, if it withstands all such tests, accept the induction as true. Or, otherwise, if there exists a pre-established induction, or an a *priori* truth (which is an induction organically registered), he may set out from this, and deduce his conclusion from it.

In his *Introduction to the Science of Religion,* Professor Mas Miiller does not adopt either of these methods. As given on page 143 (new edition of 1882), his theory is that, in the case of other races as in the case of the Turanian race there dealt with, men's religious ideas arise thus: – " First, a worship of heaven, as the emblem of the most exalted conception which the untutored mind of man can entertain," expanding to ... " a belief in that which is infinite. Secondly, a belief in deathless spirits or powers of nature; . . . Lastly, a belief in the existence of ancestral spirits." To give anything like a scientific character to this theory, he ought to do at least one of two things. Either he should cite a number of cases in which among men whose state is the rudest known, there exists this heaven-worship and resulting conception of tho infinite, or else he should prove that his theory is a necessary deduction from admitted laws of the human mind. He doeanot fulfil either of these requirements, or even attempt to fulfil cither. Not simply does he fail to give such numerous cnses of Nature-worship existing without any other kind of worship, as would serve for the bnsis of an induction, but I arn not aware that he has given a single case: the renson bcing, I believe, that no cases are to be found; for my own inquiries, which are tolerably extensive, have not brought one to my knowledge. On the other hand, so far from bcing able to deduce his conclusion from laws of mind, he is obliged deliberately to ignore laws of mind which are well established. If, as he alleges, men began with worshipping heaven as feym-1i ilizing the infinite, afterwards worshipping the powers of Mature as personalized, and finally ancestral spirits, then the progress of thought is from the abstract to the concrete: the course implied is the reverse of that known to be followed.

AVhile it cannot, I think, be admitted that what is called by Professor Max Miiller the *Science of Rnliyion* has any claim whatever to the name *science,* we find evidence that his conclusion was from the outset a foregone conclusion, and one certainly not belonging to the class distinguished as scientific. Here are two extracts which throw light on the matter: –

" The elemeuts and roots of religion were there, as far back as we can trace the history of man. . . . An intuition of God, a sense of human woakm ss and dependence, a belief in a Divine governmeat of the world, a distinction between good and evil, and a hope of a better life, these are some of the radical elements of all religions. Though sometimes hidden, they rise again and again to the surface. . . . Unless they had formed part of the original dowry of the human soul, religion itself would have been uu impossibility." *Chips, ete.,* vol. i, pref. x.

The other extract is from the closing paragraph of the preface written by Professor Max Miiller to the *Myths and Sunys from tlw South Pacific.* Speaking of that work, he says –

"But it coutains mach that . . . will comfort those who hold that God has not left Himself without a witness, even among the lowest outcasts of the human niee."

Noting how the theological here hides the scientific, I may add that anyone who reads Mr. Gill's volume and contemplates the many verifications it contains of the inference otherwise so nmply supported, that ancestor-worship is the root of all religions, will be surprised to see how readily a foregone conclusion can find for itself support in a mass of evidence which to other readers will seem fatal to it.

But now leaving this general criticism, let us examine deliberately and in detail the hypothesis of Professor Max Wiiller, and that mythological theory associated with it.

1. A more special science caunot be fully understood until

the more general science ineluding it is understood; and it is a corollary that conclusions drawn from the more special cannot be depended on in the absence of conclusions drawn from the more general. Philological proofs are therefore untrustworthy unless supported by psychological proofs. Not to study the phenomena of mind by immediate observation, but to study them immediately through the phenomena of language, is necessarily to introduce additional sources of error. In the interpretation of evolving thoughts, there are liabilities to mistake. In the interpretation of evolving words and verbal forms, there are other liabilities to mistake. And to contemplate the mental development through the linguistic development, is to encounter a double set of risks. Though evidence derived from the growth of words is useful as collateral evidence, it is of little use by itself; and cannot compare in validity with evidence derived from the growth of ideas. Hence the method of the mythologists, who argue from the phenomena which the symbols present, instead of arguing from the phenomena symbolized, is a misleading method.

One illustration will suffice. In a lecture delivered at the Royal Institution, on March 31st, 1871, Prof. Max Miiller said – " The Zulus call the soul the shadow, and *such is the influence oj law)nage* that, even against the evidence of the senses, the Zulus believe that a dead body can cast no shadow, because the shadow – or, as we should say, the ghost – has departed from it." *(Times,* 1 Ap., 1871.) Here the explanation is regarded as entirely linguistic. The course of thought which, among so many races, has led to identification of soul and shadow, and which has for its corollary the departure of the soul or shadow at death, is ignored. Those who have digested the abundant evidence given iu the text, will see how profound is the misconception caused.

2. In another way – allied though different – does the method of the mythologists reverse the right method. They set out with the ideas and feelings possessed by the civilized. Carrying these with them they study the ideas and feelings of the semi- civilized. And thence they descend by inference to the ideas and feelings of the uncivilized. Begiuning with the complex they get from it the factors of the simple. How great are the errors to be anticipated, an analogy will show. So long as biologists gathered their cardinal conceptions from much- developed organisms their interpretations were quite wrong; and they were set right only when they began to study little- developed organisms – the lower types and the embryos of the higher types. That the teeth, though rooted in the jaws, do not belong to the skeleton, but are dermal structures, is a truth which no anatomist, dealing with, adult mammals only, wouldever have imagined; and this truth is bnt one ont of many disclosed by examining animals in the order of nscending evolution. Similarly with social phenomena, inclnding tlio systems of belief men have formed. The order of ascending evolution mast be followed here too. The key to these . systems of belief can be found only in the ideas of the lowest races.

3. The distortion caused by tracing the genesis of beliefs from above downwards, instead of tracing it from below upwards, ia exemplified in the postulate of Prof. Max Miiller, that there was at first a high conception of deity which mythology corrupted. He says *(tici. of Lan.,* ii, 467) that " the more we go back, the more we examine the earliest germs of every religion, the purer, I believe, we shall find the conceptions

of the Dcity." Now, unless we assume that Prof. Max Miiller is unacquainted with such facts as are brought together in Part I, we si-all here recognize a perversion of thought caused by looking at them in the wrong order. We shall be the more obliged to recognize this, on remembering that his linguistic researches furnish him with abundant proofs that men in low stages have no terms capable of expressing the idea of a Universal Power; and can, therefore, according to his own doctrine, have no such iden. Lacking words even for low generalities and abstractions, it ia utterly impossible that the savage should have words in which to frame a conception uniting high generality with high abstractness. Holding so unwarranted a postulate, it is very improbable that Prof. Max Miiller's mythological interpreta- lions, harmonized as we must suppose with this postulate, can be true.

4. The law of rhythm in its social applications, implies that alternations of opinion will be violent in proportion ns opinions are extreme. Polities, Religion, Morals, all furnish examples. After an unqualified acceptance of the Christian creed, those who inquired pnssed to unqualified rejection of it as an invention of priests : both courses bcing wrong. Similarly, after belief in clnssic legends as entirely true, there comes repndiation of them as entirely false: now prized as historic fact, they are now thrown nside ns nothing but fiction. Both of these jndgments are likely to prove erroneous. Being sure that the momentum of reaction will carry opinion too far, we may conclnde that these legends are neither wholly true nor wholly untrue.

5. The assumption that any decided division can be made between legend and history is untenable. To suppose that at a certain stage we pass suddenly from the mythical to the historical, is absurd. Progress, growing arts, increasing knowledge, moresettled life, imply a gradual transition from traditions containing little fact and much fancy, to traditions containing little fancy and much fact. There can be no break. Hence any theory which deals with traditions aa though, before the time wlxv. i they are elassed as historic, they are entirely nnhistoric, is inevitably wrong. It must be assumed that the earlier the story the smaller the historic nueleus; but that some historic nucleus habitually exists, llythologists ignore this implication.

6. If we look at the ignoring of this implication tmder another aspect, we shall be still more startled by it. A growing society coming at length to recorded events, must have passed through a long series of unrecorded events. The more striking of such will be transmitted orally. That is to say, ever)- early nation which has a written history, had, before that, an unwritten history; the most remarkable parts of which survived in traditions more or less distorted. If, now, the alleged doings of heroes, demi-gods, and deities, which precede definite history, are recognized as these distorted traditions, the requirement is satisfied. If, otherwise, these are rejected as myths, then there conies the question – Where are the distorted traditions of actual events ? Any hypothesis which does not furnish a satis- factory answer to this question is out of court.

7. The nature of pre-historic legends suggests a further objection. In the lives of savages and barbarians the chief occurrences are wars. Hence the trait common to mythologies – Indian, Greek, Babylonian, Tibetan, Mexican, Polynesian, ete. – that the early deeds narrated, even ineluding the events of creation, take the form of fightings, harmonizes with the hypothesis that they are expanded and idealized stories of human transactions. But this trait is not congruous with the hypothesis that they are

fictions devised to explain the genesis and order of Nature. Though the mythologist imagines the phenomena to be thus naturally formulated ; there is no evidence that they tend thus to formulate themselves in the undeveloped mind. To see this, it needs but to ask whether an untaught child, looking at the surrounding world and its changes, would think of them as the products of battles.

8.   The study of superstitions by descending analTsis instead of by ascending synthesis, misleads in another way.   It suggests causes of Nature-worship which do not exist.   The undeveloped mind has neither the emotional tendencies nor the intellectual tendencies which mythologists assume.

Note, first, that the feelings out of which worship *really* grows, as shown in Part 1, are displayed by all forms *oi* theundeveloped mind – by the mind of the savage, by tne mind of tlie civilized child, by the mind of the civilized adult in its uncultured state.   Dread of ghosts is common to them all.   The horror a child feels when alone in the dark, and tlie fear with which a rustic passes through a churchyard by night, show us the still-continued sentiment which we have found to be the essential element of primitive religions.   If, then, this sentiment excited by supposed invisible bcings, which prompts the eavage to worship, is a sentiment conspicuous in the young and in tlie ignorant among ourselves; we may infer that if tlie savage hns an allied sentiment directed towards powers of nature and prompting worship, this, also, while manifest in him, must be similarly manifest in our own young and ignorant.

So, too, with the thought-element which mythologists nseribe to tlie savage. The speculative tendency which they suppose causes primitive interpretations of Nature, is a tendency which he should habitnally disp'ay, and which the least developed of the civilized should also display. Observe the facts under both these heads.

9.   The familiar Sun excites in the child no awe whatever. Reculling his boyhood, no one can recall any fieling of fear drawn out by this most striking object in Nature, or any sign of such feeling in his companions. Again, what pensant or what servant-girl betrays the slightest reverence for the Sun ? Gazed at occasionally, admired perhaps when setting, it is regarded without even a tinge of the sentiment called worship. Such allied sentiment as arises (and it is but an allied sentiment) arises only in the minds of the cultured, to whom science has revealed the vnstness of the Universe or in whom the perception of beauty has become strong. Similarly with other familiar things. A labourer has not even respect for the Earth he digs; still less any such emotion as might lead him to treat it as a dcity. It is true that the child may be awed by a thunderstorm and that the ignorant may look with superstitious terror at a comet; but these are not usual and orderly occurrences. Daily experiences prove that surrounding objects and powers, however vast, excite no religious emotion in undeveloped minds, if they are common and not supposed to be dangerous.

And this, which analogy suggests as the state of the savage mind, is the state which travellers describe. The lowest types of men are devoid of wonder. As shown in § 45, they do not marvel even at remarkable things they never saw before, so long as there is nothing alarming about them. And if thcir surprise is not aroused by these unfamiliar things, still less is it aroused by the things witnessed daily from birth upwards. What is more marvellous than flame ? – coming no one eeoswhence, moving, matmg sounds, intangible and yet hurting the hands, devouring things and then vanishing. Yet the lowest races are not characterized by fire-worship.

Direct and indirect evidence thus unite to show ns that in the primitive man there does not exist that sentiment which Nature-worship presupposes. And long before mental evolution initiates it, the Earth and the Heavens have been peopled by the supernatural beings, derived from ghosts, which really draw oat bis hopes aud fears, and prompt *his* offerings wad prayers.

10. Similarly with the im plied thought-element. The ignorant among ourselves are unspeculative. They show scarcely any rational curiosity respecting even the most imposing natural phenomena. What rustic asks a qnestion as to the constitution of the Sun ? When does he think about the cause of the Moon's changes ? What si? n does he give of a wish to know how clouds are formed ? Where is the evidence that his mind ever entertained a thought concerning the origin of the winds ? Not only is there an absence of any tendency to inquire, but there is utter indifference when explanation is offered. He accepts these common-place things as matters of course, which it does not concern him to account for.

It is thus, a'so, with, the savage. Even in the absence of proof it would be inferable that it' the great mass of minds in our own race are thus unspeculative, the minds of inferior races must be still more unspeculative. But, as was shown in § 46, we have direct proof. Absence of rational curiosity is habitually remarked by travellers amongst the lowest races. That which Dr. Rink says of the Esquimaux, that " existence in general is accepted as a fact, without any speculation as to its primitive origiu " (p. 36), is said by others in kindred ways of various rude peoples. Nay, savages even ridicule as foolish, questions about the ordinary course of Nature ; no matter how conspicuous the Ganges displayed.

Thus the intellectual factor, too, implied by tho alleged . aythopoeic tendency, is wanting in early stages ; and advancing intelligence does not begin to manifest it until long after the ghost-theory has originated a mechanism of causation.

11. Joined with these two erroneous assumptions is the assumption, also erroneous, that the primitive man is given to " imaginative fictions." Here is another mistake caused by Ascribing to undeveloped natures, the traits which developed satures exhibit. As shown in § 47, the savage conspicuously lacks imagination;' and fiction, implying imagination, arises only as civilization progresses. The man of low type no movoinvents stories than he invents tools or processes; bnt in the one case, as in the other, the products of his activity evolve by small modifications. Among inferior races the only germ of literature is the narrative of events. The savage tells the occurrences of to-day's chase, the feats of the fight that happened yesterday, the successes of his father who lately died, the triumphs of his tribe in a past generation. Without the slightest idea of making marvellous stories, he makes them unawares. Having only rude speech full of metaphor; being prompted by vanity and unchecked by regard for truth; immeasurably credulous himself and listened to by his descendants with absolute faith; his narratives soon become monstrously exaggerated, and in course of generations diverge so widely from possibility, that to ns they seem mere freaks of fancy.

On studying facts instead of trusting to hypotheses we see this to be the origin of primitive legends. Looked at apart from preconceptions, the evidence (see *Inseriptive Sociology,* " Esthetic Products ") shows that there is originally no myth- opceic tendency ; but that the so-called myth begins with a story of human adventure. Hence this assumed factor is also wanting.

12. One more supposition is made for which there is, in like manner, no warrant. The argument of the mythologists proceeds on the assumption that early peoples were inevitably betrayed into personalizing abstract nouns. Having originally had certain verbal symbols for abstractions ; and having, by implication, had a corresponding power of abstract thinking; it is alleged that the barbarian thereupon began to deprive these verbal symbols of their abstrnctness. This remarkable process is one of which ele:ir proof might have been expected; but none is forthcoming. "We have indeed, in his *Chips,* ete. (vol. ii, p. 5-5), the assertion of Prof. Max Miiller that " as long as people thought in language, it was simply impossible to speak of morning or evening, of spring and winter, without giving to these conceptions something of an individual, active, sexual, and at last personal character;" *(i. e.,* having, somehow, originally got them without concrete meanings, it was impossible to avoid making their meanings concrete) ; but to establish the alleged impossibility something more than authoritative statement is needed. And considering that the validity of the entire theory depends on the truth of this proposition, o-e might have looked for *an* elaborate demonstration of It. Surely the speech of the uncivilized should furnish abundant materials.

Instead, I find put in evidence certain personalizations of abstracts made by our-selves. Prof. Max Miiller quotes passagesin which Wordsworth speaks of Religion as a "mother," of "father Time," of " Frost's inexorable tooth," of " Winter like a traveller old," of "laughing hours." But in the first place it is to be remarked that these, where not directly traceable to the personages of elassic mythology, have obviously arisen by conscious or unconscious imitation of elassic modes of expression. to which our poets have been habituated from boyhood. And then, in the second place, we find no trace of a tendency for this fanciful personalization to generate beliefs in actual personalities; and unless such a tendency is proved, nothing is proved.

13. Sanskrit is, indeed, said to yield evidence of this personalization. But the evidence, instead of being direct, is remotely inferential; and the inferences are drawn from materials arbitrarily selected.

How little confidence can be placed in the mode of dealing with the language of the Vedas, may be inferred from the mode of dealing with the Vedic statements. Appeal is professedly made to the ideas of highest antiquity, as being, according to theory, freest from mythoposic corruptions. Bnfc only such of these ideas as suit the hypothesis are taken; and ideas of as high, and indeed of higher, antiquity, which conflict with it are ignored. Of numerous cases, here is one. Soma-worship being common to the Rig-Veda and the Zend- Avesta, is thereby proved to have existed before the diffusion of the Aryans. Further, as before shown (§ 178), the Rig-Veda itself calls Soma " the creator and father of the gods," " the generator of hymns, of Dyaus, of Prithivl, of Agni, of Surya, of Indra, and of Vishnn." According to this highest authority, then, these so-called Nature-gods were not the earliest. They were preceded by Soma, " king of gods and men," who " confers immortality on gods and men : " the alleged sun-god, Indra, being named as performing his great deeds under the inspiration of Soma. Hence if antiquity of idea, as proved both by the direct statements of the Rig-Veda itself, and by community of belief with the Zend-Avesta, is to be taken as the test, it is clear that Nature-worship was not primordial among the Aryans.

If we look more elosely at the data taken from this " book with seven seals " (which is Prof. Max Miiller's name for the book from which, strangely enough, he draws such positive conclusions) and observe how they are dealt with, we do not find ourselves reassured. The word *dyaus,* which is a cardinal word in the mythological theory, is said to bo derived from the root *dyu,* to beam. In his *Science of Language,* vol. ii, p. 4G9, Prof. Max Miiller says of it – " A root of this rich and expansive meaning would be applicable to many conceptions : thedawn. the sun, the *sky,* the daT, the stars, the eyes, the ocean, and the meadow." May we not add that a root so variously applicable, vague in proportion to the multiplicity of its meanings, lends itself to interpretations that are proportionately uncertain ? The like holds throughout. One of the personalized Vedic gods, inferred to have been originally a Nature- pod, is the Earth. We are told that there are twenty-one Vedio names for the Earth. We learn that those names were applicable to various other things; and that consequently " earth, river, sky, dawn, cow, and speech, would become homonyms " *(Cliijis,* ii, 72). On which statements oar comment may be, that as homonymous words are, by their definition, equivocal or ambiguous, translations of them in particular cases must be correspondingly questionable. No doubt roots that are so "rich," allow ample play to imagination, and greatly facilitate the reaching of desired results. But by as much as they afford scope for possible inferences, by so much do they diminish the probability of any one inference.

Nor is this all. The interpretation thus made by arbitrary manipulation of ill-understood materials, is made in pursuance of what seems a self-contradicting doctrine. On the one hand, primitive Aryans are described as having had a speech formed from roots, in such manner that the abstract idea of *protecting* preceded the concrete idea of a *father.* On the other hand, of ancient Aryans coming after these primitive Aryans, we are told that they "could only speak and think" *(ibid.,* 63) in personal figures: of necessity they spoke, not of sunset, but of the " sun growing old " – not of sunrise, but of " Night giving birth to a brilliant child" – not of Spring, but of "the Sun or the Sky embracing the earth" *(iiiitl.,* 64). So that the race who made their concretes out of abstracts, are described as led into these Nature-myths by their inability to express abstracts except in terms of concretes I

How doubtful must bo these interpretatious may be judged from the following synonyms and homonyms for the Sun, taken from the *Sanskrit Dictionary* of Mr. Municr Williams. *Sura* – a god, divinity, deity, a symbolieal expression for the number 33 ; a suge, learned man, the sun. *Sura* – the sun ; the Soma ; a wise or learned man, teacher : a hero, king. *Sura* – a hero, "warrior, champion, valiant man, great or mighty man ; a lion, a boar ; the sun, N. pr. of certain plants and trees. *Savitri* – & generator ; sun ; epithet I Indru and Siva ; a particular plant. *Arka* – a ray, flash of lightning, sun, fire, crystal, copper, N. of Indra and of a plant ; *membrum virile,* hymn, singer, learned man, elder brother, food. *Anfaman* – *a* bosom friend, playfellow, N. pr., sun, Asclepias plant. *I'ieasrut* – N. pr. of the Sun, Aruun, and others. *Sirakara*

– *Ji.* pr., a crow, the sunflower, sun. And there are several others. Though these are from a general Sanskrit Dictionary, and not from a Dictionary of Vedic . Sanskrit, yet it must be admitted that the Vedio Sanskrit is as vague or vaguer, unless it be affirmed that languages become less specific as they develop.

May we not say, then, that the doctrine of the personalizatior of abstracts, unsupported by evidence which existing races furnish, is not made probable by ancient evidence?

14. We need not, however, leave off simply with the conclusion that the hypothesis is nnsustained. There is a definite tost, which, I think, completely disproves it.

As part of the reason why abstract nouns and collective

nouns beearae personalized, Prof. Max Miiller says : – "Now in ancient languages every one of those words had necessarily a termination expressive of pender, and this naturally produced in the mind the corresponding idea of sex" *(Chips,* ii, 55). Here the implication is that the use of a name carrying with it the idea of sex in the thing named, therefore carried with it the idea of something living; since living things alone possess the differences expressed by gender. Observe, now, the converse proposition necessarily going with this. It is implied that if an abstract noun has no termination indicating a masculine or feminine nature, any liability there mav be to give more concreteness to its meaning, will not be joined with a liability to ascribe sex to it. There will be no tendency to personali/e it accompanying the tendency to make it concrete ; but it will become a neuter concrete. Unqnestionably if a termination implying sex, and therefore implying life, therefore implies personality ; where there is no termination implying sex, no implication that there is life and personality will arise. It follows, then, that peoples whose words have no genders will not personalize the powers of Nature. But the facts directly contradict this inference. " There are no terminations denoting gender in Qnichua" (Markham, p. 23), the language of the ancient Peruvians ; and yet the ancient Peruvians had personalized natural objects and powers – Mountains, Sun, Moon, the Karth, the Sea, etc.; and the like absence of genders and presence of Nature-worship, occurred among the Chibchas, and among the Central Americans. Tims personalization of the great inanimate objects and agents, can have had no such linguistic cause as that alleged.

15. The many reasons for rejecting the interpretations which mythologists offer us, thus fall into several groups.

Some of them are *a priori.* The method adopted is doubly wrong – wrong as seeking in the characters of words, explanations which should be sought in the mental phenomena symbolized by those words ; and wrong ns seeking in developed thoughts and feelings the keys to undeveloped ones, instead of the converse. The assumption, associated with this method, that the human mind had originally a conception of deity suchas we now cr. ll pure, is directly contradicted by the evidence which tlie uncivilized present; and suicidally implies that there were abstract thoughts before there was even au approach to words abstract enough to convey them.

A second group of *a priori* reasons is otherwise derived. The mythological theory tacitly assumes that some clear division pan bo made between legend and history ; instead of recognizing the truth that in the narratives of events there is a slowly increasing ratio of truth to error. Ignoring the necessary implication that before definite history, numerous partially-trne stories must be current, it recognizes no long series of distorted traditions of actual events. And then, instead of secing in the fact that all the leading so-called myths describe combats, evidence that they arose out of human transactions, mvthologists assume that the order of Nature presents itself to the undeveloped mind in terms of victories and defeats.

Of *a posteriori* rensons for rejecting the theory, come, first, those embodied in denials of its premises. It is not true, as tacitly alleged, that the primitive man looks at the powers of Nature with awe. It is not true that he speculates about their characters and causes. It is not true that he has a tendency to make fictions. Every one of these alleged factors of the mythopccic process, though present in the developed mind, is absent from the undeveloped mind, where the theory assumes it.

Yet furl her reasons are forthcoming. From premises unwarranted by evidence, the conclusions are reached by processes which are illegitimate. It is implied that men, having originally had certain signs of abstract conceptions, and therefore power of forming such conceptions, were obliged, afterwards, to speak and think in more concrete terms – a change not simply gratuitously assumed, bat exactly opposite in direction to that which the developments of thought and language actually show ns. The formation of ideal persons out of abstract nouns, which is ascribed to this necessity, ought to be clearly demonstrated from the speech of existing low races, which it is not. Instead, we have deductions from an ancient Sanskrit work, unintelligible to the extent of having " seven seals," from which conclusions called unquestionable are drawn by taking some statements and ignoring others, and by giving to words which have a scoro of meanings those most congruous with the desired conclusion.

Finally comes the fact which, even were the argument in peneral as valid as it is fallacious, would be fatal to it – the fact that personalization of natural powers, said to be suggested by verbal terminations expressive of sex, occurs just as much where there are no such terminations.

19

SECTION 19

APPENDIX C.

THE LINGUISTIC METHOD OF THE MYTHOLOGISTS.

Already in § 188, I have given an example of mTth-interpretation carried on after the current manner: the instance being the myth of Sarama, which, on the strength of the alleged derivation of the word, one mythologist regards as % figurative account of the dawn, and another as a figurative account of the storm. This conflict seems typical rather than exceptional. Concerning the true renderings of these early words, philologists are often at issue; and no wonder, considering that according to Prof. Max Miiller, Sanskrit is " a language which expressed the bright and the divine, the brilliant and the beautiful, the straight and the right, the bull and the hero, the shepherd and the king, by the same terms." *(Rig-Veda,* i, 121.) Examples of the resulting confusion are continually thrust on the attention even of outsiders. The *Academy* for January 17th, 1885, contains a letter in which, speaking patronizingly of Mr. Divijcnder Nath Tagore, a j-oung Hindoo philologist, Prof. Max Miiller quotes some passages showing that they are at issue concerning " the original meaning [Pmeanings] of Matri, 'mother', Bhratri, 'brother', and Svasrt, 'sister'." Here are passages showing the disagreement.

" Max Miiller saya that the meaning of the word Mutri is *Maker* (nirmatri); wo say that its meaning ig *measurer* (parimutiv). . . . Prof. Max Muller eays that the primary meaning of uhratri is one who bears a burden, but we uy it i bhilgin, or sharer," eto., etc.

In the same number of the *Academy* is a letter from Mr. Rhys, Professor of Celtic at Oxford, in which, after quoting Dr. Isaac Taylor's qnestion – " Does anyone doubt that Odin is the wind *?"* he says – " My impulse would have been just as confidently to ask, Does anyone still think that Odin is the wind *?"* And then he refers to the first " nmong the Norse scholars of the present day " as saying that Odin means primarily heaven, and afterwards the god of wisdom. In a subsequent number of the *Academy* (February 14th), M. Henri Gaidoz remarks on the rcepticism likely to be produced concerning

mythologicalinterpretations, when "one says Odin is the heaven; another, Odin is the wind; according to a third, Odin is the storm: " adding that " each of these opinions is supported by a learned etymology which pretends to be the genuine one."

By way of further showing on what a quicksand rests the vast and elaborate structure of mythological interpretations, let me here place for comparison two translations of the same passage in the *Rig- Veda :* –

B. V. i, 85, 1. " Those who glance forth like wives and yoke-fellows, they are the powerful sons of Rudra on their win. The Maruts have made heaven and earth to grow, the;, the strong and wild, delight in the sacrifices." – *Max duller.*

" The Jlaruts who are going forth decorate themselves like females: they are gliders (through the air), the sons of Eudra, and doers of good works, by which they promote the welfare of earth and heaven: heroes, who grind (the solid rocks), they delight in sacrifices." – *Wilson.*

Here we see how readily a language like Sanskrit lends itself to those various figurative interpretations in which the mythologists delight.

Deeper than objections hence arising, is an objection which may be made to the assumption on wliich philologists at large proceed – the assumption that there exists in all cases, or in nearly all cases, a rational root for a word – a root, that ia, to which reason may trace back the word's origin. Now any one who observes the transformations of words and strange deviations of meanings occurring among ourselves, notwithstanding the restraints imposed by education and by printing, will find reason to challenge this assumption. If at present there goes on what may be called by contrast an irrational genesis of words, we may be sure that in early times such a genesis was active, and that a considerable part of language resulted from it. To help us in conceiving the transformations which then took place perpetually, let us observe a few of the transformations which now take place occasionally.

By gardeners and greengrocers the name artichokes has been abridged to " chokes ;" and this name appears even in the bilis sent to householders. They have made a still greater transformation of the word asparagus. Misapprehension first led them to call it " asparagrass ;" then it became " sparrowgrass ;" and finally " grass;" which is the name now current in London among those who sell it. In early days before there had arisen any thoughts about correct speech, or any such check upon change as results from literature, these abbreviated and corrupted words would have replaced the original words. And then, if at a later period search had been made for the origins of them, philologists would inevitably have gone wrong. Wnat more obvious than that the name " choke" givento an article of food, must have bad reference to some alleged effect of swallowing it; or what more olivions than that the name " grass" arose from a mistaken classing of the phuit with grasses at large.

Agreeing as we must with the philologists that from the begiuning dialectical chancres have been perpetually transforming words, let us note some of the transformations which dialects of our own language exhibit, that we may help onr- selves to imagine what must have resulted from kindred divergences daring thousands of years. In the Berkshire dialect, the word " that" has become " thak ; " and in the Devonshire dialect " this " has become " thickie." On referring to "The general table of Grimm's Law," as given in Prof. Mar Aliiller's *Science of Language,* vol. ii, p. 246, I see no precedent for a change of the into the *k.* Passing over this, however, I put a further question. Possibly the additional syllable in the metamorphosed word " thickie " might not prevent identification of it as modification of " this," when its grammatical uses were studied. But suppose that in conformity with Grimm's law, which shows that in Gothic *th* may be represented by *d,* and in old high German becomes *d* ; suppose, 1 say, that this word "thickie" became " dickie," what philologist would then be able to identify it with " this" ? Again, in the Somersetshire dialect " unele " has become " nunk." Who, in the absence of written language, would find the true derivation of this word ? Who would imagine that it had descended from the Latin *avunculut?* Even were it admitted that the dropping of the first syllable and of the last two syllables, might be suspected without the aid of books (which is extremely improbable), what warrant could be given for supposing a change of the remaining syllable *vunk* into *nunk ?* Grimm's law does not show us that *v* changes into *n;* and in the absence of books there would be no clue. Once more, in the Somersetshire dialect " if " has become " nif." Instead of that abridgement commonly undergone by words in course of time, we here have expansion – a prefixed consonant. It seems not unlikely that this change arose from the habit of always using "if" with a prefixed "and" – "and if;" which, quickly spoken, became " an' if," and still more quickly spoken " nif ;" but though this supposition is countenanced by a change in the same dialect of the word "awl" into "nawl" (which, probably at first "an awl," became "a nawl "), it does not harmonize with the associated change of "lunch" into " nunch." But however it has arisen, this growth of " if " into " nif " is one which effectually hides the derivation of the word. Were the Somersetshire dialect to become an independent language, as it might have done in times like those of the primitive Aituis, 110 philologistcould have traced "nif" to its root. The conelusion that " nif," used as the sign of a hypothetical proposition, was derived from " gif." meaning to hand over something, would have seemed utterly unwarranted by the meaning, and quite at variance with the laws of phonetic, change.

Beyond such obscurations as these, there are obscurations caused by introductions of new words needed in new occupations, institutions, processes, games, etc., which are snbse.- quently transferred to other spheres of use, while their original uses cease. We have an instance in the name " bookuig- office," as applied at railway-stations. Why booking-office? Young people cannot say; though people whose memories go back fifty years can. In the old coaching-days, when the accommodation for passengers was small, it was a usual precaution to secure a place one or more days before tho day of an intended journey. A elerk entered in a book the passenger's name, the place taken by him, and the date for which he took it. He was then said to be " booked ;" and hence the office was called a booking-office. Railway-managers had at first a slightly modified system. There was a book with paper tickets and counterfoils, of a kind like that now used in post- offices for registering letters. On paying his fare the passenger had his name written on the ticket and counterfoil, and the ticket was then torn off and given to him. This method was in use on the London and North Western Railway (then the London and Birmingham) as late as 1838, if not later. Presently came the invention of that little stamping apparatus which made it economical of time and trouble to adopt the stiff tickets now universally used. The books and booking disappeared, but tho name " booking-office " survived. When all who remember pre-railway days are dead, any one who asks the derivation of the word " booking" as thus applied, will be utterly misled if he sets out with the ordinary assumption that the word has arisen by modifications of some word having an appropriate meaning. Railway-business, or rather railway- making, supplies us with another familiar instance. Labourers occupied in excavating cuttings and forming embankments, are called "navvies." Whence the name? In future times any one who asserts that "navvy" is short for navigator, will probably be laughed at. How is it credible that a man occupied in digging and wheeling earth, should be called by a name which signifies one who sails the seas, and especially one who directs the course of a ship ? Yet. impossible as this affiliation will seem to those ignorant of recent historT, it is the true one. In the days when they were made, canals were thought of as lines of inland navigation – so commonly so, that sometimes a tavern built by the side of a canal was called a " NavigationIun." Bfcnne it happened that the men employed in excavating canals were called " navigators," and for brevity " navvies." When railway-making began to replace canal-making, the same class. of men being employed in kindred work, carried wilh them this abbreviated name, now no longer having even a remotely appropriate meaning. And the name has eventually been established as applying to any man engaged on earthworks of whatever kind. Now if, even in our times, there are aberrant origins of words – if these are at present numerous among the uncultured, how multitudinous must they have been among early peoples, who, on the one hand, were not restrained by education from making changes, and who, on the other hand, were compelled by the poverty of their vocabularies to use metaphors far more than they are used now. Indeed, as extension of the meanings of words by metaphor has played a chief part in the genesis of language, we may conclude that the metaphorically-derived words which eventually became established and apparently independent, form the most numerous elass of words. And we may further conelude that sinco modifications go on veiy rapidly in early speech, the connexions of such words with the words from which they were derived were most of them soon lost, and endeavours now made to find their derivatii ns must conseqnently be futile.

It has been replied to me when I have raised objections of this kind, that philologists distinguish between words of which, the roots can be found, and words of which the roots cannot be found. At the time when this reply was given, little force was recognized in *my* rejoinder, that no trustworthy test is assignable; but I abide by this rejoinder until a trustworthy test is assigned. It seems to mo impossible to devise any method by which there may be distinguished words of which it is hopeless to find the derivations, from words of which tho derivations may reasonably be sought. Indeed, false derivations sometimes present far more the appearance of trne derivations than do many of the derivations which really are true. Here are some extracts from an imaginary dictionary of derivations, which . wo will suppose to be compiled a century hence.

Bfiike, t. *t.* From a root which meant a refuge, usually inclosed, but which from the original sense of inclosure with security came to mean inclosure with suppression. In Icelandic, Swedish, and Danish we have *torp,* "a fort or castle;" in Anglo-Saxon we have *bark, hmy;* and in middle English we have *burqh, boryh,* "a pi ice of shelter." In middle English *baricr)h* meant " a den, eave, or lurking place," whence in English eamo *burrow* and *boeuaejk.* . Anglo-Saxon had also the word *beorgan* to protect, which, as usual, dropped the terminal syllabie. Hence, as *borg, bmk, burgh* meant a place of shelter or fortified place, to *bcorg* meant to protect by inctosura ; and this *beon)* or *heorgh* changing its guttural (as the Scotch word *lorh* has changed into the English *lock),* finally beeame *burke.* But a place beeu e by walls is al-o u phK-e of imprisonment; and the meaning ofbeing shut in eveatually became the predominaat meaning. A clear analogy i-. turnished by the clni'ged use of the word *prerenl.* Of old, as in the Bible (Ps. lix, 10) and in the Chureh of England service, it meant to go before wiih the effect of helping, but it now means to go before with tlie effect of nrreting. In like maaner to *Lurrth* or *burke,* having originally meaat to inclose with the rffe.-t of protection, has come to mean to inclose with tlie effecf of suppression. Hence a diseussion is siid to be *burked* when it is suppressed. How natural is the coanexion of ideas may be perccived nt a public meeting, when, to a prosy are iker, there comes a shout of " ihut up." Here there is obviously in this process of *lmrkiug* a speech, an unconscious ivferonce to the origin il fortified place, which, while it may be shut up to Steep out foes, may also be shut up to imprison inhabitaats.

Now when, in a few generations, there has been forgotten the story of the murderers Burke and Hare, who suffocated thcir victims by clapping pitch-plnsters on thcir mouths, this might very Well pass for a true derivation. The changes are natural, and not greater than those vhich continually occur. Unt let us take another cnse.

Post, c. . To put a letter or packet iato a place whence it is taken for delivery by public olficials. This word is derived from tlie substantive *post,* a ji ecc of timber set upright, – a mime which was commonly transferred to an upright pillar of iron (at one time not unl'rcqu'-ntly an old cannon) fixed at tiio corner of a street or other public place. The hollow iron upr ght receptacles for letters, which in large towns were placed at the corners of streets, were for tins reason ealled *posts.* Hence to pot a letter meaat to put a letter into one of these hollow iron posts ; just as to warehouse goods meaat to put goods into a warehouse, or to ship a eargo meant to put a cargo iato a lliip.

I do not see how a century hence any one could, without an elaborate inquiry, detect the fallacy of tin's derivation; and in the absence of a literature, detection of the fallacy would be impossible. Far less licence is taken than philologists habitually take, and far fewer rensons for scepticism cun bo assigned. We shall at once see this when we look at some samples of the derivations which are put forth and widely accepted.

It is said that the Aryan word which in Sanskrit is *Dyaus,* eventually became *Tyr* in Old Norso. This may be true; though to establish such a strange genealogy seems to call for more evidence than has survived during the lapse of thousands of years, filled with numerous migrations and consequent social changes. One may admit it as possible that our word *daw/liter* comes from an ancient word *duhitar,* milker, from *dult,* to milk ; though in accepting this conclusion we have to suppose that an earlier word for daughter (which must have existed before. the Aryans reached the cattle-keeping stage) wns replaced by t bis new word, notwithstanding the inapplieability of the new vord to daughters in childhood and to married daughters. Prof. Max Miiller may be right in tracing back the various European names for the moon to a primitive name which in banskrit is *mns;* and it may be, as he says, that "this masin Sanskrit is clearly derived from a root ma, to measure, to mete " *(Science of Lanf)unge,* i, 7) ; though if, as he supposes, " the moon was originally culled by the farmer the mea-surer," we must suppose either that before the Arvans reached the farming stage and also the stage at which the general use of measures had generated the conception of measuring, there existed no name for the moon, or else that the pre-existing familiar name had its place usurped by this unfamiliar metaphorical name : the usurpation being one which suggests the probability that in America " shooting-iron " will by-and-by replace rille. But without contesting the correctness of theso derivations, one may naturally ask by what criterion they are distinguished from the false derivations given above: – nay, may even naturally ask how it happens that the false ones have a greater apparent probability than these alleged trne ones.

Fully to appreciate the linguistic method of interpreting myths, we must, however, contemplate an example. Here is an abbreviated passage from the *Lectures on the Science of Lnni)uaye,* vol. ii, pp. 395 – 9.

" From *rit* in the seuse of siuning, it was possible to form a derivative rfkta, in the sense of lighted np, or bright. This form does not exist in Sanskrit, but as kt in Sanskrit is liable to be changed into ks, we may recognise in riksha the same derivative of *rik.* JPiksha, in tbe sense of bi iglit, Las become tbe mime of the bear, Bo ealled eitlier from his bright eyes or from his brilliant tawny fur. The sumo name, riksha, was given in Sanskrit to the stars, the bright ones. . . . Now, remember, that the constellation here culled tbe . ffikshas, in the seuse of the bright ones, would bo homonymous in Sanskrit with the Bears. . . . You will now perceive the influence of wonts on thought, or tbe spontaneous growth of mythology. The name rikshu was applied to the bear in the seuse of the bright fuscous animal, and in that sense it beeame most popular in the later Sanskrit, and in Greek and Latin. The same name, in the sense of the bright ones, had been applied by the Vedic poets to the stars in general, and more particularly to that constellation which, in the northern parts of India, was the most prominent. . . . The Hindus also forgot the original meaning of riksha. It beeame *t* niere name, apparently with two meanings, star and bear. In India, however, the meaning of bear predominated, and as riksha becaino more and more the established name of the animal, it lost in the game degre its connection with the stars."

So that setting out from the root *riJc* shining and the derivative rikta (which *mir)ht* have existed in Sanskrit but did not), and assuming that the changed derivative riksha was applied to the bear because of his "bright eyes," or " brilliant tawny fur" (traits which do not distinguish him from other animals), we have built up for us by various other assumptions and suggestions the interpretation of the Great Bear myth!

To complete our conception we must not forget a certain postulate with which this method of interpretation sets out; – the postulate, namely, that there were originally certain roots supernaturally given. Says l'rof. Max Miiller – "nothing

has ever been added to the substance of language . . . all its changes have been changes of form . . . no new root or radical has ever been invented by later generations, ns little as one single element hns ever been added to the material world in which we live ... in a very just sense, we may be said to handle the very words which issncd from the month of the son of God, when he gave names to ' all cattle, and to the fowl of the air, and to every benst of the field!' " *(Science of Languaye,* vol. i, 28 – 9). Hence the implication is that while those divisions of language which we know anything about, have arisen by processes of evolution, there was a special creation preceding the evolution – an endowment of linguistic capital in the shape of roots having abstiact meanings. Further, we are taught that mankind lost thcir original ability to frame abstract ideas and use the corresponding abstract words; and that whether or not there was any other " fall of man," there was a linguistic fall of man.

Thus as a basis for the " seience " of language, we are asked to accept tho Hebrew legend of the creation. Then the linguistic theory built upon this foundation of legend, is used as a key to the " science " of religion; which " science " of religion sets out with absolute negations of the two fundamental methods of science. It asserts, as innate in the primitive man, a religious consciousness which instead of bcing proved to exist by an induction from many cases is not exemplified in a single cnsei and for the established deduction from the laws of thought, that the development of ideas is from concrete to abstract, it substitutes the nssertion that the development of religious ideas has been from the abstract to the concrete. Lnstly, the conclusions reached by taking a modified Babylonian superstition as a postulate, and rensoning by inverted scientific methods, we are asked to accept instead of the conclusions which observation of the languages and religions of rnde tribes of men everywhere forco upon To I

REFERENCES.

To find the authority for any statement in the text, the reader is tc proceed ns follows : – Observing the number of the section in which the statement occurs, he will first look out in the following pages, the corresponding number, which is printed in conspicuous type. Among the references succeeding this number, he will then look for the name of the tribe, people, or nation concerning which the statemeut is made (the names in the references standing in the same order as that which they have in the text); and that it may more readily eateh the eye, each such name is printed in Italics. In the parenthesis following the name, will be found the volume and page of the work referred to, preceded by the first three or four letters of the author's name; and where more than one of hia works hns been used, the first three or four letters of the title of the one coataining the particular statement. The meanings of these abbreviations, employed to save the space that would be occupied by frequeat repetitions of full titles, is shown at the end of the references ; where will be found arranged in alphabetieal order, these initial syllables of authors' names, &c., and opposite to them the full titles of the works referred to.

§3. *Congo* (Tuck. 178) – *Termite* (Seliwein. i, 350). § 16. *East Africa* (Burt. " Cen. Af." i, 94) – *Negroes* (Liv. "Miss. Tra." 78; Schwein. i, 148 ; Speke, 330). § 17. *Carol* (Dana, 289) – *Greece* (Toz. 3 ; Grote, ii, 296). § 19. *India* (Fay. "Tiger," 42-3; Fay. "Than." 32) – *Bechnana* (ref. lost) – Ormoco (Hum. ii, 273) – *East Africa* (Liv. " Zambesi," 190). – *Termite* (Hum. ii, 288). 24. *Chinooks* (Lew. & Cl. 425) – *Shoshones*

(Lew. & Cl. 312) – *Guiana* (Brett, 25) – *Arawaki* (Ber. 29) – *Guaranii* (VVaitz, iii, 413) – *Tamulian (As.* S. B. xviii. pt. ii, 710) – *Pattooa. s* (As. S. U. xxv, 296) – *Fuegian s* (Wilkes, i, 121) – *Andamanese* (Eth. S. "Trans." JT. S. iv, 210) – *Veddahs* (Eth. 8. " Turns." N. S. ii, 282) – *Bushmen* (Arb. 213 ; Bar. i, 233) – *Akka* (Schwein. ii, 140) – *Bushmen* (ref. lost). § 25. *Vstyales* (Pall. iv, 52) – *Kamschadales* (Krash. 175) – *Kookies* (As. S. B. xxiv, pt. ii, 636) – *Chinooks* (Lew. and Cl. 425) – *Gvaranis* (VVaitz, iii, 413) – *Patagoniara* (Fitz. ii, 134) – *Akka* (Schwein. ii, 129, 141). § 26.

Kamsehadales (Krush. 175) – *Bushmen* (Bar. i, 234) – *Akka* (Schwein. ii, 129, 141) – *Veddahi* (Ten. ii, 450) – *Damaras* (Gal. 192) – *Yakuts* (VVrang. 327, note; Coch. i, 255) – *Comanche* (School. i, 231) – *Bushmen* (Thomp. i, 9'J). § 27. *Tasmanians* (Bon. 120) – *Papuans* (Macgili i, 277)–

JJa. naras (Roy. GK S. xxii, 15; Gal. 173) – *Dakotahs* (Burt. "Saints," 127.) § 28. *Yakuts* (Wrong. 384) – *Tamulian (As.* S. B. xviii,

pt. u, 709). § 29. *Bushmen* (Licht. ii, 194)- *Zului* (Card. "

Abiportes (Dob. ii, 32). § 32. *Savage* (Wnl. –). § 33. *Crerl-t*

(School. v, 27-1) – *Guiana* (Ber. 46; Hum. " Trav." iii, *S)* – *Indian* (Wnl. "Amazon," 92) – *Crecks* (Suliool. v, 272) – *Chinook* (Ross, "Fur. Hun." i, 125) – *Brazilian* (South, i, 223) – *Kamsrhadales* (Lath, i, 496) – *Kirqhis* (Lath. i. 311) – *Bedouin* (Burt. " Kl Mrdinah," iii, 45) – *Arabt* (Den. i, 411 ; Palg., V. G., i, 155) – $W *African* (Burt. " Cen. Af." ii, 325-326) – *Damaras* (Gal. *233) – Hottentots* (Burch. ii, *ff!)* – *Buhmea* (Arb. 243, 245-6) – *Malagasy* (Ell. "Hisiory," i, 140) – *Papuan* (Wai. "Mai. Arch." ii, 448) – *Fijians* (Ersk. i, 263 ; Wilkes, iii, 76) – *Andamunete* (Etlu 8. "Trans." N. S. iv, 210) – *Tasma. nia. ni* (Bon. 56) – *Facgiant* (Fitz. ii, 18S 1 Eth. S. "Traus." N. S. i, 264) – *Australians* (Havg. 102; Sturt, "Cent. Austr." i, 124) – *Bushman* (Lieht. ii, 224). § 34. *Australians* (Eth. 3. " Traus." N. S. iii, *223) – Hottentots* (Kol. i, 46) – *Bushmen* (Bar. i, 24t) – *Todas* (Eth. S. "Trans." N. S. vii, 2U) – *Bhih* (As. 3. B. Ix, 506) – *Santalt* (Hun. i, 155) – *Kookies* note (As. S. B. xxir, pt. ii, 636) – *Loango* note (Pink. xvi, 563) – *Esquimaux* (Hall, i, 130). § 35. *Mantras* (Eth. S. "Trans." N. S., iii, 7:, 78) – *Borneo* (Lub. "Origin," 10) – *Bushmen* (Arb. 243-4) – *Brazil* (Bates, 16'.!) – *Car'tbs* (Edw. i, 42) – *Bhilt* (Roy. A. S. "Trans." i, 88) – *Bodo* (As. S. B. xviii, pt. ii, 746) – *Lepchas* (Eth. 8. "Journal," N. S. i, 152) – *Bedouin* (Burek. i, 250-1; Palg., W.)., i, 70) – JVio *Guinea* (Earl, "Papuans," 6) – *Kamschailales* (Krash. 175) – *Dumarat* (Gal. 232-3) – *Malag* (Wai. "Malay," ii, 443) – *ZWas* (Eth. S. "Traus."

N. S. vii, 241) – *Fijians* (Sec. 192) § 36- *Soul Ameriea (Wai.*
" Malay," ii, 460). § 37. *Australia* (. Sturt, " South Austr." ii, 143)
– Joro (Karl, "Kust. Seas," *) – Pacific* (Ersk. 318) – *Vote* (Tur. " Nine-
teen," 395) – *Makololo* (Liv. "Miss. Tra." all) – *Fuegiaus* (Wilkes, i, 126)
– *Neie Guinea* (KolCf, 301) – *Bushmen* (Mof. 58) – *Atidamanese* (Mouat, 285)
– *Bushmen* (Lieht. ii, 194-5; Mof. 156; Bur. ii, 54) – JYeio *Caledonians*
(Forst. 240) – *Taunete* (Forst. 242) – JVeio *Guinea.* (Earl, " Papuans," 49, 80)
– *Tahi)ians* (Ell. "Pol. Eea." new ed. i, H6) – *Dyaks* (Brooke, ii, 89, and i,
57) – *Jaeans* (Raf. i, 245) – *Malags* (Wai. "Malay," i, 380) – *Brazilians*
(South, i, 223) – *Fijians* (Will., T.,' i, 129) – *Damaras* (Roy. G. S. xxii, 159;
Aude. 156) – *Bhih* (Roy. A. S. "Journal," viii, 191) – *Naaas* (As. S. B.
xxiv, 6U9) – *Bodo* (As. S. B. n-iii, pt. ii, 745-6) – *Lepchas* (Hooker, i, 129,
123) – *Faus* (Kth. S. " Trans." N. S. iii, 41) – *Cucdmas* (Bates, 293).
§ 38. *lloussas* (ref. lost) – *Crecks* (School. v, 691) – *Afrieans* (Liv. " Miss.
Tin." 206) – *Duaks* (Tylor, "Prim. Cult." i, 71). " § 40. *Bushmen*
(Bar. i, 234) – *Kareus* (As. S. B. Xxxv, pt. ii, 13) – *Siberian* (Prich. iv, 449)
– *Braziliaus* (LTern. 113) – *Abipones* (Dob. ii, 32, 13) – *Veddahs* (Eth. S.
"Trans." N. S. ii, 2SS)) – *Bedouins* (Palg., W. G., ii. 240; Burt. "El
Metinah," i, 360) – *HottetMs* (Burch. i, 175) – *Damaras* (Gal. 145) – *Prairia
Indians* (Burt. "Saints," 151) – *Brazilian* (Bates, 222) – *Araieaks* (Roy.
G. S. ii. 231) – *Guiana* (Brett, 344; Subom, ii, 75) – *Esquimaux* (Etb. S.
"Journal," i, 290) – *Hottentots* (Kol. i, 241) – *Fuegians* (Fitz. i, 55) –
Toaaans (Wilkes, iii, 19) – *Santals* (As. S. B. Ix, 555). § 41. *Brazilian*
(Bn'tes, 277) – *Hast African* (Burt. " Cen. Af." ii, 337) – -Oamora (Gal. 176-7)
Be, toain (PalR., W. G., i, 137) – *Sumatraus* (Mars. 208) – *Malaga-ty*
(Ell. "History," i, 136). § 42. *Dyaks* (St. John, S., i, 28) – *Karens*
(As. S. B. xxxrii, pt. ii, 128) – *Kamsrhodales* (Kotz. ii, 16) – *Mountain-
Snnke* (Ross, "Fur. Hun." i, 250) – *Brazilian (Hern.* 236) – *Patagoniant*
(Wilkes, i, *lU)* – *Guaranis* (Dob. ii, 63) – *Fuegians* (Wed. 154) – *Anda-
manese* (Eth. S. "Trims." N. S. ii, 46) – *S. Australians* (Sturt. "Sonth.
Aust," i, 106)- § 43. *Fueyiaus* (Fitz. i, *24)* – *An-lamauese* (Eth. S.
" Traus." N. S. v, *4&)* – *Ahts* (Lub. "Origin," 9-10) – *Brazilian* (Spix, ii,
253 ; Bates, *2* – *Aoipones* (Dob. ii, 59) – *East Africans* (Burt. " Cen. Af."
ii, *WQ)* – *Malagasy* (Ell. "History," i, 136) – *Damanm* (Gal. 133) – *Hill-
tribes* (As. S. B. iriii, pt. i, 242) – *'Brazilians* (Spix, ii, 251-2). § 45.
Australians (How. i, 68) – *Patagonians* (Hawk. i, 376) – *VeH&ahs* (Prid.
460) – *Samoiedex* (Pink. i, 534). § 46. *Bushmen* (Burch. i, 461) –
Samoans (Wilkns, ii, *27)* – *Tahitiann* (Kll. "Pol. Res." ii, 19) – *Cucama
(Bates, 234, 2Tl)* – *Negroe* (Park, i, 265). § 47. *Nil? basin* (Eth. S.
"Trani." N. S. v, 233). § 48. *Erjaat. Africa* (Reade, 244) – *Negro*
(Burt. "West Af." i, 259) – *Aleuts* (ref. lost) – *East African* (Burt. "Cen.
Af." ii, *32-)* – *Australians* (Eth. S. "Trans." N. S. iii, 223). §52.
Esquimaux (Hayes, 125-6; Eth. S. " Journal." i, 141) – *FijIans* (Ersk. 435) –
Orinoco (Hum. "Trav." ii, 423) – *Dakotah* (Burt. "Saints," 144) – *Abiponc*
(Alcedo, i, 3) – *Guaranis* (South. ii, 368) – *Caribi* (Edw. i, 47) – *Bullom*

(Winter. i, 255) – *Africans* (Ast. ii, 664) – *Iroquois* (Morg. 174) – *Creeki*
(School. v. 269) – *Karens* (As. S. B. xxxir, pt. ii, 195) – *Malagasy* (Ell.
'History," i, 393). § 54. *Egyptians* note (St. John, B., 79). § 55.
Insects "(Wai. "Nat. Scl." 56, 68, 54, 59-60). § 56. *Benin* (Bas.
"Menseh," ii, 352) – *Wanika* (Bas. "Menseh," ii, *45)* – *GreenlandeTM*
(Crantz, i, 185) – *Fijians* (Will., T., 241). § 57. *Fijians* (Will., T., i,
241). § 58. *Abipones* (South. iii, 40t) – *Cumana* (Herr. iii, 311) –
Niger (Lander, R. and J., iii, 242). § 65. *New Zealanders* (Thoms.,
A. 8., ii, 203) – *Bushmen* (Ande. 28) – *Arawak* (Brett, 108) – *Esquimaux*
(Eth. 8. "Journ." i, 141). § 66. *Childv* note (Rev. Phil. i,
14). § 69. *Peravians* (Cieza, *228)* – *Abipone* (Dob. ii, 183) – *Zuni*
(Pop S. M. 1876, 580) – *Bushman and Arapahos* (Lub. " Origin," 413).
§ 70. *N. A. Indians* (School. vi, 664, – *Grcenlanders* (Crantz, i, 185) –
New Zralanders (Thoms., A. S., i, 113) – *fijl* (Will., T., i, 242) – *Dyaks*
(St. John, S., i, 189) – *Karens* (As. S. B. xxxiv, pt. ii, 199) – *Peraviant*
(Gar. i, 129) – *Jen-s* (Mills, 56). § 71. *Chitipea-as* (Keat. ii, 155) –
fifalagasif (Drur. 179) – *Sandwich Ishlrs.* (Kll. "Hawaii," 251) – *Congo*
(Rende, 24S) – *Wanika (Kruyf, 7)* – *Kaffirs* (Shooter, 399) – *Zulut* (Cal.
146-7) – *Hebrews* (Genesis xv, 1, & xx, 3; I Samuel iii, 10). – *Iliad*
(Hum. bk. xxiii). § 76. *Chippetca* (Keat. ii, *la8)* – *MytJts*
(Flake, " Myths," 78). § 77. *Zulus* (Cal. 232). § 79. *Karens*
(As. S. B. xxxiy, pt. ii, 199, and xxxv, pt. ii, *2f()* – *Algonquins* (Tyler, " Prim.
Cult." i, 436) – *Dyaks* (St. John, S., i, 189) – *Australians,* "&c. (Tylor,
"Prim. Cult." i, 439) – *Greenland era* (Crantz, i, 184) – *S. Australians*
Scheur. 2S, 73). § 81. *Death* (For. & T. iii, 316). § 82. *Bush-
men* (Arb. 2o5) – *Tnsmanians* (Bon. 1740 – *Toda* (Per. 314) – *Damara*
(Gal. 190) – *Tupis* (South. i, 24S). § 83. *Arawaks* (Roy. G-. S. ii, 70)
– *Banks' Islanders* (Anth. I. " Jovir." x, 281) – *Hos* (As. S. B. ix. pt. ii, 705) –
Fantees (Cruic. ii, 216) – *Caribs* (Heriot, 515) – *Samoa* (Turn. "XIX" 272)
– *Loango* (Ast. iii, 222) – *Gold Coast* (Beech. 227) – *Hebrews* (Gru. 19) –
Todas (Hark. 52) – *Bcchnana* (Mof. 308) – *Ianuits* (Hall, ii, 197) – *Bagos*
(Ca. il. i, 164) – *Kookies* (As. S. B. xxiv, *62)* – *Malagasy* (Drur. 235) –
Mexicans (Clav. i, 322-3) – *Peravians* (Vncns, 44). '§ 84. *Arr a* (Kolff,
167) – *Tahitians* (Ell. "Pol. Res." i, 524) – *Mafanans* (Brooke, i, 78) –
Curumlars (Hark. 133) – *Fantees* (Beech. 228) – *Karens* (As. S. B. xxxv, pt.
ii, 28) – *New Zealanders* (Ang. ii, 71) – *Brazilians* (Herr. iv, 97) – *Peravians*
(rof. lost) – *Sherbro* (Schon,31) – *Loango* (Pink. xvi,597) – Daliomans (Burt.
" Dahomo," ii, *&l)* – *Bhil* (As. S. B. xx, 507) – Caribs (Irv. *ty* – *Chibchii a*
(Sim. 258) – *Peravians* (Tsehu. ii, 398) – *Kookies* (But. 86) – *Ceatral Am.*
(Ori. pi. iii, 49). § 85. *Bodo* (As. S. B. xyiii, pt. ii, 736) – *Kookies*
(A?. Rs. vii, 194) – *Innuits* (Hall, ii. 197) – *K. American Indians* (School. iv,
66) – *Mexico* (Tor. 31) – *Peravians* (Yueas, 47-8 ; Piz. 238-40). § 86.
Guaranis (South. ii, 371) – *Esquimaux* (Lub. " Prehistoric," 524) – *Peru-
vians* (Arri. 41) – *Iroquois* (Morg. 175) – *Brazilians* (Burt. " Brazils," ii, 50)
– *Kherbro* (Schon, 31) – *W. Australians* (Eth. Soc. " Trans." N. S. iii, 245).

§ 87. *Chihchas* (Sim. *2a8)* – *Egyptian* (Kbers, i, 334) – *Damaras* (Chap. ii, 282) – *Matiamba* (Bas. " MenVch," ii, 378) – *Kamichadales* (Krash. 220) – *If ew Zealand* (Thoms., A. S., i, 188) – *Muruts* (St. John, S., ii, 1291 – *Tahitiaus* (Kll. "Pol. Res." i, 525) – *Bechuana* (Liv. "Miss. Tra." 90) – *Bogota* (Sim. 271) – *Urna* (Cam. ii, 110) – *Mandaus* (Cot. " N. A. Indiaus'," i, 89) – *Guiana* (Hum. ii, 488) – *Chibchas* (Sim. 258) – *Peruvians (Cieza,* ch. 63) – *Mandingoes* (Park, i, 271) – *Esquimaux* (Crantz, i, 217) – *Bodo* (An. S. B. xviii, pt. ii. 736) – *Damara* (Ande. 228) – *Inland Nearoes* (Park, ii, 196) – San *Salvador* (Squier, 341) – *Guatemala* (Xim. 213) – *Chibchat* (Cieza, ch. 63 ; Acos., Joaq., 126-7). § 88. *Mexicaus* (Herr. iv, 126). – *Peruvians* (Gar. i, 127) – *Loanqo* (Pink. xvi, 596) – *Chibchat* (Sim. 258) – *Psrumans* (Gar. ii, 92). § 89. *Patroclus* (Hom. " Iliad," Long, bk. xxiii, p. 454) – *Tasmania* (Bon. 97) – *Soosoos* (Winter, i, 239) – *Coast Negroes* (Cruic. ii, 218) – *Damaras* (Ande. 227) – *Hawaii* (Ell. "Hawaii," 146) – *Samoa* (Tur. "Nineteen," *227)* – *Tongans* (Marin. i, 393) – *Ken Zeal unders* (Thoms., A. S., i, *SS)* – *Tmnes'e* (Tur. " Nineteen," 319) – *Madaaascar* (" Eng. Indep." July 30, 186S, p. 810) – *Greenlander* (Cr:intz, i, 219) – *Chinook (Ross,* "Oregon," 97) – *Todas* (Eth. S. "Trans." N. S. vii, 214) – *Arabs* (Burek. i. 101) – *Ahiponet* (Dob. ii, 274) – *Peruvians* (Cieza, 151) – *Tasmaniaus* (lion. 97) – *Gretnlanden* (Crantz, i, 219) – *Chinookt* (Ross, "Oregon," 97) – *Comanches* (SchooL ii, 133-4) – *Dakotahs* (Burt. "Saints," 150) – *Sandwich Isldrs.* (Kll. "Hawaii," 147-8) – *Dahomant* (Burt. "Dahome," ii, *V,7)* – *Mexico* (Tor. 22; Ilevr. iii, 209 and 216) – *Samoa* (Tur. "Nineteen," 227). §90. *Ambamba* (Bns. " Af. R." 82) – *Inland Negroes* (Lander, Ii. & J., iii, 113) – *Zambesi* (Liv. " Miss. Tra." 578) – *Fijians* (Will., T., i, 201) – *Peru,* (Gar. i, 127) – *Moslem* (Burt. "El 3Ied." ii, *W)* – *Cremntiot (*" Times," Julv 6, 1874). § 91. *Keijro* (Park, i, 91). – *Man* (Genesis, ii, 7). § 92. *Australiaus* (Bon. 185) – JV'eio *Caledoniaus* (Tur. "Nineteen," 424) – *Darnley Island* (Macgill. ii, 29) – *Krumen* (Burt. " Dahome," ii, 165) – *Karens* (As. S. B. xxxiv. pt. ii, 198) – *Araueaniaus* (Aleedo, i, 411) – *Qaimlaga* (Fern. 297) – *Peruvians* (Gar. i, 127; Acos., Jos. de, ii, 314) – *Samoa* (Tur. "Hundred," 150) – *Peruvians* (Arri. *3l)* – *Amasulu* (Cal. 354) – *Fiji* (Will., T., i, 248) – *Ama:ulu* (Cnl. 855). §93. *Tahiti-ins* (Kll. "Pol. Res." i, 516) – *Yakuts* (Hill, ii, 278) – *Yn.-atan* (Oroz. 157) – *Nicobar* (As. S. B. Xv, *3V3)* – *Eqiiptians* (Rev. Scien. 1 March, 1879) – *Grecks* (Thirl. i, 224; Hom. " Iliad," Buckley, bk. xxiii, p. 420) – *Semi-substantiality* (Tylor, "Prim. Cult." i, 455-6).

§ 94. *Niearaguans* (Ovi. pt. iii, 43, 45) – *Chancas* (Cieza, 316) – *Central Amer.* (Ovi. pt. iii, 42) – *Dying men* (Reit.) – *Greenlanilcrs* (Crantz, i, 185) – *Amazulu* (Cal. 91) – *Iraijnois* (Morg. 176) – *Fraser Island* (Srayth, i, 121) – *Ansai)rii* (Wnlpole, iii, 3J9). § 95. *Tasmaniaus* (Roy. S. V. D. iii, 180) – *Aztees* (lirin. 50). § 96. *Kareus* (As. S. B. xxsiv, pt ii, 211) – *Chippewas* (Keat. ii, 158) – *Fijians* (See. 398; Will., T., i. 2H) – *Mexieans* (Tern. *iv, Wo)* – *Laches* (Fern. 14). § 97. *Bongo* (Schwein. i, 307) – *Karens* (As. S. B. xxxiv, pt. ii, 196) – *Malagasy* (Kll. " History," i, 429) –

Mexicans (Clav. i, *2-M*) – *Malaiiasi)* (Ell. " History," i, 429-30). § 98. *Basutos* (Lnb. " Origin," 219) – *Fij ian* (Will., T., i, 245). § 99. *Coma a- chfs* (School. i, 237) – *Guatemala* (Brin. 2 16). § 100. *Manganias a:id Negroes* (Lub. "Origin," 216, 234). §101. *Chinooks* (Wilk, V, U) – *Comancbes* (School. v, ti85) – *Yucatan* (steph. i, 421) – *Tupis* (South, i, 248) – (Will., T., i, 247). § 102. *Creck* (School. v, 269) – *Comanches* (School. i, *23)* – *Palanuniant* (Falk. 114) – jVw *Hebrides* (Eth. S. " Journal," iii, 62) – *Peruvians* (Arri. 41) – *Todas* (Marsh. 125) – *Tasmaniant* (Tas. "Jour." i, 253) – *Itakotahs* (School. ii, 178). § 103. *Tongous* (Atk. 483) – *Ahiponet* (Dob. ii, 269) – *Dahomaia* (Burt. "Dahome," ii, 164) – *Patagoniaus* (Fulk. 119) – *Nagas* (As. S. B. xxxiv, 015) – *Guiana.* (RaL 109, note) – *Papuan* (Earl, "Papuans," 85) – *Ynea* (Pres. " Peru," i, 29) – *Ancient Mexiean* (Tern. i, 213) – *Chibcha* (Sim. 258) – *Malagasy* (" Eng, Indep." July 30, 18G8, p. 810) – *Miskmis* (At. S. B. xir, pt. ii, 488) – *Otd Calabar* (Burt. "Daltome," ii, 262) – *F, mfres* (Beech. 229) – *DitnJes* (Low, 203-4) – *Kirghiz* (Atk. 483) – *Toda.* (Eth. S. "Trans." JJ.8. vii, 24T. 1 – *Vatean* (Tur. "Nineteen," 450) – *Peru* (Tselra. ii, 355). §104. J/im iraan (Herr. Hi, 220-21) – *Vera Pax* (Xim. 212) – *Mexicans* (Clav. i, 325) – *Pern* (Pres. " Peru," i, 29-30) – *Japanese* (R. iv. Scien. Jan. 18, 1879) – *Quuranis* (Waitz, iii, 419) – *Yiwa* (Oar. – ; Cieza, 223) – *Chibrhas* (Sim. 258) – *Tonqnin* (Tav. plate) - -*Yorubans* (Lan. –) - *Conao* (Aet. iii, 2BO) – *Chinook* (Kane, ITS) – *Anciteum* (Tur. "Nineteen," 372). § 105. *Tahiti an s* (Hawk. ii, 239; Ell. " Pol. Res." i, 328) – *Tunaans* (Marin. ii, 103-4) – *Fiji* (Will., T., i, 1SS) – *Chibchas* (8im. 258) – A'lVeiw (As. S. B. xsxiv, pt. ii, 205) – *Kookie* (A?. S. It. xxiv, 632) – *Dahomans* (Forb. i, 170) – *Kaffirs* (Sliooter, 161) – *Akkra* (Has. " Menseh," ii, 91) – *Axxiirian* (Re- cords, i, 143-6) – *Greeks* (Hom. " Odyssey," bk. *x.)* – *Zcns (ret. ost)* – *Petit* (Mons. i, 247). § 106- *Dahomey* (Burl. " Dahome," ii, 24) – *Kafirs* (Shooter. 161) -*Amn:t. ln* (t'ul. 3. Vt) – Jcn (Sup. Bel. i, 110). § 107. . JV/iVm (lirsk. 247 ; Will., T., i, 218-246) – *Ureeks* (Hlaekio, 6, note ; limn. "iliad,"bk. *v)* – *Amazulu* (Cal. 203-4) – *Tahltians* (Ell. " Pol. Res." i, 517). § 108. *Kaffirs* (Shooter, 210) – *Australian* (Lub. " Origin," 37S) – *Koossas* (Licht. i, 260) – *Bagos* (('ail. i, 1U1-5) – *Comanrhes* (St-hool. V, *6m)* – *Chippeieayant* (Frank. 132) – *Chinese* (Thoms., J., "Straits," 393). § 110. *Sandwich Isldrs.* (Ell. "Hawaii," 251) – *3Iaitaqatar* (Kll. "His- tory," i, 3!i; l) – *Guinna* (Her. 100) – *Gold Const* (Cruio. ii, 135) – *East Africans* (Liv. –) – *Zambesi* (Liv. " Miss. Trav." 4-3i) – *Atet-tltm* (Bas. –) – *Kamschmlnles* (Krash. *2-i)* – *Lepchas* (Eth. S. "Journal," N. S. i, 149) – *Creek* (School. v, 27u) – *BalonJd* (Liv. "Miss. Trav." 314) – *HoHentots* (Kol. i, 12(t) – *Boobies* (Bas. "Af. R." 320) – *Berhurma* (Thomp i, 214). § 111. *Keto Caledonia and Eromangn* (Tur. "Nineteen," 428 and 496) – *Gold Co-ist* (Bas. " Menseh," ii, 56) – *Bnlloms* (Winter. i, 222-3) – *Carilm* (Brett, 125) – *Comanchet* (School. ii, 133) – *Patagonians* (Fitz. ii, 158) – *Arabia* (Burek. i, 280) – *Ditaki* (Low, 245 ; St. John, S., i, 172) – *Tahiti* (EH. "Pol. Res."i. 5Ki) – *India* (Lub. "Origin," *S7-l)-Ktion, ls* (Roy. A. S.

"Journal," vii, 197) – *Care-burial* (Nil-son, 15."i) – *PalaiJonians* (Falk.
115). § 112. *Peravians* (I'res. " Peru," i, 29) – *Manduns* (Lew. & Cl.
Q'i) – Mangaia (Gill, –) – *Nem Zealand* (Thoms., A. S. i, 9tt) – *Santal*
(Hun. i, 153) – *Teutonic* (ref. lost) – *Chonos* (Eth. S. –) – *Araucanians*
(Alcedo, i, 410) – *Peravians* (Tsi-lm. ii, 3!IS) – *Ollomack* (Schom. ii, 319) –
Central Americans (Ovi. pt. iii, 43) – *Chinooks* (Wnitz, iii, 339) – *Chippewns*
(Keat. ii, *M*) - *Kalmucks* (Pall. i, 574) – *Kookies* (As. S. B. xxiv, 632) –
Todns (Marsh. l6) – *Eroman, ja* (Tur. "Nineteen," 4%) – Zi/t fTur.
'Niaett-en." *-Wri – Mapachei* (Smith, E. R., 173) – . *Dam'iras* (Ande. 22fJ) –
Bechnanas (Mof. 307) – *America* (Cat. "Last Ram." 3-'5) – *Basnto* (Arb.
131) – *Secltcle* (Tylor, " Researches," 35H) – *Todas* (Marsh. 125) – *Fiji* (Will.,
T., i, 188) – *New Caledonians* (Tur. "Nineteen," 425) – *Mexicans* iClav. i,
822-3) – *Esquimaux* (Lub. "Prehistoric," 521) – *Gold Coast* (Bos. 156) –
South America (Hum. ii, 361) – *Kanowits* (St. John, S.. i, 42) – *Malanaus*
(Brooke, i, 78) – *Chinootrs* (Ban. i, 247) – *Fijian* (See. 399) – *Samoan* (Tur.
"Nineteen," 235 & *3'22) – Sandimch Is.* (Ell. " Uawaii." 106) – *New Zea-
land* (Ang. ii, 71, 154; Thoms., A. S., i, 187) – *Chonos* (Eth. S. " Trans." –)
– *Arancanians* (Waitz, iii, 520) – *Australians* (Bon. 92; Aug. ii, 228) –
Chinooks (Ross, " Oreg. m," 97) – *Oityaki* (Bas. "Mensch," ii, 331).
§ 113. *Samoan* (Tur. "Nineteen," 237) – *Tonaans* (Marin. i, 55; ii, 99,
128) – *Nicaragua* (Ovi. pt. iii, 42) – *Patatfonian* (Fulk. 115) – *Iiabylonians*
note (Smith, "Ass. Dis." 212). § 114. *Borneo* (St. John. S., i, 172) –
Mexico (Tern. i, 158) – *Panches* (Fern. 319) – *Peravians* (Ull . a, i, 473l –
Morneo (Brooke, i, 235; n, 106-57) – *Dunks* (St. John, S., i, 189-90(-
Zulia (Cal. 380, 385) -*Ancieut Mexicans* note (Clav. i, 251-2;. § 117.
Co
Australians (Eth. S. "Trans." N. S. iii, 22S) – *Vedd , Jis* (Eth. 8. "Tmn"
N. S. ii. 301) – *Tasmaniant* (Roy. S. V. D. iii, 180) – *Amazon* (WalL
"Amazons," *4M)-Karen* (A. 8. B. xxxiv, pt. ii, 196) – *Tahitians* (Ell.
" Pol. *Res." i*, 523) – *Nienh"v* (A. S. B. xv, 3 IS-19) – *Arab* (Bas. "Menseh:"
ii, 109-10). § 11G. *Kjrrns* (As. S. B. xxxiv, pt. ii, 204) – *Nicobar*
(Bas. –) – *Rocks iLiv.* –) – *D'makil* (Hurr., W. C., i, 3521 – *Tropical*
(llurr. iii, ls:i) – *Aniacanians* (A'9-do, i, 111) – *Puhono* note (Ban. iii, 1 26).
§119. *Veddah* (Eth. S. "Trans." N. S. ii, 301-i) – *Australian* (Ror.
S. V. D. iii, 179) – *Ash antnei* (Beech. 181 2) *Homeric* (Hom. "HiaiV'
Baeklcv, *passim) – Aranraaian* (Alft-do, i, 4lo). – *Afriean* (Lir. " Mim.
Trav." 67). § 120. *lingks* (&t. Jolm, S., ii, 6U). § 122. *Congo*
(Roade, 250) – $n *Africans* (Bmt. "Cen. Af." ii, 3."i4) – *Arabic* (Bas.
"Measch," ii,591) – ma/K(L'n1.263,36l,3fi8). § 123. *Amazafu* (Cal.
18"i) – *Abilsxiaians* (Parkvns, ii, 14o) – *Tungans* (Marin. i, 102-3) – -*Amazulu*
(Cul. 2li3') – ATAonrfs (l'Jr. 333) – !'.(ars (Couh. i, 293) – *Kirghiz* (Atk.,
Mrs., 154). § 124. TM4s (IVtli. 221) – *Sumoans* (Tur. "Nineteen,"
221) – *Snmatrans* (Mars. 191) – iW (Ramb. 190) – *Jctcs* (Sup. Rel. i, 120,
113) – *Church* (Burn. iv, 651). § 125. *Anwzulu* (fal. 209) – *Samoani*
(Tnr. " Nineteen," 23fi) -*Dyaki* (St. John, S., i, 62) – *Araieaki* (Brett, 362)

– *Land Dyaks* (St. John, S . i, 178) – *Karens (As.* S. B. xxxv, pt. ii, 24) –
Lepchas (Hooker, i, 135) – *Bodo and Dhimals* (As. S. B. xviii. pt. ii, 722)
– *Coast Negroes* (Wiater. i, 23fi) – *Koussas* (Licht. i, 25S) – *Zulu* (Cal. 201)
– *Comanchet* (Eth. S. "journal," ii. 2GS) – *Mun:lrui-ns* (Horn. 315) –
Iinhylunlans (Smith, " As?. D'sc." 176) – *Greeks l* Horn. " Hiiui," Lang, bk. i,
2-3i – fixUationqf theick (Prayer). § 126. *Unnies* (Wai. "Amazon,"
500) – *Chippewayan s* (Hearne, 338j – *Kalmucks* (Pall. –) – *Kookies* (As.
S. B. Miv, 630) – *Khonds* (Roy. A. S. "Journal," vii, 197) – *Bushmen* (Arb.
254) – *Bechuanat* (Bart-li. ii, 551) – *Coast Kegroes* (Winter. i, 235) – *Afriea*
(Kth. S. "Trans." N. S. iii, 45) – *Loanilo* (Ast. iii, *2'H)* – *Tahitians* (Ell.
"Pol. Res."i, 515) – *Kaga* (Hut. 150) – *Tasmanians* (Bon. 180) – *Kara-
Hotlentots* (Liclit. ii, Appendix ii). § 129. *Iiigniede* (Hom. " Iliad."
Lang, bk. v, p. *86)* – *Kgilpiiann* (Hccords, ii, 70-72). § ISO.
TahUians (Ell. " Pol. Res.'" ii, 23. i) – *Homeric* (Hluekie, 11) – *Helen* (Hom.
"Hind," Lang, bk. iii, p. 53) – *Homeric* (lUnckie, 15, *H)* – *Congoese* (Tuck.
162) – *Tahkalis* (Brin. 253) - *Ordaining Priests* (Prayer). § 131.
Amazulu (Cal. 387, 259, 264, 260, 273) – *Fijian* (Will., T., i, 221) – *Sunlal
(As.* S. B. xx, 571) – *Homer* (Blackie, 43) – *Zulu* (Cal. 265). § 132.
Mishmis (As. S. B. xiv, pt. ii, 487) – *Sumatrans.* (Mara. 191) – *Californiau*
(Ban. iii, 160) – *Koniaija* (l!an. i, 85) – *Colum'nans (Ban.* i, 286) – *Cumana*
(Herr. iii, 310) – *Raphael* (Sup. Eel. i, 102) – *Exorcism* (Hook, 38; Lee, i,
59-W. l)-Amazulu (Cnl. 161). § 133. *Kaffirs (Kth.* S. "Trans." X S.
V, *2. M)* – *Tahtiians* (Ell. "Pol. Eos." i, *l-l)* – *Auslrniian s* (Eth. S. "Trans."
N. S. iii, 235) – *Jewish* (ref. lost) – *Australians* (Eth. S. "Trans." N. S. i,
289) – *Caeamat* (Gar. i, 56) – *Taridnat* (Wai. "Amazon," 4:'S) – *Anaonkt*
(Waitz, iii, 388) – *Koniaga* (Ban. i, 76) – *Chinooks* (Han. i, 245) – *MapucMi*
(Smith, E. R.'222) – JV. *Americans* (Hurt. "Saiats," 142) – S. *Amerieans*
(Smith, E. R. 222) – *Chinook* (Kane, 205 ; Ban. i, 215) – *DiJaks* (St. John,
B., i, 197) – *Tasmanians* (Tas. " Jour." i, 253-1) – *Pufugonians* (Fitz. ii, 16 i)
– *!feai Zealandert* (ref. lost) – *Amnzntu* (Cal. 270) – *Ancient Fernna is*
(Arn. 21-22) – *Taunese* (Tur. "Nineteen," 89, 91) – *Chippeieas* (Keat. ii,
163) – *Ardrah* (Bas. " Menscii," ii, 357) – *Ancient Peravians* (Arri. 21-2) –
Europe (ref. *lost)* – *England* (Stat. Xv. pt. 2, W – *Thlinkeeti* note (Ban.
iii, 147) – *Koniaga-whalers* (Ban. i, 7b) – *Ashantee* (Beech. –) – *Damaru*
(Ande. 179, 33n) – *Dyak* (Boyle, 207) – *Brazilian* (Spix, ii, 244). § 134.
Eechuanas (Bas. "Menseh," ii, 265) – *Yorubas* (Burt. " Abeokuta," i, 3O3)
– *Umgnskana* (Cal. 3U1, *319)-Iirazilian* (Stade, 106-7). § 136.
Dakotahs (School. ii, 193) – *Hottentots* (Kol. i, 138) – *Tonga* (Marin. i, 88)
– *Keio Zealand* (Ans. i, 279) – *Tahitians* (Couk, –) – *Neio Zealanders*
(Ang. ii, 71) – *Aneiteutn* (Tur. " Nineteen," 3711 – *Ashantis* (Beech. 213) –
Sandieicft Isdrt. (Cook, –). § 137. *Veddahs* (Eth. S. " Trans."
N. S. ii, 2i16) – *Bontjo* (Srhwein. i, 23t) – *Lohaheng* (Liv. " Miss. Trav." 124)
– *Arawaku* (Schom. ii, -158) – *Guiana* (Hum. ii, 488) – *Creeks* (School. v,
270) – *Fantees* (Beech. *2. i)* – *Dahomans* (Burt. " Dahomey ii, 164) – IVa-
tanese (Landa, 196) – *Caribs* (Edw. i, *60)* – *Brazilian* (Spix, ii, 250) –

Peravians (Tsehu. ii, 393) – *New Guinea* (Earl, " Papnans," 85) – *Tahilian s* (Hawk. ii, 95 ; Ell. " Pol. Res." i, 519) – *Sumatra* (Mars. 388) – *Tonga* (Murin. i, 144) – *Dyaks* (Brooke, ii, *270)* – *Fijians* (VVilkes, iii, 119) – *Tamilian* (Ell. "Pol. Res." i, 521) – *Peravians* (Aeos., Jos. do, ii, 312) – *Collas* (Cieza, 364) – *Egyptians* (Diod. 60-61 ; Mur. i, 89) – *Etruria* (Ferg. " Hist. of Arch." i, 284.) – *Darins* (Ferg. " Hist. of Arch." i, 194) – *Chaldean* (Ferg. "Hist. of Areh." i, 158). § 138. *Tope* (Ferg. "Tree," 88; Cun.'ll) – CAoiVya (Gun. 9) – *Tahiti* (Hawk. ii, *ltiS)* – *Cenlft! Amerioans* (Xim. *23)* – *Egyptian* (Wilk. iii, 85, 430) – *Bedouins* (Burck. i, 101; Pale., W. GK, i, 10) – *European* (Bluat, 16; Ferg. "Tree," 89). § 139. *Lower Californians* (Bun. i, 569) – *Coras* (Ban. i, 641) – *Damaras* (Ande. 222) – *Vancoaver Island* (Roy. G. 3. nvii, 301) – *MosqnUo* (Ban. i, 744) – *Karen* (As. S. B. xxxiv, pt. ii, 196; xxxv, pt. ii, 29) – *Bodo and Dhimdt* (As. 8. B. xviii, pt. ii, 708) – *Mexican. (Tian.* i, 641) – *Pueblos* (Ban. i, 555, note) – *Sea Dyaks* (St. John, S., i, 71) – *Hottentot* (Ande. 327) – *Samoa* (Tur. "Nineteen," 349) – *Fiji* (See. 392) – *Bhils* (Roy. A. S. "Trans." i, 88) – *Araucanians* (Smith, E. R., 275) – *Virzimbers* (Drur. 406) – *Berotse* (Liv. " Miss. Trav." 331) – *Kaffirs* (Gard. 314) *Amazulu* (Cal. 175) – *Sandwich Is.* (Cook –) – *Greeks* (Blackie, 4S) – *Agamemnon* (Hom. "Iliad," bk. ii, Lang, p. 33-4) – *Amazulu* (Cal. 239, 197) – *Kaffirs* (Shooter, 165) – *Zeus* (Hom. "Iliad," bk. v, Lang, p. 6o) – -*Athene* (Hom. "Odyssey," bk. iii, Lang. p. 45) – *Sandwich Istdrs.* (Ell. "Hawaii," 136i – *Egyptians* (Wilk. iii, 427-9). § 140. *Dyaks* (Low, 204) – *Gold Coast* (Beech. 229) – *Toda* (Eth. S. "Trans." N. S. vii, 2to) – *Indians* (Ban. i, 126) – *Baqos* (Gail. i, 164) – *Gold Coast* (Cruic. ii, 218) – *Dahomans* (Burt. "Dahome'," ii, 163) – *Yacatanese* (Landa, l'J6) – *Egyptians* (Wilk. iii, 443) – *Politnenian* (Grey, " Pfll. Myth." 43). § 141. *Samoa* (Tur. "Hundred," 48-9) – *Fijians* (Will., T., i, 231) – *Mexicans* (Clav. i, 279) – *Chibchas* (Fern. 141 ; Acos., Joaq., 213) – *Khonds* (Camp. 2111 – *Tahitians* (Ell. "Pol. Res." i, 488) – *Tongans* (Marin. ii, 208) – *Mexicans* (Ulav. i, 325) – *Dahomey* (Burt. " Da-honig," ii,25) – *Australia* (Eth. S. "Trans." N.9. ii, 246) – *Fijian* (Will., T., i, *20)* – *yaieans* (Ersk. 334) *Jfaidahs* – *(Bnn.* iii, 150) – *Nootkas* (Ban. iii, 152) – *Dahomey* (Burt. "Dahome," ii, 16t) – *Ulysses* (Hom. "Odyssey," bk. ii, Lang, p. 179) – *Dahomans* (Burt. " Dahome," ii, 167) – *Mexicans* (Herr. iii, 210-13) – *Baal* (i Kings, xviii, 28) – *Nateotetains* (Ban. i, 127) – *Mexicans* (Jfen. 108) – *Guancavilcas* (Cieza, 181) – *Sandwich Is.* (Ell. "Hawaii," 147, 30) – *Peravians* (Gar. i, 118; Acos., Jos. de, ii, 309). § 142. *Aleutian* (Ban. iii, *5W)* – *Tupis* (South. i, 219) – *Californiaus* (Bun. i, 570) – *Chippewas* (School. " Mississippi," 122) – *San Salvador* (Pala. 81) – *Chibchas* (Sim. 259) – *Peravians* (Cieza, 365) – *Tahiti* (Ell. "Pol. Res." i, 630) – *Mandingoes* (Cail. i, 341-) – *Egyptians* (Wilk. iii, 443, 450) – *Brazilian* (Heriot, 539) – *Peru* (Gar. ii, 111; Pres. "Peru," i, 30) – *Amazulu* (Cal. 147, 145, 239, 203). § 143. *Bambiri* (Liv. "Miss. Trav." fi05) – *Africa* (Reade, 24'.)) – *Amazulu* (Cat. 140) – *Veddahs* (Eth. S. "Trans." N. S. ii, SOI–2) – *Dakolah* (School. iii, 226) – *Bankn' IMrs.* (Aath. i, x, 285) –

Vateans (Tur. "Nineteen," 394) – *Taanese* (Tur. "Nineteen," 88) – *Chruses*
(Hom. "Iliad," Lang, bk. i, p. 2) – *Bameses* (Records, ii, 70) – *Biff Veda*
note (Raj. i, 427). § 144. *East Africans* (Liv. –) – JT. *Amer. In-
diara* (School. Iv, 65) – *Turkomans* (Tam. 61) – *Troqnoii* (Morg. 119) –
Egyptiaus (Vilk. iii, 430, 378) – *Malagasy* (Drur. 233) – *Chinese* (Edk. 71)
Tonga (Marin. i, 88) – *Gold Coast* (Beech. 190) – *Nasamonians* (Herod, iii,
150) – *Sumatra* (Mars. 242) – *Me-Iiamal Europe* (Smith, W., " Christian," ii,
1417) – *Turkomaus* (Vam. 210) – *Negroes* (Bas. "Meusch," iii, 118) –
Mosquito (Ban. i, 740-1) – *Aztees* (Men. 108) – *Blood-drinking* note (Mich.
ii, 35). § 145. *Mexieaus* (Dur. i, 193) – *Santals* (Hun. i, 18S).
§ 146. *California* (Ban. i, 400) – *South Ameriean* (Gar. i, 50 ; Bnl. eh. r,
67 ; Aven. –). § 147. *Juangs* (Dalt. 157-8) – *Fuegiaus* (Hawk. –)
– *Andamanese* (Eth. S. "Trans." N. S. ii, 35) – *Australians* (Sturt, "South
Austr." i. 107) – *Tasmanians* (Roy. S. V. D. iii, 180) – *Yeddahs* (Eth. S.
"Traus." N. S. ii, 301-2) – *Fiji an s* (See. 301) – *Taunese* (Tur. 88) – *Sumatrant*
(Mars. 289, 291) – *Angola* (Liv. " Miss. Trav." 440) – *Bambiri* (Liv. "Miss.
l'rav." 605) – *Kaffirs* (Shooter, 161) – *Santals* (Hun. i, 182) – *Khondt* (Roy.
A. S. "Journal," vii, 189) – *Hindu,* (Fort. Feb. 1872, 133-5). § 148.
Amazulu (Cal. 63, 21, 22, 32, 8, 1, 40, 58, 35, 7, 2, 33, 18, 51, 33, 17, 91).
§ 149. *Greek* (Grote, i, 110) – *Peru* (Aven. –) – *Niearaguans* (Ovi. pt. iii,
40-43, 44,46) – *Vedic* note (Muir, iii, 332). § 150. *Indra* (Muir, iii,
226-27, 238) – . fly *J'eda* (ref. lost) – *Menu* (Jones, iii, *passim*) – *Jehovah*
(DeuteronomT, xxvi, 14 ; Ecclesiasticus, Tii, 33 ; Tobit, iv, 17) – *Yemen*
(Acad6m. Comptesrendus –) – *Arabia* (Caus, i, 348-49; Palg., W. G., i, 10).
§ 151. *Nicaraguans* (Ovi. pt. iii, 41) – *Menu* (Jones, iii, 146) – *Amazula*
(Cal. 202,175) – *Menu* (Jones, iii, 147) – *Iranians* (Zend Av. iii, 231) – *Romans*
(Smith, W., " Gr. and Rom." 559). § 152. *Catholic* note (Roch.
323-4). § 153. *Greet* (Blnckie, ii) – *Romans* (ref. lost) – *Hebrews*
(Isaiah, viii, 19 ; 1 Samuel, xxviii, 13; n"te, Cheyne, i, 58; Bible
" Speaker's," ii, 358 ; Kuenen, i, 221). § 154. *Central Ameriean*
(Landa, 198) – *Peruvians* (Yncas, 107) – *Sandwich Is.* (Ell. " Hawaii,"
334) – *Crees* (Kane, 127) – *Caribs* (Brett, 129) – *Tasmaniaus* (Tas. Jour.
i, 253; Bon. *W)* – *Andamanese* (ref. lost) – it/a (Ersk. 369) – *New
Caledoniaus* (Tur. " Nineteen," 425) – *Badagry* (Lander, R., ii, 252) –
Mandaus (Cat. " N. A. Indiaus," i, 9j). § 155. *Yucatanese* (Landa,
198) – *Mexicaus* (Nouv. 1843, ii, 202) – *Yucatanese* (Landa, 198) – *Mexieaus*
(Lop. de Gorn. 437). § 156. *Mexicans* (Clav. i, 389 ; Torq. ii, P9) –
Africa (Baa. "Af. R." 164) – *Abyssiniaus* (Parkyus, ii, 60-63) – *Papuan*
(Kolff, 62) – *Javans* (Raf. i, 331) – *France* (Mous. vi, 4; Cher, i, 458) –
Coast Negroes (Bos. 232) – *Araveaniaus* (Smith, E. R., 309) – *Jfem Zealand-
ers* (Thoms., A. S., i, 88) – *Peruviaus* (Acos., Jos. de, ii, 312; Anda. 57) –
Yucatanese (Lop. Cog. i, 316). § 157. *North Am. Indians* (Kane,
202) – *Okanagans* (Ban. i, 284) – *Mandaus* (Cat. " N. A. Indians," i, 107)
– *Madagascar* (Ell. "Three Visits," 414). § 158. *Egyptians ("* Rev.
Scien." 1 March, 1879) – *Samoiedes* (Bas. " Meusch," ii, 377) – *Ostyales*

(Erm. ii, 51; Felius. ii, 21) – *Samoiedes* (Bas. "Meusch," ii, 85) – *Russiaus*
Erm, ii, 177) – *Sandwich Isldrs.* (Ell. "Hawaii," 251) – *Yueatanese* (Fan.
307-8, 316) – *Quiche* (Ban. iii, 52-3) – *Arabiaus* (Dozy, i, 22) – *Memnon*
(Roy. S. of Lit. ii, 45) – *Early Christiaus* (Bible, " Codex Apoo." i, 670,
G81). §159. *Ladies* (Fern. 14) – *Peruvians* (Arri. 11; Avon. – 1
Arri. 89 ; Monies. 147 ; Yneas, *61)* – *Bulloms* (Winter, i, 240. 241) – *Vera
Paz* (Xim. 211) – *Mexicaus* (Clav. i, 323) – *Kew Zealanders* (White, 30S).
§ 160. *Bulloms* (Winter, i, 222) – *Congo* (Pink. xvi, 158) – *Little Addoh*
(Laird, ii, 32) – *Polynesia* (Ell. " Hawaii," 102) – *Fiji* (Will., T., i, 99) –
Dakotah (School. iv, 642) – *Mandana* (School. iii, 248) – *Indiaus* (Buch. 228)
– *Peruviaus* (Acos , Jos. de, ii, 3 8) – *Chibchas* (Sim. 249) – *Hindu* (" Fort."
Feb. 1872, 127). § 161. *East Afriea* (Burt. " Cen. Af." ii, 346) –
Coast Negroes (Winter, i, 123 ; Cruic. ii, 135; Bas. "Meuseh," ii, 2UO) –
Higer (Lander, E. & J., iii, *Wo)* – *Dahomey* (Burt. "DahomeY' ii, 361) –
Pelich (Beech. 179-80) – *Congo* (Bus. "Af. R." 82). § 162. *Jujngs*
(Dalt. 157-8) – *Andaman* (Eth. S. " Trans." If .8. ii, 42, 35) – *Damarat (R.
Or. S.* xxii, 159) – *CJiirihnanas* (Gar. i, 50) – *Peravians* (Gar. i, 47) – *India*
(Lub. "Origin," 286; "Fort." F.-b. 1872, 131). § 164. *Peravians*
(Gnr. i, 75 ; Cieza, cli. 90). § 165. *Brazil* (Burt. " Brazils," ii, 366).
§ 166. *Thlinkeets* (Ban. iii, 129) – *Karens* (As. S. B. xxxiv, pt. ii, 217) –
Abasstnia (Parkyns, ii, 144 ; Wilk. iii, 285) – *Khondi* (Camp. *ii)* – *Bultoins*
(Winter. i, 256)' – *Mexicans* (Nfen. 10U) – *Honduras* (Herr. iv, 141) – *Chib-
ehas* (iim. 245; Fern. 50) – *Africans (Liv.* " Mus. Trav." 615) – *Gallabat*
(Schwcin. i, 307-8) – *Tele (Liv. "* Miss. Trav." 642) – *Guiana* (Brett, 374)
– *Sumatrans* (Mars. 292) – *Apache's* (Ban. iii, 135) – *Californians* (Ban. iii,
131) – *Tlaseala* (Clav. i, 243) – *Calabar* (Hutch. 163). ' § 167. *Zulus*
(Cal. 130, 196, 197, 197, 198, 199, 368, 362, 202, 200, 201) – *Culiacan* (Ban.
i, 587) – *Amninlv* (Cal. 215, 200) – *Few Zealanders* (Thoms., A. S., i, 29)
– *Russian* (ref. lost) – *Babylonians* (Smith, "Ass. Disc." 191) – *Animal-
Worship* ("Fort-" Feb. 1870,196; Nov. 1869, 566). § 168. *Idzubar*
(Smith, "Ass. Disc." 202-3) – *Ishtar* (Records, i, 143) – *Ventriloquists* (Del.
"Isaiah," i, 240) – *Greeki* (Hom. "Odyssey," Lang, bk. xi, p. 190) –
Philippine (Jag. 169) – *Assyrians* (Records, iii, 134) – *Arabt* (Cans. i, 349).
§ 169. *Dakotahs* (Burt. " Saints," 153) – *Bongo* (Schwein. i, 311) –
Damara (Gal. 132) – *Abipones* (Dob. ii, 166) – *South Brazil* (Spix, ii, 255)
– *Abipones* (Dob. ii, 183) – *Koossa* (Licht. i, App.) – *Guaranis* (Dob. ii,
18J-). § 170. *Australians* (Ang. i, 92) – *Damara* (Ande. 225) – *Bodo
ff Dhimals* (As. S. B. xviii, pt. ii, 734) – *Kaffir* (Shooter, 219) – *Comanches*
(Seiiool. ii, *32)* – *ChiPpeivailan* (Hearne, 93) – *Bedouins* (Burck. i, 97) –
Kaffirs (Eth. S. "Trans." N. S. v, 295) – *Tapis* (South. i, 239) – *Karens*
(As. S. B. xxxv, pt. ii, 10) – *Nea Zealand* (Ang. ii, 88) – *Dakotah* (Burt
" Saints," 141) – *Yornbans* (Lander, R., ii, 228) – *Hottentots* (Pink. xvi, 141)
– *Makololo* (Liv. " Miss. Trav." 221) – *King Koffi* (Rams. *72)* – *Tothmes*
(Records, *passim) – Assyrian* (Smith, " Ass. Disc." 171) – *Bameses* (Records,
ii, 75, 76). § 171. *Mahomet* (Kor. eh. xciv) – *Central Asiatic*

(Michell, 96) – *Sea Dyaks* (Brooke, i, 62) - *Bechuana* (Liv. "Miss.. Trav."
13) – *Patagonians* (Falk. 114) – *Columbia* (Ross, "Oregon," 88) – *California*
(Ban. iii, *87)* – *Zapotees* (Ban. iii, *7l)* – *Haidahs* (Ban. iii, 97) – *Ahts* (Ban.
iii, *96)* – *Chippeioaitans* (Ban. i, 118) – *Koniagas* (Ban. iii, 104) – *Califor-
nians* (Ban. iii, 88, *92)* – *Doa-rib* (Frank. 293). § 172. *Papaaos*
(Ban. iii, 76) – *Kamsehadales* (Krash. 205) – *Dakotahx* (School. –) – *Negro*
(Liv. "Miss. Trav." 60S) – *Chippeiaas* (School. "Mississippi," 98-99) –
Ostyaks (Harr., J., ii, 924) – *Kookies* (Ind. xxvii, 63) – *Indian* (Ban. iii, 93)
– *Berhuanas* (Liv. "Miss. Trav." 13) – *Australia* (Lub. "Origin," 261).
§173. *Congo* (Bas. " Menseh," iii, 199) – *Thlinkeets* (Bun. i, 10LI) –
A. shantee (Rams. 306) – *Madagascar* (Ell. " History," i, 356) – *Egitptians*
(Records, ii, 70-76, iv, 56 ; Brugseh, i, 74) – *Vedd'ahs* (Kth. S. " trans."
N. S. iii, 71). § 174. *Aleutians* (Ban. iii, 104) – *Kirghiz* (" Fort."
Oct. 1839, 418) – *"Egypt* (Wilk. iii, 312). § 175. *Pacifie States* (Ban.
iii, *27)* – *Salish $c.* (Ban. iii, *9)* – *Land Ditaks* (St. John, S., i, 196) –
Eatavian s (Hawk. iii, 756). § 177. *Opinm-eaters* (Yam. 14) – *Wan-
dingoes* (Bas. "Mensch," iii, 194) – *Arafura* (Kolff, 161). §178.
Soma (Muir, i, ii, iii, v, *passim)* – *Peru* (Gar. i, 88 ; Mark. " Travels," 232)
– *Chibchat* (Fern. 20) – *North Mexico* (Ban. i, 587) – *Philippine Is.* (Jag.
267-9) – Soma, note (Muir, *passim)* – *Peruv* note (ref. lost). § 179.
Bechuanas (Mof. 262) – *Basuto* (Gas. 240; Arb. 131) – *Damaras* (Roy. G.
8. xxii, p. 159; Ande. 218; Gal. 204, 18S) – *Congoese* (Bas. " Af. R." 81,
172). § 180. *Arabic* (Palg., W. G., i, *4a)* – *Santali* (Hun. i, 173) –
Kamschadales (Hill, ii, 402) – *Damaras* (Gal. 176) – *Great Xicobar* (R8ep.
6). § 181. *TasmaniaTM* (Roy. S. V. D. iii, 281) – *Karens* (As. S. B.
ixxv, pt. ii, 10-11) – *If. Ameriean Ind.* (Cat. "N. tmd S. Am. Tad." 18, 14
Ifi) – *Armmks* (Biett, 367) – *Perurians* (Ciezn, 232, note *2)* – *Puebhs* (Ban.
i'i, 81') – *Isaima* (Wul. " Aniu/. ous," 506) – *Karens* (As. S. B. xxxv, pt. ii,
IIHI). §182. *Conqo-people* (Lub. "Origin," 289) – *AddacoodaA*
(Lub. "Origin," 281) – J/r. nVo (Tvlor, " Annhnac," 215) – *Beerbhoom*
(Hun. i, 131) – *Land l!vaks* (Low, 273) – *Iroquois* (Alorg. 161) – *Santals*
(Hun. i, 184). § 184. *Muleor* (Somer. 9) – *Inland Negroes* (Lir.
"Miss. Trav." 888) – *Ashantee* (rcf. lost) – *Beckuana* (Cos. 235) – *Wanika*
(Krapf, 168). § 185. *OjMieiceu* (Cat. " N. and S. Am. Ind." 19, 20)
– *Karens* (As. S. B. xxxv, pt. ii, 10) – *Tasmanias* (Roy. S. V. D. iii,
281) – *American* (Cht. w . swra, 20, 4c.). § 186. *Pacific States* (Ban.
i'i, 155 ; iii, 121) – *Mexieaus* (Pivs. " Mexico," ii, 41) – *Peruviaus* (Mem.
i, 37; Yncas, 13, 17, 25, 57, *3S)* – *Suntals* (Hun. i, 1S6) – *Araueaniaia*
(Al9edo, i, 416). § 187. *Peruviaus* (Arri. 31; Ben. 253) – *Iroquoit*
(Morg. 227). § 188. *Dawn-myth* (Mitl. " Lectures," ii, 506-13) –
Kareus (As. S. B. Xxxy, pt. ii, 10) – *Tapis* (Stade, 142) – *Kew Zealand*
(Thoms., A. S., *passim).* § 189. *Jew:s* (Sup. Bel. i, 105) – *Patagoniaas*
(Falk. 115) – *Fiji* (Ersk. 293) – *Herrey Isldrs.* (Anth. I, vi, 4) – *South
Australians* (Ang. i, 89) – *Tasmanianx* (Roy. S. V. D. iii, 274) – *N. Amerieaus*
(Tylor, "Prim. Cult," i, 359) – *Californian t* (Robin. 259-262; Ban. iii,

138-9) – *Amazon* (Wai. "Amazon," 506) – *Dyak* (Brooke, i, 189) – *Assgria*
(Roy. A. S. –). § 190. *Loucheax* (Ban. iii, 141) – *Esquimaux*
(Hayes, 253) – *South Australians* (Ang. i, 89, 109) – *Chibchax* (Fern. 18) –
Mexiean (Men. 81) – *Kareus* (As. S. B. xxxr, pt. ii, 10) – *Aryan* (Cox, ii,
139, 138). §191. *Comanches* (Eth. S. "Journal," ii, 268) – *Che-
ckt-mecas* (lit. 45) – *Olchoacs* (Ban. iii, 161) – *Tiuneh* (Ban. iii, 142) – *Satire*
(Hum. ii, 221) – *Barotse (L.* "Miss. Trav." 220) – *Tlascala-* (ouv. –)
– *Quiche* (Ban. iii, 60) – *Mizieea* (Ban. iii, *73*) – *Mexicans* (Men. 79 ; Waitz,
iv, 141 ; Men. 81) – *Damaras* (Gal. 138, 137) – *Diuneh* (Frank. 155) – *Peruviaus* (Yncas, xii; Pres. " Peru," i, 29) – *Mexicaus* (Herr. iii, 204) – *Panrfies*
(Herr. v, 86) – *Chibchas* (Sim. 244; Lugo, 7) – *Sun* (Sbakesp. " Heary viii,"
act i, se. i ; "Julius Caesar," act v, sc. 3) – *Alrarado* (Pres. "Mexico," i,
438) – *Peruvians* (Gar. i, 229) – *Central Amerieans* (Cop. 33) – *Karens* (As
S. B. xxxv, pt. ii, 10) – *N. A. Indiaus* (Cat. " N. and S. Am. Ind." 32, 14) –
Egyptians (Brit. Mm. " Papyri," 2-3 ; WTilk. iii, 5:3) – *Aryans* (Cox, ii, 30
et seq.). § 192. *Egiipiians* (Soc. B. A. iii, 93, S8, 93,94 ; Records, ri,
100). § 195. . BecAaaiKW (Thomp. i, 341) – *Chippeicas* (Buch. 228)
– *Fijian* (Will., T., i, 216) – *Malagasy* (Ell. "History," i, 390) – *Todas*
(Marsh. 123-4). § 196. *Todas* (Marsh. 136, 142) – *Talligue* (Montg.
184-5) – *Kamschada-les* (Krash. 183). §197. *Fijians* (Ersk. 247;
Will., T., i, 233) – *Tahiti* (Kll. "Pol. Res." new ed. iii, 113, 114) – *Benin*
(Bas. "Meusch," ii, 413) – *Loango* (Ast. iii, 223) – *Msambara* (Krapf, 384)
– *Peru* (Xer. 62; Ac-os., Jos. de, ii, 433; Gar. i, 54; Bal. ch.) – *Semites*
(Pnlg., W. G., i, 87) – Prmce *of Wales* ("Times" –) – *Peru* (Acos., Jos.
de, ii, 412) – *Yuealanese* (Lop. Cog. i, 318) – *Mexicans* (Men. 86; Waitz, ir,
33) – *Sandwich Isdrs.* (Ell. "Hawaii," 138) – *Tonga* (Marin. ii, 97) – *New Zea.
landers* (Thoms., A. S., i, 110) – *Shoa* (Harr., W. C., iii, 2!)1) – *Yoruba* (B:is.
" Mcusch," iii, 312) – *Ramses* (Records, viii, *passim*) – *Babylonian* (Smith,
"Ass. Disc." 189) – Note *Kelmchaduexznr* (rcf. lost). § 198.
Loango (Ast. iii, *2ZA*) – *Futgiaus* (Fitz. ii, *8tt*) – *Pnlagouiuns* (FalV. 116) –
Chippeieas (School. V, 149) – *CaJiroes* (Can. iii, *6)–llamaras* (Gnl. 202,
190) – . SnurfiricA *Isdrs.* (Ell. " Hawaii," 309) – *Mejrieaus* (Men. 84) – *Taouism*
(Edk. 59) – *Scandinavian* (Heims. i, 220, 218, 218-9, 224,224-5; note,
Das Ixii) – *JF. swlapius* (Num. ser. iii, vol. 2, 5-6) – *Braziliaus* (U'titz, iii,
417) – *Chinook* (Ban. iii, 95-6) – *Mexican* (I'res. "Mexico," i, 53-4; Sain.
lik. 1, chs. 7, 9, 17, 19, 20) – *Central Americaus* (Lop. Cog. i, 316-17).
§ 199. *Bushmen* (Chap, ii, 436) – *Africans* (Lir. " Mise. Trav." 271) –
Congo (Tuck. 380 ; Bas. " Af. E.") – *Niger* (Lander, R. & J., iii, 7!)) –
Jiec'nuana (Thompson, i, 171) – *Fulahs* l!irth ii, 429) – *Khond* (Camp. 220)
– *Nicobarians* (As. S. B. xv, 3 19) – /"'/"ut (Ersk. 24t1) – ,4rrs (Wai.
"Malay," ii, 263) – *Dyakt* (Low, 224, 247) – *Mexican* (Men. 81) – *South
America* (Hum. ii, *4T3)* – *Wanikas* (Krapf, 168) – *Sandwich Islands* (Ell.
"Hawaii," 104) – *Mexicans* (Nouv. 1843, iii, 140) – *Chibchat* (Fern. 155).
? 200. *Thlinkeets* (Bun. i, 94) – *Mosquitoes* (Pim, 305-6) – *Karens* (As. S.
lt. xxxv, pt. ii, 2) – *Kamschadales* (Kotz. ii, 12) – *Rude Nations* (Nilsson,

211, 176) – *Tupis* (South, i, 227) – *Seaadinaria* (Heims. *passim*) – *Greeks*
(ret. lost)- *Uehreic* (Genesis, vi, 2). § 201. *Fijians* (Will., T., i, 233,
218, 230, 21)- *Grecks* (Hom. "Iliad" and "Odyssey," Buckley, *pas-
rim).* § 202. *Fijianx* (Sec. 401) – *Semitic* (Palc.. W. G., i, 33) – *Arabt*
(link. 130) – *Shaddai* (Kuenen, *i,271)* – *Tiglalh-PJlaer* (Roy. A. S. –) –
Abraham (Genesis, xvii, 8, 7, 14; xviii, 2, 3, 5, 12). § 203. *Eesa*
(Burt. "East Af." 51) – *Hottentots* (Mof. 258) – *Santal* (Hun. i, 181) –
Egyptians (Ren. 85-6) – *Quiche* (Ban. –) – *I'edic* (Mnir, *pansim)* – *Buddha*
(ret". *ue)* – *Equptian* (Wilk. ii, 4H7) – *Arcadian* (ref. lost). §207.
J/exico (Lop. de Gom. 3i) – *Angola* (Liv. "Miss Trav." 440). § 218.
Sponge (Hnx. 16) – *Mgriothela Sf Blood-corpuscles* (Brit. Ass. 10,
9). " § 226. *Anrianianese* (ilouat, 30 i) – *Bushmen* (Licht. ii, 104) – -
– *Comanches* (School. i, 260; Eth. S. "Journal," ii, 267) – *Dakotahs* (Burt.
"Saints," 116; Cut. " JN. A. Indiaus," i, 2ii0) – *Karens* (As. S. B. xxxvii, pt. ii,
130) – *Africa* (Liv. –) – *Ashantee* (Beech. *H6)* – *$aiipt* (Musp. " Histi. ire,"
1S). § 228. *Cayaguat* (Sonth, ii, 373) – *Pa'taauniaut* (Fitz. ii, 166) –
Chinooks (Ross, "Oregon," *92)* – *Beluchi* (Eth. S. "Journal," is 18, i, 112)
– *Gold Coa. st* (Beech. *'Afi)* – *Frlaiahs* (Den. ii, 94). § 230. *Tauna*
(Tur. "Ninetoen Years," 811) – *Fiji* (Will., T., i, 22!)) – *Sandwich Isdrs.* (Ell.
"Hawaii," II8) – *NewZealautler. i*(Thoms., A. S., i. 116) – *K, iffirs* (Bnck. 230)
Merico (Clav. i, 272). § 232. *Fuegiaia* (Fitz. ii, 186) – *Shasta* (Ban.
i, 313) – *Const Ner)roes* (Winter, i, 89) – Peru (Pret. "Peru," i, 138) –
Mexicans (Clav. i, 338) – *Roman* (Palg., F., " Kng. Com." pt. i, 332) – *Enqlixh*
(Kem. ii. 340 ; Bren. exxix-xxx). § 236. *Mexieans* iZur. *WA)* – l*Jrru*
(Pres. " Peru," i, 138). § 241. *Fiji Is.* (Ersk. 457) – Samoa (Tur.
'-Nineteen Years," 271) – *Loango* (Pink. xvi, 56O, 574) – *Ashanlie*
(Beech. 148) – *Mexicans* (Cortes, 59; ClaT, i, 386) – *Peruvians* (Gar. ii,
18). § 242. *Flanders* (Hallam, "Mid. Ages," iii, 324) – *English*
(Stubbs, " Const. Hist." i. 130) – *France* (Fust. 7). § 245. *Nagat*
(As. 8. B. ix, pt. ii, 957) – *Bechuanas* (Thomp. i, 214) – *Eastern Africa*
(Burt. " Cen. Af." i, 335) – *Atyssinia* (Parkjus, i, 213) – *Brchuanas* (Burch.
ii, 306-7) – *East African* (B'urt. "Cen. Af." i, 335) – *Dahomey* (Burt.
"Dahome," ii, 248; i, 280) – *Ashantee* (Beech. 132) – *London* (Beck. ii,
29-30) – *Hearif VIII* (Smiles, i, l. r,!0 – $otrfon (Smiles, i, 204) – A'orM-
England (Smi'h-c, i, 16O). § 246. *Sandwich Isldrs.* (Ell. "Hawaii,"
29ij) – *Fijiaas* (Will., T., i, 93) – *Laioer Niger* (Allen, i, 3!tS) – *Sansandinq*
(Pa-k, ii, 273-1) – *Bnlta* (Mnre. 379) – *tiadagascar* (Kll. "History," i, 332)
– *Chibchas* (Sim. 257) – *Mexico* (Clav. i, 385 ; Saha. i, 29). §250.
Esquimaux (Hearne, 161) – *Abon* (As. S. B. xiv, pt. i, 426) – *Arafuras*
(Kolff, 161) – *Todas* (Marsh. 41-45 ; Eth. S. "Traus." N. S. vii, 241) – *Boda
and tihimals* (As. S. B. xviii, pt. ii, 745-6 ; Hodg. 156-60) – *Lepchas* (Hooker,
i, 129; Eth. S. " Journal," i, 150-1) – *Cants* (Edw. i, 49 ; Hum. iii, 89) –
Crecks (School. v, 27!') – *Tasmanians* (Bon. 81) – *Kamschadales* (Kotz. ii,
13 ; Krash. 175) – *r, il, i,, oniaus* (Fulk. 123) – *Samoa* (Tur. " Nineteen Yeart,"
287, *291)* – *Kir:ihiz* (Miehell, 278-9) – *Niamnianu* (Schwein. ii, 22)

– *Ashantee* (Beech. 96) – *Fiji* (Ersk. 464). §251. *Sandwich Isdrs.*
(Ell. "Hawaii," *392)* – *Tahiti* (Forst. 355; Ell. ' PoL Res." ii, 306-
67) – *Koo'sax* (Licht. i, 2S6) – *AsJiantea* (Cruie. ii, 242) – *Araucaniant*
(Albedo, i, 405). § 252. *Sandwich I.* t. (Ell. " Hawaii." 402) – *Tahi-
tian* (Ell. "Pol. Res." *ii, 3)* – *Samoa* (Tur " Ninrteen Years," 284) –
Btetjuans (Licht. ii, 329 and *2.'S)* – *Bachapin* (Burch. ii, 431) – *Koossas*
(Lieht, i, 2SH) – *Zulus* (Arb. 140) – *Dahomey* (Dalz. 121 ; Burt. " Daljome,"
i, 53, 276) – *William* (Stubbs, "Select Charters," 16-17). § 253.
Fuegians (l)ur. iii, 238) – *Tasmaniuna* (Bon. 21) – *Taunese* (Tur. "Nineteen.
Years," 32U) – *Fijians* (Willies, iii, 332) – *Neic Zealanders* (Thoms., A. S., i,
77) – *Mexicaus* (Clav. i, 345) – *Peruvians* (Gar. ii, 119-20) – *Persians*
(Herod, iv, 314) – *Elizabeth* – *Cromwell* (Smiles, i, 185). § 254.
Mandaas (Lew. and Cl. 113) – *Cumanches* (Marcy, 29) – *Kookies* (As. S. B.
xxiv, 635) – *Santals* (Hun. i, 217) – *New Zealand* (Ang. ii, 50) – *Sandwich
Isdrs.* (Ell. "Hawaii," 202) – *Tonaa* (Wilkes, iii, 22) – *Kadaganx* (St. John,
S., ii, 269) – *Celebes* (Wai. "Many," i, 337) – *East Afriea* (Burt. "Cen.
Af." ii, 365) – *Inland Nearoet (Aen, i, 321)* – *San Salvador* (Pala. 83) –
Mvndurucvs (Bates, 274) – *Pafartoniuns* (Wilkes, i, 115) – *Sakarran* (Low,
184) – *Dahomans* (Burt. "Dahome," i, 52) – *Guatemala* (Xim. 203) – *Mexico*
(Zur. 56-7) – France (Levas. i, 167 ; Bourq. ii, 208-9) – *English* (Lap. ii,
352 3 and ii, 355-6; Hallam, "Con. Hist." eh. viii; Maeaulay, i, 416).
§259. *Zulus* (Shooter, 268 ; Gard. 34) – *Fijians* (Ersk. 431) – *Mexico*
(Clav. i, 342) – *Fiji* (Will., T., i, 32) – *Madagasear* (Ell. " History," i, 346-9)
– *Dahomans* (Burt. " Dahomo," i, 22d) – *Ashantee* (Bas. " Mensch," ii, 333)
– *Mexico* (Suha. iii, 1, *&c.)* – *Perv* (Gar. i, 143) – *Fijians* (Will., T., i., 20S)
– *Dahomey* (Burt. " Dahome," ii, 19, 167) – *Mexieaus* (Herr. iv, 213) –
Peru (Ynros, 54-6) – *Peru* (Gar. i, 132) – *Mexico* (Clav. i, 271) – *Fijiani*
(Ersk. 250) – *Tahiti* (Ell. "Pol. Res." ii, 208; Hawk. ii, 240) – *Mexico*
(Clav. i, 270 ; Saha. i, 277) – Peru (Gar. i, 132) – *Ancient Peruvians* (Gar.
ii, 3t) – *Madagasear* (Ell. "History," i, J.97) – *Peru,* (Gar. ii, 34) – *Efiup-
tianx* (Wilk. *i,299)* – *Fiji* (Will., T., i, 30) – *Peruvians* (Gar. ii, 113) – *Per-
sians (ret.* lost). § 260. *Arafuras* (Kolff, 161) – *Tudat* (Eth. S.
"Traus." N. S. vii, 239, 241) – *liodo $ Dhimdls* (As. S. B. xviii, pt. ii, 741)
– *Mishmis* (As. S. B. xiv, pt. ii, 491, and ri, 332) – *Pueblos* (ban. i, 536,
546) – *Samoa* (Tur. "Nineteen Years." 28) – *Phoenicia* (Ezekiel, xxviii, 3,
4, 5). § 265. *Ktchabite* (Jeremiah, xxxv, 7) – *Nabat&an* (Robert,
xxiii) – *//i'// Tribes* (As. S. B. xv, 65) – *Afriea* (ref. lost) – *Equatorial
Afriea* (Keade, 535) – *Bectmanas* (Thomp. i, 314). § 269. *Sfatet*
(Plato, iii, 432; Hobbes, iii, ix-x). § 277. *Offspring* note (Fiske,
" Outlines." ii, 342-3). § 278. *Chipfiewauans* (llcarne, 104) – *Slavt
Indian* (Hooper, 303) – *Bushmen* (Lieht. ii, 48) – *Queessland Australians*
("Times," July 21, 1875) – *Dogrib* (Lub. "Prehistoric," 533) – *Qstensl,, nd
Australians* ("Times," July 21, 1875) – *Australiaus* (Mit. i, 307).
§ 279. *Bushmen* (Spar, i, 357) – *Chippewat* (Kent, ii, 157) – *Esquimaux*
(Hall, ii, 312) – *Aleuts* (Ban. i, 92) – *Arawdks* (Brett, *W)* – *Veddahs* (Ten.

lahs, Keriahs, $'c. (Lub. "Origin," S3-4) – *N. American* (Lub. "Origin,"
&l) – Busiimcn (Lub. "Origin," 85) – *Teehurs* (Lub. " Orisin," 8U),
§ 294. *Andamanese* (Eth. S. "Trans." N. S. v, 45). § *297Fuegians*
(Fitz. ii, 182) – *Tudas* (Eth. S. "Trans." N. S. vii, 240) – *Nairs* (McLen.
"Prim. Marr." 184-5) – *TahiHans* (Ell. "Pol. Res." ii, 571). § 298.
Aleutians (Bns. "Menseh," iii. 299) – *Lancerota* (Hum. i, 32) – *Kaxias, Sfc.*
(McLen. "Prim. Marr." 183) – *Ceitlon* (Ten. u,42S) – *Avaroes, e.* (McLen.
"Prim. Marr." 195) – *Arabia Felix* (Bas. "Menseh," iii, 293) – *Hindu*
(Mfil. "Hist." *4K) – Aneient Britons* (Cffisar. "Do Bcllo," bk. v. c. 14).
§ 299. *Todas* (Eth. S. "Trans." N. S. vii, 240) – *Tahiti* (ref. lost).
§ 301. *Tibetan* (Wils. 215-6, 215-6 ; Bogle, 123). § 302. *Fdv-*
audrff (McLen. " Prim. Marr." 245, 199, 203, 203-4) – *Thibet* (Penna, 71)
– *Haidahs* (Ban. i, 169) – *Zulus* (Arb. 13S) – *Damara* (Ande. *76) – Cungo*
(Ast. iii, 254) – *Samoa* (Tur. "JNineteen Years," 190) – Tern *Paz* (Xim.
207) – *Ni-. w Zealanders* (Tlioms., A. S., i, 178) – *Mishmis* (As. S. B. xiv, pt. ii,
438) – *JUixico* (Torq. ii, *42') – Ettbas* (Hurt- "Abeokuta," i, 208) – *Slare*
Coast (Bos. 31U) – *Dahomeit* (Biirt. " Uahome," i, 367). § 304.
Bushmen (Burch. ii, *&) – Gunds* (For.-y. 14S) – *Veddabs* (Ten. ii, 441) –
Ostyaks (Lath. i, 457) – *Lifu* (Tur. "Nineteen Years," 401) – *Mandinaoea*
(1'a'rk, i, 261) – *Damara* (Ancle. 225) – *Yatcaut* (Les. ii, 285) – *Hai'dahs*
(Ban. i, 169) – *Comanches* (Ban. i, 512) – *Nnffi* (SchBn, 161) – *Fijian* (Ersk.
254) – *Mixhmee* (Grif. 35) – *Knossas* (Licht. i, 2til) – *Java* (Raf. i, 73) –
t-umatrans ([urs. 270) – *Mexico* (Tern. i, 210-11) – *Honduras* (Herr. iii,
367) – *Kiearagna* (Ovi. p. iii, 37). § 305. *Apache* (Ban. i, 512) –
Mexico (Clar. i, 206) – *MaAagatcar (KSL* "History," i, NS8) – *EottAfricnt*
(Kurt. "Cen. Af." ii, *332) – Athantee* (Beech. 124) – *Germanx* (Tac. ch.
xriii, p. *&3) – 3ieromngian* (Montesq. i, 402) – Ar *Caledonia* (Tur. " Nineteen Years," 424) – *Uandingo* (CoiL i, 34) – *Knffirs* (Shooter, 79) – *Chip-*
pevauans (Kent, ii, 155) – *Comanckes* (Ban. i, 512) – *itakololo* (Lir. –).
§ 307. *kaffirs* (Licht. i, 214) – *Damarat* (Ande. 22S) – *Koossa Kaffirt*
(Licht. i, 2-) – *Chippewat* (Kent, ii, 171) – *Ostqakt* (Lath, i, 457) – *$-i!.?*
(Oor. *13)) – Madagasear* (Ell. "History," i, IRS) – *Hebrewt*(Miseh. 201) –
Battas (Mars. 3S1) – *Mishmi* (As. Res. xvii, 374) – *Africa* (Monteiro, i, 241)
– *Hottentots, Ifc.* (Lub. " Origin," 72-3). 308. *Atatralians* (Hit. i,
131) – *Buthmin* (Bar. i, 232) – *Damara* (Ande. 225) – fY/7oa (Ersk. 254) –
raAdiaM (Kll. " Pol. Res." ii, 571 – *Ckibckat* (Fern. 23) – *Hebrtwi* (Deu-
teronomy, xxi, 10-14) – *Persiant* (Kawl., O., ir, 171) – *P,-rurian* (Gar. i,310)
– *Abyisinia* (Bruce, iv, 463). 6 310. *Hudsons fia. y and Copper*
Indians (Lub. "Origin," 101-2) – *Btdouin s* (Burek. i, 112). §311.
Land Dyakt (Low, 300). § 315. *PortDory* (Earl, '- Paeuans," 81) –
Dyakt (Low, 1U5) – *Fuegians* (Fitz. ii, 182) – *Todat* (Eth. S. "Trans." N. S.
vii, 240) – *Etquimaux* (Crantz, i, 147 ; Eth. S. " Journal," i, 147) – *Caribt*
(Hum. ii, 455-6) – *Port Dory* (Earl, " Papuaus," 81) – *Land Dyakt* (Low,
300) – *Bodo and DhimaU* (As. S. B. xviii, pt. ii, 744) – *Iroquoit* (Morg. 324)
– *Pueblos* (Ban. i, *Wo-tty – Dalrymplt Itland* (Jukes, i, *M) – HiU-Dyakt*

(Low, 290) – *Bodo if Dhimdls* (Hodg. 156-60) – *Lepcha* (Eth. 8. "Journal,"
N. S. i, 152) – *Pueblo* (Ban. i, 546) – *Fijians* (Will.,!., i, 26) – *Athanti* (Beech.
122, 124) – *Dahomey (Bas.* "Meusch," iii, 302) – *Peruvians* (Gar. i, 309) –
Mexicans (Clav. i, 206, 322) – *Chitehas* (Sim. 254) – *Kicaraguan s* (Ovi. pt.
iii, *y1)* – *Carolingian* (Bouquet, xi, 88) – *Touloute* (Kcenigs. fi8). § 317.
Error, c. (Maine, "An. Law," 121; Maine, " Ear. Inst." IIS) – *Rudiments*
(Maine, "An. Law," 120) – *Obedience* (Maine, "An. Law," 136) – *Mantra
(ret.* lost) – Cart (Edw. i, 42) – *Mapuche* (Smith, E. R., 231) – *Brazilxm*
(Bates, 169) – *Gallinomeros* (Ban. i, 390) – *Shothones* (Ban. i, 437) – *Narajns*
(Ban. i, 507-8) – *Californianx* (Ban. i, 413, 566) – *Comanches* (Ban. i, 514)
– *Bedouin* (Burck. i, 355) – *Ancient Societies* (Maine. " An. Law," 128-9) –
Commonwealth (Maine, " An. Law," 128) – *Greekt* (School. V, 4!)8; v, 262;
i, 275) – *Iroguoit* (Hind, ii, 147) – *Kutchins* (Ban. i, 132) – *Creeks* (School.
v, 273). § 318. *Infancy of Society* (Maine, "An. Law," 130, 124-5)
– *TahUiant* (Ell. " Pol. Res." ii, 346) – *Tongant* (Ersk. 158) – *Chllchat*
(Fern. 23) – *Iroqvoit* (Hind, ii, 147-8; Morg. 84, 62, 71,184,311,313) –
Coatt Negroet (Bo?. 203; Ouic. ii, 280) – *Congo* (Pink. rri, 571) – *Sumatrans* (Mars. 376) – *Family-Corporate, S(c.* (Maine, "An. Law," 183-4, 124)
– *Palria Pnlestat* (Maine, "An. Law," 13S, 141) – *Tiuneh* (lian. i, 13U) –
Tntelage (Maine, "An. Law," 152-3) – *KuccJi* (As. S. *K.* xviii, pt, r, 708,
7iV) – *K; iren s* (As. S. B. xxxvii. pt, ii, 112) – *Khasias* (Eth. S. " Traus." N. S.
vii, 30S) – *Sea Dyaks* (St. John, S., i, 57 ; Brooke, i, 07) – *Aleutian* (Ban. i,
92) – *Nootkat* (Ban. i, 197) – *Spokanet* (Ban. i, 277) – *Iroywis* (Morg. S4,
826) *-Pueblos* (Ban. i, 545) – *Timbuctoo* (Sha. 18) – *Yellala* (Tuck, ISO).
§ 319. *Comanches* (Marcy, 20) – *Hottentots* (Kol. i, 300-1) – *Kajprt*
(. Shootcr, *'J7-H)* – *Peruvians* (Lop. de Gom. 231) – *Coast Negroes* (Bos. 203)
–*Duhomey* (Forb. i, 27) – *Biology* (Maine, "Early Inst." IIS).
§320. *Patriarchal family* (Maine, "Early Inst," 311, 99-100) – *Bid-
parians* (ref. lost). – *Disintegration* (ref. lost). – *Sclavonic* (Evans, 55).
§ 321. *Children* ("Times," Feb. 28, 1877). § 324. *Puttonahs* (Ai.
S. B. Xxv, 296) – *Corea* (Gutz. i, 17U) – *Kirghiz* (Wood, 214) – *Dyat*
(Brooke, i, 131) – *African* (Reade, 366-9). § 325. *Fveqians* (Eth. 8.
" Traus." N. S. i, 264) – *Australiaus* (Mit. ii, 346) – *llaitlaha* (lian. i, 167) –
Chippewagan (Hearne, 55) – *Kajpr* (Shooter, 84) – CVtirAas (Sim. 253) –
Mandaa (Cnt. 'N. A. Indians," i, 120) – *Yueatanese* (Nouv. 1843, i, 46) –
Easr Africa (Burt. *"Cert. At."* ii, 332) – *Ulapuenes* (Smith, K. R., 218).
I 326. *Tasmanians* (lion. 55) – *Fuegiant* (r'itz. ii, 185-6) – *Antiamanes*
(Eth. S. "Trans." N. S. ti, 36) – *Australiaus* (Hit. i, *Zffl)* – *Chippeimyaus*
(Hearne, 90) – *Comanches* (School. i, 23fi) – *Esnu-imaux* (Orantz, i, 154) – -
Tasmanian (Bon. 55) – iinmara (Gal. *W7)* – *Tnpis* (South, i. 250) – *South
Brazil* (Spix, ii, 246) – *Abipones* (Dob. ii, *18)* – *Ber1manat* (Burcli. ii, 564)
– *Kaffirs* (Licht. i, 266) – *Damara-t* (Gal. *lo7)* – *Oufana)as* (Karl, "Papu-
aus," 51) – *Coroados* (Spix, ii, 259) – *Samoa* ('fur. " Nineteen Years," 196)
– *Java* (Raf. i, 353) – *Angola (Ast.* iii, 276) – *Peru* (Cicza, *16)* – *Abyssinia*
(Bruce, iT, 474) – *Arabs* (Peth. *136)* – *Dahomaus* (Forb. i, *23)* – *Chippetrag-*

an s (School. T, 176) – *Clatsops* (Lew. & Cl. 441) – *Cveba* (Ban. i, 764) – *Xtahomey* (Burt. "Dahome," ii, 72 note) – Gonds (Forsy. 148) – Prru (Herr. iv, 342) – On/raZ *Ameriea* (Juar. 192). § 327. ZV; d, w (Eth. S. "Trans." K. S. Tii, 242) – *Bodo $ Dhimdls* (As. S. B. xviii, pt. ii, 744) – *Diiaks* (St. John, S., i, 55; Brooke, ii, 101) – *Pueblos* (Ban. i, 547, 549) – *Fijiaus* (Vilkes. iii, 77; Ersk. 24S; See. *23*) – *Samoaus* (Tur. "Nineteen Tears," 280-4, 261, 264, 322, *lfJO*) – *Iroquois* (Kcriot, *331*) – *Egyptians* (Ebers, 3O8) – *Reman* (Mom. i, 71). § 328. *Mediaral Europe* (Maine, "Ear. Iust." 337) – *Napoleon* (Leg. 171) – -France (Scgur, i, 391-2) – *China* (Gutz. i, 294 *ft seq.; i,* 493-4) – *Japan* (Alcock, ii, 143). § 329. *Lapps* note (Will., W. M., 162-3). § 330. *Andaman* (Mount, 295) – *Futgiaus* (Eth. S. "Trans." N. S. i, 262) – *Australians* (Sturt, "Central Austr.'" ii, 137; Eyre, i, 8P ; Ang. i, 73) – *Sound Indians* (Ban. i, 218) – *Pi-Eda* (Ban. i, 436) – *Macusi* (Schom. ii, 315) – *Prairie Tribes* (Cat. " N. A. Indians," i, 217) – *Hudson's Bail* (Ileriot, 53. r,) – *Assinihoine* (Kane, 139). § 331. *Chechemeeas* (Nouv. 1843, ii, 147) – *Panches* (Fern. 11) – *Persian* (Herod, i, 277) – *Hebrews* (Ecclesiasticus, ch. xxx, v. 6) – *Brantóme* (Peign. I, 296) – *Chinese* (Mas, i, 52). § 332. *Fijians* (Will., T., i, 181 ; Ersk. 201) – *Chechemecas* (Ban. i, 632) – *Mexieans* (Clav. i, 331) – *Peru,* (Gar. ii, *20'i*) – *Bodo $ Dlmnals* (As. S. B. xviii, pt. ii, 744, 719 ; Hodg. 160 ; As. S. B. xviii, pt. ii, 708; Hodg. 160) – *Dyal-s* (Brooke, ii, 337) – *Samoans* (Tur. " Nineteen Years," 175, 188) – *Tuunese* (Tur. " Nineteen Years," 87) – *Pueblos* (Bun. i, 538, 547). § 333. *China* (Gut/., i, 493-4-5; Du If. i, 278, 318) – *Japanese* (Mitford, i, 58 ; . Alcock. ii, 242, 251) – *Semites* (ii Kings, iT, 1 *;* Job, xxiv, 9 ; Exodus, xxi, 7 ; Ecelesiasticus, xxx) – *Homans* (Mom. i, 64). § 334. *Ctlli* (Ciesar, "de Bella," bk. Ti, ch. 18) – *Meroringian* (Pard. 455) – *French* (Taiue, 174-5 ; Scgur, i, 376) – *Fifteenth Century* (Wright, 3H1-2) – *Seventeenth Cenfvry* (Cra. ik. ii, 884-5). § 336. *i'"tt Afrieans* (Burt. " Con. Af." ii, 333). § 337. *France* (Koenigs. 253 ; Thier. i, 49). § 339. *Pataaonian* (Falk. 126). S 342. *Mexieaus* (Torq. ii, 184 -6) – *Eoossa-KaJfirs* (Li'cht. i, 2UO).

TITLES OF WORKS REFERRED TO.

Acad *Aeademy (The).* January 27, 1873.

Aeadem Aeademic des Inscriptious. *Camples rendus.*

Acos., Joaq. Acosta (Joaq.) *Compendio hisforico del descubrimiento ycotenizacion de la- Nueva Granada-.* Paris, 184S, Svo.

Aco., Jos. de Acusta (Jos. de) *Natural and moral history of the Indies. Trans.* (Ilakluyt Soc. vol. 60-1.) Lon'd. 1880, 2 voU. Svo.

Aduius Adaius (F. O.) *History of Japan.* Loud. 1875, 2 Tola. 8vo,

Alf. .... A'feilo (A. de) *Geographical and historieal dictionary of America. Trans,* by O. A Thompson. Lend. 1812, 5 vols. 4to. Alcoek Alcock (Sir R.) *The eapital of the Tycoon.* Lond. 1863, 2 vols. Svo. Allen Allen (W.) and T. B. H. Thomson, *Narrative of expedition to R. Niger.* Lond. 1848, 2 vols. Svo. Anda . . Andngova (V. de) *Narrative of the proceedingt of Pedrariat*

Daeila (Hakluyt Soc. vol. 34). Lond. 1865, 8ro.

Anda Andersson tC. J.) *Lake Ngami.* Lond. 1850, roy. Svo.

Ang Atigas (O. F.) *Savage life and seenes in Australia and Netf Zealand.* Lond. 1847, 2 vols. sm. Svo. Angl Anglerius (Petrus Martyr) *De rebus Oceanicis decodes tret.*

Colon. 1574, sm. Svo.

Anth. I Anthrnpologicnl Iustitute. *Journal.* Lond. 1871-6, vols. 1-6.

Arb Arbousset (T.) and F. Daumas, *Explor. tour to K. E. of Cape Colong. Trans.* Caiic Town, 1846, Svo. Arri Arriaga (P. J. de) *Extirpacion de la idolatria del Pint.*

Lima, 1621, 4to.

As. K! *Asiatic Researches.* Calcutta, 1788-1839, 21 vols. 4to.

. As. S. li Asiatic Society of Bengal. *Journal.* Calcutta, vols. 9-35, Svo.

Ast Astley (T.) *New general collection of foitages and travelt lbif J.* Green]. Lond. 1745-7, 4 vola. 4to. Atk Atkiuson (T. V.) *Travels in the regions of the vpper and lower Amoor.* Lond. 186t1, rov. 8vo. Atk., Mrs Atkinson (Mrs. T. V.) *Secollections of Tartar Steppes.*

Lond. 1863, sm. 8vo. Aven Arendnflo (Fern. de) *Sermones de lot misierios de nuestra S. fe eatolica.* Lima, 16t9, 4to. Buck Baokhouse (J.) *Narrative of visit to the Mauritius and South Afriea.* Lond. 1844, Svo. Bak Baker (Sir S. W.) *The Nile tributaries of Abyssinia.* Lond.

1867, Svo. Bal Balboa (M. C.) *Sistoire du Peroa* [1576-86]. *Trad, par H. Ternaux-Compaus.* Paris, 1840, Svo. Baluz Baluziua (S.) *Capitularia regum Francorum.* Parisiis, 1667,

2 vols. folio. Ban Bancroft (II. II.) *The native races of the Pacific states of N. Ameriea.* Lond. 1875-6, 5 vols. Svo. Bar Barrow (Sir J.) *Travels into the interior of Southern Africa.*

Lond. 1806, 2 vols. 4to. Barth Barth (II.) *Travels and discoveries in north and central Afriea.* Lond. 1857-8, 5 vols. Svo.

Bas Bastian (A.) *Afrieanische Seisen.* Bremen, 1859, Svo.

. . *Der Menseh in der Oeschichte.* Leipzig, I860, 3 volt.

sm. Svo. ,, ... *Beitrdye tur vergleichenden Psychologic.* Berlin, 1868,

Svo. Bate8 Bates (H. W.) *Naturalist on river Amazons.* 2nd ed.

Lond. 1864, sm. Svo. Beck Beekmann (J.) *History of inventions and discoveries. Traus.*

2ud cd. Lond. 1814, 4 vols. 8ro. Bsceh Beecham (John) *Askantee and the Qold Coast.* Lond. 1841,

em. 8vo. Ban Benzoni (Gir.) *History of the neio World. Trans.* (linkluvt Soc. vol. 21.) Lond. 1857, Svo.

Bible *Sible (The Holy) according to the iiuthorised rersion, Kith a
commentaril* [" *The Speaker's"* ed. *by Canon F. C. Cook.*
Lond. 1871-81, 11 vols. §& *Bible. Corlex apoernphus Nori Testamenti; ed. J. A..
Fabri-
i-iia.* IIamb. 1719, 2 vols. sm. 8vo. Ber Bcmau (Rev. J. H.) *Missionary lab'juri
in British Quiana.*
Lond. 1847, sm. 8vo.
Blackie Blaekie (Prof. J. S.) *Horis Hellenics.* Lond. 1874, 8o.
Jllmit Blunt (Rev. J. H.) *Dictionary of doctrinal and historical
theology.* Lond. 871, imp. 8vo. liogle Bogle (Ci.) *Karraf. ce of mission to Tibet,
and journey of
T. Maaning to Lnsa; ed. by C. B. Markham.* Lond.
1876, Svo.
Bol Boiler (II. A.) *Amoxy the Indians.* Philad. 1868, sm. 8vo.
Bon Bonwick (J.) *Daily life and origin of the Tasmanians.*
Lond. 1870, 8vo. Bos Bosman (W.) *Deseription of the coast of Guinea. Trans.*
Lond. 1721, 8vo. Bouq Bouquet (Dom. M.) *Reraeil de his!oriens des Gaulet et de
la France.* Paris, 17H8-1855, 22 vols. folio. Bourke Bourke (J. G.) *The snake-
dance of the JUoyuis of Arizona.*
Lond. 1884. 8vo. Bourq Bourquelot (F. de) *Eludes snr lei foires de la Champagne.*
(In *Memoires presentees par dirers savants a l'Acad. des
Inser.* 2e Serie, Tome V. Paris, 1865, 4lo.) Bovle Boyle (F.) *Adrentures among the
Dyaks of Borneo.* Lond.
1865, 8vo. Bren Brontano (L.) *Preliminary essay on gilds: English gild*
(Early Eng. Text Soc.). Lond. 1870, 8vo.
Brett Brett (Rev. W. H.) *Indian tribes of Quiana.* Lond. 186S.8vo.
Brin Briaton (D. G.) *The myths of the new World.* New York,
1868, sm. 8vo. Brit. *Ass* British Association for the advancemeat of Science.
*Report
of the 49th meeting at Sheffield, Aug.* 1879. Lond. 1879,
8vo. Brit. *Mus* British Museum. *Select papyri in the hieratic character.*
Lond. 1842-60, 3 vols. folio.
Britt Britton (H.) *Loloma, or two yean in cannibal-land.* Melbourne, 1884. sm.
Svo.
Brooke Brooke (C.) *Ten years in Sarawak.* Lond. 18t56, 2 vols. 8vo.
Bruce Bruce (J.) *Tracels to discover the source of the Kile.*
Edinb. 1805, 7 vols. 8vo. and plates. Brug Brul$soh-Bey (H.) *History of Ey. ift
under the Pharaohs.
Trans.* Lond. 1881, 2 vols. 8vo." Bach Buchanan (J.) *History, maaners and
customs of the North
American Indians.* Lond. 1824, 8vo. Bun Bunsen (C. C. J.) *Egvpfa place in
univerial history.
Trans.* Lond. 1848-67, 5 vols. 8vo. Burch Bureliell (VV. J.) *Travels in southern
Africa.* Lond. 1822-4,
2 vols. 4to. Burck Burckhardt (J. L.) *Notes on the Bedouins and Wahdbys.*

Lond. 1831, 2 vols. 8vo. Burn Burn (R.) *The ecclesiastieal law.* 9tL ed. Lond. 1842,

4 vols. 8vo. Burt. ... Burton (J. H.) *History of Scotland.* Lond. 1867-70, 7 vols. Svo.

Bi:rt Burton (Capt. R. F.) *Pilgrimage to El Medina and*
Loud. lSj5-6, 3 vols. 8vo.

, *firt/oottepsineatAfrica.* Lmd. 1856. 8vo.

, *Luke regions of central Africa.* Ion i. 18ti0, 8vo.

, *City of the Saints.* Loud. -1861, 8vo.

, *Wanderings in west Africa.* Lond. 1863, 2 vola.

sm. 8vo. , *Abeokuta and the Cameroon Mountains.* Lond. 1863, 2 vols. sm. 8vo. *Mission to ;.".; King of Dahome.* Lond. 1864, 2 vols. sm. 8vo.

2'Ae *Highlands of the Brazils.* Lond. 1869, 2 vols.

8vo. But Bull r (Major J.) *Travelt and adventures in Assam.* Lend.

1855, 8vo. Ca-sar Caesar (C. J.) *Commentarii, recog. F. Oehler.* Lips. 1863, sm. 8vo. Call. Call lie (R.) *Trarels through central Africa to Timbnctoo.* Trans. Lond. 1S30, 2 vols. 8vo.

Calo *Calentta Review.* Ot-t. 1883, vol. 77. Calc. 1883, 8vo.

Cal Callnway (Bp. H.) *The religious system of the Amazulm.*
Natal" 1SBS-70, 3 pts. 8vo. Cam Cameron (C-unmaadcr V. L.) *Across Africa.* Lond. 1877,

2 vols. 8vo. Camp Campbell (Gun. J.) *The tcild tribes of Khondistan.* Lond.

lb'64, 8vo. Cas Casalis (Rev. E.) *The Basutos.* Trans. Lond. 1861, sm.

8vo. Cat Catlin (G.) *Illustrations of the North American Indiana,*
with letters and notes. Lond. 187li. 2 vols. 8vo.   *Last rambles amongst the Indians.* Lond. 1868, sm.

8vo. *North and fonlh American Indians: Catalogue of*
Cattin's Indian cartoons. New York, 1871, 8vo. Caus Causia de Perocval (. P.) *Histoire des Arabes arant*

f'Islarnisme. Paris, IS t7-9. 3 vols. 8vo. Chap Chapman (J.) *Trarels in the interior of South Afriea.*

Lond. 1868, 2 vols. 8vo. Cher Chmiel (A.) *Dictiounaire historique de la France.* Paris,

1855, 2 vols.   sm.   8vo.   Clievne Clieyne (Rev.   T. K.) *The Boak of Isaiah chronologieally*

arranged. Lond. 1870, sm. 8vo. *The prophecies of Isaiah.* 2nd ed. Lond. 1SS2, 2 vols. 8vo. Cieza Cieza de Leon (P. de) *Travelt: A. D.* 1532-50 (Hakluvt

Soc. vol. 33). Lond. 18fi-t, 8vo. CIny Clavigero (F. 8.) *The history of Mexico,* Trans. Lond.

1787, 2 vols. 4to. Coch Cochrane (Capt. J. D.) *Pedestrian journey through Ruseia and Siberian Tartara.* Lond. 1825, 2 vols. sm. 8vo.

Cook Cook (Capt. J.) *Second voyage.* Lond. 1777-8, 4 vols. 4to.

, *Third and last eoilaye.* Loud. 1784, 3 vols. 4to.

Cop Copway (G.) *Traditional history and characteristic sketeft*

of the OJiktcait nation. Boston, 1851, 8vo. Cortes Cortes (II.) *Despatcltei* [1520 etc.]. *Trans.* New York,
18t3, 8vo.
Cox Co (Kev. Sir Q-. W.) *Mythology of Ike Aryan nations.*
Lond. 1870, 2 vols. 8vo. Craik Craik (G. L.) and G. Maefarlane. *Pictorial history of*
England. Loud. 1847, 8 vols. 8vo. Craatz Craatz (D.) *History of Greenland. Trans.* Lond. 1820,
2 vols. 8vo. Crich Crichton (A.) and H. Wheaton. *Scandinavia, ancient and modern.* Kdinb. 1S3S, 2 vols. sm. 8vo. Oruic Cruickshank (Broilie) *Eighteen $ears on the Gold Coast of*
Africa. Lond. 18ii3, 2 vols. sm. 8vo.
Can Cunningham (Gen. A.) *The Bhilsa lopes.* Lond. 1854, 8vo.
Dalt Dalton (E. T.) *Deseriptive ethnology of Bengal.* Cal.
1872, 4to.
Dalz Dalzel (A.) *History of Dahomy.* Lond. 1793, 4to.
Dana Dana (j. D.) *On coral reefs and islands.* Lond. 1872, 8vo.
Dap Dapper (O.) *Africa. Trans. byJ. Ogiltat.* Lond. 1670, folio.
Dar Darwin (0.) *Journal* (in *Voyages of the "Adrenturer" and*
"Beagle," by Ad. R. Fitzron, London, 1840, vol. iii). Das Daseat (Sir Or. W.) *Popular tales from the Norse.* Kdinb.
1859, sm. 8vo. Del Dclilzseh (Franz) *Biblical commentary on Isaiah. Trans.*
Edinb. 1873, 2 vols. 8ro. Den. Donliam (Maj. D.), Capt. H. Clapperton, and Dr. Oudnev.
Trarels in northern and central Africa. 3rd ed. Lond.
1828, 2 vols. 8vo. Dcut. m. *Gr.* ... Deutsehe morgenlandiselie Gesellsehaft. *Zeitschrift.* Berlin,
18(39, 8vo. Diod Diodorus Siculus. *Bill. Historicd, ed. P. Wesselingius.*
Amst. 1746, 2 vols. folio. Dob Dobrizlioffer (M.) *Account of the Abipunes. Trans.* Lond.
1822, 3 vols. 8vo. Dozy Dozy (R. P. A.) *Histoire dei 2$uiulmans d'E. ipagne.* Leyde,
1861, 4 vols. 8vo.
Drur Drury (B.) *Madagascar, or journal during fifteen years' eaptivity.* Lond. 1731, 8vo. Du II Du Halde (J. B.) *Description of the empire of China.*
Trans. Lond. 1733-41, 2 vols. folio. Dur Duran (D.) *Historia de las Indias de Nueva Espaiia.*
Mexico, 1867, 2 vols. sm. folio.
Earl Earl (U. W.) *The eastern seas.* Lond. 1837, 8vo.
M *Native races of the Indian archipelago: Papnans.*
Lond. 1853, em. 8vo. Ebers Ehers (G.) *Aegnpten und die Biicher Mose'.* Vol. I.
Leipzig, 18C8. la. 8vo.
Eiik Edkins (J.) *Religion in China.* Lond. 1877, 8vo.
Edw. Edwards (Bryan) *History of the British colonies in (It*
West Indies. Loud. ISO l-19, 5 voU. 8vo.

Ell Kills (Rev. W.) *Tour through Hawaii.* J, ond. 1826, 8vo.

Polynesian researches. Lond. 1829, 2 vols. Svo.

,, Tiie same. New ed. Lond. 18o9, 4 vols. sm. 8vo.

Jt *History of Madaifazear.* Lond. 1838,2 vols. 8vo.

Three visits to Madagasear. Lond. 1858, 8vo.

Elt Ellon (C.) *Origins of English history.* Lond. 1822, la. 8vo.

Eng. Indep. *Eniflish Independent (The),* July 30, 186S.

$rui. J'. rmun. (Adolph) *Travels in Siberia Trans.* Lond. *83,*Ersk Erskine (Capt.
J. E.) *Cruise among the Ielandi of the Western

Pacific.* Lond. 1853, Svo. Kst Esteto (M. de) *Expedition to Pacharamac* (in
*Beports on

the diseovery of Peru)* (Hukluvt Soc. vol. 46). Loud.
1872, 8vo.

Eth. S. .. . Ethnological Society. *Journal.* Vols. i-v, N. S. i-ii.
Lond. 1848-70, 6 vols. 8vo.

,, *Transactions.* Vols. i-ii, N. S. i-vii. Lond. 1859-69, Svo.

Evans Evans (A. J.) *Through Bosnia and the Hertegoeiba.* Loud.
1876, Svo. Eyre Eyre (K. J.) *Ejrpeditions of discovery into Central Australia,*
Lond. 18Vj, 2 vols. Svo.

Falk Falkner (T.) *Description of Patagonia.* Hereford. 1774, Svo.

Fan Fancourt (C. St. J.) *The history of Yueatan.* Lond. 1851,
Svo. Fay Fayrir (Sir J.) *The Thanatophidia of India.* 2nd ed. Lond
1874, folio.

., *The ro'ial tiger of Bengal.* Lorid. 1875, Cp. Svo.

Felins [P'eliuska (Eva)]. *Iferelations of Siberia; by a banished
lady.* Lond. Isfii, 2 vols. Svo. Ferg. FerRusson (J.) *Tree and serpent worship.* 2nd
ed. Lond.
1873, Svo.

, *History of Architecture.* Lond. 1874-6, 4 vols. Svo.

Frrn Fernandez de i'ieilraliita (L.) *llistoria de las c.'mquijta-'i del
nueroreyno de Granada.* Amberes [ItiSi], folio.

Fiske Fiske (J.) *Myths and muth-makers,* Lond. 1S73. sm. Svo.

Fitz Fitzrov (Admiral K.) *1'o:iages of the "Adtenturer" and
"Beagle."* Lond. 18; i9-.1O, 3 vols. 8ro. For. & T Forbes (J.), A. Tweedie and J.
Conolly. *Cyclopredia of
practieal medicine.* Lond. 1S33-5, 4 vols. la. Svo.

Forst Forster (J. R.) *Voyage round the irorld.* Lond. 1778. 4to.

Foray . . Forsyth (Capt. J.) *Highlands of central India.* Loud. 1871,
Svo.

Fort *Fortnightly Review (TJit).* Lond. 1869-72, Svo.

Frank 1'ranklin (Capt. Sir J.) *Narratiee of two journeys to the
shores of the Polar Sea.* Lond. 1823, 2 vols. 4to. Fust Fustel de Coulauges (X.
D.) *Institnlions politiyues de
Vancieune France.* Ire Partie. Parisi, 1875. Svo. Gal Galton (F.) *Narratire of an
explorer in tropieal Sonth*

Africa. Lond. 1S53, Svo. Gar Garrilasso tle la Vega. *The royal commentaries of the*
Yncas. Traus. (Uuklut Soc. vols. 41 and 45.) Lond.
1869-71, 2vols. Svo. Gard Gardiner (Capt. A. F.) *Narrative of a journey to the Zoolu*
country. Lond. 1836, Svo. Gill Gill (Rev. W. W.) *Life in the southern Isles.* Lond. [1876],
em. Svo. , *Myths and songs from the South Pacific.* Lond. 1876,
sm. Svo. Gor Gordon (Lady L. DulT) *Letters from Eflvpt.* Lond. 1865,
sm. Svo.
Grey Grey (. Sir G.) *Polynesian mytholofli).* Lond. 1855, sm. Svo.
Grimm Grimm (Jacob) *Tenlonic mylholoyy. Trans.* Lond. 1880-3,
3 vols. Svo. Gnf Griffiths (W.) *Journal of travels in Assam, Burma, $e.*
Calcutta, 18i7, Svo.
Grote .... Grote (G.) *History of Greece.* Lond. 1846-56, 12 vols. 8vo.
Gru. .... Gruntlt (P. I.) *Die Trauergebrauche der Hebracr.* Leipzig,
1868, Svo. Gutz ...... Gutzlnff (Eev. K. F. A.) *China opened. Sensed l, y A. Seed.*
Loud. 1838, 2 vols. Svo. Hall .... Hall (Capt. C. F.) *Life with the Esquimaux.* Lond. 1864,
2 vols. Svo.
Hallam Hallani (11.) *State of Europe in the middle ages.* Lond.
1868, 3 vole. Svo. ..... *Constitutional History of England.* Lond. 1867,
3 vols. Svo.
Han. Hanusch (I. J.) *Vie Wisseuschaft det Slatuischen Milthus.*
Lemberg, 1842, Svo. Hark . Harkness (Capt. H.) *Description of an aboriginal race of*
the Neilgherry Hills. Lond. 1832, Svo. Hair., J. Harris (J.) *Collection of voyages and travels.* Lond. 1764,
2 vols. folio.
Harr., "W. 0. Harris (Sir W. 0.) *Highlandt of Ethiopia.* Lond. 1844,
3 vols. Svo.
Hawk Hawkesworth (J.) *Account of voyages in the Southern Hemi-*
sphere. Lond. 1773, 3 vols. 4to.
Hayes ...... Hayes (I. I.) *Arctic boat journey.* Lond. 1860, sm. Svo.
Hayg , Havgarth (H. W.) *Secollectious of bush life in Australia.*
Lond. 1848, um. Svo. Hearne Hearne (S.) *Journey to the Northern Ocean.* Lond. 1795,
4to. Heims *Heimskringla: or Chronicle of the I:ings of Norwag ; by S.*
Laing. Lond. 1844, 3 vols. Svo. Herb Herberstein (Seb. von) *Notes upon Russia. Traus.* (Hak-
luyt Soo. vol. I and xii.) Lond. 1851-2, 2 vols. Svo. Heriot Heriot (G.) *Travels through the Canadas.* Lond. 1807,
4to. Hern .... Herndon (Lieut. W. L.) *Exploration of the valley of the*
Amazon. Wash. 1853, Svo. Herod Herodotus. *History. Trans, by Q-. Bawliuson.*
Lond. 1858,

4 vols. Svo.

Heir. Herrera (A. de) *General history of the continent and islands of America. Traus.* Lond. 1725-26, 6 vols. Svo.

Hill Hill (S. S.) *Travels in Siberia.* Lond. 1854, 2 vols. sm. Svo.

Hind Hind (H. Y.) *Canadian Red Biver exploring expedition.* Lond. 1860, 2 vols. Svo. Hobbei Hobbes (T.) *English works; edited by Sir W. Molesworth.*

Lond. 1839-46, 11 vols. Svo. Hodg. Hodgson (B. H.) *Kocch, B6do and Dhimdl tribes.* Calcntta,

1847, Svo. Horn. Homer. *The Iliad, literally traus, by T. A. Buckley.* Lond,

1870, sm. Svo. *The Iliad, done into English prose by A. Lang, W. Leaf and E. Myers.* Lond. 1883, sm. Svo. *The Odyssey, literally trans, by T. A. Buckley.* Lond.

1878, sm. Svo. *The Odyssey, done into English prose by S. H. Butcher and A. Lang.* Lond. 1879, sm. Svo.

Hook Hook (Dean W. F.) *A church dictionary.* Lond. 1859, Svo.

Hooker Hooker (Sir J. D.) *Himalagan journals.* Lond. 1854, 2 voln, Svo.

Hooper .... Hooper (Lieut. "W. H.) *Ten moaths among tie tents vf the Tusti.* Lond. 1853, 8vo. How . Howitt (W.) *History of discovery in Australia, Tasrn-min,*

and New Zealand. Lond. 1865, 2 vols. 8vo. Hum Humholdt (A. V.) *Trareli to the Equinoctial regions of*

America. Trans. Lond. 1852-3, 3 vols. sm. 8vo.

Hun. Hunter (W. W.) *Annals of rnral Bengal.* Lond. 1868. 8vo

Brief history of the Indian people. Lond. 1882, sin

8vo. Hutch Hutehinson (T. J.) *Impressions of Western Africa.* Locd.

1858, em. 8ro. Hax. Huxley (Prof. T. H.) *Introdaction to ike classification nj animalt.* Lond. 1869, 8vo. Ind ...... *India i selections from government recordt* (Forcign Dqi.)

XXVII. Calcutta, 1857, folio. Lmes Innes (Prof. C.) *Scotland in the middle ages.* Edinb. 1860,

8vo.

, *Sketehes of early Scoteh history.* Edinb. 1861, Sro.

Irr Irving (Wash.) *Voyages of the companions of Columbui.* Lond. 1831, sm. 8vo. Ixt. . Ixtlilxochitl (D. Fern. d'Alva) *Histoire de Chichimeques*

[1600]. *Trad. (Voyages, ifc.,par H. Ternaux-Compans,*

Vol.7). Paris 1810,' 8vo. Jag Jagor (F.) *Travelt in the Philippines.* [Trans.] Lond. 1875,

8vo.

Jer Jervise (A.) *History and traditions of the land of the Lindsays.* Edinb. 1882, 8vo. Jew. .... Jewitt (J. R.) *Narrative of a eaptivity among the sar-ages of Nootka Sound.* Middletown, 1816, sm. 8vo.

Jones Jones (Sir W.). *Works.* Lond. 1799-1804. 9 vols. 4to.

Jour. IT. S *Journal of Hellenic Sluilies.* Vol. v. Lond. 18S4, 8vo.

Jour. P *Journal of Philology.* Vol. ix. Lond. 1880, 8vo.

Jnar Jnarros (D.) *Statistieal ami commercial history of Ouatr-mala. Trans.* Lond. 1824, 8vo. Jub *Jubbalpore Exhibition* of 1866-7: *Report of the Ethnological*

Cummitlee. Nagpore, 1868, 8vo. Juk Jukes (J. B.) *Narrative of the Surreying Voyage ofH. M. S.*

"Fly." Lond. 1847, 2 vols. 8vo.

Jus Justi (F.) *Handbuck der Zendsprache.* Leipzig, 1864, 4to.

Kane Kane (P.) *Wanderings of an artist among the Indians uf North America.* Lond. 1859, 8vo. Keat Kenling (VV. H.) *Expedition to source of St. Peter't riier.*

Phil. 1824., 2 vols. 8vo. Kem Kemble (J. M.) *The Saxons in England.* Lond. 1849, 2 vols.

8vo. Kcenigs Koonigswarter (L. J.) *Histoire de Forganisation de lafamiHe rn France.* Paris, 1851, 8vo. Kol Kolben (P.) *Present state of the Cape of Good Hope. Ttans.*

Lond. 1731, 2 vols. 8vo. Kolff Kolff (D. K.) *Voyage of the Duteh brig of war " Dourya."*

Trans. by G. W. Earl. Lond. 1840, 8vo.

$or *Koran (The). Trans. by ?. Sale.* Lond. 1774, 2 vols. 8vo.

Koli Kotzebue (O. von) *Neie voyage round the world. Trans.*

Loud. 1830, 2 vols. sm. 8vo. Krapf Krapf (Kev. J. L.) *Travels, researches and missionary labour*

in Eastern Afriea. Lond. 1800, 8vo.

Krash Krasheninnikov (S. P.) *History of KamschatJea. Trans. by*

J. Oriece. Glocester, 17ti4, 8vo. Kacnen Kuenen (A.) *The religion of Israel. Trans.* Lond. 1874-5.

3 vols. 8vo. Laird Lain! (M.) and B. A. K. Oldfield. *Expedition iuto iuterior of Africa.* Lond. 1837, 2 vols. 8vo. Lumla Landa (Diego de) *Relacion de lo cosas de Yacatan.* (In

Collection de Document; par Brasseur de Bourbourg.

Paris, 1864, Vo!. iii.) Lander, B Lauder (R.) *Records of Capt. Clapperton's last expedition.*

Lond. 1830, 2 vols. um. 8vo. Lander, B.&J. Lander (R. & J.) *Journal of an expedition to th Niger.*

Lond. 1832, 3 rols. sm. 8vo.

Lap Lappenberg (J. M.) *History of England under the Anglo-Saxon tings. Trans.* Lond. 1845, 2 vols. 8vo.

Lath Latham (B. G.) *Deseriptive ethnology.* Lond. 1859, 2 vols.

8vo. Lee Lee (Rev. Dr. F. (J.) *Glimpses of the supernatural.* Lond.

1875, 2 vols. sm. 8vo. Leg Legoave' (E.) *Histoire morale des fentmes.* Paris, 1874,

sm. 8vo. Len Lonormaat (F.) *Les sciences occultes en Asie: la magie chez les Chaldcens.* Paris, 1874, 8vo. Les Lesscps (M. de) *Journal de son voyage depuis Kamchatka*

jusju'en France. Paris, 1780, 2 vols. 8vo. Leras Levasseur (E.) *Histoire des classes oavr&res.* Paris, 1859,

2 vols. 8vo. Lew. & Cl Lewis (M.) and Capt. W. Clarke. *Travels to the source of the Missouri.* Lond. 1814, 4to. Licht Liclitenstein (H.) *Travels in Southern Africa. Trans.*

Lond. 1812-5, 2 vols. 4to. Lit Livingstone (D.) *Missionary travels and researches in South*

Afriea. Lond. 1S57, 8vo. Livingstone (D. and C.) *Narratire of an exploration to the*

Zambezi and its tributaries. Lonri. 1865. 8vo. Lloyd Lloyd *(Or. T.) Thirty-three yean in Tasmania and Victoria.*

Lond. 1862, er. 8vo. Lop. Cog Lopez Cogolludo (D.) *Hisloria de Yueatan.* Merida, 1S67-8,

2 vols. sm. 4to. Lop. de Gom. Lopez de Gomara (F.) *Historia general de las Indias* (in

jfistoriadores primitivos de Indias, tumo i, Madrid,

1852, la. 8vo). Low Low (H.) *Sarawak, its inhabitants and prodactions.* Lond. 184S, 8vo. Lub Lubbock (Sir J.) *Origin of civilization.* 4th ed. Lond. 1882, 8vo.

Prehistoric times. 4th ed. Lond. 1878, 8vo.

[, ngo Lugo (B. de) *Gramatica en la lengna general del nuevo reimo llamado Moaca.* Madrid, 1(i1'J, sm. 8vo.

Lyall Lyail (Sir A. C.) *Asiatic studies.* Lond. 1882, 8vo.

Macaul Macaulay (Lord) *History of England.* Lond. 1849-61,

5 vols. 8vo. Mnedon Maedonald (Rer. Duff) *Africana ; or the heart of heathen Afrlea.* Lond. 1882, 2 vols. 8vo. Macgill Mactjillivray (J.) *Voyage of H. M. S. " Rattlesnake."* Lond.

1852, 2 vols. 8vo.

MeLen McLermnn (J. F.) *Primitive marriage.* Lend. 1SG5, sm. Svo.

Stadia t'a *ancient history: Primitive marri ige* [a reprint]. Lend. 187G, sm. Svo.

Maine - Maine (Sir H. S.) *Ancient lav.* Lond. 1S61, Svo.

.... *Village communities in tke eatl and wrst.* Lond. 1871, Svo.

Early history of inrtitutions. Lond. 1875, Svo.

Mall. Mallet (P. H.) *Korthem antiquities. Trans.* Lond. 1847, sm. Svo.

Marcr Marcy (CoL B. B.) *Thirty year s of army life on the border.* New York, 1866, Svo.

Mari . Mnriette-Ber (A. F. F.) *The monuments of Upper Egypt.*

Trans. Alexandria, 1S77, sm. Svo. V.. iin. .... lloriner (W.) *Account of the natives of the Tonga Islands.*

2nd ed. Lond. 1818. 2 vols. Svo.

Mark Markham (C. R.) *Travels in Peru and India.* Lond. 1S62,

Svo. *Grammar and dictionary of Qvichua.* Lond. 1864,

8vO.

Mars Mars'len (W.) *History of Sumatra.* 3rd ed. Lond. 1811,4to.

Marsh. Marshall (Col. VT. E.) *Travels amongst the Todas.* Lond.

1873, Svo. Mas . Ma S (Sinibaldo de) *La Chine et let puissances c&retieanes.*

Paris, 1861, 2 vola. sm. Svo. Masp Maapero (G.) *Histoire ancieune det penplet de FOrient.*

Paris, lh8, sm. Svo. *Un enquitejudiciaire a Thebes* (In *Memoiret de TAead.*

des laser., tome riii, Paris, 1871, 4to.). Med Mediums (W. H.) *China, iU ttate and prospects.* Lond.

1S38, sm. Svo. Mem *Hfemorias de loi vireyes qne han goternado el Peru durante el tiempo del coloninjc Expaiiol.* Limn, 1859, tomo 1, 4to. Men. llendieta (Geron. de) *Historia ecclesiastiea Indiana.*

Mexico, 1870, 4to. Mich Michclet (J.) *Origines du droit Franeais.* Bruxelles, 1838,

2 vols. sm. Svo.

Michell Mic-hell (J. and R) *The Ensriaus in Central Aria; by Russian travellers.* Traus. Lond. 1S65, Svo.

Mills Mills (Rev. J.) *The British Jeies.* Lond. 1853, sm. Svo.

Mind *Uind.* April, 1877. Lond. 1877, Svo.

Misch *Jlischua: eighteen treatiset translated by Rettv. D. A. it*

Sola and M. J. Eaphall. Lond. 1845, Svo. Mit., A. Mitchell (A.) *The past in the present (Rhind Lectures).*

Kdinb. 1880, Svo. Mit. Mitchell (Sir T. L) *Three expeditions into the interior of Eastern Australia.* Lond. 1839, 2 vols. Svo. MiLfoid Mitford (A. B.) *Tales of old Japan.* Lond. 1871, 2 vcli.

Svo. Mof Moffat (R.) *Missionary labours and scenes in Sonlh Africa.*

Lond. 1842, Svo. Mom Jfonunsen (T.) *History of Some.* Traus. Lond 1S63,

4 vols. Svo. Mous Mouslrnlct (Engucrrand de) *Chronicles.* Traus. Lond.

1S10, 12 vols. Svo. Monteil Monteil (A.) *llisluire des francais des dirers (tats.* 4e &l

Pan, ljJ, 5 vols. sm. Svo.

875

Moateiro .... Montciro (J. J.) *Angola and th river Congo.* Lend. 1875,

2 vols. sm. 8vo. Monies Montesinos (F.) *Sffm. historiques sur l'ancien Perou.* Trad.

(In *Voyages, relations, Jfc., par H. Ternaux-Compans,*

Paris, 1840, tome viii, 8vo.) Montesq Montesquieu (C. S. de) *lie l'esprit des lois.* (In *(Eurres.*

Amst. 1758, 3 vols. 4to.) Moatg Montgomery (G. W.) *Narrative of a journey to Gnatemala.*

New York, 1839, 8vo. Morg Morgnn (L. li.) *League of the Ho-de-no-iau-nee, or Iroquois.*

Rochester, U. S. 1851, 8vo..

Monat Mouat (F. J.) *Adcentures and researches among the Andaman Islanders.*
Lond. 1863, 8vo. Muir Mmr (J.) *Original Sanskrit Texts.* 2nd ed. Lond. 1868-
70, 5 vols. 8vo. Miil Miiller (F. Jinx) *History of ancieat Sanskrit literature.*
Lond. 1859, 8vo. *H Chips from a German workshop.* Lond. 1867-75,
4 vols. 8vo. , *Lectures on the science of langnage.* 7th ed. Lond.
1873, 2 voh. nm. 8vo. *Lectures on the origin and growth of religion in India*
(Hibbert L.). Lond. 187S, 8vo. *Introdaction to the. zeience of religion.* Lond.
18S2,
sm. 8vo. Nebel .... Ifebel (C.) *Vo'iane dans la parlie la plus inleressante da
Mexique.* Pitris, 1836, folio. Nes Nesfield (J. C.) *Account of the Kanjars of Upper
India*
(Calcutta Ben. Oct. 1833). Cnlc. 18S3, 8vo. Nieb Niebulir (C.) *Deseription de
l'Arabia. Trad.* Amst. 1774,
4to. Nilsson Kilson (Sven) *The primilire inhabitants of Scandinavia.*
Trans. 3rd ed. Lond. 1SOS, Svo. Noav *Ifourelles annale des voyages.* 4e serie.
Paris, 1840-4,
20 vols. 8vo.
Num *Kumismalic Chronicle.* Ser. iii, vol. 2. Lond. 1882, 8vo.
Oroz Ororco y Berra (M.) *Geograjia de las lengnas y carta elno-
grafica de Mexico.* Mexico, 1S61, folio. Ovi. .... Oviedo y Vaides (Q-. *"F.*
de) *Historia general y natural de
las Indiat.* Mtulrid 1851-5, 4 vols. 4to. Palo. Palncio (D. G. de) *Carta dirijida al
re de Espaiia.*
Spanish and English; by E. G. Syuier. Jfew l'ork,
1S60, sm. 4to. Palg., F Palgrave (8ir F.) *The rise and progress of the English Common'. cealth : Anglo-saxon period.* Lond. 1S3, 2 vols. 4lo. Palg., W. G. Palgrave
(W. G-.) *A'arralire of a year's journey through
central and eastern Arabia.* Lond. IS'Jo, 2 vols. 8vo. Pall Pallas (P. S.) *Voyages
dans les nom'ernements meridionaiue
de la Russie.* Paris, I-su5, 3 vols. 4to.
Pard Pardessus (J. II.) *Loi saliqne.* Paris, 1843, 4to.
Park Park (Mimgo) *Trarel in the interior districts of Africa.*
Loud. 1816, 2 vols. 4to.
Parkyns Parkyns (M.) *Life in Abyssinia.* Lond. 1853, 2 vois. 8vo.
Parl *Parliamentary history of England from the earliest period
to* 1803. Lond., T. C. Hansard, 1806-20, 36 vols. *la.* 8vo. Pcig Pcignot (Q-.)
Choix de teslamens. Paris, 1829, 2 vols. Svo.
Perm Peuna di Billi (F. O.) *Notizia del regno del Thibet:* 1750
(In *Noureau Journal Asiatique,* Paris, 1S35, Svo.). Per Percival (Rcv. P.) *The land
of the Veda.* Lond. 1S54,
Sui. Svo. Peth. Fetherick (J.) *Egypt, the Soudan, and central Africa.*
Lond. 1S61, 8vo.' Pim Pim (Com. B.) and B. Seemaun. *Dottings on the roadside
in Panama.* Lond. 1869, 8vo. Pink Pinkertcn (J.) *General collection of voyaget
and travelt.*

Loud. 1808-14, 17 vols. 4to. Pis. .... Pi/arro (P.) *Relacion del acecubrimiento*
y conquista de lui
Reinos del Peru, ano 1571. (In *Coleccion de documentor*
iniditoi para la Historia de Espaiia, tomo T, Madrid,
1844, 4to.) Pls. .... Plato. *The Sepublic.* (In *Dialoguet. Trans, by B. Joirett,*
Oxford, 1875, 5 vols. Svo.) Pop Popul Vuh. (In *Collection de documents, par*
Srasseur de
BourbourtT, vol. i, Paris, 1861.)
Pop. S. M *Popular Science Monthly.* New York, 1876, Svo.
Prayer Prayer. *Book of common Prager.* Oiford, 1852, Svo.
Pret. .. . Preacott (W. II.) *History of tke conquest of Mexico.* Lond.
1843, 3 vols. Svo. - *History of the conquest of Peru.* Loud. 1S47, 2 vols.
8vo. Prich Priehard (J. C.) *IJesearcJiet into the pTtii. ncal history of*
mankind. 3rd cd. Lond. 1836-47, 5 vols. 8vo. Prid Pridham (C.) *Historical,*
politieal, and statistieal account of
Ceylon. Lond. 1849, 2 vols. 8vo.
Kaf Ruffles (Sir T. S.) *History of Java.* Lond. 1817, 2 vols. 4to.
Rai Bujendralala Mitra. *Indo-Aryaus.* Lond. 1S81, 2 vols. Svo.
EaL Ealcgh (Sir W.) *Discovery of Guiana, ed. by Sir R. H.*
8chombargk (Hakluvt Soc. vol. iii). Lond. 1848, Svo. Eals Ealston (W. K,. S.)
The songs of the Russian people. Lond.
1872, Svo.
Eamb ... *Eambles in the deserts of Sgria.* Lond. 1S64, em. Svo.
Eams Eamscyer (F. A.) and J. Kuhne. *Four year s ta Ashantee.*
Trant. Lond. 1875, Svo. Eawl., 0- Eawliuson (Eev. Prof. G.) *The fee great*
monarcJiies of the
ancient Eastern World. Lond. 18H2-7, 4 vols. Svo.
Eawl., H Euwliuson (Gen. Sir. H. C.) *Cuneiform inseriptious of Wen- tern Asia.*
Lond. 1861-70, 3 vols. folio.
Eeade Eeade (W. W.) *Savage Africa.* Lond. 1863, Svo.
Rccords *Records of the Past, leing English trauslatious of the As*
syrian and Egyptian monumentt. Loud. 1S74-S1, 12 vols.
sm. Svo.
Ecit Eeitterius (C.) *Jtlorlilogus.* [Aug. Vind.], 1508, 4to.
Ken Benouf (P. Le P.) *Lectures on the origin and growth of re*
ligion in ancient Egypt (Hibbert L.). Lond. 1880, Svo. Eev. Phil *Seeue*
Philosvphique. Paris, 1876, vol. i, Jau, ; 1877, vol. iii,
May.
Eev. Scion *Revue Scienlifigve.* Paris, 1879.
Rig – . *Eiff-Veda-XanhUd. Trans, by H. H. Wilson.* Lond. 1850-7,
3 vols. Svo.
, *Trans, by F. 3fax Miiller.* Lond. 1S69, vol. i, Svo.
Eiuk Eink (H.) *Tales and tradition, of the Eskimo. Tranf*
Lond. 1875, sm. Svo.
Robert Robertson (E. "W.) *HMorical essays.* Edinb. 1872, 8vo.

Robin [Robinson (A.)] *Life in California.* New York, 1846,
sm. 8vo. Rocli Rochholz (E. L.) *Deutscher Glaube und Branch.* Berlin,
1867, 2 vols. 8vo. Roep Roepstorff (F. A. de) *Vocabulary of dialects spoken in the
Kicobar and Andaman Isles.* Calcutta, 1875, 8vo. Ross Ross (A.) *Adventures of
the first settlers on the Oregon*
Loml. 1849, 2 vols. sm. 8vo. *Fur hunters of the far West.* Lond. 1855, 2 *tols.* sm.
8vo. Itoss, J Ross (Rev. J.) *History of Cored, ancieat and modern.*
Paislev, 1880, 8vo. Roll Rouge (Vte. E. de) *Les monuments qu'on peut attribaer*
am

six premieres dynasties de Manethon. (Tn *Mem. dc*
l'Acad. des. fnscr., tome xxx, pt. 2, Paris, 1877, 4to.) Rov. A. S Royal Asiatic
Society. *Transactions.* Lond. 1S27-35,
3 vols. 4to.
.... *Journal,* vols. vii to viii. Lond. 1843-6, 8vo.
Roy. Q-. S Roval Geographical Society. *Journal,* voU. ii to Txvii.
Lond. 1SS2-57, 8vo. Roy. S. of Lit. Royal Society of Literature. *Transactions.*
Lond. 1829-39,
3 vols. 4to.
Roy. V. D. S. Royal Society of Van Diemen's Land. *Proceedings.* Tasmania, 1S55,
vol. iii, 8vo. Sahn. Sahauun (B. de) *Historia general de lo cosa ie Nueva*
Espaita. Mexico, 1S2J-30, 3 vols. 8vo. St. John, B. St. John (B.) *Two years'*
residence in a Levantine family.
London, 1850, sm. 8vo. St. John, S. St. John (Sir S.) *Life in the forests of the far*
east. Lond.
18R2, 2 vols. 8vo. Schef. Sclieffer (Prof. J.) *The history of Lapland. Trans.*
Oxon,
1674, folio.
Schom Schomburgk (Sir R-. H.) *Reisen in Britisch-Ouiana.* Lcipzig, 1S47-9, 3
vols. 8vo.
Schon Schon (Rev J. F.) and S. Crowther. *Journals during expedition up the Niger.*
Lond. 1842, sm. 8vo. School Schoolcrut't (H. R.) *Information respecting the Indian*
tribes
of the United States. Lond. 1853-6, 5 vols. 4to. *Expedition to the sources of the*
Mississippi ricer. Lond.
1855, 8vo. Schuer Schnermann (C. "W.) *Vocabulary of the Parntalla langnage.*
Adelaide, 1844, 8vo. Schwein Sehwcinfnrth (G.) *The heart of Africa.* Lond. 1873,
2 vols. Svo See Seeman (B.) *Viti; an account of a mission to the Vitian or*
Fijian Islands. Cnmb. 1802, Svo. Segur Segur (Vte. A. J. A. P. de) *Leu femmes:*
leur condition el
leur influence Paris, 1820, 2 vols. Svo. Sol Selden (J.) *Titles of honour.* (In *Opera*
omnia Jo. Seldeni,
vol. iii. Lond. 1726, folio.) 8ha Shabeeny (El Ha;; e Abd Salam) *Account of*
Timbactoo and
Housa in Africa. Trans. by J. G. Jackson. Lond.
1820, 8vo. Blkesp Shakespeare (W.) *Works. edited by W. G. Clark, J. Glover,*

and It'. A. Wright. Camb. 1863-6, 9 vols. 8vo.

Shooter .... Shooter *(Rev.* J.) *The Kaffirs of Natal and the Zulu country.*
Loud. 1857, Svo. Sim .... Simon (P.) *Koliciashistoriales.* (In Kingsboroush's
(Lord)

Antiquities of Mexico, vol. viii. Loud. 1830, folio.) Smiles .... Smiles iS.)
Lires of the engineers. Lond. 1S61-2, 3 vols. Svo.

Smith, E. II. Smith (E. R.) *The Araueanians.* Lond. 185."i, sm. Svo.

Smith, G ..... Smith (0.) *Assgrian discoreries.* Lond. 1875, Svo.

.... - *Chaldean account of Genesis. Keto ed. by A. H. Sayce.*

Lond. 1880, 8vo. Smith, W. .... Smith (W.) *Dictionary of Greek and Roman
antiquitiej.*

Lond. 1856, Svo. .... - *and* S. Chectham, *Dictionary of Christian antiquities.*

Lond. 1875-80, 2 Vo!s. Svo. Smyth .... Smyth (R. B.) *The aborigines of
Victoria.* Melb. 1878,

2 vols. la. 8vo. Soc. B. A. .... Society of Biblical Archaeology. *Trausactions.*
Lond. 187-1,

vol. iii, Svo. Somer .... Somerville (Mrs. M.) *Personal recollections.* Lond.
1873,

gm. Svo. South .... Southey (R.) *History of Brazil.* Lond. 1810-19, 3 voh.

4to. Spar .... Sparrman (A.) *Voifaqe to Cape of Good Hope.* 2nd ed.

Lond. 1786, 2 vol3.'4to. Speke .... Speke (Capt. J. H.) *What led to the
discoteru of the tourct*

of the Ai7e. Lond. 1864, Svo. Spen .... Spencer (Herbert) *First principles.*
6th ed. Lond. 1884, Svo.

, ... - *Principles of biology.* 4th ed. Lond. 188!. 2 vols. Svo.

.... - *Principles of psychology.* 4th ed. Lond. 1881, 2 Tols.

Svo. .... - *Social Statics.* Lond. 18G8, Svo.

,, ... - *Essags.* First Series. Lond. 1858, Svo.

.... - *Essags.* Lond. 1883, 3 vols. Svo.

.... - - *Itescrilitive sociology.* Lond. 1873-81, 8 parts, folio.

No. 1.

,, 2. Mr&icans, Central Amerieans, Chibehas, and Peruvians.

n 3. Lowest races, Negruto raws, and . Matayo-Putyoesian race.

i, 4. Afriean races.

5. Asiauc races.

6. Aincriciui races.

!, 7. Hebrews and l'hIniciant,

8. French.

Spieg .... Spiegel (Fr.) *Erdnische AUerthumstunde.* Leipzig, 1871-8,

3 vols. Svo. Spix .... Spir (J. li.) and C. F. P. von Martins. *Travels in Brazil*
[ZVan,.] Lond. 1824, 2 Vo!s. Svo. Squier .... Squirr *(K.* G.) *The states of
central Amerioa.* New York,

1858, 8vo. Slade .... Stado (H.) *Captivity in Brazil. Traus.* (Haklnyt Soc.

vol. li.) Lond. 1874, Svo. Stat .... *Statutes of the Sealm.* Lond. 1810, 11
vols. folio.

Steph .... Stepheus (J. L.) *Incidents of travel i Yueatan.* Lond.
1813, 2 vols. Svo. Stubbs .... Stubbs (Bp. W.) *The constitnlional history of England.*
Oxford, 1880, 3 vols. Svo. ,, ... *- Select charters.* Lond. 1S70, em. Svo.
Start .... Start (Capt. C.) *Tiro expeditions into the interior of Southern Australia.* Loud. 1S33, 2 Vo!. Svo.
Sturt Sturt (Capt. C.) *Expedition into Central Australia.* Lond.
184:i, 2 Vols. 8vo. Sup. Eel... *Supernatural religion: an inquiry into the reality of divino*
   revelation. Lond. 1874-7, 3 vuls. 8vo. Tac Tacitus (C. C.) *Germaaia ; by Ii. Q-.* Latham. Lond. 1851,
   8vo.
Taine Taino (H.) *Vancien regime.* Paris, 1876, 8vo.
Tnfl . *Tastnanian Journal of Natural Science, Sfe.* Hobart, 1841,
vola. i and iii, 8vo. Tav Tavernier (J. B.) *Voyage to Tunkin and Japan. Trans.* Lond. 16SO, folio.
Ton Tenneat (Sir J. E.) *Ceylon.* Lond. I860, 2 vols. 8vo.
Tern Ternaux-Compans (H.) *;'oyages, relations et mcmoires pour servir a I ' kistoire de la decoaverte de I ' Amerique.* Paris,
1837-41, 10 vols. 8vo. Thier Thierry (A.) *Formation and progress of the Tiert $tat. Trans.* Lond. 1859, 2 vols. sm. 8vo. ThirL Tliirlwall (Bp. C.) *History of Greece.* Lond. 1845-52,
   8 vols. 8vo. Xhomp Thompson (G.) *Travels and adventures in Southern Africa.*
   2nd edit. Lond. 1827, 2 void. 8vo. Thoms., A. S. Thomson (A. S.) *The story of New Zealand pat and present.*
   Lond. 1859, 2 vols. sm. 8vo.
Thoms., J Thomson (J.) *The straits of Malacca.* Lond. 1875, 8vo.
Times *Times (The).* July 21, 1875; Feb. 2S. 1877.
Tor Torihio de Benavente, o Motolinia. *Historia de las Indias:*
15U9 (in Garcia Icuzbalceta, J., *Coleccion de documento,*
tomo i. Mexico, 1S58, 8vo.) Torq. .... Torquemada (J. de) *Monarquia Indiana.* Madrid, 1723,
   3 vols. folio. Toz Tozer (Rev. II. F.) *Lectures on the geography of Greece.*
   Lonrl. 1873, sm. 8vo. Tschu Tsehudi (J. J. von) *Pent: Reiseskizzen,* 1834-42. St. Gullen,
   1846, 2 vols. 8vo. Tack Tackey (('apt. J. K.) *Narrative of an expedition to the river*
   Zaire. Lond. 1818, 4to.
Tur Turner (Rev. G.) *Nineteen years in Samoa.* Lond. 186O, 8vo.
Samoa a hundred years affo. Lond. 1881, em. 8vo.
Tylor Tylor (E. B.) *Anahnac, or Mexico and the Mexicans.* Lond.
"1861, 8vo.
... *Researches into the early history of mankind.* Lond.
1865, 8vo.
, *Primitive culture.* 2nd ed. Lond. 1873, 2 vols. 8vo.

Ulloa Ulloa *(Gr.* J. and A. de) *Voyage to South America. Trans.*
Lond. 1772, 2 vols. Svo.
Vam Viimbery (A.) *Sketches of Central Aria.* Lond. 1868, 8vo.
Virg. Virgilins Maro (P.) *Poems, translated into English prose
by J. Conington.* Lond. 1882. 8vo.
Wahl Wahl (O. W.) *The land of the Czar.* Lond. 1875, 8vo.
Waitz Wnitz (T.) *Anthropolotjie der Naturcolker.* Lcipzig, 1859,
6 vols. 8vo. WaL Wallace (A. R.) *Travels on the Amazon and Rio Negro.*
Lond. 1853, la. 8vo.
.. *The Malay archipelago.* Lond. 1869, 2 vols. Svo.
Contributions to the theory of natural selection. Lond
1871, sm. Svo.
Walpole Walpole (Lieut. Hon. F.) *The Ansagrii or the assattius.*
Lond. 1851, 3 vols. 8vo.
Wed Weddell (J) *Voyage towardt the South Pole.* Lond. 1827,
8vo.
Wheat Wheatley (J? ev. Ch.) *Rational illustration of the Boot of
Common Prager.* Oxford, 1839, Svo.
White White (J.) *Te Sou; or the Maori at home.* Lond. 1874,
m. Svo.
Wilkes Wilkes (Comm. C.) *Jfarratine of United States' exploring
expedition.* Phil. 1S45, 5 vols. Svo. and atlas.
Wilkin Wilkiuson (Sir J. G.) *Mauners and customs of the ancient
Eguptians.* New ed. Lond. 1S7S, 3 vols. Svo.
Will., M. Williams (Prof. M.) *Sanskrit-English Dictionary.* Oxford,
1872, 4to.
Will., T Williams (T.) and J. Calvert. *Fiji and the Fijians.* Lond.
1858, 2 vols. sm. Svo.
Will., W. M. Williams (W. M.) *Through Norwag tmth ladies.* Lond.
1877, sm. Svo.
Wils Wilson (A.) *The abode of snov,.* Edinb. 1876, sm. Svo.
Winter Winterbottom (T.) *Account of the natire Afrieans in the
neighbourhood of Sierra Leone.* Lond. 1803, 2 vola. Svo.
Wood ..... . Wood (Capt. J.) *Journey to source of river Oxus.* New ed.
Lond. 1S72, Svo.
Wrang Wrangel (F. V.) *Expedition to the Polar Sea. Trans.* Lond.
1840, Svo.
Wright .... Wright (T.) *Domestic mauners and sentiments in England
during the middle ages.* Lond. 1862, em. 4to.
Xer . . Xeres (F. de) *Account of Cu:co. Traus.* (In *Reports on the
discorery of Pern.* Hakluvt Soc. Vo!, xlvi.) Lond. 1872,
Svo.
Xim. ... . Ximenez (F.) *Las historias del origen de los Indies de Guate-
mala* [1721] ; *publ. par C. Scherzer.* Tiena, 1857, Svo.
Yncas *Ynta-s. Karrat'ires of the rites and laws of the Yneas;* tran-,.

bjC. R. Slarkham. (Uakluyt Soc. Vo!, xlvii). Lond. 1873,
S'vo.

Zend. Av. ... *[Zend] Aveata: Die Heiligen Schriften der Parsen ; uberselzt von F. Spiegel.* Leipzig, 1852-63, 3 vols. Svo.

Zur. Zurita tA. de) *Rnppurts sur Iet differentes classes de chfft ic la Sonrelle Espagne. Trad.* (In Ternaux-Compaus (II.)
fc. Yd. *Ti.)* Paris, 18-ift Sto.

HU 1UM7 S I